Microsoft® Office PowerPoint® 2003

ILLUSTRATED, CourseCard Edition

INTRODUCTORY

THOMSON
COURSE TECHNOLOGY

Microsoft Office Specialist Program

Microsoft® Office
Specialist
Approved Courseware

WHAT DOES THIS LOGO MEAN?

It means this courseware has been approved by the Microsoft® Office Specialist Program to be among the finest available for learning one or more of the applications of the Microsoft Office 2003 Suite. It also means that upon completion of this courseware, you may be prepared to take an exam for Microsoft Office Specialist qualification. If "1 of 2" or "2 of 2" appears below the logo on the cover, this indicates this courseware has been approved as part of a sequence of texts for preparation to become a Microsoft Office Specialist. See the table below for more information.

WHAT IS A MICROSOFT OFFICE SPECIALIST?

A Microsoft Office Specialist is an individual who has passed exams for certifying his or her skills in one or more of the Microsoft Office desktop applications such as Microsoft Word, Microsoft Excel, Microsoft PowerPoint®, Microsoft Outlook®, Microsoft Access, or Microsoft Project. The Microsoft Office Specialist Program is the only program in the world approved by Microsoft for testing proficiency in Microsoft Office desktop applications and Microsoft Project. This testing program can be a valuable asset in any job search or career advancement.

ILLUSTRATED TITLES FOR OFFICE 2003 MICROSOFT OFFICE SPECIALIST CERTIFICATION

The Illustrated Series offers a growing number of Microsoft-approved courseware products that cover the objectives required to pass a Microsoft Office Specialist exam. After studying with any of the books listed below, you should be prepared to take the Microsoft office Specialist Program exam indicated. The following titles have certification approval as courseware for the Microsoft Office Specialist program:

Exam	Course Technology Illustrated Series Textbook
Microsoft Office Access 2003	Microsoft Office Access 2003 – Illustrated Introductory, CourseCard Edition (1-4188-4298-2) or Microsoft Office Access 2003 – Illustrated Complete, CourseCard Edition (1-4188-4299-0)
Microsoft Office Excel 2003	Microsoft Office Excel 2003 – Illustrated Introductory, CourseCard Edition (1-4188-4295-8)
Microsoft Office Excel 2003 Expert	Microsoft Office Excel 2003 – Illustrated Complete, CourseCard Edition (1-4188-4296-6)
Microsoft Office PowerPoint 2003	Microsoft Office PowerPoint 2003 – Illustrated Introductory, CourseCard Edition (1-4188-4304-0)
Microsoft Office Word 2003	Microsoft Office Word 2003 – Illustrated Introductory, CourseCard Edition (1-4188-4301-6)
Microsoft Office Word 2003 Expert	Microsoft Office Word 2003 – Illustrated Complete, CourseCard Edition (1-4188-4302-4)
Microsoft Office 2003 (separate exams for Word, Excel, Access and PowerPoint)	Microsoft Office 2003 – Illustrated Introductory (0-619-05789-0) and Microsoft Office 2003 – Illustrated Second Course (0-619-18826-X) when used in a sequence, meet the requirements for Microsoft Office Specialist for Word, Excel, Access, and PowerPoint.

MORE INFORMATION:

To learn more about becoming a Microsoft Office Specialist, visit www.microsoft.com/officespecialist.

To learn about other Microsoft Office Specialist approved courseware from Course Technology, visit www.course.com.

The availability of Microsoft Office Specialist certification exams varies by application, application version, and language. Visit www.microsoft.com/officespecialist for exam availability.

Microsoft® Office PowerPoint® 2003

ILLUSTRATED, CourseCard Edition

INTRODUCTORY

Microsoft® Office Specialist
Approved Courseware

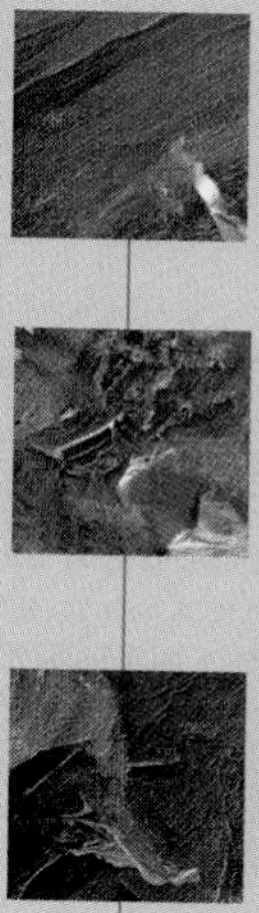

David W. Beskeen

THOMSON
COURSE TECHNOLOGY™

Australia • Canada • Mexico • Singapore • Spain • United Kingdom • United States

THOMSON

COURSE TECHNOLOGY

Microsoft® Office PowerPoint® 2003—Illustrated Introductory, CourseCard Edition

David W. Beskeen

Managing Editor:
Marjorie Hunt

Production Editors:
Philippa Lehar
Danielle Slade

QA Manuscript Reviewers:
Jeff Schwartz, Sean Franey
Alex White

Product Managers:
Christina Kling Garrett
Jane Hosie-Bounar

Developmental Editor:
Rachel Biheller Bunin

Text Designer:
Joseph Lee, Black Fish Design

Associate Product Manager:
Emilie Perreault

Editorial Assistant:
Shana Rosenthal

Composition House:
GEX Publishing Services

Printed in the United States of America

6 7 8 9 BM 09 08 07

For more information, contact Thomson Course Technology, 25 Thomson Place, Boston, Massachusetts, 02210.

Or you can visit us on the World Wide Web at www.course.com

ISBN-10: 1-4188-4304-0
ISBN-13: 978-1-4188-4304-5

The Illustrated Series Vision

Teaching and writing about computer applications can be extremely rewarding and challenging. How do we engage students and keep their interest? How do we teach them skills that they can easily apply on the job? As we set out to write this book, our goals were to develop a textbook that:

- works for a beginning student
- provides varied, flexible, and meaningful exercises and projects to reinforce the skills
- serves as a reference tool
- makes your job as an educator easier, by providing resources above and beyond the textbook to help you teach your course

Our popular, streamlined format is based on advice from instructional designers and customers. This flexible design presents each lesson on a two-page spread, with step-by-step instructions on the left, and screen illustrations on the right. This signature style, coupled with high-caliber content, provides a comprehensive yet manageable introduction to Microsoft Office PowerPoint 2003—it is a teaching package for the instructor and a learning experience for the student.

About This Edition

New to this edition is a free, tear-off PowerPoint 2003 CourseCard that provides students with a great way to have PowerPoint skills at their fingertips!

Acknowledgments

I would like to thank Rachel Biheller Bunin for her tireless efforts and editorial insights, which have made my work better. I would also like to thank Thomson Course Technology for all of their vision and support over the last 10 years; I look forward to many more!

David W. Beskeen
and the Illustrated Team

Preface

Welcome to *Microsoft® Office PowerPoint® 2003–Illustrated Introductory, CourseCard Edition.* Each lesson in this book contains elements pictured to the right.

How is the book organized?

The book is organized into eight units on PowerPoint, covering creating, editing, and formatting presentations, as well as creating charts, inserting WordArt, and using advanced features.

What kinds of assignments are included in the book? At what level of difficulty?

The lessons use MediaLoft, a fictional chain of bookstores, as the case study. The assignments on the light purple pages at the end of each unit increase in difficulty. Data Files and case studies, with many international examples, provide a great variety of interesting and relevant business applications. Assignments include:

- **Concepts Reviews** include multiple choice, matching, and screen identification questions.
- **Skills Reviews** provide additional hands-on, step-by-step reinforcement.
- **Independent Challenges** are case projects requiring critical thinking and application of the unit skills. The Independent Challenges increase in difficulty, with the first one in each unit being the easiest (most step-by-step with detailed instructions). Independent Challenges 2 and 3 become increasingly open-ended, requiring more independent problem solving.
- **E-Quest Independent Challenges** are case projects with a Web focus. E-Quests require the use of the World Wide Web to conduct research to complete the project.
- **Advanced Challenge Exercises** set within the Independent Challenges provide *optional* steps for more advanced students.
- **Visual Workshops** are practical, self-graded capstone projects that require independent problem solving.

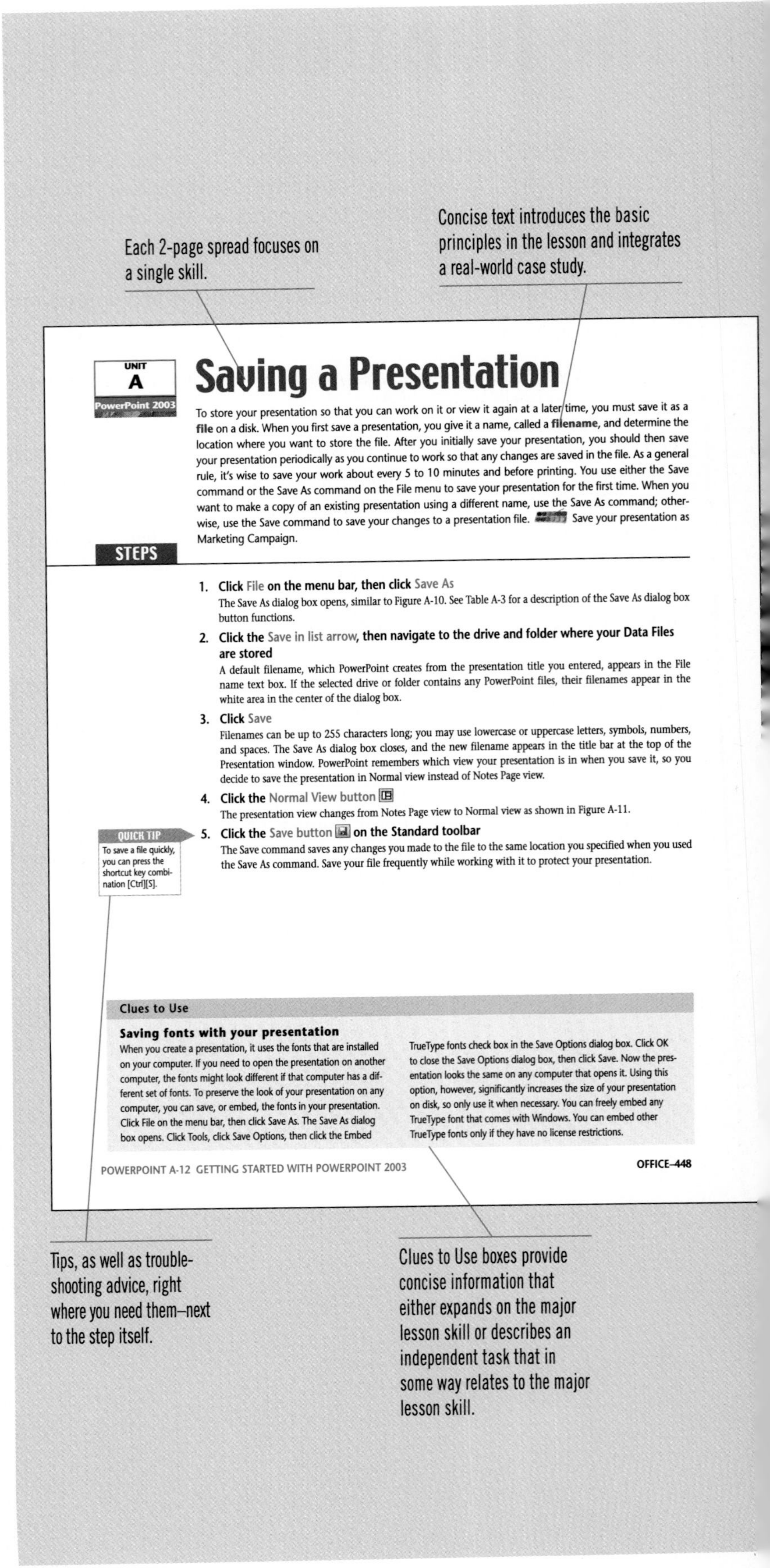

Each 2-page spread focuses on a single skill.
Concise text introduces the basic principles in the lesson and integrates a real-world case study.
Tips, as well as trouble-shooting advice, right where you need them–next to the step itself.
Clues to Use boxes provide concise information that either expands on the major lesson skill or describes an independent task that in some way relates to the major lesson skill.

UNIT A PowerPoint 2003

Saving a Presentation

To store your presentation so that you can work on it or view it again at a later time, you must save it as a **file** on a disk. When you first save a presentation, you give it a name, called a **filename**, and determine the location where you want to store the file. After you initially save your presentation, you should then save your presentation periodically as you continue to work so that any changes are saved in the file. As a general rule, it's wise to save your work about every 5 to 10 minutes and before printing. You use either the Save command or the Save As command on the File menu to save your presentation for the first time. When you want to make a copy of an existing presentation using a different name, use the Save As command; otherwise, use the Save command to save your changes to a presentation file. Save your presentation as Marketing Campaign.

STEPS

1. **Click File on the menu bar, then click Save As**
   The Save As dialog box opens, similar to Figure A-10. See Table A-3 for a description of the Save As dialog box button functions.
2. **Click the Save in list arrow, then navigate to the drive and folder where your Data Files are stored**
   A default filename, which PowerPoint creates from the presentation title you entered, appears in the File name text box. If the selected drive or folder contains any PowerPoint files, their filenames appear in the white area in the center of the dialog box.
3. **Click Save**
   Filenames can be up to 255 characters long; you may use lowercase or uppercase letters, symbols, numbers, and spaces. The Save As dialog box closes, and the new filename appears in the title bar at the top of the Presentation window. PowerPoint remembers which view your presentation is in when you save it, so you decide to save the presentation in Normal view instead of Notes Page view.
4. **Click the Normal View button**
   The presentation view changes from Notes Page view to Normal view as shown in Figure A-11.
5. **Click the Save button on the Standard toolbar**
   The Save command saves any changes you made to the file to the same location you specified when you used the Save As command. Save your file frequently while working with it to protect your presentation.

QUICK TIP
To save a file quickly, you can press the shortcut key combination [Ctrl][S].

Clues to Use

Saving fonts with your presentation

When you create a presentation, it uses the fonts that are installed on your computer. If you need to open the presentation on another computer, the fonts might look different if that computer has a different set of fonts. To preserve the look of your presentation on any computer, you can save, or embed, the fonts in your presentation. Click File on the menu bar, then click Save As. The Save As dialog box opens. Click Tools, click Save Options, then click the Embed TrueType fonts check box in the Save Options dialog box. Click OK to close the Save Options dialog box, then click Save. Now the presentation looks the same on any computer that opens it. Using this option, however, significantly increases the size of your presentation on disk, so only use it when necessary. You can freely embed any TrueType font that comes with Windows. You can embed other TrueType fonts only if they have no license restrictions.

POWERPOINT A-12 GETTING STARTED WITH POWERPOINT 2003 OFFICE-448

Every lesson features large, full-color representations of what the screen should look like as students complete the numbered steps.

FIGURE A-10: Save As dialog box

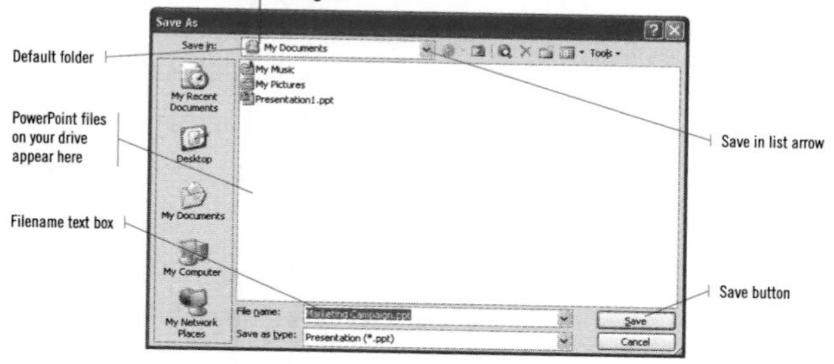

FIGURE A-11: Presentation in Normal view

TABLE A-3: Save As dialog box button functions

button	button name	used to
	Back	Navigate to the drive or folder previously displayed in the Save in list box
	Up One Level	Navigate to the next highest level in the folder hierarchy
	Search the Web	Connect to the World Wide Web
	Delete	Delete the selected folder or file
	Create New Folder	Create a new folder in the current folder or drive
	Views	Change the way folders and files are viewed in the dialog box
Tools	Tools	Open a menu of commands to help you work with selected files and folders

OFFICE-449

GETTING STARTED WITH POWERPOINT 2003 POWERPOINT A-13

PowerPoint 2003

Tables provide quickly accessible summaries of key terms, toolbar buttons, or keyboard alternatives connected with the lesson material. Students can refer easily to this information when working on their own projects at a later time.

The pages are numbered according to application and unit. PowerPoint indicates the application, A indicates the unit, 13 indicates the page.

What online content solutions are available to accompany this book?

Visit www.course.com for more information on our online content for Illustrated titles. Options include:

MyCourse 2.0

Need a quick, simple tool to help you manage your course? Try MyCourse 2.0, the easiest to use, most flexible syllabus and content management tool available. MyCourse 2.0 offers you brand new content, including Topic Reviews, Extra Case Projects, and Quizzes, to accompany this book.

WebCT

Thomson Course Technology and WebCT have partnered to provide you with the highest quality online resources and Web-based tools for your class. Thomson Course Technology offers content for this book to help you create your WebCT class, such as a suggested Syllabus, Lecture Notes, Practice Test questions, and more.

Blackboard

Thomson Course Technology and Blackboard have also partnered to provide you with the highest quality online resources and Web-based tools for your class. Thomson Course Technology offers content for this book to help you create your Blackboard class, such as a suggested Syllabus, Lecture Notes, Practice Test questions, and more.

Is this book Microsoft Office Specialist Certified?

Microsoft Office PowerPoint 2003—Illustrated Introductory, CourseCard Edition covers the objectives for Microsoft Office PowerPoint 2003 and has received certification approval as courseware for the Microsoft Office Specialist program. See page ii (the back of the title page) for more information on other Illustrated titles meeting Microsoft Office Specialist certification.

The first page of each unit indicates which objectives in the unit are Microsoft Office Specialist skills. If an objective is set in red, it meets a Microsoft Office Specialist skill. A document in the Review Pack cross-references the skills with the lessons and exercises.

Instructor Resources

The Instructor Resources CD is Course Technology's way of putting the resources and information needed to teach and learn effectively into your hands. With an integrated array of teaching and learning tools that offers you and your students a broad range of technology-based instructional options, we believe this CD represents the highest quality and most cutting edge resources available to instructors today. Many of these resources are available at www.course.com. The resources available with this book are:

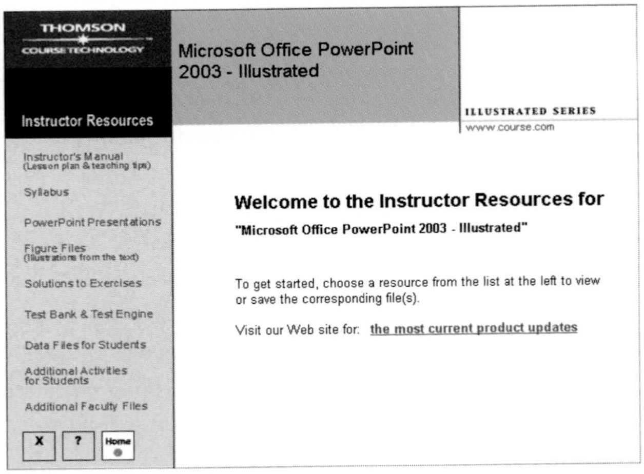

- **Data Files for Students**—To complete most of the units in this book, your students will need **Data Files**. Put them on a file server for students to copy. The Data Files are available on the Instructor Resources CD-ROM and in the Review Pack, and can also be downloaded from www.course.com.

  Instruct students to use the **Data Files List** located in the Review Pack and on the Instructor Resources CD. This list gives instructions on copying and organizing files.

- **Solutions to Exercises**—Solutions to Exercises contains every file students are asked to create or modify in the lessons and End-of-Unit material. A Help file on the Instructor Resources CD includes information for using the Solution Files. There is also a document outlining the solutions for the End-of-Unit Concepts Review, Skills Review, and Independent Challenges.
- **PowerPoint Presentations**—Each unit has a corresponding PowerPoint presentation that you can use in a lecture, distribute to your students, or customize to suit your course.
- **Instructor's Manual**—Available as an electronic file, the Instructor's Manual is quality-assurance tested and includes unit overviews, and detailed lecture topics with teaching tips for each unit.
- **Sample Syllabus**—Prepare and customize your course easily using this sample course outline.
- **ExamView**—ExamView is a powerful testing software package that allows you to create and administer printed, computer (LAN-based), and Internet exams. ExamView includes hundreds of questions that correspond to the topics covered in this text, enabling students to generate detailed study guides that include page references for further review. The computer-based and Internet testing components allow students to take exams at their computers, and also saves you time by grading each exam automatically.
- **Figure Files**—The figures in the text are provided on the Instructor Resources CD to help you illustrate key topics or concepts. You can create traditional overhead transparencies by printing the figure files. Or you can create electronic slide shows by using the figures in a presentation program such as PowerPoint.

SAM 2003 Assessment & Training

SAM 2003 helps you energize your class exams and training assignments by allowing students to learn and test important computer skills in an active, hands-on environment.

With SAM 2003 Assessment, you create powerful interactive exams on critical applications such as Word, Outlook, PowerPoint, Windows, the Internet, and much more. The exams simulate the application environment, allowing your students to demonstrate their knowledge and think through the skills by performing real-world tasks.

Designed to be used with the Illustrated series, SAM 2003 Assessment & Training includes built-in page references so students can create study guides that match the Illustrated textbooks you use in class. Powerful administrative options allow you to schedule exams and assignments, secure your tests, and run reports with almost limitless flexibility.

Brief Contents

	Preface	vi
POWERPOINT 2003	Getting Started with PowerPoint 2003	A-1
POWERPOINT 2003	Creating a Presentation	B-1
POWERPOINT 2003	Modifying a Presentation	C-1
POWERPOINT 2003	Enhancing a Presentation	D-1
POWERPOINT 2003	Customizing a Presentation	E-1
POWERPOINT 2003	Enhancing Charts	F-1
POWERPOINT 2003	Working with Embedded and Linked Objects and Hyperlinks	G-1
POWERPOINT 2003	Using Advanced Features	H-1
	Glossary	1
	Index	5

Contents

Preface vi

POWERPOINT 2003

Getting Started with PowerPoint 2003 A-1

Defining Presentation Software A-2
Starting PowerPoint 2003 ..... A-4
    Creating a PowerPoint shortcut on the desktop
Viewing the PowerPoint Window A-6
    Toolbars and menus in PowerPoint 2003
Using the AutoContent Wizard A-8
    About wizards and the PowerPoint installation
Viewing a Presentation A-10
Saving a Presentation A-12
    Saving fonts with your presentation
Getting Help and Researching Information A-14
    Recovering lost presentation files
Printing and Closing the File, and Exiting PowerPoint A-16
    Viewing your presentation in grayscale or black and white
Concepts Review A-18
Skills Review A-20
Independent Challenges A-21
Visual Workshop A-24

POWERPOINT 2003

Creating a Presentation B-1

Planning an Effective Presentation B-2
Using templates from the Web
Entering Slide Text B-4
Using Speech Recognition
Creating a New Slide B-6
Entering Text in the Outline Tab B-8
What do I do if I see a lightbulb on a slide?
Adding Slide Headers and Footers B-10
Entering and printing notes
Choosing a Look for a Presentation B-12
Using design templates
Checking Spelling in a Presentation B-14
Checking spelling as you type
Evaluating a Presentation B-16
Concepts Review B-18
Skills Review B-19
Independent Challenges B-21
Visual Workshop B-24

POWERPOINT 2003

Modifying a Presentation C-1

Opening an Existing Presentation C-2
Setting permissions
Drawing and Modifying an Object C-4
Understanding PowerPoint objects
Editing Drawn Objects C-6
More ways to change objects
Aligning and Grouping Objects C-8
Adding and Arranging Text C-10
Review a presentation
Formatting Text C-12
Replacing text and attributes

Importing Text from Microsoft Word C-14
Inserting slides from other presentations
Customizing the Color Scheme and Background C-16
Concepts Review C-18
Skills Review C-20
Independent Challenges C-22
Visual Workshop C-24

POWERPOINT 2003

Enhancing a Presentation D-1

Inserting Clip Art D-2
Find more clips online
Inserting, Cropping, and Scaling a Picture D-4
Using graphics in PowerPoint
Embedding a Chart D-6
Entering and Editing Data in the Datasheet D-8
Series in Rows vs. Series in Columns
Formatting a Chart D-10
Customizing data series in charts
Creating Tables in PowerPoint D-12
Using Slide Show Commands D-14
Setting Slide Show Timings and Transitions D-16
Rehearsing slide show timing
Setting Slide Animation Effects D-18
Presentation checklist
Concepts Review D-20
Skills Review D-21
Independent Challenges D-22
Visual Workshop D-24

POWERPOINT 2003
Customizing a Presentation E-1
Understanding PowerPoint Masters E-2
Accessing the Internet from the Desktop
Formatting Master Text E-4
Exceptions to the slide master
Changing Master Text Indents E-6
Restoring the master layout
Adjusting Text Objects E-8
Changing margins around text in shapes
Using Advanced Drawing Tools E-10
Drawing a freeform shape
Using Advanced Formatting Tools....................E-12
Applying a color scheme to another presentation
Insert and Format WordArt E-14
Using the Style Checker
Creating a Template....................E-16
Applying a template from another presentation
Concepts Review E-18
Skills Review....................E-19
Independent Challenges E-21
Visual Workshop E-24

POWERPOINT 2003
Enhancing Charts F-1
Inserting Data from a File into a Datasheet....................F-2
Data series and data series markers
Formatting a Datasheet F-4
Formatting datasheets and charts
Changing the Chart Type F-6
Customized chart types
Changing Chart Options F-8
Working with Chart Elements F-10
Moving and sizing chart elements

Animating Charts and Adding Sounds F-12
Adding voice narrations
Embedding an Organization Chart F-14
Modifying an Organization Chart F-16
Concepts Review F-18
Skills Review F-19
Independent Challenges F-21
Visual Workshop F-24

POWERPOINT 2003

Working with Embedded and Linked Objects and Hyperlinks G-1

Embedding a Picture G-2
Exporting a presentation
Embedding an Excel Chart G-4
Embedding a worksheet
Linking an Excel Worksheet G-6
Linking objects using Paste Special
Updating a Linked Excel Worksheet G-8
Using the Links dialog box
Inserting an Animated GIF File G-10
Inserting movies
Inserting a Sound G-12
Playing music from a CD
Inserting a Hyperlink G-14
Creating a Photo Album G-16
Concepts Review G-18
Skills Review G-19
Independent Challenges G-21
Visual Workshop G-24

Using Advanced Features **H-1**

Sending a Presentation for Review H-2
    Other ways to send a presentation for review
Combining Reviewed Presentations H-4
    Reviewing a presentation
Setting Up a Slide Show H-6
    Hiding a slide during a slide show
Creating a Custom Show H-8
    Using action buttons to hyperlink to a custom slide show
Rehearsing Slide Timings H-10
    Changing the page setup
Publishing a Presentation for the Web H-12
    Online meetings
Packaging a Presentation H-14
    Using the Microsoft PowerPoint Viewer
Broadcasting a Presentation H-16
    Record and save a broadcast
Concepts Review H-18
Skills Review H-19
Independent Challenges H-21
Visual Workshop H-24

Glossary **1**

Index **5**

Read This Before You Begin

Software Information and Required Installation

This book was written and tested using Microsoft Office 2003 - Professional Edition, with a typical installation on Microsoft Windows XP, including installation of the most recent Windows XP Service Pack, and with Internet Explorer 6.0 or higher. Some of the exercises in this book assume that your computer is connected to the Internet. If you are not connected to the Internet, see your instructor.

Tips for Students

What are Data Files?

To complete many of the units in this book, you need to use Data Files. A Data File contains a partially completed presentation, so that you don't have to type in all the information yourself. Your instructor will either provide you with copies of the Data Files or ask you to make your own copies. Your instructor can also give you instructions on how to organize your files, as well as a complete file listing, or you can find the list and the instructions for organizing your files in the Review Pack. In addition, because there are no Data Files supplied for Unit A or Unit B, you will need to create folders for A and B at the same level as your other unit folders in order to save the files you create.

If you are using floppy disks to complete the exercises in this book, then you will need to use multiple disks to complete all of the work in Unit G. Because of the size of the Data Files in Unit H and the nature of some of PowerPoint's features, it will be necessary for you to use some hard disk space to complete the exercises.

Why is my screen different from the book?

Your desktop components and some dialog box options might be different if you are using an operating system other than Windows XP.

Depending on your computer hardware and the Display settings on your computer, you may also notice the following differences:

- Your screen may look larger or smaller because of your screen resolution (the height and width of your screen).

- Your title bars and dialog boxes may not display file extensions. To display file extensions, click Start on the taskbar, click Control Panel, click Appearance and Themes, then click Folder Options. Click the View tab if necessary, click Hide extensions for known file types to deselect it, then click OK. Your Office dialog boxes and title bars should now display file extensions.

- Depending on your Office settings, your toolbars may be displayed on a single row and your menus may display a shortened list of frequently used commands. Office menus and toolbars can modify themselves to your working style by displaying only the most frequently used buttons and menu commands. To view buttons not currently displayed, click a Toolbar Options button at the end of either the Standard or Formatting toolbar. To view the full list of menu commands, click the double arrow at the bottom of the menu.

Toolbars in one row

Toolbars in two rows

In order to have your toolbars displayed in two rows, showing all buttons, and to have the full menus displayed, you must turn off the personalized menus and toolbars feature. Click Tools on the menu bar, click Customize, select the show Standard and Formatting toolbars on two rows and Always show full menus check boxes on the Options tab, and then click Close. This book assumes you are displaying toolbars in two rows and displaying full menus.

UNIT
A
PowerPoint 2003

Getting Started with PowerPoint 2003

OBJECTIVES

- Define presentation software
- Start PowerPoint 2003
- View the PowerPoint window
- Use the AutoContent Wizard
- View a presentation
- Save a presentation
- Get Help and research information
- Print and close the file, and exit PowerPoint 2003

If you have a SAM user profile, you may have access to hands-on instruction, practice, and assessment of the skills covered in this unit. Log in to your SAM account and go to your assignments page to see what your instructor has assigned.

Microsoft Office PowerPoint 2003 is a computer program that enables you to create visually compelling presentations. With PowerPoint, you can create individual slides and display them as a slide show on your computer, video projector, or even via the Internet. Maria Abbott is the general sales manager at MediaLoft, a chain of bookstore cafés founded in 1988. MediaLoft stores offer customers the opportunity to purchase books, music, and movies while enjoying a variety of coffees, teas, and freshly baked desserts. As her assistant, Maria needs you to learn the basics of PowerPoint so you can create presentations for the sales department.

UNIT
A
PowerPoint 2003

Defining Presentation Software

Presentation software is a computer program you can use to organize and present information and ideas. Whether you are giving a sales pitch or explaining your company's goals and accomplishments, presentation software can help you communicate effectively and professionally. You can use PowerPoint to create presentations, as well as notes for the presenter and handouts for the audience. Table A-1 explains the items you can create using PowerPoint. Maria wants you to create a presentation that explains a new marketing campaign that the MediaLoft Sales Department is developing. Because you are not that familiar with PowerPoint, you get to work exploring its capabilities. Figure A-1 shows a handout you created using a word processor for a recent presentation. Figure A-2 shows how the information might look in PowerPoint.

DETAILS

You can easily complete the following tasks using PowerPoint:

- **Present information in a variety of ways**
  With PowerPoint, you can present information using a variety of methods. For example, you can print handout pages or an outline of your presentation for your audience. You can display your presentation as an electronic slide show on a computer. If you are presenting to a large group in a conference room, you can use a video projector. If you want to reach an even wider audience, you can post your presentation so it can be viewed over the Internet.

- **Enter and edit data easily**
  Using PowerPoint, you can enter and edit data quickly and efficiently. When you need to change a part of your presentation, you can use the word processing and outlining capabilities of PowerPoint to edit your content rather than re-create it.

- **Change the appearance of information**
  PowerPoint has many features that can transform the way text, graphics, and slides appear. By exploring some of these capabilities, you discover how easy it is to change the appearance of your presentation.

- **Organize and arrange information**
  Once you start using PowerPoint, you won't have to spend much time making sure your information is correct and in the right order. With PowerPoint, you can quickly and easily rearrange and modify text, graphics, and slides in your presentation.

- **Incorporate information from other sources**
  Often, when you create presentations, you use information from other sources. With PowerPoint, you can import text, graphics, and numerical data from spreadsheet, database, and word processing files such as Microsoft Excel, Microsoft Access, Microsoft Word, and Corel WordPerfect. You can also import graphic images from a variety of sources such as the Internet, image files on a computer, or other graphics programs. Likewise, you can also incorporate changes made to your presentation by others who review it.

- **Show a presentation on any computer that doesn't have PowerPoint installed**
  By using the Package for CD feature, you can copy your presentation and its supporting files to a CD to be viewed on another computer, even if the computer doesn't have PowerPoint installed. The PowerPoint Viewer, which is included on the CD when you package a presentation, displays a presentation as an on-screen slide show on any compatible computer. To package a presentation directly to a CD, your computer must be running Windows XP or later.

FIGURE A-1: Traditional handout

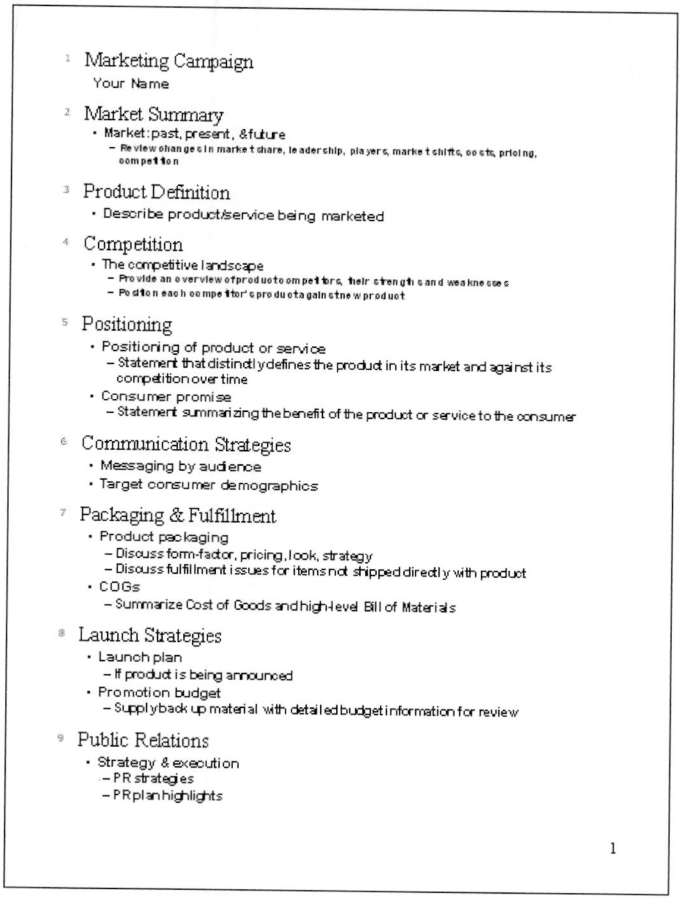

1 Marketing Campaign
Your Name

2 Market Summary
- Market: past, present, & future
  - Review changes in market share, leadership, players, market shifts, costs, pricing, competition

3 Product Definition
- Describe product/service being marketed

4 Competition
- The competitive landscape
  - Provide an overview of product competitors, their strengths and weaknesses
  - Position each competitor's product against new product

5 Positioning
- Positioning of product or service
  - Statement that distinctly defines the product in its market and against its competition over time
- Consumer promise
  - Statement summarizing the benefit of the product or service to the consumer

6 Communication Strategies
- Messaging by audience
- Target consumer demographics

7 Packaging & Fulfillment
- Product packaging
  - Discuss form-factor, pricing, look, strategy
  - Discuss fulfillment issues for items not shipped directly with product
- COGs
  - Summarize Cost of Goods and high-level Bill of Materials

8 Launch Strategies
- Launch plan
  - If product is being announced
- Promotion budget
  - Supply back up material with detailed budget information for review

9 Public Relations
- Strategy & execution
  - PR strategies
  - PR plan highlights

1

FIGURE A-2: PowerPoint handout

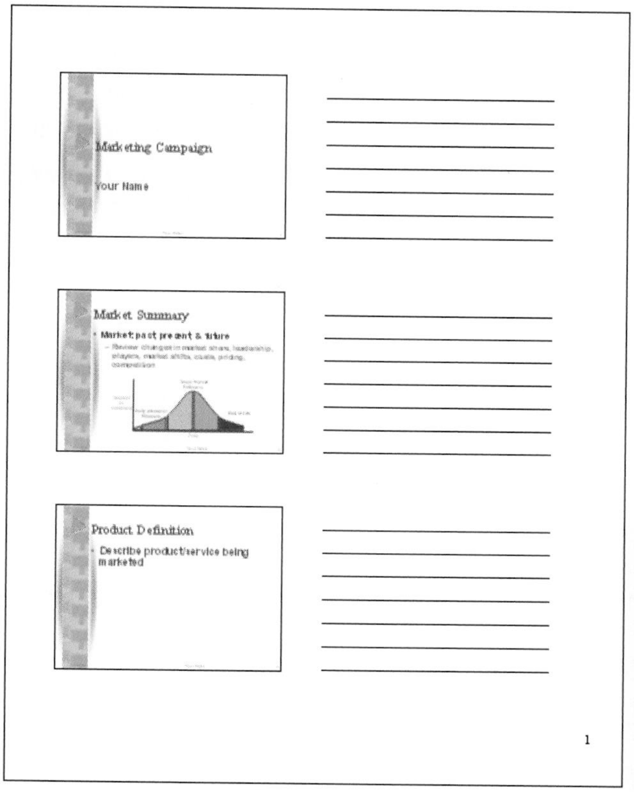

TABLE A-1: Presenting information using PowerPoint

item	use
On-screen presentations	Run a slide show directly from your computer
Web presentations	Broadcast a presentation on the Web or on an intranet that others can view, complete with video and audio
Online meetings	View or work on a presentation with your colleagues in real time
Color overheads	Print PowerPoint slides directly to transparencies on your color printer
Black-and-white overheads	Print PowerPoint slides directly to transparencies on your black-and-white printer
Notes	Print notes that help you remember points about each slide when you speak to a group
Audience handouts	Print handouts with two, three, or six slides on a page
Outline pages	Print the outline of your presentation to highlight the main points

Starting PowerPoint 2003

To start PowerPoint 2003, you must first start Windows. You have to click the Start button on the taskbar, then point to All Programs to display the All Programs menu. Point to Microsoft Office to open the Microsoft Office menu which contains the Microsoft PowerPoint program name and icon. If Microsoft PowerPoint is not in the All Programs menu, it might be in a different location on your computer. If you are using a computer on a network, you might need to use a different starting procedure. Start PowerPoint to familiarize yourself with the program.

STEPS

1. **Make sure your computer is on and the Windows desktop is visible**
   If any program windows are open, close or minimize them.
2. **Click the Start button start on the taskbar, point to All Programs**
   The All Programs menu opens, showing a list of icons and names for all your programs.
3. **Point to Microsoft Office**
   You see the Microsoft Office programs installed on your computer, as shown in Figure A-3. Your screen might look different, depending on which programs are installed on your computer.
4. **Click Microsoft Office PowerPoint 2003 on the Microsoft Office menu**
   PowerPoint starts, and the PowerPoint window opens, as shown in Figure A-4.

TROUBLE

If you have trouble finding Microsoft PowerPoint on the Programs menu, check with your instructor or technical support person.

Clues to Use

Creating a PowerPoint shortcut on the desktop

You can make it easier to start PowerPoint by placing a shortcut on the desktop. To create the shortcut, click the Start button start, then point to All Programs. On the All Programs menu, point to Microsoft Office, point to Microsoft Office PowerPoint, then right-click Microsoft Office PowerPoint 2003. In the shortcut menu that appears, point to Send To, then click Desktop (create shortcut). Windows places a Microsoft PowerPoint shortcut icon on your desktop. In the future, you can start PowerPoint by simply double-clicking this icon, instead of using the Start menu. You can edit or change the name of the shortcut by right-clicking the shortcut icon, clicking Rename on the shortcut menu, and then typing a new name as you would name any item in Windows. If you are working in a computer lab, you may not be allowed to place shortcuts on the desktop. Check with your instructor or technical support person before attempting to add a shortcut.

FIGURE A-3: All Programs menu

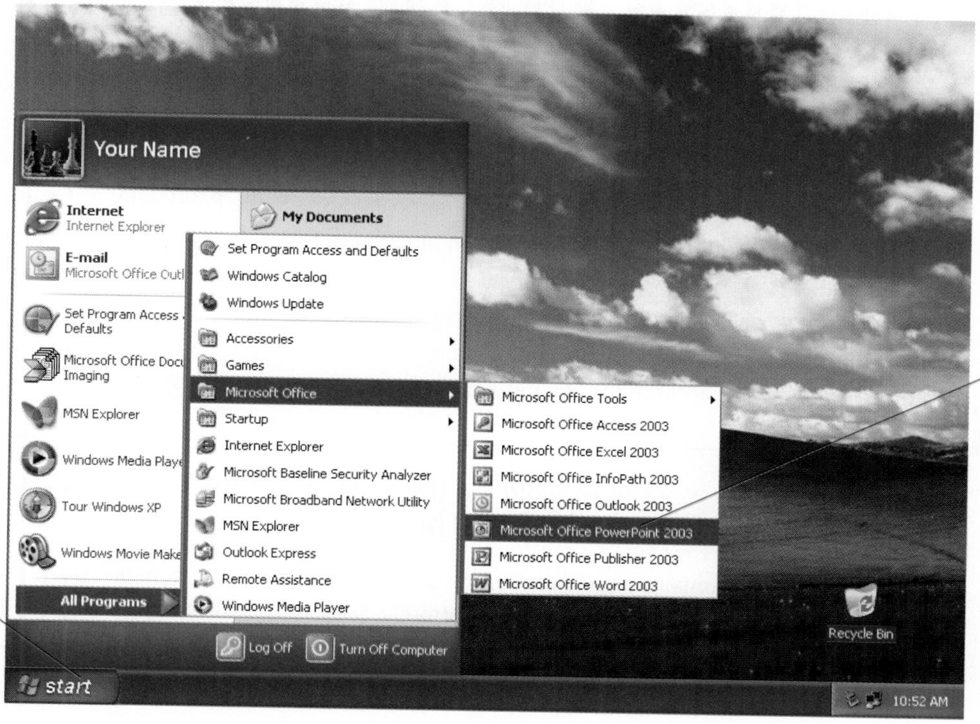

Start button

Microsoft Office PowerPoint 2003 program

FIGURE A-4: PowerPoint window

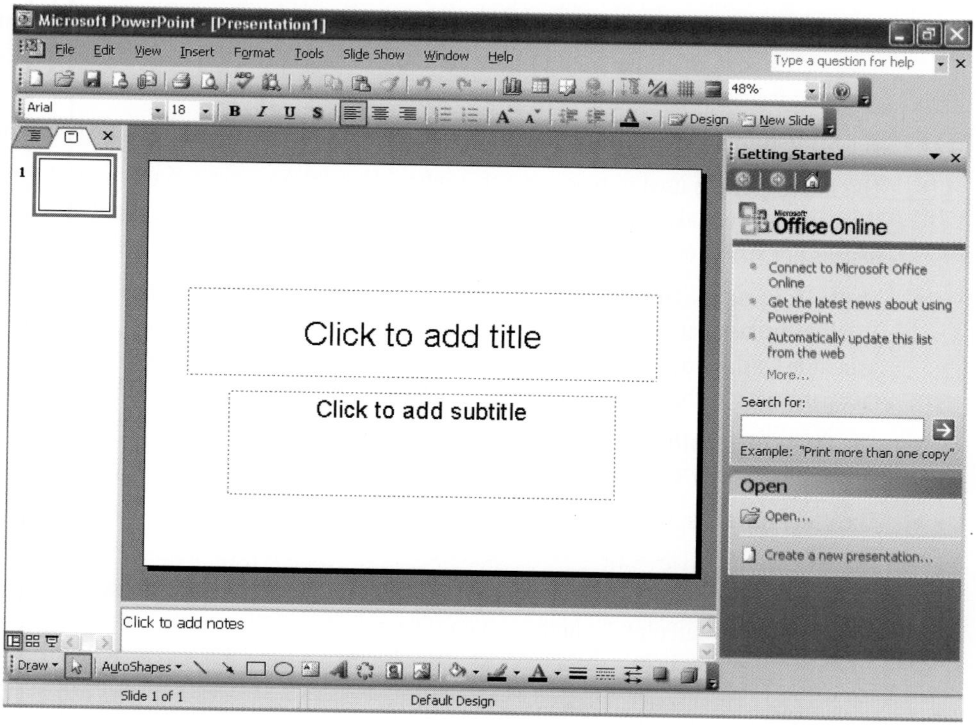

UNIT A

PowerPoint 2003

Viewing the PowerPoint Window

When you first start PowerPoint, a blank slide appears in the PowerPoint window. PowerPoint has different **views** that allow you to see your presentation in different forms. By default, the PowerPoint window opens in **Normal view**, which is the primary view that you use to write, edit, and design your presentation. Normal view is divided into three areas called **panes**: the pane on the left contains the Outline and Slides tabs, the Slide pane, and the notes pane. You move around in each pane using the scroll bars. The PowerPoint window and the specific parts of the Normal view are described below.

DETAILS

Using Figure A-5 as a guide, examine the elements of the PowerPoint window, then find and compare the elements described below:

- The **title bar** contains a program Control Menu button, the program name, the title of the presentation, resizing buttons, and the program Close button.
- The **menu bar** contains the names of the menus you use to choose PowerPoint commands, as well as the Type a question for help box and the Close Window button.
- The **Standard toolbar** contains buttons for commonly used commands, such as copying and pasting. The **Formatting toolbar** contains buttons for the most frequently used formatting commands, such as changing font type and size. The toolbars on your screen may be displayed on one line instead of two. See the Clues to Use for more information on how toolbars are displayed.
- The **Outline tab** displays your presentation text in the form of an outline, without graphics. In this tab, it is easy to move text on or among slides by dragging text to reorder the information.
- The **Slides tab** displays the slides of your presentation as small images, called **thumbnails**. You can quickly navigate through the slides in your presentation by clicking the thumbnails on this tab. You can also add, delete, or rearrange slides using this tab.
- The **Slide pane** displays the current slide in your presentation, including all text and graphics.
- The **notes pane** is used to type notes that reference a slide's content. You can print these notes and refer to them when you make a presentation or print them as handouts and give them to your audience. The notes pane is not visible to the audience when you show a slide presentation in Slide Show view.
- The **task pane** contains sets of hyperlinks for commonly used commands. The commands are grouped into 16 different task panes. The commands include creating new presentations, opening existing presentations, searching for documents, and using the Office Clipboard. You can also perform basic formatting tasks from the task pane such as changing the slide layout, slide design, color scheme, or slide animations of a presentation.
- The **Drawing toolbar**, located at the bottom of the PowerPoint window, contains buttons and menus that let you create lines, shapes, and special effects.
- The **view buttons**, at the bottom of the Outline tab and Slides tab area, allow you to quickly switch between PowerPoint views.
- The **status bar**, located at the bottom of the PowerPoint window, shows messages about what you are doing and seeing in PowerPoint, including which slide you are viewing.

FIGURE A-5: Presentation window in Normal view

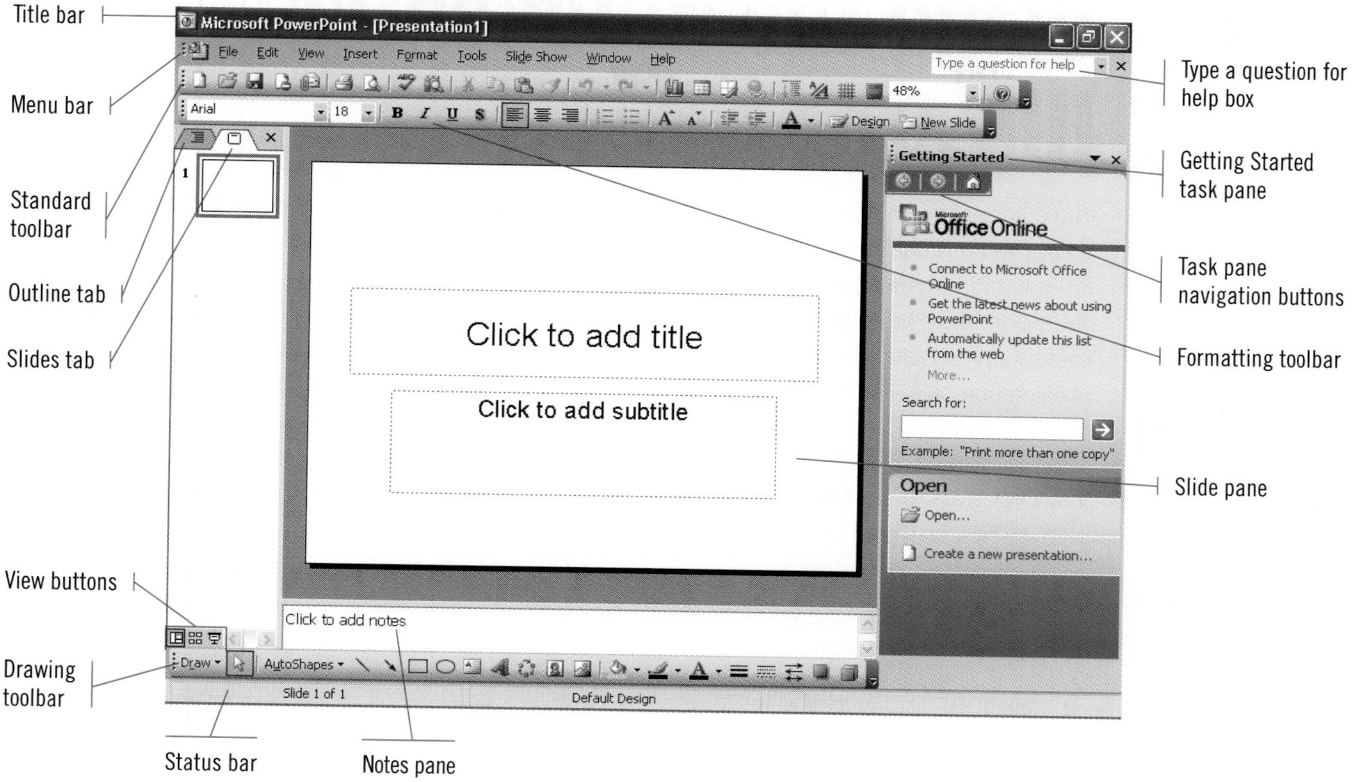

Clues to Use

Toolbars and menus in PowerPoint 2003

PowerPoint 2003 offers personalized toolbars and menus, which modify themselves to your working style. When you use personalized toolbars and menus, the Standard and Formatting toolbars appear on the same row and display only the most frequently used buttons. To use a button that is not visible on a toolbar, click the Toolbar Options button at the end of the toolbar, and then click the button that you want. As you work, PowerPoint adds the buttons you use to the visible toolbars and drops the buttons you haven't used in a while to the Toolbar Options list. Similarly, PowerPoint menus adjust to your work habits, so that the commands you use most often appear on shortened menus. To view additional menu commands, you can either double-click the menu name or click the Expand button (double arrows) at the bottom of a menu.

The lessons in this book assume you have turned off personalized menus and toolbars and are working with all menu commands and toolbar buttons displayed. To turn off personalized toolbars and menus so that you can easily find the commands that are referenced in this book, click Tools on the menu bar, click Customize, select the Show Standard and Formatting toolbars on two rows and Always show full menus check boxes on the Options tab, and then click Close. The Standard and Formatting toolbars appear on separate rows and display all the buttons, and the menus display the complete list of menu commands. (You can also quickly display the toolbars on two rows by clicking either Toolbar Options button and then clicking Show Buttons on Two Rows.)

UNIT A
PowerPoint 2003

Using the AutoContent Wizard

The quickest way to create a presentation is with the AutoContent Wizard. A **wizard** is a series of steps that guides you through a task (in this case, creating a presentation). Using the AutoContent Wizard, you choose a presentation type from the wizard's list of sample presentations. Then you indicate what type of output you want. Next, you type the information for the title slide and the footer. The AutoContent Wizard then creates a presentation with sample text you can use as a guide to help formulate the major points of your presentation. You decide to start your presentation by opening the AutoContent Wizard.

STEPS

QUICK TIP

You can also access the New Presentation task pane by clicking Create a new presentation in the Open section on the Getting Started task pane.

1. **Click the Other Task Panes list arrow ▼ in the task pane title bar, then click New Presentation**

   The New Presentation task pane opens.

2. **Point to the From AutoContent wizard hyperlink in the New section of the task pane**

   The mouse pointer changes to the Hyperlink pointer. The pointer changes to this shape any time it is positioned over a hyperlink.

3. **Click the From AutoContent wizard hyperlink**

   The AutoContent Wizard dialog box opens, as shown in Figure A-6. The left section of the dialog box outlines the contents of the AutoContent Wizard, and the text in the right section explains the current wizard screen.

4. **Click Next**

   The Presentation type screen appears. This screen contains category buttons and types of presentations. Each presentation type contains suggested text for a particular use. By default, the presentation types in the General category are listed.

5. **Click the Sales/Marketing category, click Marketing Plan in the list on the right, then click Next**

   The Presentation style screen appears, asking you to choose an output type. The On-screen presentation option is selected by default.

6. **Click Next, click in the Presentation title text box, then type Marketing Campaign**

   The Presentation options screen requests information that appears on the title slide of the presentation and in the footer at the bottom of each slide. The Date last updated and the Slide number check boxes are selected by default.

7. **Press [Tab], then type Your Name in the Footer text box**

8. **Click Next, then click Finish**

   The AutoContent Wizard opens the presentation based on the Marketing Plan presentation type you chose. Sample text for each slide is listed on the left in the Outline tab, and the title slide appears in the Slide pane on the right side of the screen. Notice that the task pane is no longer visible. The task pane can be easily opened the next time you need it. Compare your screen to Figure A-7.

FIGURE A-6: AutoContent Wizard opening screen

FIGURE A-7: Presentation created with AutoContent Wizard

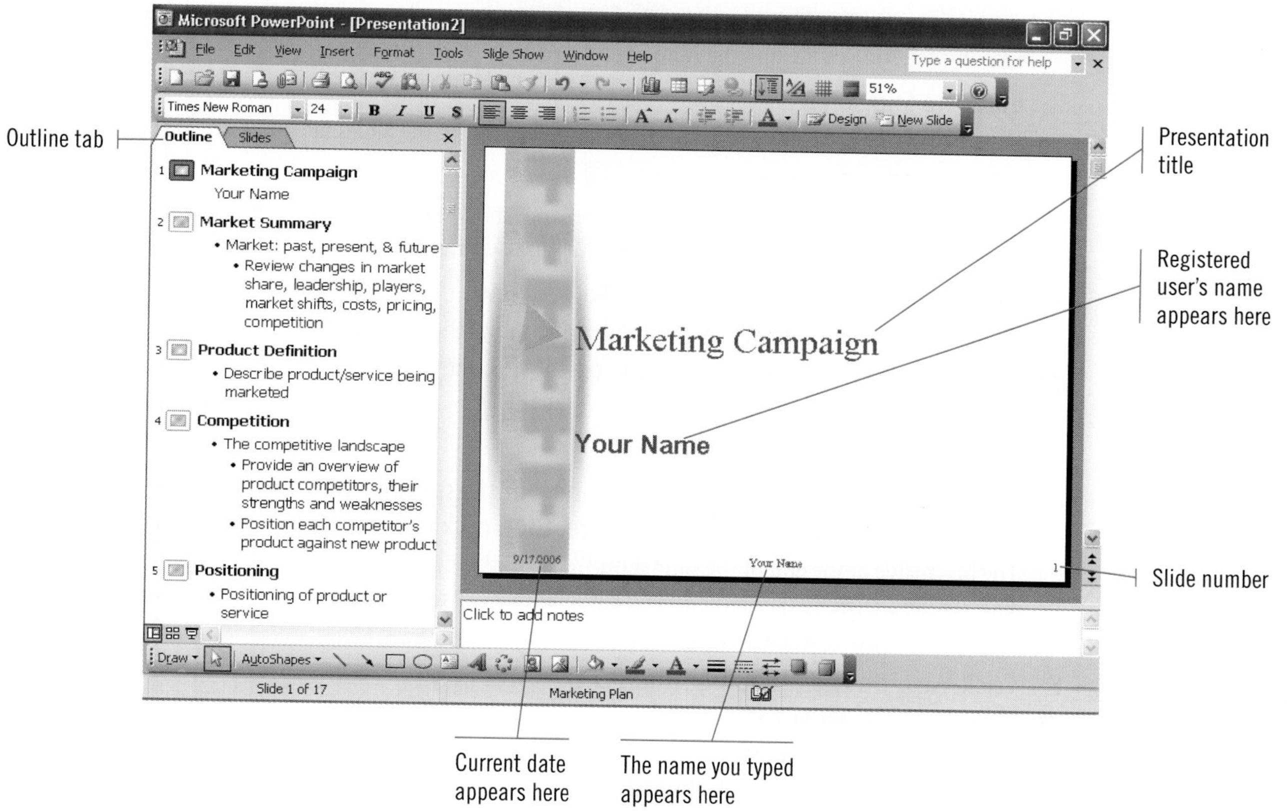

Clues to Use

About wizards and the PowerPoint installation

As you use PowerPoint, you may find that not all AutoContent Wizards are available to you. The wizards that are available depend on your PowerPoint installation. A typical installation of PowerPoint provides you with many wizards, templates, and other features. However, some features may require you to run an install program before you use the feature for the first time. If you find a feature that is not installed, run the install program as directed. In some instances you may be required to insert the Office CD in order to install a feature. If you are working on a networked computer or in a lab, see your technical support person for assistance.

UNIT A

PowerPoint 2003

Viewing a Presentation

This lesson introduces you to the four PowerPoint views: Normal view, Slide Sorter view, Slide Show view, and Notes Page view. Each PowerPoint view shows your presentation in a different way and allows you to manipulate your presentation differently. To move easily among most of the PowerPoint views, use the view buttons located at the bottom of the pane containing the Outline and Slides tabs. Table A-2 provides a brief description of the PowerPoint views. Examine each of the PowerPoint views, starting with Normal view.

STEPS

1. **In the Outline tab, click the small slide icon next to Slide 4**
   The text for Slide 4 is selected in the Outline tab and Slide 4 appears in the Slide pane as shown in Figure A-8. Notice that the status bar also indicates the number of the slide you are viewing, the total number of slides in the presentation, and the name of the AutoContent wizard you are using.
2. **Click the Previous Slide button at the bottom of the vertical scroll bar three times so that Slide 1 (the title slide) appears**
   The scroll box in the vertical scroll bar moves back up the scroll bar. The gray slide icon on the Outline tab indicates which slide is displayed in the Slide pane. As you scroll through the presentation, read the sample text on each slide created by the AutoContent Wizard.
3. **Click the Slides tab**
   Thumbnails of all the slides in your presentation appear on the Slides tab and the Slide pane enlarges.
4. **Click the Slide Sorter View button**
   A thumbnail of each slide in the presentation appears as shown in Figure A-9. You can examine the flow of your slides and drag any slide or group of slides to rearrange the order of the slides in the presentation.
5. **Double-click the first slide in Slide Sorter view**
   The slide appears in Normal view. The Slide pane shows the selected slide.
6. **Click the Slide Show from current slide button**
   The first slide fills the entire screen. In this view, you can practice running through your slides as they would appear in the slide show.
7. **Press the left mouse button, press [Enter], or press [Spacebar] to advance through the slides one at a time until you see a black slide, then click once more to return to Normal view**
   The black slide at the end of the slide show indicates that the slide show is finished. When you click the black slide (or press [Spacebar] or [Enter]), you automatically return to the slide and view you were in before you ran the slide show, in this case Slide 1 in Normal view.
8. **Click View on the menu bar, then click Notes Page**
   Notes Page view appears, showing a reduced image of the current slide above a large text box. You can enter text in this box and then print the notes page for your own use to help you remember important points about your presentation. To switch to Notes Page view, you must choose Notes Page from the View menu; there is no Notes Page view button.

TROUBLE

If you don't see a menu command, click the Expand button at the bottom of the menu.

FIGURE A-8: Normal view with the Outline tab displayed

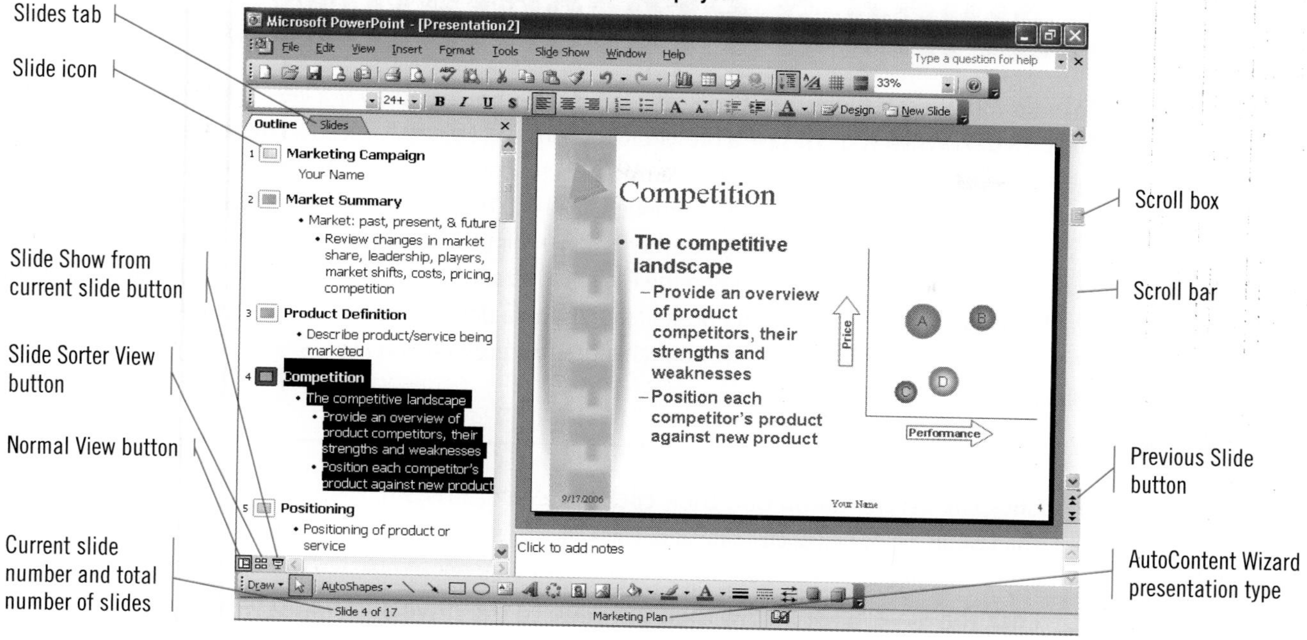

FIGURE A-9: Slide Sorter view

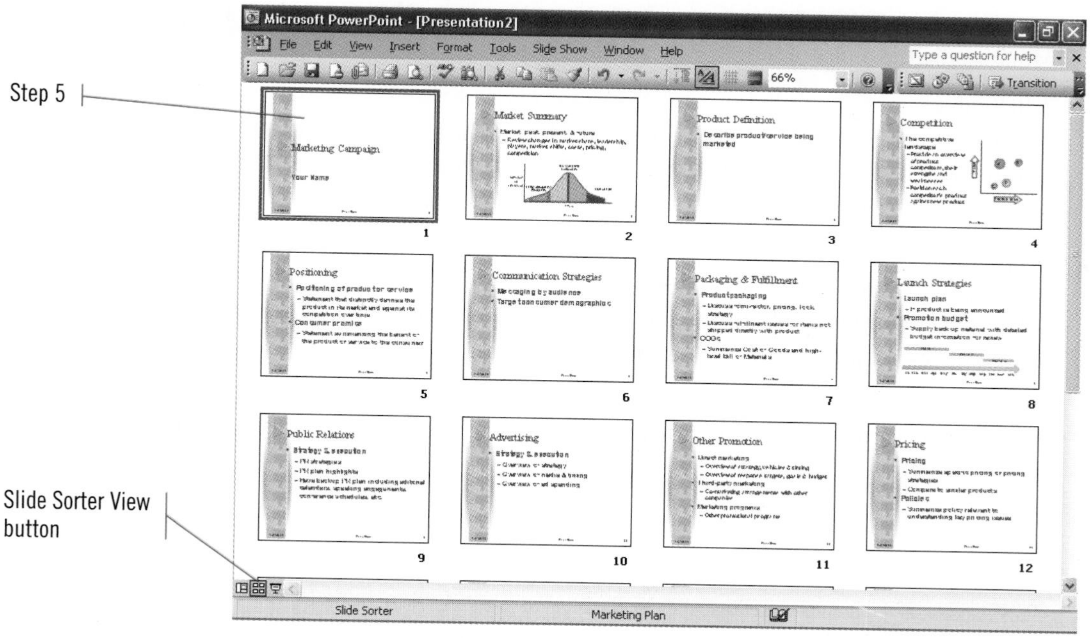

PowerPoint 2003

TABLE A-2: PowerPoint views

view name	button	button name	description
Normal		Normal View	Displays the pane that contains the Outline and Slides tabs, Slide pane, and notes panes at the same time; use this view to work on your presentation's content, layout, and notes concurrently
Slide Sorter		Slide Sorter View	Displays thumbnails of all slides in the order in which they appear in your presentation; use this view to rearrange and add special effects to your slides
Slide Show		Slide Show from current slide	Displays your presentation as an electronic slide show
Notes Page			Displays a reduced image of the current slide above a large text box where you can enter or view notes

Saving a Presentation

To store your presentation so that you can work on it or view it again at a later time, you must save it as a **file** on a disk. When you first save a presentation, you give it a name, called a **filename**, and determine the location where you want to store the file. After you initially save your presentation, you should then save your presentation periodically as you continue to work so that any changes are saved in the file. As a general rule, it's wise to save your work about every 5 to 10 minutes and before printing. You use either the Save command or the Save As command on the File menu to save your presentation for the first time. When you want to make a copy of an existing presentation using a different name, use the Save As command; otherwise, use the Save command to save your changes to a presentation file. Save your presentation as Marketing Campaign.

STEPS

1. **Click File on the menu bar, then click Save As**
   The Save As dialog box opens, similar to Figure A-10. See Table A-3 for a description of the Save As dialog box button functions.
2. **Click the Save in list arrow, then navigate to the drive and folder where your Data Files are stored**
   A default filename, which PowerPoint creates from the presentation title you entered, appears in the File name text box. If the selected drive or folder contains any PowerPoint files, their filenames appear in the white area in the center of the dialog box.
3. **Click Save**
   Filenames can be up to 255 characters long; you may use lowercase or uppercase letters, symbols, numbers, and spaces. The Save As dialog box closes, and the new filename appears in the title bar at the top of the Presentation window. PowerPoint remembers which view your presentation is in when you save it, so you decide to save the presentation in Normal view instead of Notes Page view.
4. **Click the Normal View button**
   The presentation view changes from Notes Page view to Normal view as shown in Figure A-11.
5. **Click the Save button on the Standard toolbar**
   The Save command saves any changes you made to the file to the same location you specified when you used the Save As command. Save your file frequently while working with it to protect your presentation.

QUICK TIP
To save a file quickly, you can press the shortcut key combination [Ctrl][S].

Clues to Use

Saving fonts with your presentation

When you create a presentation, it uses the fonts that are installed on your computer. If you need to open the presentation on another computer, the fonts might look different if that computer has a different set of fonts. To preserve the look of your presentation on any computer, you can save, or embed, the fonts in your presentation. Click File on the menu bar, then click Save As. The Save As dialog box opens. Click Tools, click Save Options, then click the Embed TrueType fonts check box in the Save Options dialog box. Click OK to close the Save Options dialog box, then click Save. Now the presentation looks the same on any computer that opens it. Using this option, however, significantly increases the size of your presentation on disk, so only use it when necessary. You can freely embed any TrueType font that comes with Windows. You can embed other TrueType fonts only if they have no license restrictions.

FIGURE A-10: Save As dialog box

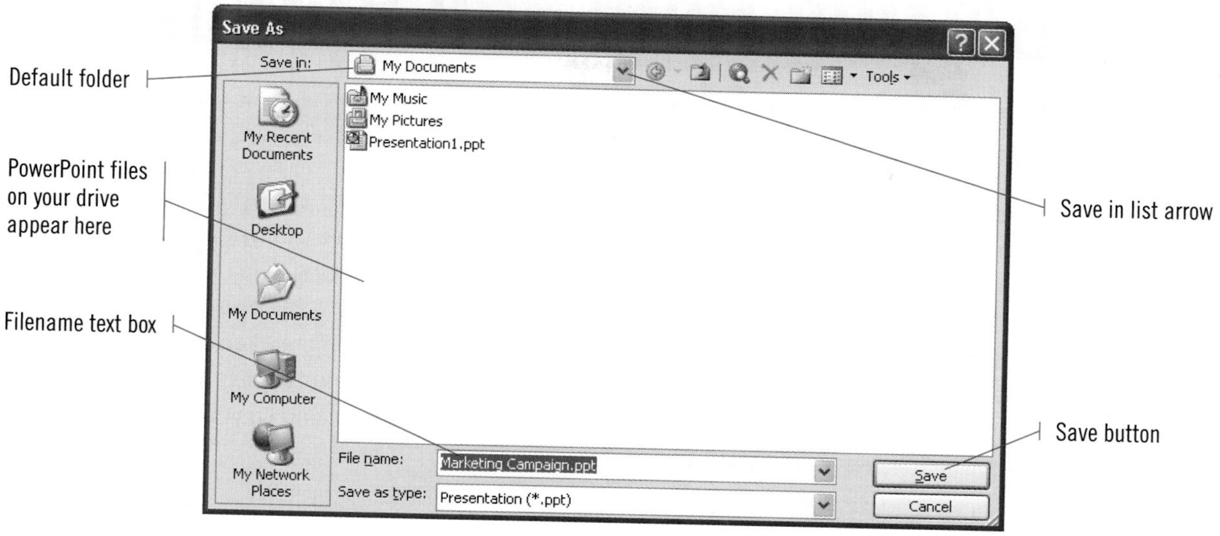

FIGURE A-11: Presentation in Normal view

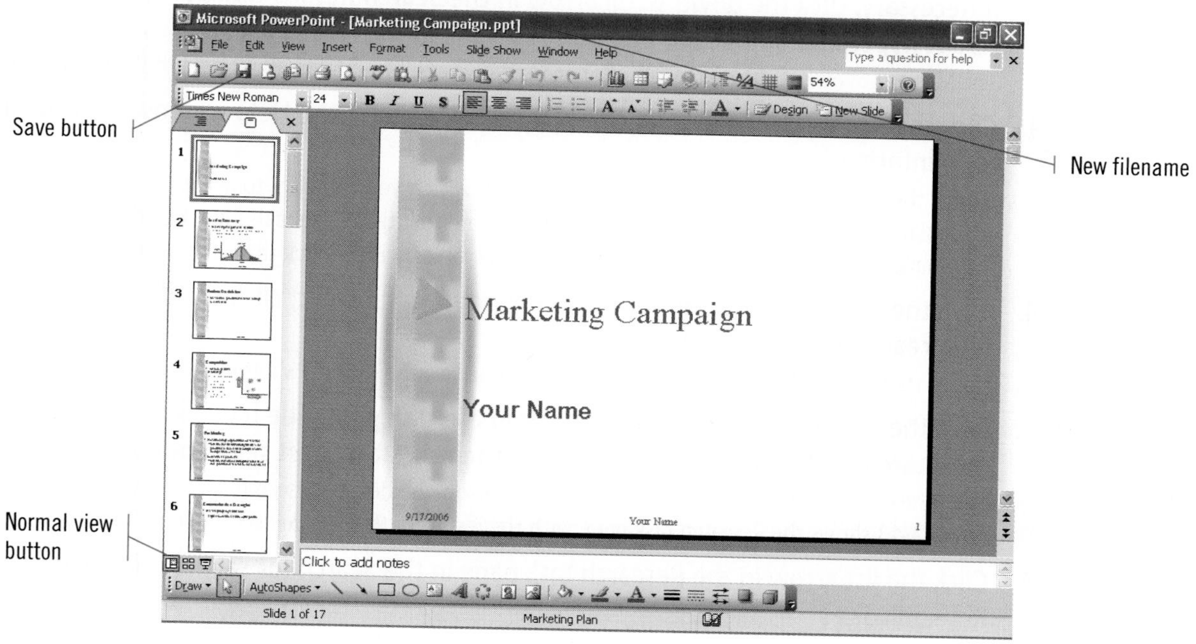

TABLE A-3: Save As dialog box button functions

button	button name	used to
	Back	Navigate to the drive or folder previously displayed in the Save in list box
	Up One Level	Navigate to the next highest level in the folder hierarchy
	Search the Web	Connect to the World Wide Web
	Delete	Delete the selected folder or file
	Create New Folder	Create a new folder in the current folder or drive
	Views	Change the way folders and files are viewed in the dialog box
Tools ▾	Tools	Open a menu of commands to help you work with selected files and folders

UNIT A

PowerPoint 2003

Getting Help and Researching Information

PowerPoint has an extensive Help system that gives you immediate access to program definitions, reference information, and feature explanations. To access Help information, you can type a word, phrase, or question in the Type a question for help box on the menu bar or you can click the Help button on the Standard toolbar. Help information appears in a separate window that you can move and resize. You can also access other resources such as dictionaries, thesauruses, or Web sites to research information on various topics related to PowerPoint. If the information you are looking for does not appear in the Help window, you can rephrase your question and try your search again. You are finished working on your presentation for now and you decide to learn about hyperlinks.

STEPS

TROUBLE

If your search results are not from www.microsoft.com, then you may not be connected to the Internet. Check with your instructor or technical support person for help. If you are unable to connect to the Internet, you will not be able to complete all of the steps in this lesson.

TROUBLE

A dialog box may open telling you that the Research feature is not installed. Install the Research feature using the Office CD or check with your instructor or technical support person for help.

1. **Click in the Type a question for help box on the menu bar, type hyperlinks, then press [Enter]**
   The Search Results task pane appears showing Help topics related to hyperlinks. See Figure A-12.
2. **If necessary, click the down scroll arrow in the Search Results task pane, then click the About hyperlinks and action buttons hyperlink in the results list**
   The Microsoft PowerPoint Help window opens and displays information about hyperlinks and action buttons.
3. **Click the down scroll arrow on the vertical scroll bar in the Help window to read all of the Help information**
   Notice the hyperlinks (blue words) in the Help text, which you can click to get further information on that particular subject. Two subtopic hyperlinks, which are identified by small blue arrows, are below the Help information. To view information on either of these topics, simply click the topic hyperlink.
4. **Click the Testing and repairing broken hyperlinks subtopic, click the down scroll arrow, then read the information**
   Notice that the small blue arrow now points down indicating that the subtopic is displayed.
5. **Click the Other Task Panes list arrow ▼ in the task pane title bar, click Research, click in the Search for text box, type hyperlinks, then click the Start searching button ➔**
   The Research task pane displays information found in the default research Web sites and reference books. Figure A-13 shows the Research task pane with the results of the research on the term 'hyperlinks'.
6. **Click the list arrow in the Research task pane in the Search for section, then click All Research Sites**
   PowerPoint researches the currently available Web sites for information on hyperlinks and displays the information in the Research task pane. To further help your ability to research topics, PowerPoint allows you to choose which reference books, research Web sites, and other research services you can use when doing research.
7. **Click the Close button ☒ in the Microsoft PowerPoint Help window title bar**
   The Help window closes, and your presentation fills the screen again. The Research task pane should still be visible.
8. **Click the Research options hyperlink at the bottom of the Research task pane**
   The Research Options dialog box opens. The options in this dialog box allow you to customize the tools that will be used to research information.
9. **Click the down scroll arrow in the dialog box to view all of the available options, then click Cancel**

FIGURE A-12: Search Results task pane showing Help topics

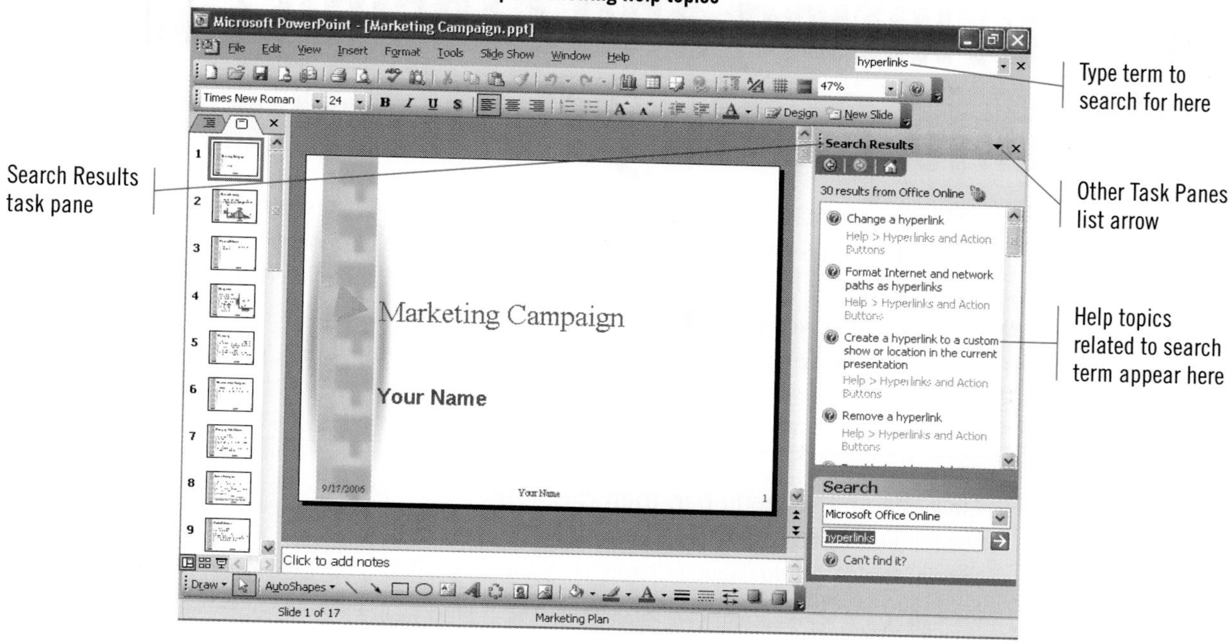

FIGURE A-13: PowerPoint window showing Research task pane

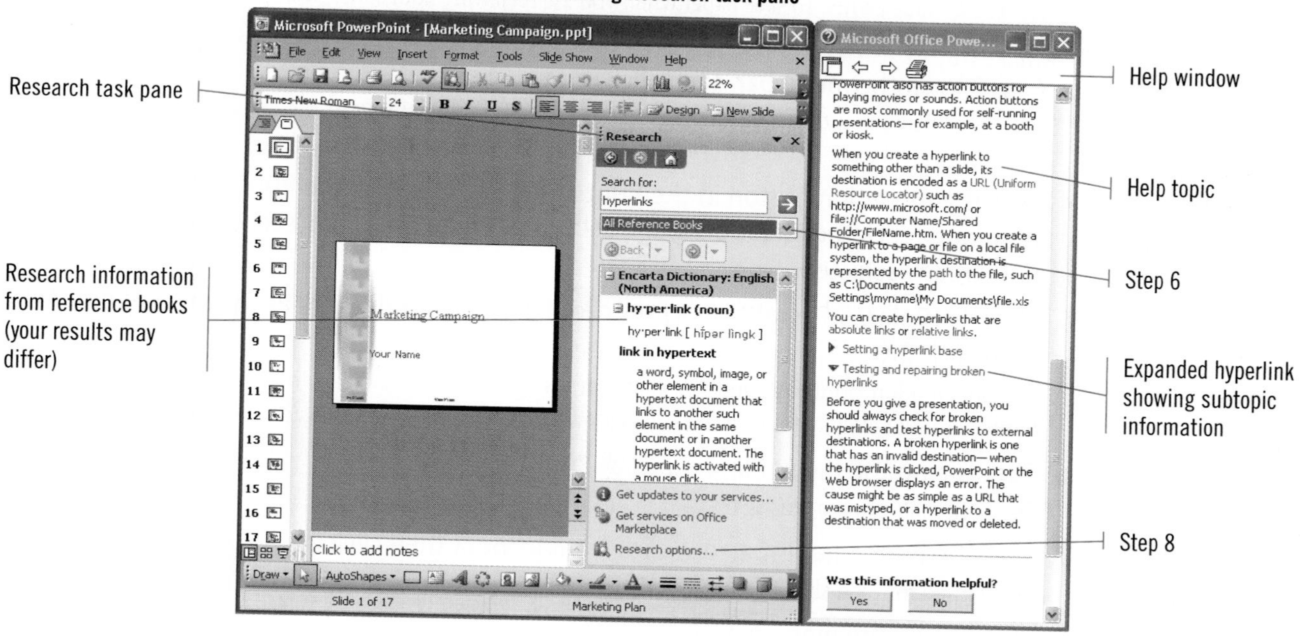

Clues to Use

Recovering lost presentation files

Sometimes while you are working on a presentation, PowerPoint may freeze, making it impossible to continue working on your presentation, or you may experience a power failure that causes your computer to shut down. If this type of interruption occurs, PowerPoint has a built-in recovery feature that allows you to open and save files that were open during the interruption. When you start PowerPoint again after an interruption, the Document Recovery task pane opens on the left side of your screen, displaying both original and recovered versions of the PowerPoint files that were open. If you're not sure which file to open (original or recovered), it's usually better to open the recovered file because it will have retained the latest information. You can, however, open and review all the versions of the file that was recovered and select the best one to save. Each file listed in the Document Recovery task pane has a list arrow with options that allow you to open the file, save the file, delete the file, or show repairs made to the file.

UNIT
A
PowerPoint 2003

Printing and Closing the File, and Exiting PowerPoint

You print your presentation when you have completed it or when you want to review your work. Reviewing hard copies of your presentation at different stages gives you an overall perspective of its content and look. When you are finished working on your presentation, even if it is not yet complete, you can close the presentation file and exit PowerPoint. You are done working on the presentation for now, so after you save the presentation, you print the slides and notes pages of the presentation so you can review them later; then you close the file and exit PowerPoint.

STEPS

QUICK TIP
If you have a color printer, Color appears in the Color/grayscale list box.

QUICK TIP
To quickly print the presentation with the current Print options, click the Print button on the Standard toolbar.

QUICK TIP
To print slides in a size appropriate for overhead transparencies, click File, click Page Setup, click the Slides sized for list arrow, then select Overhead.

1. **Click File on the menu bar, then click Print**
   The Print dialog box opens. See Figure A-14. In this dialog box, you can specify which slide format you want to print (slides, handouts, notes pages, etc.), the slide range, the number of copies to print, as well as other print options. The default options for the available printer are selected in the dialog box.
2. **In the Print range section in the middle of the dialog box, click the Slides option button to select it, type 4 to print only the fourth slide, then click OK**
   The fourth slide prints. To save paper when you are reviewing your slides, it's a good idea to print in handout format, which lets you print up to nine slides per page.
3. **Click File on the menu bar, then click Print**
   The Print dialog box opens again. The options you choose in the Print dialog box remain there until you close the presentation.
4. **Click the All option button in the Print range section, click the Print what list arrow, click Handouts, click the Slides per page list arrow in the Handouts section, then click 6 if it is not already selected**
5. **Click the Color/grayscale list arrow, click Pure Black and White as shown in Figure A-15, then click OK**
   The presentation prints as handouts that you can give to your audience on three pages. The presentation prints without any gray tones. The pure black-and-white printing option can save printer toner.
6. **Click File on the menu bar, then click Print**
   The Print dialog box opens again.
7. **Click the Print what list arrow, click Outline View, then click OK**
   The outline for each slide in the presentation prints on three pages.
8. **Click File on the menu bar, then click Close**
   If you have made changes to your presentation, a Microsoft PowerPoint alert box opens asking you if you want to save changes you have made to the Marketing Campaign file.
9. **If necessary, click Yes to close the alert box**
10. **Click File on the menu bar, then click Exit**
    The presentation and the PowerPoint program close, and you return to the Windows desktop.

FIGURE A-14: Print dialog box

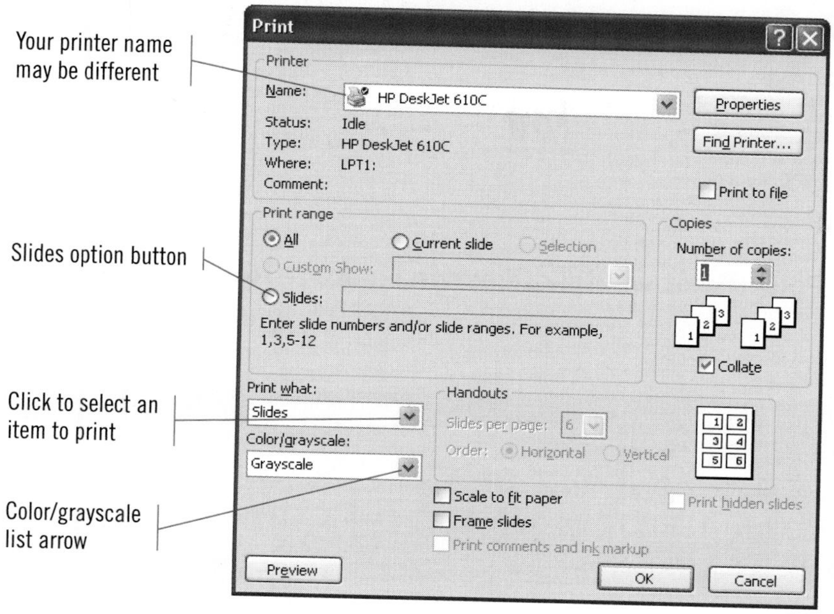

FIGURE A-15: Print dialog box with Handouts selected

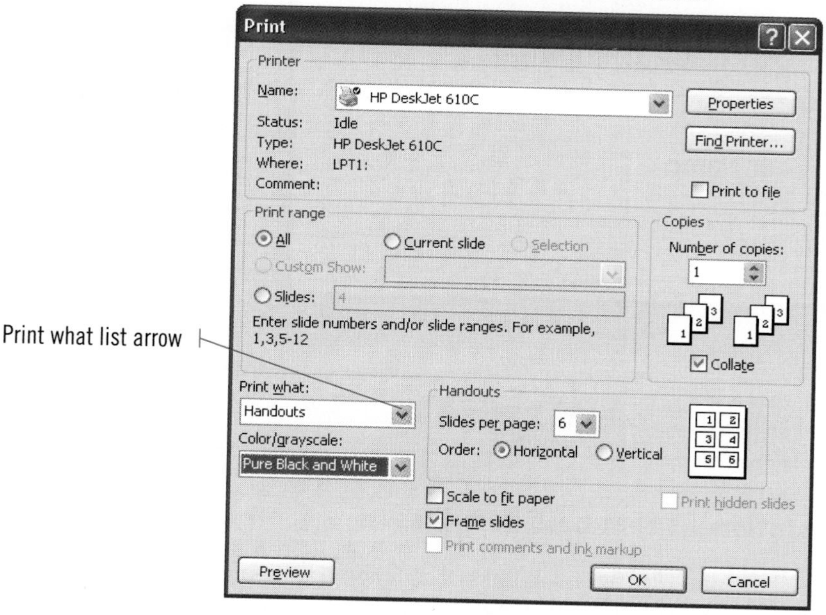

Clues to Use

Viewing your presentation in grayscale or black and white

Viewing your presentation in pure black and white or in grayscale (using shades of gray) is very useful when you are printing a presentation on a black-and-white printer and you want to make sure your text is readable. To see how your color presentation looks in grayscale or black and white, click the Color/Grayscale button on the Standard toolbar, then click either Grayscale or Pure Black and White. The Grayscale View toolbar appears. You can use the Grayscale View toolbar to select different settings to view your presentation. If you don't like the way an object looks in black and white or grayscale view, you can change its color. Right-click the object, point to Black and White Setting or Grayscale Setting (depending on which view you are in), and choose from the options on the submenu.

Practice

▼ CONCEPTS REVIEW

Label each element of the PowerPoint window shown in Figure A-16.

FIGURE A-16

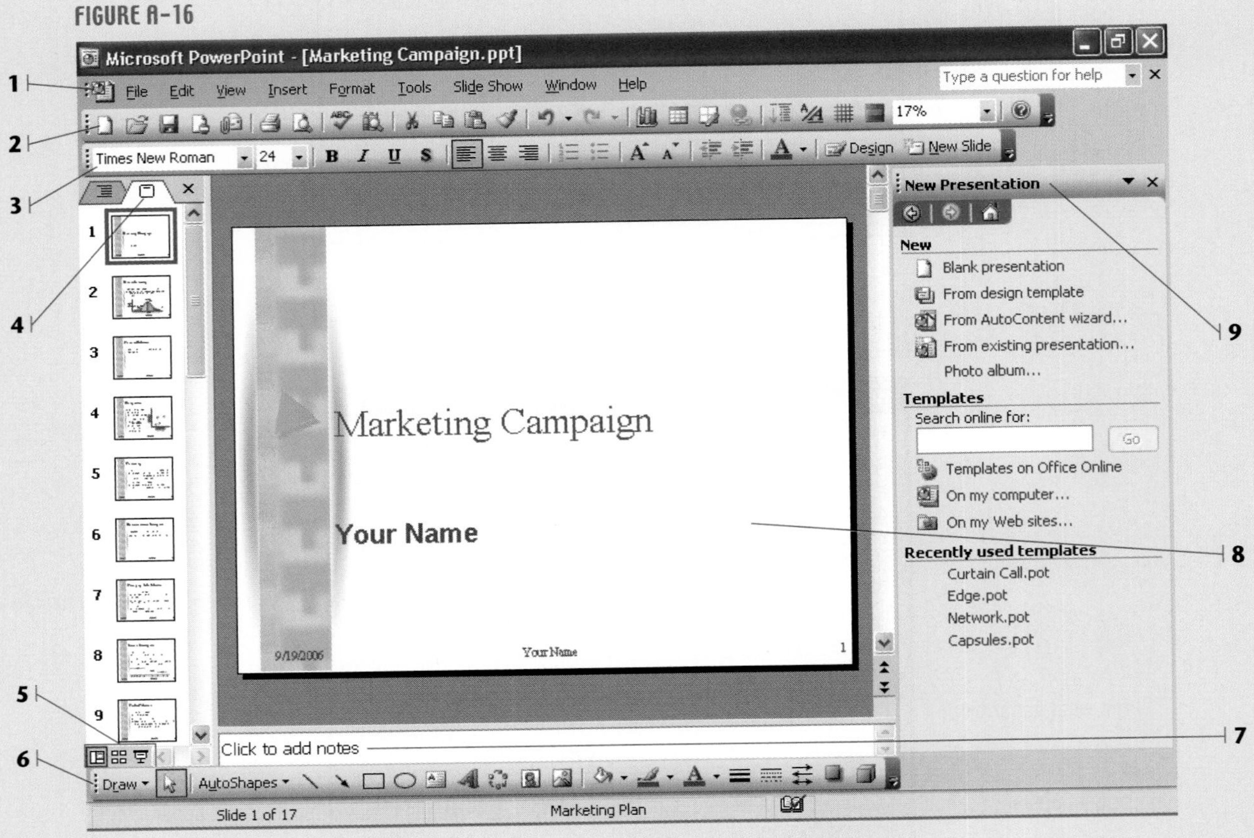

Match each term with the statement that best describes it.

10. Notes pane
11. Slide Sorter view
12. Task pane
13. Normal view
14. Slides tab

a. Displays hyperlinks of common commands
b. Displays the slides of your presentation as thumbnails in Normal view
c. A pane in Normal view that allows you to type notes that reference a slide's content
d. Displays the Outline and Slides tabs, as well as the slide and notes panes
e. A view that shows all your slides as thumbnails

Select the best answer from the list of choices.

15. All of the following are PowerPoint views, *except*:

- **a.** Slide Sorter view
- **b.** Notes Page view
- **c.** Current Page view
- **d.** Normal view

16. PowerPoint can help you create all of the following, *except*:

- **a.** A Web presentation
- **b.** Outline pages
- **c.** An on-screen presentation
- **d.** A digital movie

17. The buttons you use to switch between the PowerPoint views are called:

- **a.** Screen buttons
- **b.** View buttons
- **c.** PowerPoint buttons
- **d.** Toolbar buttons

18. The view that allows you to view your electronic slide show with each slide filling the entire screen is called:

- **a.** Slide Sorter view
- **b.** Presentation view
- **c.** Slide Show view
- **d.** Electronic view

19. How do you switch to Notes Page view?

- **a.** Press [Shift] and click in the notes pane.
- **b.** Click the Notes Page View button.
- **c.** Click View on the menu bar, then click Notes Page.
- **d.** All of the above.

20. How do you save changes to your presentation after you have saved it for the first time?

- **a.** Click Save As on the File menu, select a filename from the list, then assign it a new name.
- **b.** Click the Save button on the Standard toolbar.
- **c.** Click Save As on the File menu, then click Save.
- **d.** Click Save As on the File menu, specify a new location and filename, then click Save.

21. Which wizard helps you create and outline your presentation?

- **a.** Presentation Wizard
- **b.** OrgContent Wizard
- **c.** AutoContent Wizard
- **d.** Topic Wizard

▼ SKILLS REVIEW

1. Start PowerPoint and view the PowerPoint window.

a. Identify as many elements of the PowerPoint window as you can without referring to the unit material.

b. Describe the purpose or function of each element.

c. For any elements you cannot identify, refer to the unit.

2. Use the AutoContent Wizard.

a. Start the AutoContent Wizard, then select a presentation category and type. (*Hint*: If you see a message saying you need to install the feature, insert your Office CD in the appropriate drive and click OK. If you are working in a networked computer lab, see your technical support person for assistance. If you are unable to load additional templates, click No as many times as necessary, then select another presentation type.)

b. Select the output option of your choice.

c. Enter an appropriate title for the opening slide, enter your name as the footer text, and complete the wizard to show the first slide of the presentation.

3. View a presentation and run a slide show.

a. View each slide in the presentation to become familiar with its content.

b. When you are finished, return to Slide 1.

c. Click the Outline tab and review the presentation contents.

d. Change to Notes Page view and see if the notes pages in the presentation contain text, then return to Normal view.

e. Examine the presentation contents in Slide Sorter view.

f. View all the slides of the presentation in Slide Show view, and end the slide show to return to Slide Sorter view.

4. Save a presentation.

a. Change to Notes Page view.

b. Open the Save As dialog box.

c. Navigate to the drive and folder where your Data Files are stored.

d. Name your presentation **Practice**.

e. Click Tools on the menu bar, then click Save Options.

f. Choose the option to embed the fonts in your presentation, as shown in Figure A-17, then click OK.

g. Save your file.

h. Go to a different view than the one you saved your presentation in.

i. Save the changed presentation.

FIGURE A-17

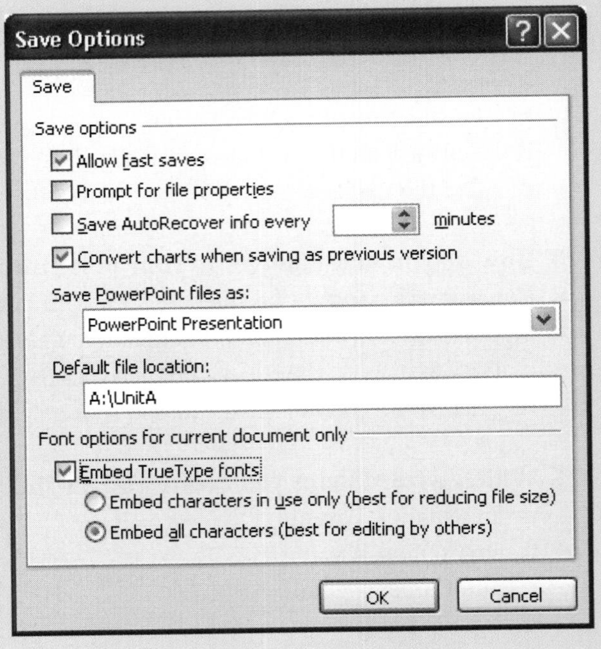

▼ SKILLS REVIEW (CONTINUED)

5. **Get Help and Research Information.**
   - **a.** Type **creating presentations** in the Type a question for help box, then press [Enter].
   - **b.** Click the down scroll arrow in the results list, then click the Create a presentation using a design template hyperlink.
   - **c.** Read the information, then click and read the Tip hyperlink.
   - **d.** Click the Help Window Close button.
   - **e.** Click the Other Task Panes list arrow, then click Research.
   - **f.** Type **PowerPoint presentations** in the Search for text box.
   - **g.** Click the Search for list arrow, then click All Research Sites.
   - **h.** Read the results that appear.

6. **Print and close the file, and exit PowerPoint.**
   - **a.** Print slides 2 and 3 as slides in grayscale. (*Hint*: In the Slides text box, type **2-3**.)
   - **b.** Print all the slides as handouts, 9 slides per page, in pure black and white.
   - **c.** Print the presentation outline.
   - **d.** Close the file, saving your changes.
   - **e.** Exit PowerPoint.

▼ INDEPENDENT CHALLENGE 1

You own a small photography business where most of your revenue comes from customized portraits for special occasions, such as weddings. In an effort to expand your business and appeal to more consumers, you decide to investigate various ways for you to display and send customer's personal photographs over the Internet. You have recently been using PowerPoint to create marketing presentations and you decide to learn more about PowerPoint's Photo Album feature using PowerPoint Help.

- **a.** If PowerPoint is not already running, start it.
- **b.** Use PowerPoint Help to find information on how to publish a photo album to the Web. (*Hint*: Type **photo album** in the Type a question for help box.)
- **c.** Write down the steps you followed to get this information, then add your name to the document.
- **d.** Print the Help window that shows the information you found. (*Hint*: Click the Print button at the top of the Help window.)

Advanced Challenge Exercise

ACE

- Use the Research task pane to search for Web sites that relate to photo albums on the Web.
- Click a Web site hyperlink in the Research task pane results list to explore the Web page contents.
- Print the Home page of the Web site you visit.
- Close your Web browser program.

- **e.** Exit PowerPoint.

PowerPoint 2003

▼ INDEPENDENT CHALLENGE 2

You are in charge of marketing for ArtWorks, Inc., a medium-size company that produces all types of art for corporations to enhance their work environment. The company has a regional sales area that includes areas throughout Western Europe. The president of ArtWorks asks you to plan and create the outline of the PowerPoint presentation he will use to convey a new Internet service that ArtWorks is developing.

a. If necessary, start PowerPoint.
b. Start the AutoContent Wizard. (*Hint*: If the task pane is not visible, click View on the menu bar, then click Task Pane.)
c. On the Presentation type screen, choose the Sales/Marketing category, then choose Product/Services Overview from the list.
d. Choose the Web presentation output, then assign the presentation an appropriate title, and include your name as the footer text.
e. Scroll through the outline that the AutoContent Wizard produces. Does it contain the type of information you thought it would?
f. Plan and take notes on how you would change and add to the sample text created by the wizard. What information do you need to promote ArtWorks to companies?
g. Switch views. Run through the slide show at least once.
h. Save your presentation with the name **ArtWorks Online** to the drive and folder where your Data Files are stored.
i. Print your presentation as handouts (six slides per page).
j. Close the presentation and exit PowerPoint.

▼ INDEPENDENT CHALLENGE 3

You have recently been promoted to sales manager at Turner Industries. Part of your job is to train sales representatives to go to potential customers and give presentations describing your company's products. Your boss wants you to find an appropriate PowerPoint presentation template that you can use for your next training presentation to recommend strategies to the sales representatives for closing sales. She wants a printout so she can evaluate it.

a. If necessary, start PowerPoint.
b. Start the AutoContent Wizard. (*Hint*: If the task pane is not visible, click View on the menu bar, then click Task Pane.)
c. Examine the available AutoContent Wizards and select one that you could adapt for your presentation. (*Hint*: If you see a message saying you need to install additional templates, insert your Office CD in the appropriate drive and click OK. If you are working in a networked computer lab, see your technical support person for assistance. If you are unable to load additional templates, click No as many times as necessary, then select another presentation type.)
d. Choose the On-screen presentation type, then enter an appropriate slide title and include your name as the footer text.
e. Print the presentation as an outline, then print the first slide in pure black and white.
f. Write a brief memo to your boss describing which wizard you think is most helpful, referring to specific slides in the outline to support your recommendation.
g. Save the presentation as **Turner Training** to the drive and folder where your Data Files are stored.
h. Close the presentation and exit PowerPoint.

▼ INDEPENDENT CHALLENGE 4

In this unit, you've learned about PowerPoint basics such as how to start PowerPoint, view the PowerPoint window, use the AutoContent Wizard, and run a slide show. There are many Web sites that provide information about how to use PowerPoint more effectively.

Use the Microsoft Web site to access information about the following topic:

- Presentation Tips

a. Connect to the Internet, then go to Microsoft's Web site at www.microsoft.com.

b. In the Search for text box, type **Dale Carnegie Training**, then press [Enter].

c. Locate the hyperlink that provides information on presentation tips from Dale Carnegie Training, then click the hyperlink. See Figure A-18.

d. Print and read the article, then write your name and course identification on the printed document.

Advanced Challenge Exercise

- Create and save a document as **Presentation Tips** to the drive and folder where your Data Files are stored.
- Type your name and course identification at the top of the document.
- The Web article identifies a four-step process for delivering an effective presentation. Using the information in the Web article, identify each of these steps and the most important subpoint. Explain your answers.
- Save your final document, print it, close the document, then exit your word processing program.

e. Exit your Web browser program.

FIGURE A-18

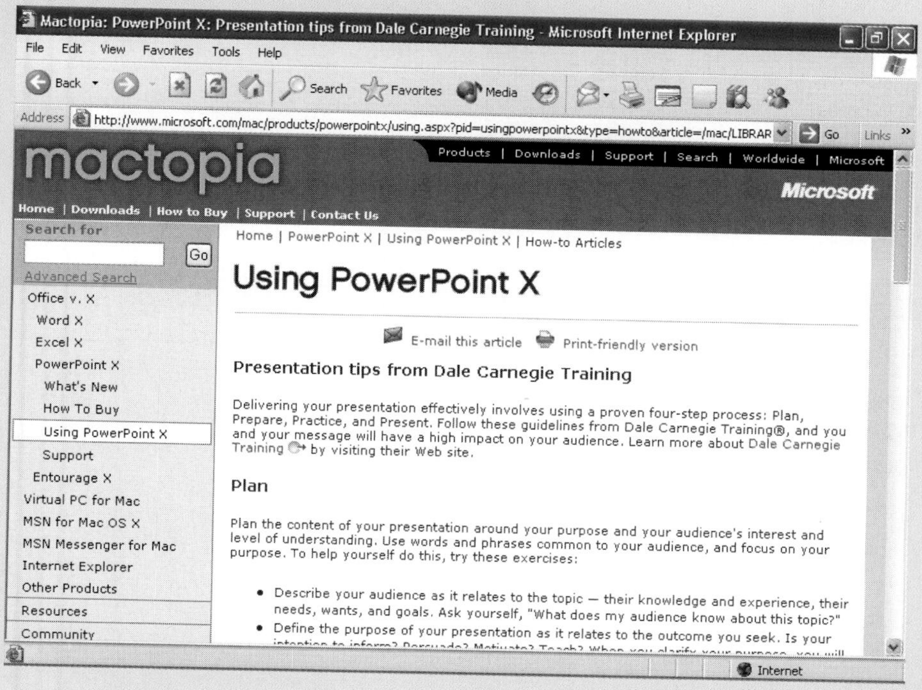

▼ VISUAL WORKSHOP

Create the presentation shown in Figure A-19 using the Project Post-Mortem AutoContent Wizard in the Projects category. Make sure you include your name as the footer. Save the presentation as **Triad** to the drive and folder where your Data Files are stored. Print the slides as handouts, six slides per page, in pure black and white.

FIGURE A-19

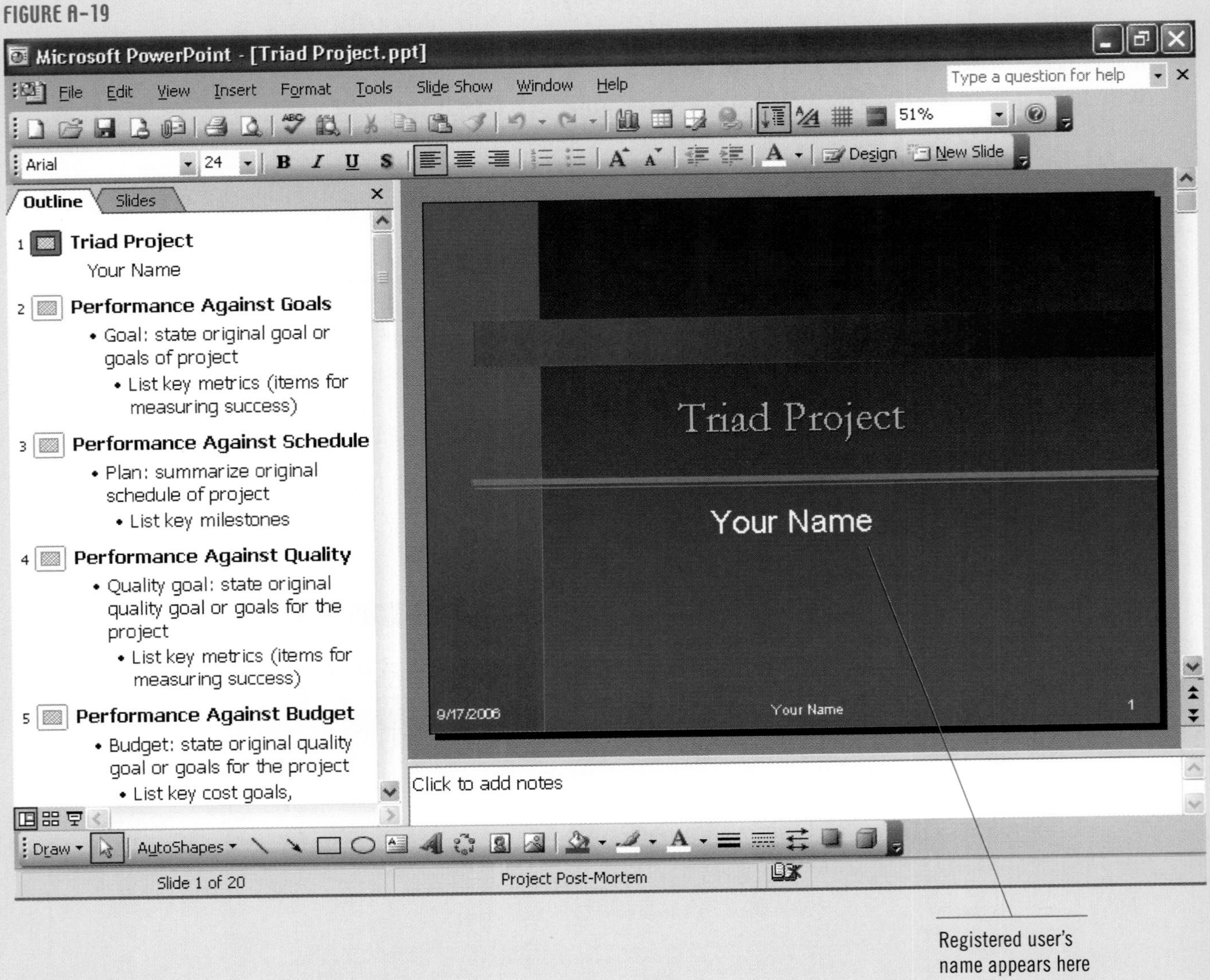

UNIT
B
PowerPoint 2003

Creating a Presentation

OBJECTIVES

- Plan an effective presentation
- Enter slide text
- Create a new slide
- Enter text in the Outline tab
- Add slide headers and footers
- Choose a look for a presentation
- Check spelling in a presentation
- Evaluate a presentation

SAM

If you have a SAM user profile, you may have access to hands-on instruction, practice, and assessment of the skills covered in this unit. Log in to your SAM account and go to your assignments page to see what your instructor has assigned.

Now that you are familiar with PowerPoint basics, you are ready to plan and create your own presentation. To do this, you first enter and edit the presentation text, and then you can focus on the design and look of the presentation. PowerPoint helps you accomplish these tasks. You can start with the AutoContent Wizard and then enhance the look of your presentation by selecting a design from a collection of professionally prepared slide designs, called **design templates.** In this unit, you create a presentation using a PowerPoint design template. Maria Abbott, general sales manager at MediaLoft, asks you to prepare a marketing presentation on a new service that MediaLoft is planning to introduce. You begin by planning your presentation.

UNIT
B
PowerPoint 2003

Planning an Effective Presentation

Before you create a presentation using PowerPoint, you need to plan and outline the message you want to communicate and consider how you want the presentation to look. When preparing the outline, you need to keep in mind where you are giving the presentation and who your audience is. It is also important to know what equipment you might need, such as a sound system, computer, or projector. Use the planning guidelines below to help plan an effective presentation. Figure B-1 illustrates a well thought-out presentation outline.

DETAILS

In planning a presentation, it is important to:

- **Determine the purpose of the presentation**
  When you have a well-defined purpose, developing an outline for your presentation is much easier. You need to present a marketing plan for a new Internet service that MediaLoft is planning to launch later in the year.
- **Determine the message you want to communicate, then give the presentation a meaningful title and outline your message**
  If possible, take time to adequately develop an outline of your presentation content before creating the slides. Start your presentation by defining the new service, describing the competition, and stating the product positioning. See Figure B-1.
- **Determine the audience and the delivery location**
  The presentation audience and delivery location can greatly affect the type of presentation you create. For example, if you had to deliver a presentation to your staff in a small, dimly lit conference room, you may create a very simple presentation with a bright color scheme; however, if you had to deliver a sales presentation to a client in a formal conference room with many windows, you may need to create a very professional-looking presentation with a darker color scheme. You will deliver this presentation in a large conference room to MediaLoft's marketing management team.
- **Determine the type of output—black-and-white or color overhead transparencies, on-screen slide show, or an online broadcast—that best conveys your message, given time constraints and computer hardware availability**
  Because you are speaking in a large conference room to a large group and have access to a computer and projection equipment, you decide that an on-screen slide show is the best output choice for your presentation.
- **Determine a look for your presentation that will help communicate your message**
  You can choose one of the professionally designed templates that come with PowerPoint, modify one of these templates, or create one of your own. You want a simple and artistic template to convey the marketing plan.
- **Determine what additional materials will be useful in the presentation**
  You need to prepare not only the slides themselves but also supplementary materials, including speaker notes and handouts for the audience. You use speaker notes to help remember a few key details, and you pass out handouts for the audience to use as a reference.

FIGURE B-1: Outline of the presentation content

1. eMedia
   - Proposed Marketing Plan
   - Your Name
   - August 12, 2006
   - Director of Internet Services
2. Product Definition
   - Internet media provider
     - Music and video
     - Articles and trade papers
     - Historical papers archive
   - On-demand publishing
     - Articles, books, research papers, games, and more…
3. Competition
   - Bookstores
   - Internet services
   - Media services
   - Ratings
4. Product Positioning
   - Licensed media download service provider
   - Interactive service provider
   - Publishing service provider

PowerPoint 2003

Clues to Use

Using templates from the Web

When you create a presentation, you have the option of using one of the design templates supplied with PowerPoint, or you can use a template from another source, such as a Web server or the Template Gallery on the Microsoft Office Web site. To create a presentation using a template from a Web server, start PowerPoint, open the New Presentation task pane, then click the On my Web sites hyperlink under Templates. The New from Templates on my Web Sites dialog box opens. Locate and open the template you want to use, then save it with a new name. To use a template from the Microsoft Office Online Web site, open the New Presentation task pane, then click the Templates on Office Online hyperlink. Your Web browser opens to the Microsoft Office Online Templates Web site. Locate the PowerPoint template you want to use, then click the Download Now button to open and save the template in PowerPoint. The first time you use the Templates Web site, you must install the Microsoft Office Template and MediaControl and accept the license agreement.

UNIT
B
PowerPoint 2003

Entering Slide Text

Each time you start PowerPoint, a new presentation with a blank title slide appears in Normal view. The title slide has two **text placeholders**—boxes with dashed-line borders—where you enter text. The top text placeholder on the title slide is the **title placeholder**, labeled "Click to add title". The bottom text placeholder on the title slide is the **Subtitle text placeholder**, labeled "Click to add subtitle". To enter text in a placeholder, simply click the placeholder and then type your text. After you enter text in a placeholder, the placeholder becomes a text object. An **object** is any item on a slide that can be manipulated. Objects are the building blocks that make up a presentation slide. Begin working on your presentation by starting PowerPoint and entering text on the title slide.

STEPS

1. **Start PowerPoint**
   A new presentation appears displaying a blank title slide in Normal view.
2. **Move the pointer over the title placeholder labeled "Click to add title" in the Slide pane**
   The pointer changes to I when you move the pointer over the placeholder. In PowerPoint, the pointer often changes shape, depending on the task you are trying to accomplish.
3. **Click the title placeholder in the Slide pane**
   The **insertion point**, a blinking vertical line, indicates where your text appears when you type in the title placeholder. A **selection box**, the slanted line border, appears around the title placeholder, indicating that it is selected and ready to accept text. See Figure B-2.
4. **Type eMedia**
   PowerPoint center-aligns the title text within the title placeholder, which is now a text object. Notice that text appears on the slide thumbnail in the slides tab.
5. **Click the subtitle text placeholder in the Slide pane**
   A wavy red line may appear under the word "eMedia" in the title text object indicating that the automatic spellchecking feature in PowerPoint is active. If it doesn't appear on your screen, it may mean that the automatic spellchecking feature is turned off.
6. **Type Proposed Marketing Plan, then press [Enter]**
   The insertion point moves to the next line in the Subtitle text object.
7. **Type Your Name, press [Enter], type August 12, 2006, press [Enter], then type Director of Internet Services**
   Notice that the AutoFit Options button appears near the text object. The AutoFit Options button on your screen indicates that PowerPoint has automatically decreased the size of all the text in the text object to fit in the text object.
8. **Click the Autofit Options button, then click Stop Fitting Text to This Placeholder on the shortcut menu**
   The text in the Subtitle text box changes back to its original size.
9. **Position I to the right of 2006, drag to select the entire line of text, press [Backspace], then click outside the main text object in a blank area of the slide**
   The text and the line the text was on are deleted and the Autofit Options button closes, as shown in Figure B-3. Clicking a blank area of the slide deselects all selected objects on the slide.
10. **Click the Save button on the Standard toolbar, then save your presentation as eMediaB to the drive and folder where your Data Files are stored**

TROUBLE
If you press a wrong key, press [Backspace] to erase the character.

TROUBLE
If the insertion point is blinking in a blank line after completing this step, press [Backspace] one more time.

FIGURE B-2: Slide with selected title text placeholder

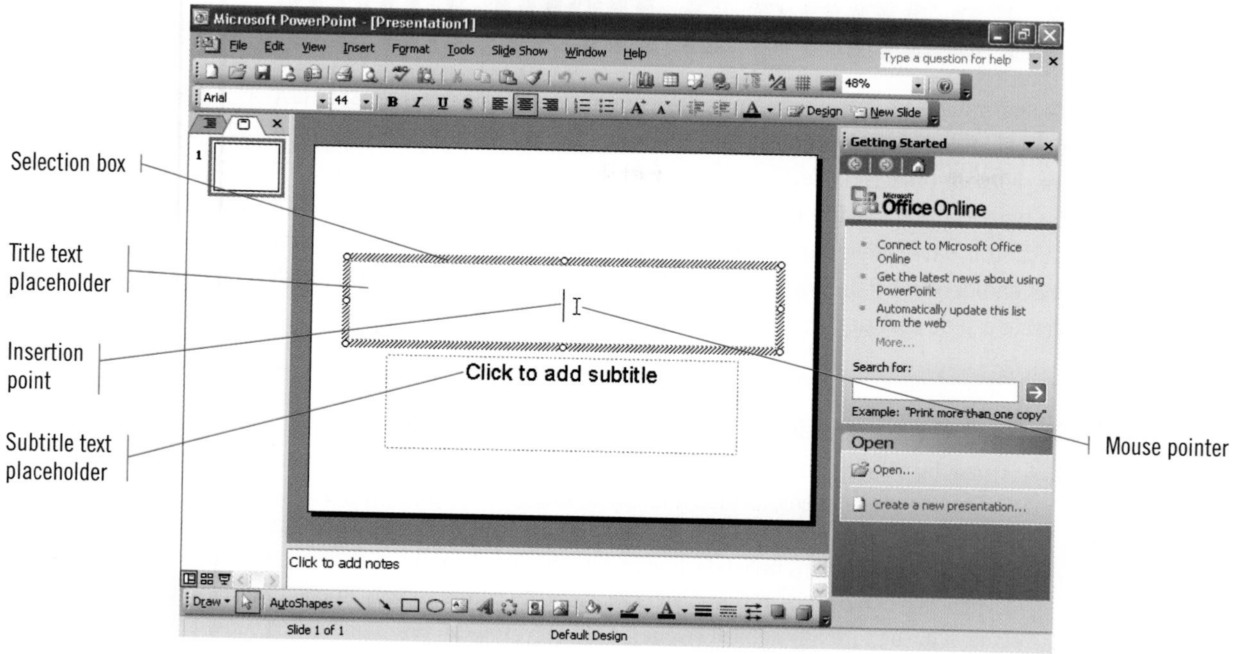

FIGURE B-3: Title slide with text

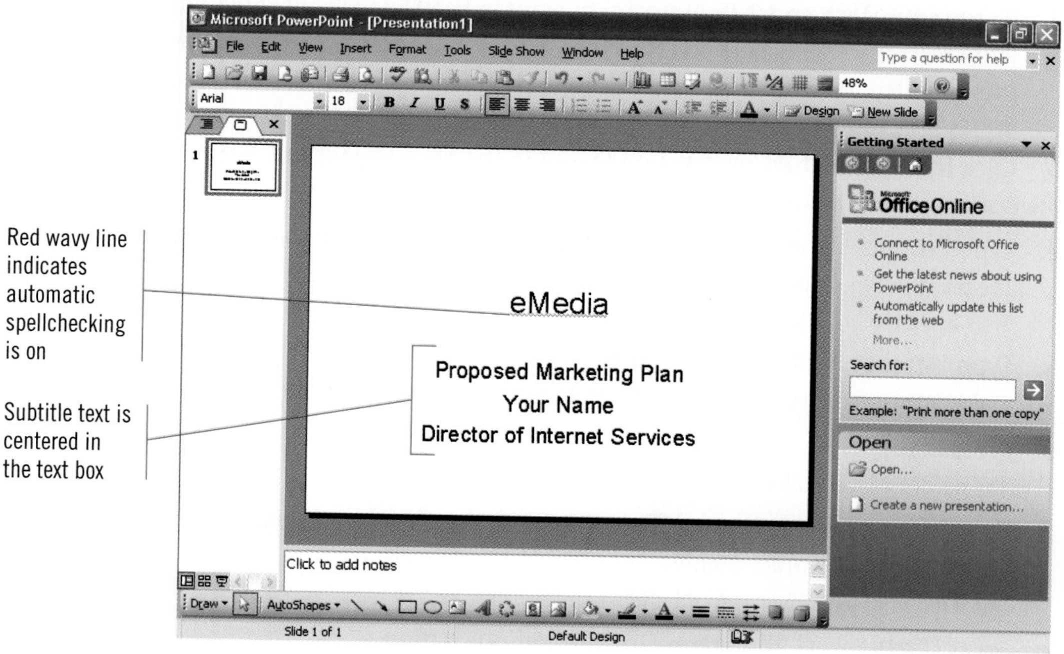

PowerPoint 2003

Clues to Use

Using Speech Recognition

Speech recognition technology lets you enter text and issue commands in PowerPoint by talking into a standard microphone connected to your computer. It is an Office-wide program that you must install and set up before you can use it. To set up Speech Recognition, start Microsoft Word, click Tools on the menu bar, then click Speech. You might be prompted to install the Speech Recognition files using the Office CD. Once you have installed the Speech Recognition files, the Speech Recognition component is available in all Office programs, including PowerPoint. To begin using Speech Recognition, you first need to train your computer to understand how you speak by using a Training Wizard. A Training Wizard is a series of paragraphs that you read into your computer's microphone. These training sessions teach the Speech module to recognize your voice. They also teach you the speed and level of clarity with which you need to speak so that the program can understand you. Training sessions improve the performance of the Speech Recognition module. If you don't use the training sessions, the Speech Recognition module may be inaccurate.

UNIT B

PowerPoint 2003

Creating a New Slide

To help you create a new slide easily, PowerPoint offers 27 predesigned slide layouts. A **slide layout** determines how all of the elements on a slide are arranged. Slide layouts include a variety of placeholder arrangements for different objects, including text, clip art, tables, charts, diagrams, and media clips. Layouts are organized by type in the following categories: text layouts, content layouts, text and content layouts, and other layouts. You have already used the Title Slide layout in the previous lesson. Table B-1 describes some of the placeholders you'll find in PowerPoint's slide layouts. To continue developing the presentation, you create a slide that defines the new service MediaLoft is developing.

STEPS

QUICK TIP

You can also insert a new slide from the Slide Layout task pane: point to the slide layout you want, click the slide layout list arrow, then click Insert New Slide.

1. **Click the New Slide button on the Formatting toolbar**
   A new blank slide (now the current slide) appears as the second slide in your presentation and the Slide Layout task pane opens, as shown in Figure B-4. The new slide in the Slide pane contains a title placeholder and a **body text placeholder** for a bulleted list. Notice that the status bar indicates Slide 2 of 2 and that the Slides tab now contains two slide thumbnails. The Slide Layout task pane identifies the different PowerPoint slide layouts that you can use in your presentation. A dark border appears around the Title and Text slide layout identifying it as the currently applied layout for the slide. You can easily change the current slide's layout by clicking a slide layout icon in the Slide Layout task pane.
2. **Point to the Title and 2-Column Text layout in the Slide Layout task pane**
   When you place your pointer over a slide layout icon, a selection list arrow appears. You can click the list arrow to choose options for applying the layout. After a brief moment, a ScreenTip also appears that identifies the slide layout by name.
3. **Click the Title and 2-Column Text layout in the Slide Layout task pane**
   A slide layout with two text placeholders replaces the Title and Text slide layout for the current slide.
4. **Type Product Definition, then click the left body text placeholder in the Slide pane**
   The text you type appears in the title placeholder, and the insertion point appears next to a bullet in the left body text placeholder.
5. **Type Internet media provider, then press [Enter]**
   A new first-level bullet automatically appears when you press [Enter].
6. **Press [Tab]**
   The new first-level bullet indents and becomes a second-level bullet.
7. **Type Music and video, press [Enter], type Articles and trade papers, press [Enter], then type Historical papers archive**
   The left text object now has four bulleted points.
8. **Press [Ctrl][Enter], then type On-demand publishing**
   Pressing [Ctrl][Enter] moves the insertion point to the next text placeholder on the slide. Because this is a two-column layout, the insertion point moves to the other body text placeholder on the slide.
9. **Press [Enter], click the Increase Indent button on the Formatting toolbar, enter the four second-level bulleted items shown in Figure B-5, click in a blank area of the slide, then click the Save button on the Standard toolbar**
   The Increase Indent button indents the first-level bullet, which changes it to a second-level bullet. Clicking the Save button saves all of the changes to the file. Compare your screen with Figure B-5.

TROUBLE

When AutoCorrect is active, if you mistype a common word, PowerPoint automatically corrects it when you press [Spacebar] or [Enter]. You know PowerPoint has automatically corrected a word when you point to a word and a small rectangle appears under the word. To see a list of common typing errors that PowerPoint corrects automatically, click Tools on the menu bar, then click AutoCorrect Options.

FIGURE B-4: New blank slide in Normal view

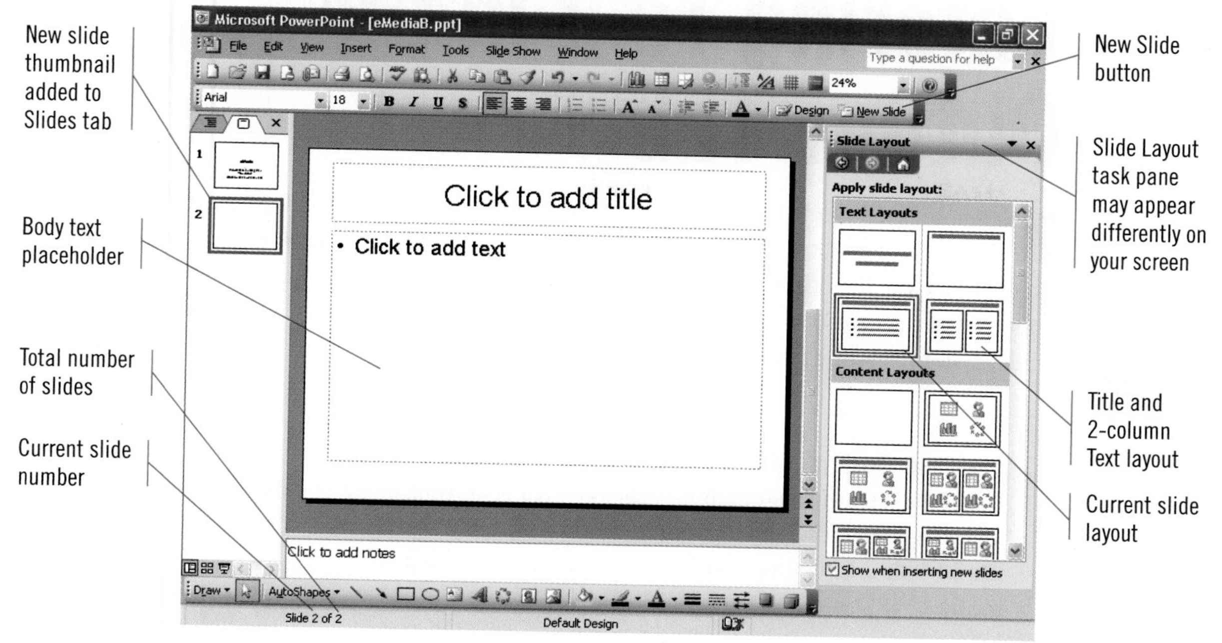

FIGURE B-5: New slide with Title and 2-Column Text slide layout

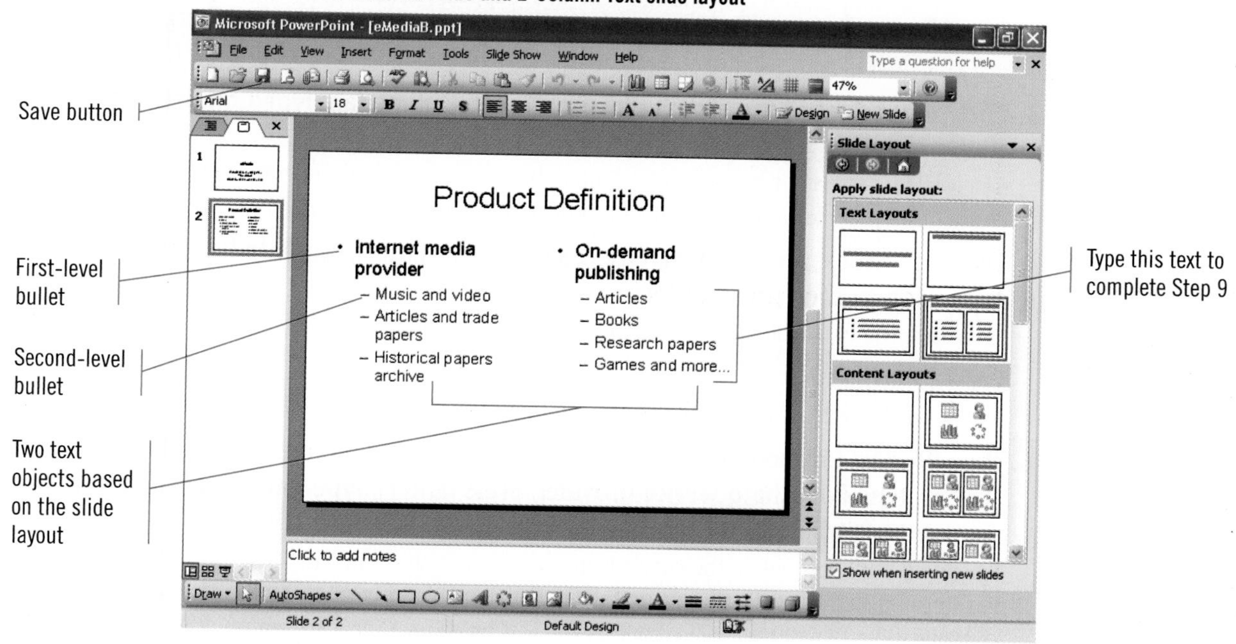

TABLE B-1: Slide Layout placeholders

placeholder	symbol	description
Bulleted List		Inserts a short list of related points
Clip Art		Inserts a picture from the Clip Organizer
Chart		Inserts a chart created with Microsoft Graph
Diagram or Organization Chart		Inserts a diagram or organizational chart
Table		Inserts a table
Media Clip		Inserts a music, sound, or video clip
Content		Inserts objects such as a table, a chart, clip art, a picture, a diagram or organizational chart, or a media clip

Entering Text in the Outline Tab

You can enter presentation text by typing directly on the slide, as you've learned already, or, if you'd rather focus on the presentation text without worrying about the layout, you can enter it in the Outline tab. As in a regular outline, the headings, or titles, appear first; beneath the titles, the subpoints, or body text, appear. Body text appears as one or more lines of bulleted text indented under a title. You switch to the Outline tab to enter body text for two more slides.

STEPS

QUICK TIP

The commands on the Outlining toolbar can be helpful when working in the Outline tab. To open the Outlining toolbar, click View on the menu bar, point to Toolbars, then click Outlining.

1. **Click the Outline tab to the left of the Slide pane**

   The Outline tab enlarges to display the text that is on your slides. The slide icon for Slide 2 is highlighted, indicating that it's selected. Notice the numbers 1 and 2 that appear to the left of each of the first-level bullets for Slide 2, indicating that there are two body text objects on the slide.

2. **Point to the Title and Text layout in the Slide Layout task pane, click the list arrow, then click Insert New Slide**

   A new slide, Slide 3, with the Title and Text layout appears as the current slide below Slide 2. A selected slide icon appears next to the slide number in the Outline tab when you add a new slide. See Figure B-6. Text that you enter next to a slide icon becomes the title for that slide.

3. **Click to the right of the Slide 3 slide icon in the Outline tab, type Competition, press [Enter], then press [Tab]**

   A new slide is inserted when you press [Enter], but because you want to enter body text for the slide you just created, you press Tab, which indents this line to make it part of Slide 3.

4. **Type Bookstoes, press [Enter], type E-sites, press [Enter], type Media services, press [Enter], type Ratings, then press [Enter]**

   Make sure you typed "Bookstoes" without the "r" as specified in the step.

5. **Press [Shift][Tab]**

   The bullet that was created when you pressed [Enter] changes to a new slide icon.

6. **Type Product Positioning, press [Ctrl][Enter], type Licensed media download provider, press [Enter], type Publishing service provider, press [Enter], type Interactive service provider, then press [Ctrl][Enter]**

   Pressing [Ctrl][Enter] while the cursor is in the title text object moves the cursor into the body text object. Pressing [Ctrl][Enter] while the cursor is in the body text object creates a new slide with the same layout as the previous slide. Two of the bulleted points you just typed for Slide 4 are out of order, and you don't need the new Slide 5 you just created.

QUICK TIP

If you click the Undo button list arrow, you can select which actions you want to undo.

7. **Click the Undo button on the Standard toolbar**

   Clicking the Undo button undoes the previous action. Slide 5 is deleted and the insertion point moves back up to the last bullet in Slide 4.

8. **Position the pointer to the left of the last bullet in Slide 4 in the Outline tab**

   The pointer changes to ✥.

TROUBLE

If your screen does not match Figure B-7, drag the text to the correct location.

9. **Drag the mouse up until the pointer changes to ↕ and a horizontal indicator line appears above the second bullet point in Slide 4, then release the mouse button**

   The third bullet point moves up one line in the outline and trades places with the second bullet point, as shown in Figure B-7.

10. **Click the Slides tab, click the Slide 2 thumbnail in the Slides tab, then save your work**

    Slide 2 of 4 should appear in the status bar.

FIGURE B-6: Normal view with Outline tab open

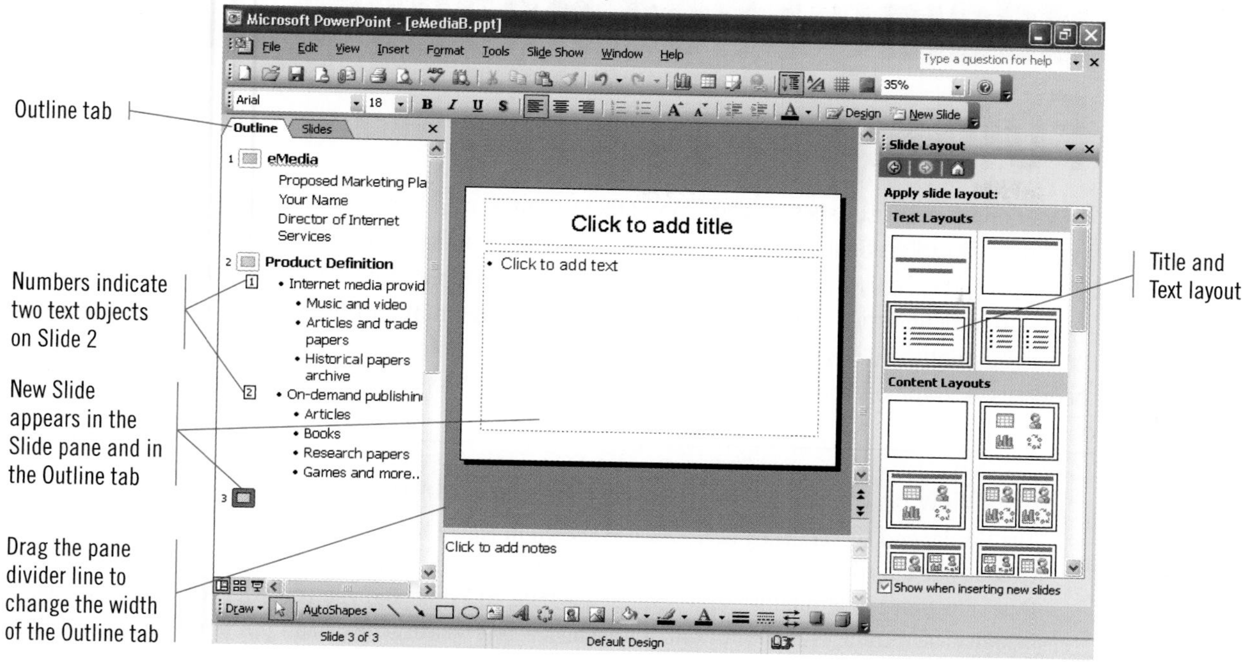

FIGURE B-7: Bulleted item moved up in the Outline tab

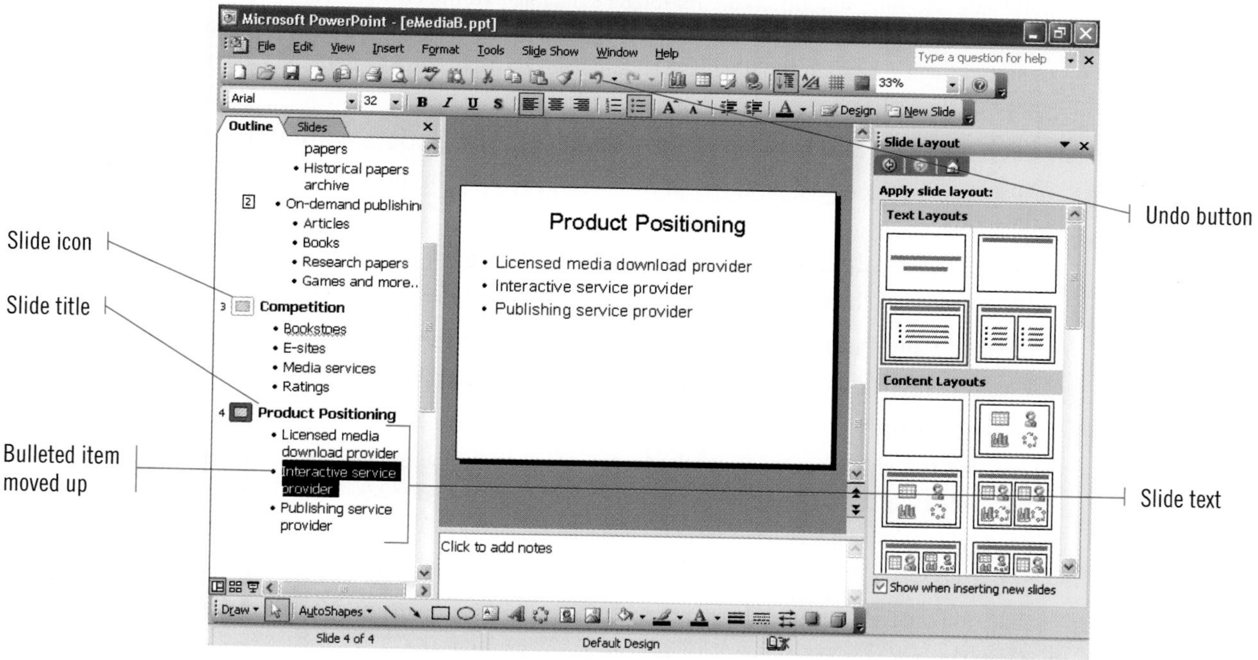

Clues to Use

What do I do if I see a lightbulb on a slide?

If you are showing the Office Assistant, you may see a yellow lightbulb in your presentation window. The lightbulb is part of the PowerPoint Help system and it can mean several things. First, the Office Assistant might have a suggestion for an appropriate piece of clip art for that slide. Second, the Office Assistant might have a helpful tip based on the task you are performing. This is known as a context-sensitive tip. Third, the Office Assistant might have detected a style, such as a word in the slide title that should be capitalized, which is inconsistent with preset style guidelines. When you see a lightbulb, you can click it, read the dialog balloon, and click the option you prefer, or you can ignore it. If the Office Assistant is hidden or turned off, the lightbulb does not appear.

UNIT B

PowerPoint 2003

Adding Slide Headers and Footers

Header and footer text, such as your company or product name, the slide number, and the date, can give your slides a professional look and make it easier for your audience to follow your presentation. On slides, you can add text only to the footer; however, notes or handouts can include both header and footer text. Footer information that you apply to the slides of your presentation is visible in the PowerPoint views and when you print the slides. Notes and handouts header and footer text is visible when you print notes pages, handouts, and the outline. You add footer text to the slides of your presentation.

STEPS

1. **Click View on the menu bar, then click Header and Footer**

   The Header and Footer dialog box opens, as shown in Figure B-8. The Header and Footer dialog box has two tabs: a Slide tab and a Notes and Handouts tab. The Slide tab is selected. There are three types of footer text, Date and time, Slide number, and Footer. The Date and time and the Footer check boxes are selected by default. The rectangles at the bottom of the Preview box identify the default position and status of the three types of footer text on the slides. Two of the rectangles at the bottom of the Preview box have dark borders.

2. **Click the Date and time check box to deselect it**

   The date and time suboptions are no longer available and the far-left rectangle at the bottom of the Preview box has a light border. The middle rectangle identifies where the Footer text—the only check box still selected—will appear on the slide. The rectangle on the right shows where the slide number will appear if you select that check box.

3. **Click the Date and time check box, then click the Update automatically option button**

   Now every time you view the slide show or print the slides in this presentation, the current date appears in the footer.

4. **Click the Update automatically list arrow, then click the fourth option in the list**

   The date format changes to display the Month spelled out, the date number, and four-digit year.

5. **Click the Slide number check box, click in the Footer text box, then type Your Name**

   The Preview box now shows that all three footer placeholders are selected.

6. **Click the Don't show on title slide check box**

   Selecting this check box prevents the footer information you entered in the Header and Footer dialog box from appearing on the title slide. Compare your screen to Figure B-9.

7. **Click Apply to All**

   The dialog box closes and the footer information is applied to all of the slides in your presentation except the title slide. You can click the Apply button to apply footer information to just one slide in the presentation if you want.

8. **Click the Slide 1 thumbnail in the Slides tab, click View on the menu bar, then click Header and Footer**

   The Header and Footer dialog box opens, displaying all of the options that you specified for the presentation. You want to show your company slogan in the footer on the title slide.

9. **Click the Date and time check box, the Slide number check box, and the Don't show on title slide check box to deselect them, then select the text in the Footer text box**

10. **Type "All Media...All the Time", click Apply, then save your work**

    Only the text in the Footer text box appears on the title slide. Clicking Apply applies the footer information to just the current slide.

QUICK TIP

If you want a specific date (such as the original date that the presentation was created) to appear every time you view or print the presentation, click the Fixed date option button, then type the date in the Fixed text box.

TROUBLE

If you click Apply to All in Step 10, click the Undo button on the Standard toolbar and repeat Steps 9 and 10.

FIGURE B-8: Header and Footer dialog box

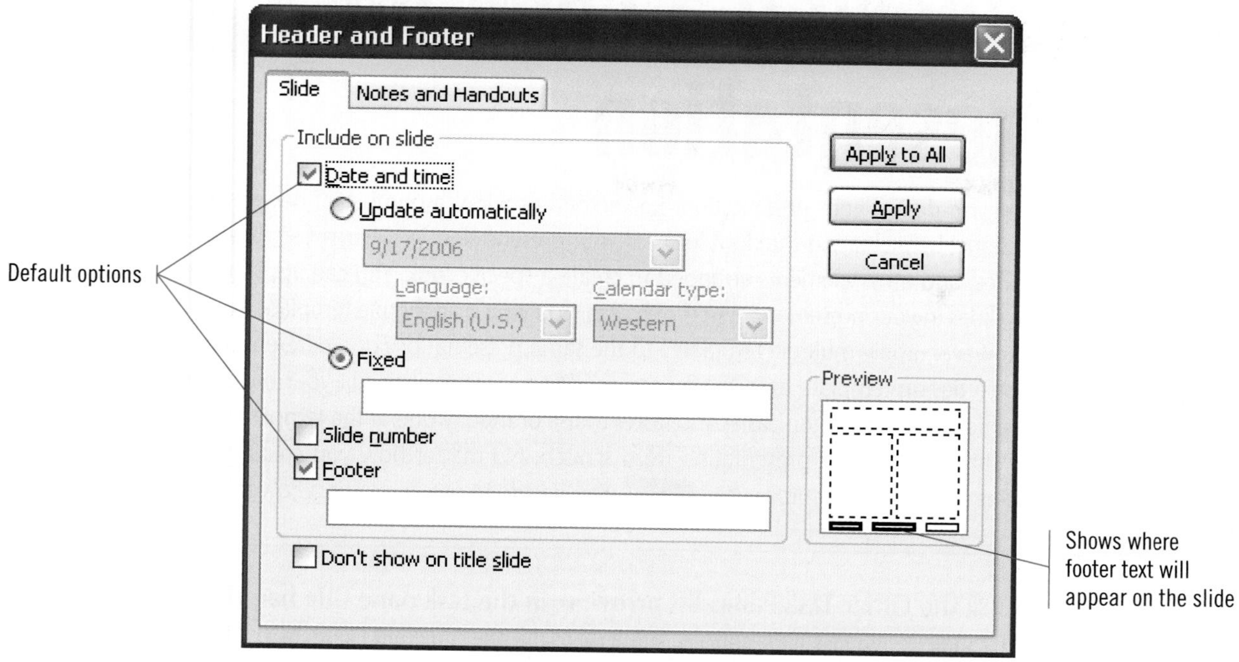

FIGURE B-9: Completed Header and Footer dialog box

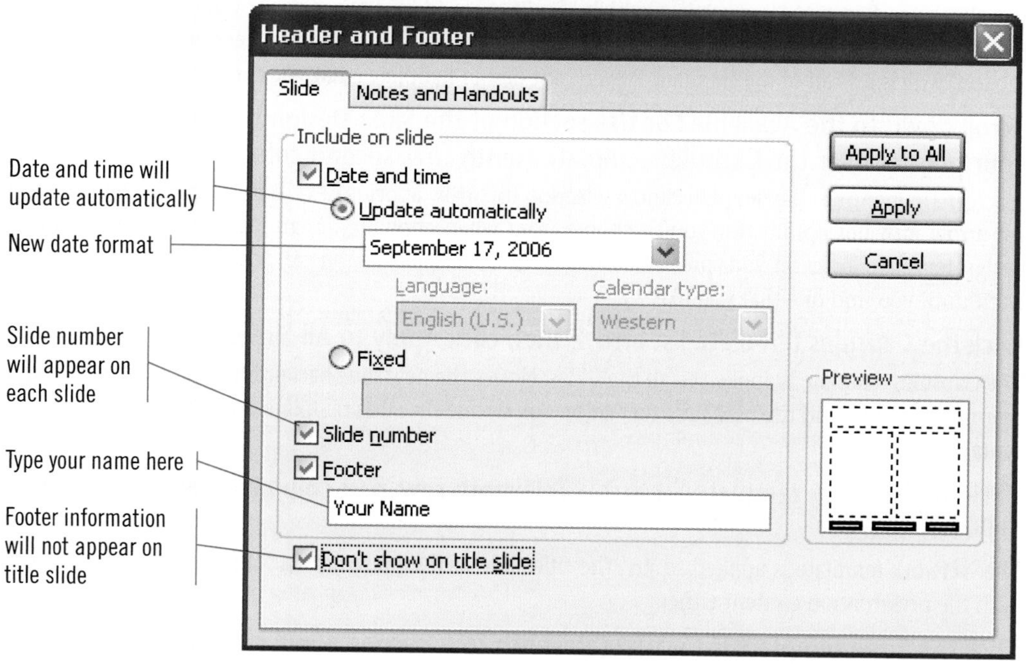

Clues to Use

Entering and printing notes

You can add notes to your slides when there are certain facts you want to remember during a presentation or when there is information you want to hand out to your audience. Notes do not appear on the slides when you run a slide show. Use the Notes pane in Normal view or Notes Page view to enter notes for your slides. To enter text notes on a slide, click in the Notes pane, then type. If you want to insert graphics as notes, you must use Notes Page view. To open Notes Page view, click View on the menu bar, then click Notes Page. You can print your notes by clicking the Print what list arrow and then clicking Notes Pages in the Print dialog box. The notes page can be a good handout to give your audience to use during the presentation and then after as a reminder. If you don't enter any notes in the Notes pane, and print the notes pages, the slides print as thumbnails with blank lines to the right of the thumbnails to handwrite notes.

Choosing a Look for a Presentation

To help you design your presentation, PowerPoint provides a number of design templates so you can have professional help creating the right look for your presentation. A **design template** has borders, colors, text attributes, and other elements arranged to create a specific look. You can apply a design template to one or all the slides in your presentation. In most cases, you would apply one template to an entire presentation; you can, however, apply multiple templates to the same presentation, or a different template on each slide. You can use a design template as is, or you can modify any element to suit your needs. Unless you have training in graphic design, it is often easier and faster to use or modify one of the templates supplied with PowerPoint, rather than design your presentation from scratch. No matter how you create your presentation, you can save it as a template for future use. You decide to use an existing PowerPoint template.

STEPS

QUICK TIP
You can click the Slide Design button Design on the Formatting toolbar to open the Slide Design task pane.

QUICK TIP
If you know what design template you want to use for a new presentation, you can apply it before you enter the presentation content. Open a new blank presentation, open the Slide Design task pane, then apply the template.

QUICK TIP
One way to apply multiple templates to the same presentation is to click the Slide Sorter View button, select a slide or a group of slides, then click the template.

1. **Click the Other Task Panes list arrow ▼ in the task pane title bar, then click Slide Design**
   The Slide Design task pane appears, similarly to the one shown in Figure B-10. This task pane is split into sections: the hyperlinks that open sub task panes are at the top of the pane; the Used in This Presentation section, which identifies the templates currently applied to the presentation (in this case, the Default Design template); the Recently Used section, which identifies up to four templates you have applied recently (this section does not appear on your screen if you have not used any other templates); and the Available For Use section, which lists all of the standard PowerPoint design templates that you can apply to a presentation.
2. **Scroll down to the Available For Use section of the Slide Design task pane, then place your pointer over the Capsules template (tenth row, second column)**
   A ScreenTip identifies the template, and a selection list arrow appears next to the Capsules template icon. The list arrow provides options for you to choose from when applying design templates. To determine how a design template looks on your presentation, you need to apply it. You can apply as many templates as you want until you find one that you like.
3. **Click the Capsules template list arrow, then click Apply to All Slides**
   The Capsules template is applied to all the slides. Notice the new slide background color, the new graphic elements, new fonts, and the new slide text color. You decide that this template doesn't work well with the presentation content.
4. **Click the Network template list arrow (eleventh row, first column), then click Apply to Selected Slides**
   The Network template is applied to just the title slide of the presentation. This design template doesn't fit with the presentation content either.
5. **Click the Edge template list arrow (eleventh row, second column), then click Apply to All Slides**
   This simple design template looks good with the presentation content and fits the MediaLoft company image.
6. **Click the Next Slide button ▼ three times**
   Preview all the slides in the presentation to see how they look.
7. **Click the Previous Slide button ▲ two times to return to Slide 2**
   Compare your screen to Figure B-11.
8. **Save your changes**

FIGURE B-10: Normal view with Slide Design task pane open

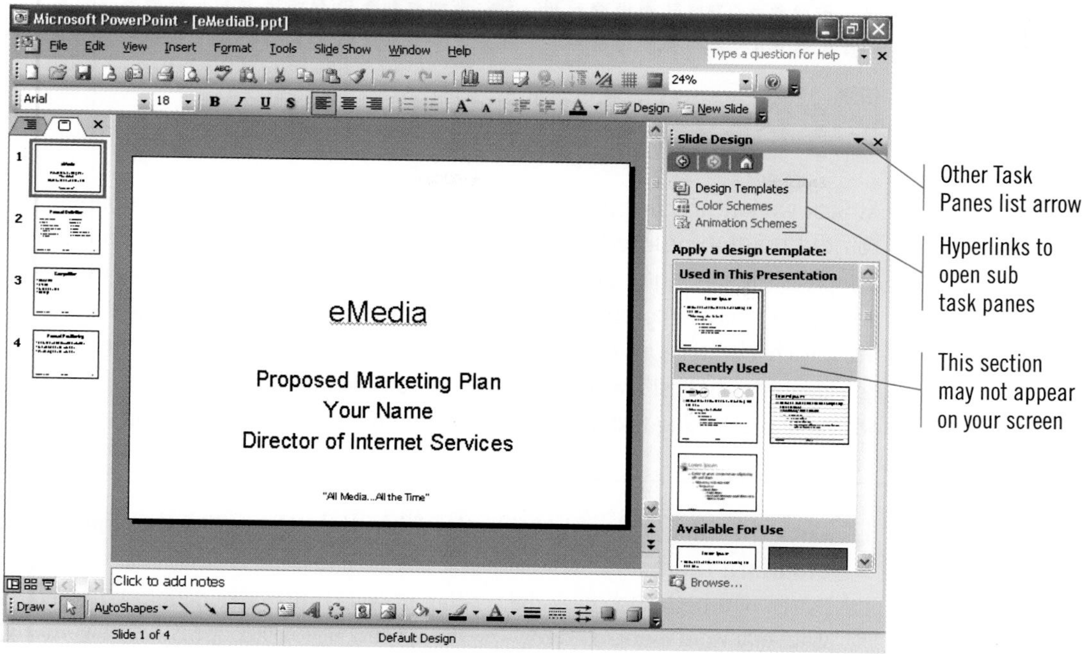

FIGURE B-11: Presentation with Edge template design applied

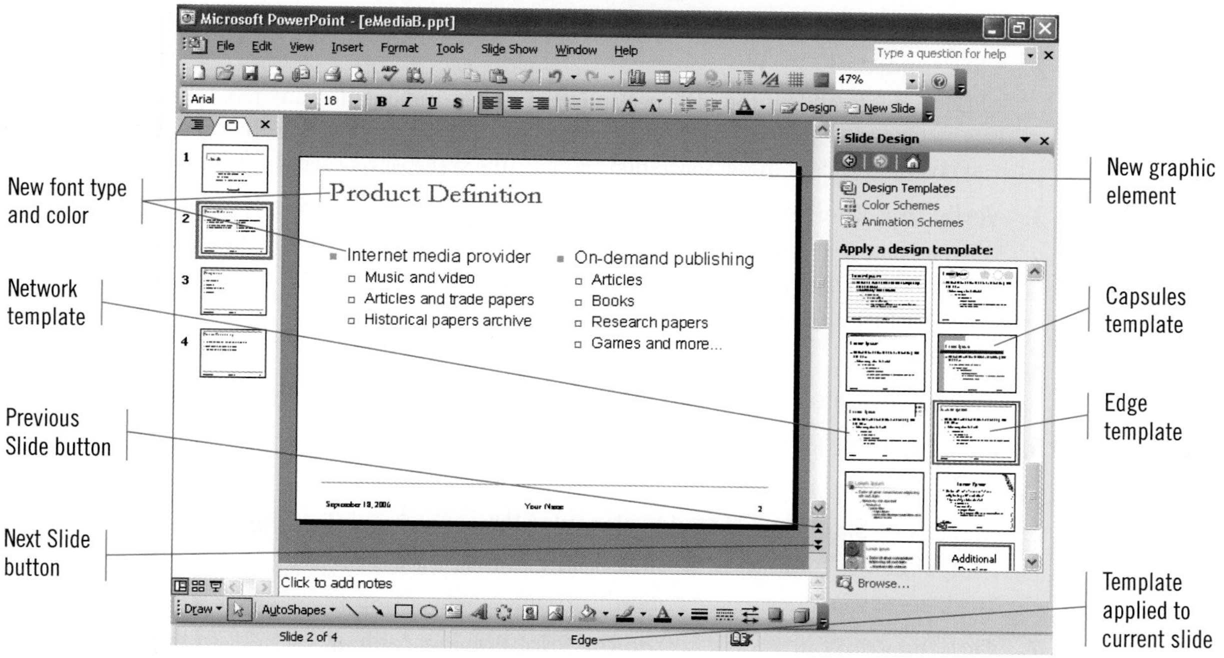

Clues to Use

Using design templates

You are not limited to using the templates PowerPoint provides; you can also modify a PowerPoint template or even create your own. For example, you might want to use your company's color as a slide background or incorporate your company's logo on every slide. If you modify an existing template, you can keep, change, or delete any color, graphic, or font. To create a new template, click Blank Presentation on the New Presentation task pane. Add the design elements to the slide to create the look you want for the presentation. Open the Save As dialog box, click the Save as type list arrow, choose Design Template, name your template, then click Save. PowerPoint automatically adds the file extension .pot to the filename, saves the template to the Templates folder, and adds it to the Slide Design task pane so that you can use your customized template as a basis for all future presentations. To apply a template that you created to an existing presentation, open the presentation, then choose the template in the Slide Design task pane.

Checking Spelling in a Presentation

As your work nears completion, you need to review and proofread your presentation thoroughly for errors. You can use the spellchecking feature in PowerPoint to check for and correct spelling errors. This feature compares the spelling of all the words in your presentation against the words contained in its electronic dictionary. You still must proofread your presentation for punctuation, grammar, and word-usage errors because the spellchecker recognizes only misspelled words, not misused words. For example, the spellchecker would not identify "The test" as an error, even if you had intended to type "The best." You're finished adding and changing text in the presentation, so you can now check the spelling in the presentation.

STEPS

TROUBLE

If your spellchecker doesn't find the word "eMedia," then a previous user may have accidentally added it to the custom dictionary. Skip Steps 1 and 2 and continue with the lesson.

1. **Click the Slide 1 thumbnail in the Slides tab, then click the Spelling button on the Standard toolbar**

   PowerPoint begins to check the spelling in your entire presentation. When PowerPoint finds a misspelled word or a word it doesn't recognize, the Spelling dialog box opens, as shown in Figure B-12. For an explanation of the commands available in the Spelling dialog box, see Table B-2. In this case, PowerPoint does not recognize "eMedia" on Slide 1. It suggests that you replace it with the word "media". You want the word to remain as you typed it.

2. **Click Ignore All**

   Clicking Ignore All tells the spellchecker not to stop at and question any more occurrences of this word in this presentation. The next word the spellchecker identifies as an error is the word "Bookstoes" in the body text object on Slide 3. In the Suggestions list box, the spellchecker suggests "Bookstores."

QUICK TIP

The spellchecker does not check the text in inserted pictures or objects.

3. **Verify that Bookstores is selected in the Suggestions list box, then click Change**

   If PowerPoint finds any other words it does not recognize, either change them or ignore them. When the spellchecker finishes checking your presentation, the Spelling dialog box closes, and an alert box opens with a message that the spelling check is complete.

4. **Click OK**

   The alert box closes. You are satisfied with the presentation so far and you decide to print it.

TROUBLE

If your preview window does not show the slide in color it is because you have selected a black and white printer.

5. **Click the Print Preview button on the Standard toolbar**

   The Print Preview window opens, displaying the presentation's title slide as shown in Figure B-13.

6. **Make sure Slides is selected in the Print What list box, click the Options list arrow on the Print Preview toolbar, then click Frame Slides**

   The slides of your presentation print with a frame around each page.

7. **Click the Print button Print... on the Print Preview toolbar, click OK in the Print dialog box, click the Close Preview button Close on the Print Preview toolbar, then save your presentation**

Clues to Use

Checking spelling as you type

PowerPoint checks your spelling as you type. If you type a word that is not in the electronic dictionary, a wavy red line appears under it. To correct an error, right-click the misspelled word, then review the suggestions, which appear in the shortcut menu. You can select a suggestion, add the word you typed to your custom dictionary, or ignore it. To turn off automatic spellchecking, click Tools on the menu bar, then click Options to open the Options dialog box. Click the Spelling and Style tab, and in the Spelling section, click the Check spelling as you type check box to deselect it. To temporarily hide the wavy red lines, click the Hide all spelling errors check box to select it.

FIGURE B-12: Spelling dialog box

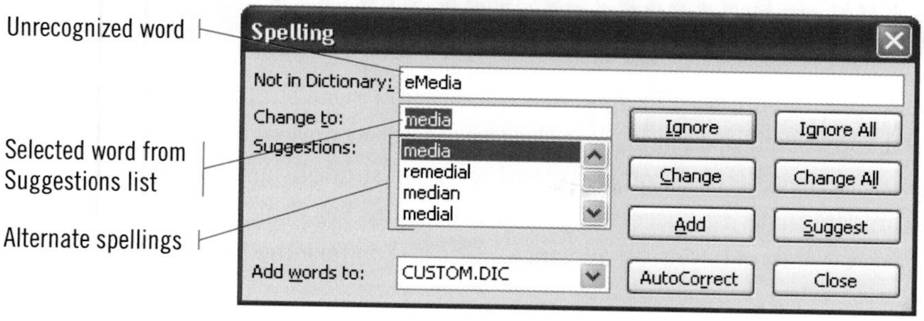

FIGURE B-13: Print Preview window

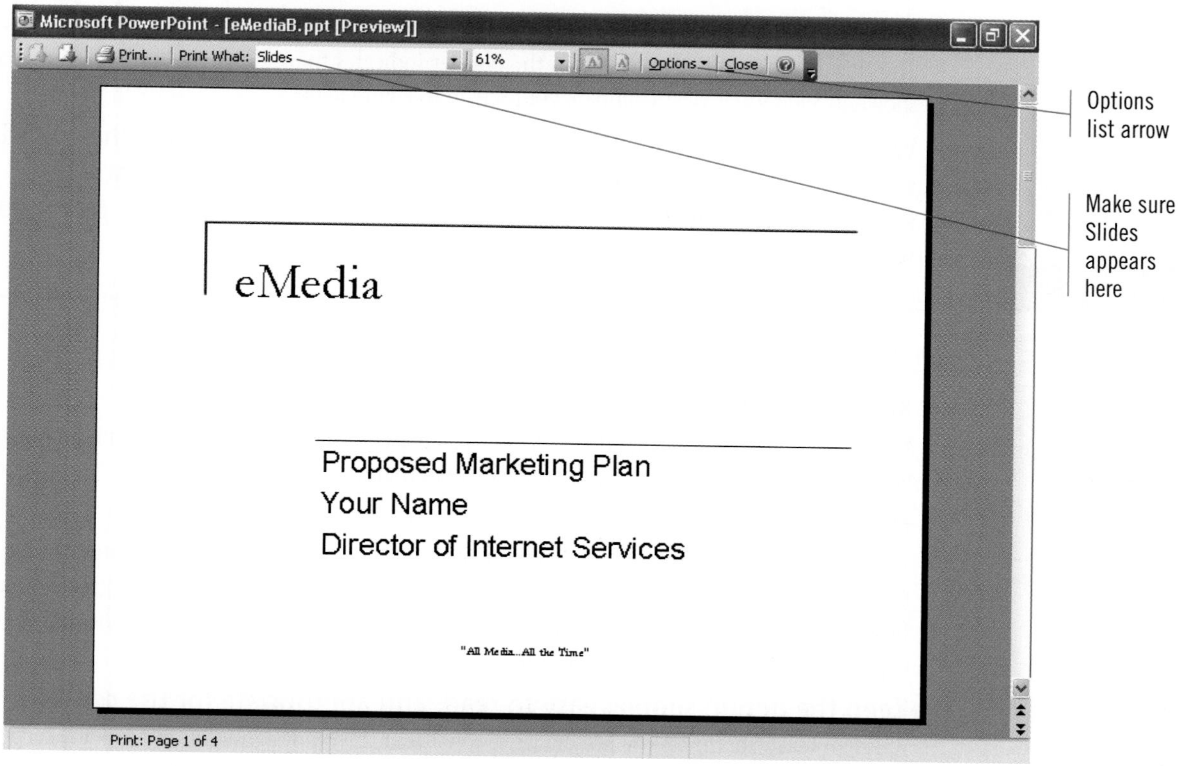

TABLE B-2: Spelling dialog box commands

command	description
Ignore/Ignore All	Continues spellchecking without making any changes to the identified word (or all occurrences of the identified word)
Change/Change All	Changes the identified word (or all occurrences) to the suggested word
Add	Adds the identified word to your custom dictionary; spellchecker will not flag it again
Suggest	Suggests an alternative spelling for the identified word
AutoCorrect	Adds the suggested word as an AutoCorrect entry for the highlighted word
Add words to	Lets you choose a custom dictionary where you store words you often use but that are not part of the PowerPoint dictionary

UNIT B
PowerPoint 2003

Evaluating a Presentation

As you create a presentation, keep in mind that good design involves preparation. An effective presentation is both focused and visually appealing—easy for the speaker to present and easy for the audience to understand. The visual elements (colors, graphics, and text) can strongly influence the audience's attention and interest and can determine the success of your presentation. See Table B-3 for general information on the impact a visual presentation has on an audience. You take the time to evaluate your presentation's effectiveness.

STEPS

1. **Click the Slide Show button, then press [Enter] to move through the slide show**
2. **When you are finished viewing the slide show, click the Slide Sorter View button**
   You decide that Slide 4 should come before Slide 3.
3. **Drag Slide 4 between Slides 2 and 3, then release the mouse button**
   The thin black line that moved with the pointer indicates the slide's new position. The final presentation is shown in Slide Sorter view. Compare your screen to Figure B-14.
4. **When you are finished evaluating your presentation according to the guidelines below, save your changes, then close the presentation and exit PowerPoint**
   Figure B-15 shows a poorly designed slide. Contrast this slide with your eMedia presentation as you review the following guidelines.

DETAILS

When evaluating a presentation, it is important to:

- **Keep your message focused**
  Don't put everything you plan to say on your presentation slides. Keep the audience anticipating further explanations to the key points shown in the presentation.
- **Keep your text concise**
  Limit each slide to six words per line and six lines per slide. Use lists and symbols to help prioritize your points visually. Your presentation text provides only the highlights; use notes to give more detailed information. Your presentation focuses attention on the key issues and you supplement the information with further explanation and details during your presentation.
- **Keep the design simple, easy to read, and appropriate for the content**
  A design template makes the presentation consistent. If you design your own layout, keep it simple and use design elements sparingly. Use similar design elements consistently throughout the presentation; otherwise, your audience may get confused. You used a simple design template; the horizontal lines give the presentation a somewhat artistic look, which is appropriate for a casual professional presentation.
- **Choose attractive colors that make the slide easy to read**
  Use contrasting colors for slide background and text to make the text readable. If you are giving an on-screen presentation, you can use almost any combination of colors that look good together.
- **Choose fonts and styles that are easy to read and emphasize important text**
  As a general rule, use no more than two fonts in a presentation and vary the font size, using nothing smaller than 24 points. Use bold and italic attributes selectively.
- **Use visuals to help communicate the message of your presentation**
  Commonly used visuals include clip art, photographs, charts, worksheets, tables, and movies. Whenever possible, replace text with a visual, but be careful not to overcrowd your slides. White space on your slides is OK!

FIGURE B-14: The final presentation in Slide Sorter view

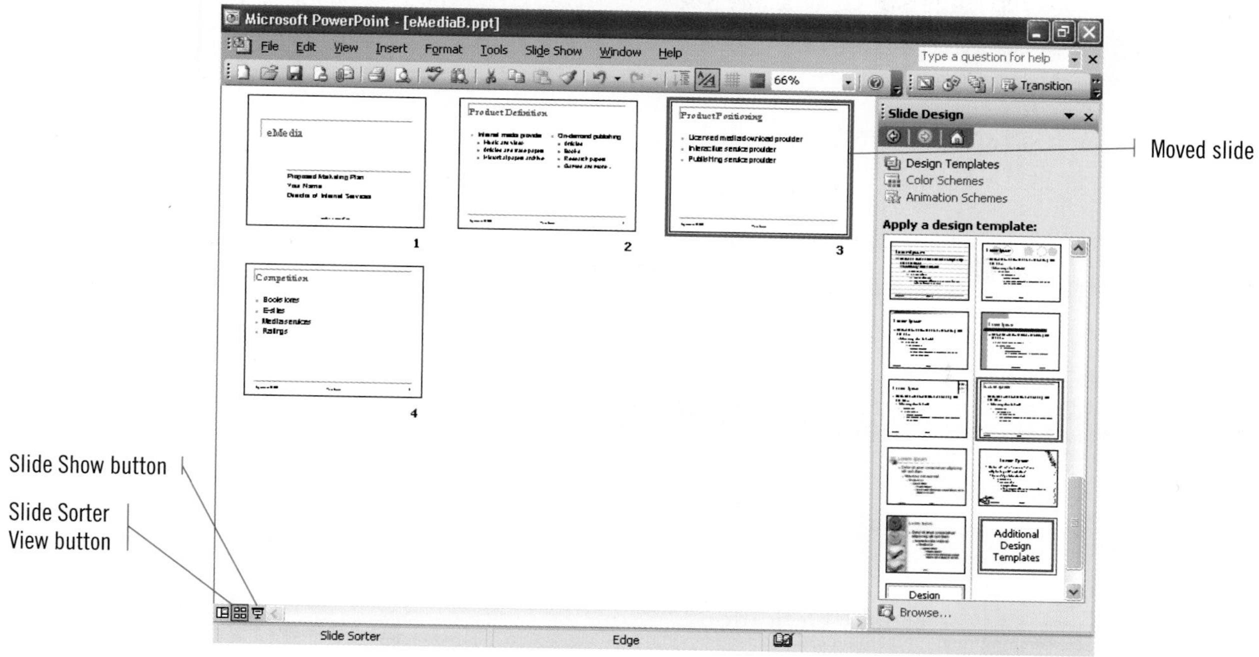

FIGURE B-15: A poorly designed slide in Normal view

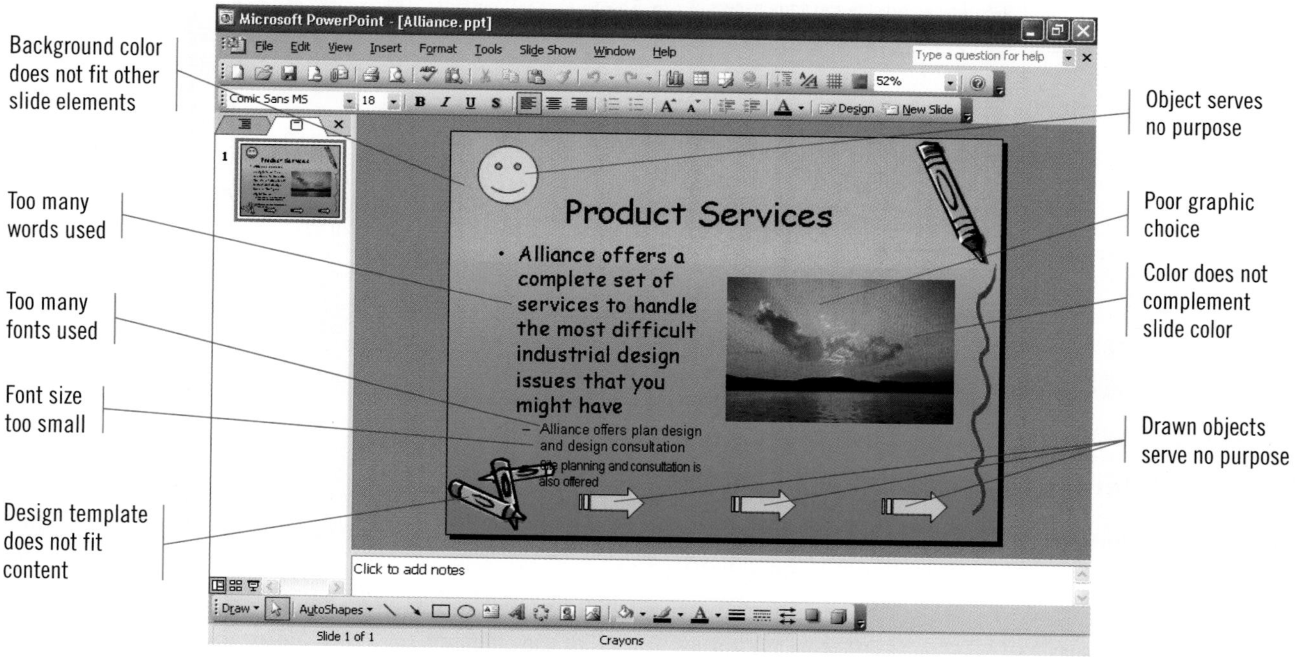

TABLE B-3: Audience impact from a visual presentation

impact	description
Visual reception	Most people receive up to 75% of all environmental stimuli through the human sense of sight
Learning	Up to 90% of what an audience learns comes from visual and audio messages
Retention	Combining visual messages with verbal messages can increase memory retention by as much as 30%
Presentation goals	You are twice as likely to achieve your communication objectives using a visual presentation
Meeting length	You are likely to decrease the average meeting length by 25% when you use visual presentation

Source: Presenters Online, www.presentersonline.com

Practice

▼ CONCEPTS REVIEW

Label each element of the PowerPoint window shown in Figure B-16.

FIGURE B-16

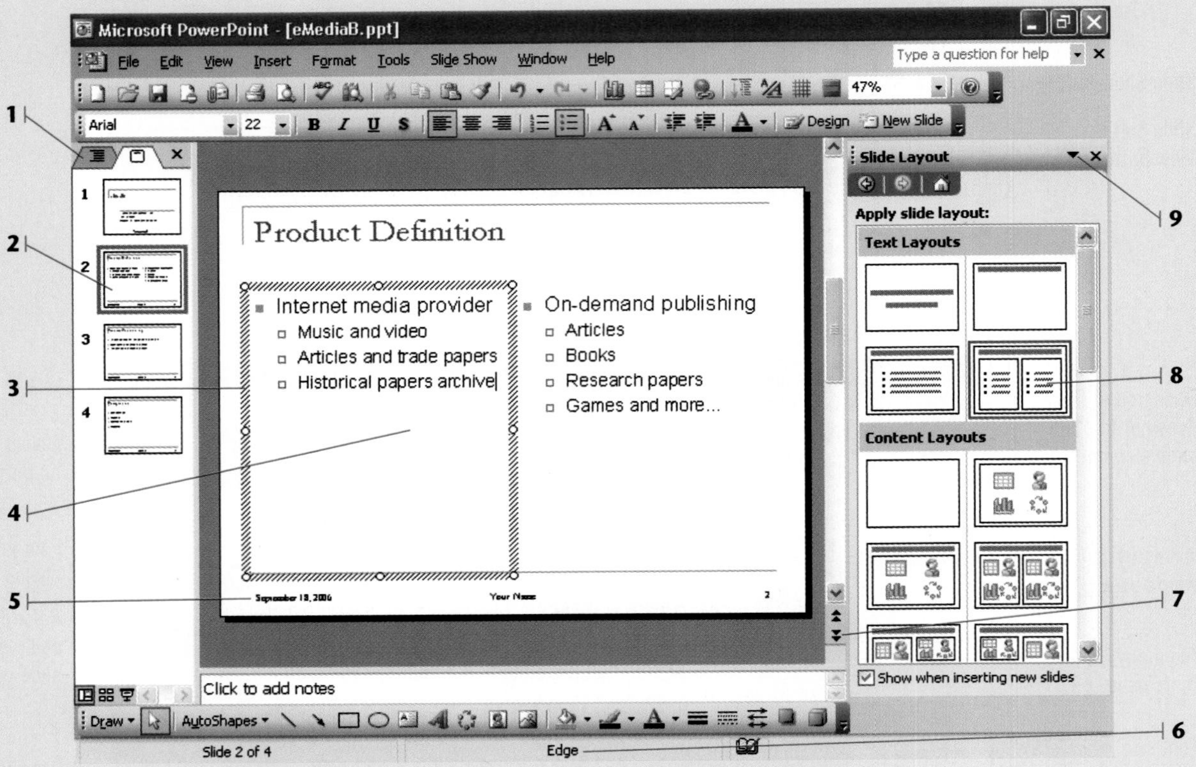

Match each term with the statement that best describes it.

10. Text placeholder
11. Slide layout
12. Selection box
13. Design template
14. Slide icon
15. Insertion point

a. A specific design, format, and color scheme that is applied to all the slides in a presentation
b. Indicates where your text will appear when you type in a text object
c. Determines how all of the elements on a slide are arranged
d. The slanted line border that appears around a text placeholder, indicating that it is ready to accept text
e. A box with a dashed border in which you can type text
f. In Outline view, the symbol that represents a slide

Select the best answer from the list of choices.

16. According to the unit, which of the following is *not* a guideline for planning a presentation?
  a. Determine the purpose of the presentation.
  b. Determine what you want to produce when the presentation is finished.
  c. Determine which type of output you need to best convey your message.
  d. Determine who else can give the final presentation.

17. Other than the Slide pane, where else can you enter slide text?
  a. Outline tab
  b. Print Preview
  c. Notes Page view
  d. Slides tab

18. Which of the following statements is *not* true?
  a. You can customize any PowerPoint template.
  b. The spellchecker identifies "there" as misspelled if the correct word for the context is "their".
  c. Speaker notes do not appear during the slide show.
  d. PowerPoint has many colorful templates from which to choose.

19. When you evaluate your presentation, you should make sure it follows which of the following criteria?
  a. The slides should include every piece of information to be presented so the audience can read it.
  b. The slides should use as many colors as possible to hold the audience's attention.
  c. Many different typefaces make the slides more interesting.
  d. The message should be clearly outlined without a lot of extra words.

20. What is the definition of a slide layout?
  a. A slide layout automatically applies all the objects you can use on a slide.
  b. A slide layout determines how all the elements on a slide are arranged.
  c. A slide layout applies a different template to the presentation.
  d. A slide layout puts all your slides in order.

21. When the spellchecker identifies a word as misspelled, which of the following is *not* a choice?
  a. To ignore this occurrence of the error
  b. To change the misspelled word to the correct spelling
  c. To have the spellchecker automatically correct all the errors it finds
  d. To ignore all occurrences of the error in the presentation

22. When you type text in a text placeholder, it becomes:
  a. A label.
  b. A title.
  c. A selection box.
  d. A text object.

▼ SKILLS REVIEW

1. Enter slide text.
  a. Start PowerPoint if necessary.
  b. In the Slide pane in Normal view, enter the text **Product Marketing** in the title placeholder.
  c. In the main text placeholder, enter **Rueben Agarpao**.
  d. On the next line of the placeholder, enter **Manager**.
  e. On the next line of the placeholder, enter **April 14, 2006**.
  f. Deselect the text object.
  g. Save the presentation as **RouterJet Tests** to the drive and folder where your Data Files are stored.

▼ SKILLS REVIEW (CONTINUED)

2. **Create new slides.**
   a. Create a new slide.
   b. Review the text in Table B-4, then select the appropriate slide layout.
   c. Enter the text from Table B-4 into the new slide.
   d. Create a new bulleted list slide using the Slide Layout task pane.
   e. Enter the text from Table B-5 into the new slide.
   f. Save your changes.
3. **Enter text in the Outline tab.**
   a. Open the Outline tab.
   b. Create a new bulleted list slide after the last one.
   c. Enter the text from Table B-6 into the new slide.
   d. Move the third bullet point in the second indent level to the second position.
   e. Switch back to the Slides tab.
   f. Save your changes.
4. **Add slide headers and footers.**
   a. Open the Header and Footer dialog box.
   b. Type today's date into the Fixed text box.
   c. Add the slide number to the footer.
   d. Type your name in the Footer text box.
   e. Apply the footer to all of the slides.
   f. Open the Header and Footer dialog box again, then click the Notes and Handouts tab.
   g. Enter today's date in the Fixed text box.
   h. Type the name of your class in the Header text box.
   i. Type your name in the Footer text box.
   j. Apply the header and footer information to all the notes and handouts.
   k. Save your changes.
5. **Choose a look for a presentation.**
   a. Open the Slide Design task pane.
   b. Locate the Profile template, then apply it to all the slides.
   c. Move to Slide 1.
   d. Locate the Pixel template, then apply it to Slide 1.
   e. Save your changes.
6. **Check spelling in a presentation.**
   a. Perform a spelling check on the document and change any misspelled words. Ignore any words that are correctly spelled but that the spellchecker doesn't recognize.
   b. Save your changes.
7. **Evaluate a presentation.**
   a. View Slide 1 in the Slide Show view, then move through the slide show.
   b. Evaluate the presentation using the points described in the lesson as criteria.
   c. Preview your presentation.
   d. Print the outline of the presentation.
   e. Print the slides of your presentation in grayscale with a frame around each slide.
   f. Save your changes, close the presentation, and exit PowerPoint.

TABLE B-4

text object	text to insert
Slide title	RouterJet Project Tests - Rueben
First indent level	Focus: Component System
Second indent level	User access components Security components Network components System components
First indent level	Data Files and Report
Second indent level	Compile component data files Define component interface parameters Write function data report

TABLE B-5

text object	text to insert
Slide title	RouterJet Project Tests - Jeremy
First indent level	Focus: Network Integration
Second indent level	Server codes and routes File transfer Data conversion Platform functionality ratings

TABLE B-6

text object	text to insert
Slide title	RouterJet Project Tests - Nura
First indent level	Focus: Software QA
Second indent level	User access testing Software compatibility testing Platform testing

▼ INDEPENDENT CHALLENGE 1

You have been asked to give a one-day course at a local adult education center. The course is called "Personal Computing for the Slightly Anxious Beginner" and is intended for adults who have never used a computer. One of your responsibilities is to create presentation slides that outline the course materials.

Plan and create presentation slides that outline the course material for the students. Create slides for the course introduction, course description, course text, grading policies, and a detailed syllabus. Create your own course material, but assume the following: the school has a computer lab with personal computers running Microsoft Windows software; each student has a computer; the prospective students are intimidated by computers but want to learn; and the course is on a Saturday from 9 a.m. to 5 p.m., with a one-hour lunch break.

a. Write a short paragraph that explains the results you want to see, the information you need, and the type of message you want to communicate.

b. Write an outline of your presentation. Indicate which content should go on each of the slides. Remember that your audience has never used computers before and needs computer terms defined.

c. Start PowerPoint and create the presentation by entering the title slide text.

d. Create the required slides as well as an ending slide that summarizes your presentation.

Advanced Challenge Exercise

- Open the Notes Page view.
- To at least three slides, add notes that you want to remember when you give the class.
- Print the Notes Page view for the presentation.

e. Check the spelling in the presentation.

f. Save the presentation as **Computer Class 101** to the drive and folder where your Data Files are stored.

g. View the presentation in Slide Show view.

h. Add your name as a footer on the notes and handouts, print handouts (six slides per page), and then print the presentation outline.

i. Save your changes, close your presentation, then exit PowerPoint.

▼ INDEPENDENT CHALLENGE 2

You are the training director for Catch Up, Ltd., a German company in Berlin that coordinates special events, including corporate functions, weddings, and private parties. You regularly train groups of temporary employees that you can call on as coordinators, kitchen and wait staff, and coat checkers for specific events. The company trains 10 to 15 new workers each month for the peak season between May and September. One of your responsibilities is to orient new temporary employees at the next training session.

Plan and create presentation slides that outline your employee orientation. Create slides for the introduction, agenda, company history, dress requirements, principles for interacting successfully with guests, and safety requirements. Create your own presentation and company material, but assume the following: Catch Up, Ltd. is owned by Jan Negd-Sorenson; the new employee training class lasts four hours, and your orientation lasts 15 minutes; the training director's presentation lasts 15 minutes; and the dress code requires uniforms, supplied by Catch Up, Ltd. (white for daytime events, black and white for evening events).

a. Think about the results you want to see, the information you need, and the message you want to communicate.

b. Write a presentation outline. What content should go on the slides?

c. Start PowerPoint and create the presentation by entering the slide text for all your slides.

d. Create a slide that summarizes your presentation, then add an appropriate design template.

e. Create an ending slide with the following information:

Catch Up, Ltd.
Gubener Strasse 765, 10243 Berlin
(Berlin-Friedrichshain)
TEL.: 393795, FAX: 39375719

f. Check the spelling in the presentation.

▼ INDEPENDENT CHALLENGE 2 (CONTINUED)

g. Save the presentation as **Catch Up Training** to the drive and folder where your Data Files are stored.

h. View the slide show, then view the slides in Slide Sorter view. Evaluate your presentation; make any changes necessary so that the final version is focused, clear, concise, and readable.

i. Add your name as a footer on the notes and handouts, print the presentation as handouts (two slides per page), then print the presentation outline.

j. Save your changes, close your presentation, then exit PowerPoint.

▼ INDEPENDENT CHALLENGE 3

You are an independent distributor of natural foods in Albuquerque, New Mexico. Your business, All Natural Foods, has grown progressively since its inception eight years ago, but sales and profits have leveled off over the last nine months. In an effort to stimulate growth, you decide to acquire two major natural food dealers, which would allow All Natural Foods to expand its territory into surrounding states. Use PowerPoint to develop a presentation that you can use to gain a financial backer for the acquisition.

a. Start PowerPoint. Choose the Maple design template. Enter **Growth Plan** as the main title on the title slide, and **All Natural Foods** as the subtitle.

b. Save the presentation as **Growth Plan Proposal** to the drive and folder where your Data Files are stored.

c. Add five more slides with the following titles: Slide 2–Background; Slide 3–Current Situation; Slide 4–Acquisition Goals; Slide 5–Our Management Team; Slide 6–Funding Required.

d. Enter text into the text placeholders of the slides. Use both the Slide pane and the Outline tab to enter text.

e. Check the spelling in the presentation.

f. View the presentation as a slide show, then view the slides in Slide Sorter view.

g. Add your name as a footer on the notes and handouts, save your changes, then print handouts (six slides per page).

h. Close your presentation, then exit PowerPoint.

Advanced Challenge Exercise

ACE

- Create a new slide at the end of the presentation. Enter concluding text on the slide, summarizing the main points of the presentation.
- Apply at least one design template to the presentation.
- Evaluate your presentation using the points identified in the Evaluating a Presentation lesson. Use a word processor to write a short paragraph explaining how your presentation met the goals for proper presentation development.
- Make any changes you feel are necessary, then identify the changes and explain your reasoning in a word processing document.
- Save the presentation as **Growth Plan Proposal 2** to the drive and folder where your Data Files are stored.
- Print the presentation outline, close your presentation, then exit PowerPoint.

E-QUEST

▼ INDEPENDENT CHALLENGE 4

One of the best things about PowerPoint is the flexibility you have in creating your presentations, but that same flexibility can result in slides that may appear cluttered, unorganized, and hard to read. Unit B introduced you to some concepts that you can use to help create good presentations using PowerPoint. Use the Web to research more guidelines and tips on creating effective presentations.

Plan and create a presentation that explains these tips to an audience of beginning PowerPoint users. The information you find on the Web should include the following topics:

- Message organization
- Text arrangement and amount
- Slide layout and design
- Presentation development
- Room layout and delivery
- Equipment

a. Connect to the Internet, then use your favorite search engine to locate Web sites that have information on presentations. Use the keywords **presentation tips** to conduct your search.
b. Review at least two Web sites that contain information about presentation tips and guidelines.
c. Start PowerPoint. Title the presentation **Presentation Tips**.
d. Create a presentation with at least five slides. Each slide should contain one main tip with supporting information about that tip.
e. Add a final slide titled **Presentation Tip URLs**. List the Web site addresses—the URLs—from which you obtained the information you used in your presentation.
f. Apply an appropriate design template.
g. Save the presentation as **Presentation Info** to the drive and folder where your Data Files are stored.
h. Add your name as a footer to the slides, notes, and handouts, check the spelling in the presentation, then view the final presentation as a slide show.
i. View your presentation in Slide Sorter view and evaluate it. Make any changes necessary so that the final version is focused, clear, concise, and readable.
j. Save your final presentation, print the slides as handouts (two per page), then close the presentation and exit PowerPoint.

▼ VISUAL WORKSHOP

Create the marketing presentation shown in Figures B-17 and B-18. Add today's date as the date on the title slide. Save the presentation as **Trade Proposal** to the drive and folder where your Data Files are stored. Review your slides in Slide Show view, add your name as a footer to the slides, notes, and handouts. Print the first slide of your presentation as a slide, then print the outline. Save your changes, close the presentation, and exit PowerPoint.

FIGURE B-17

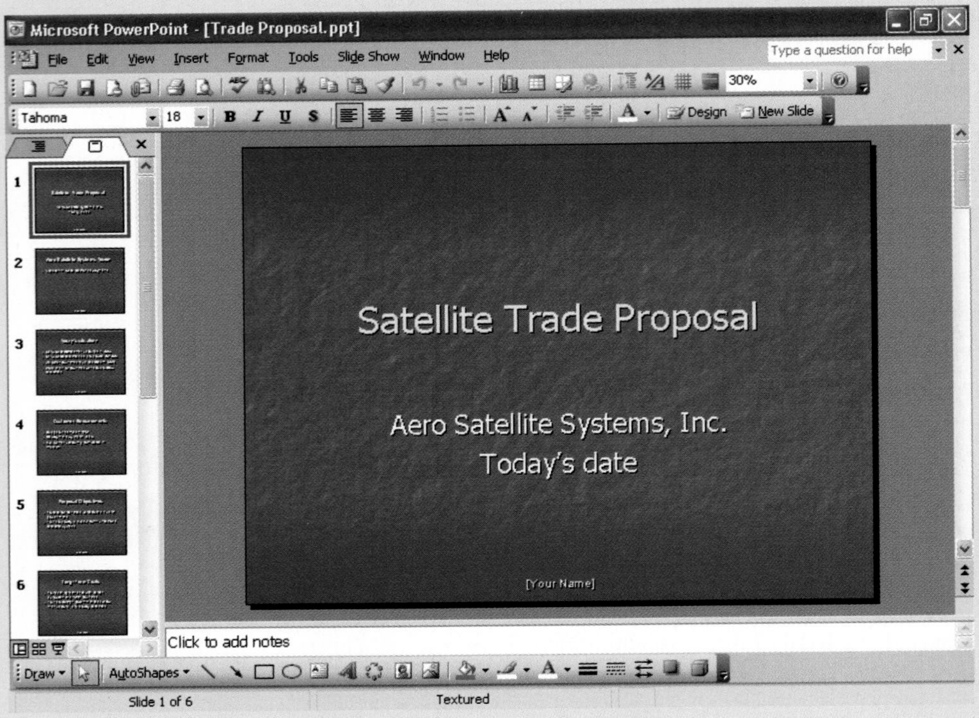

FIGURE B-18

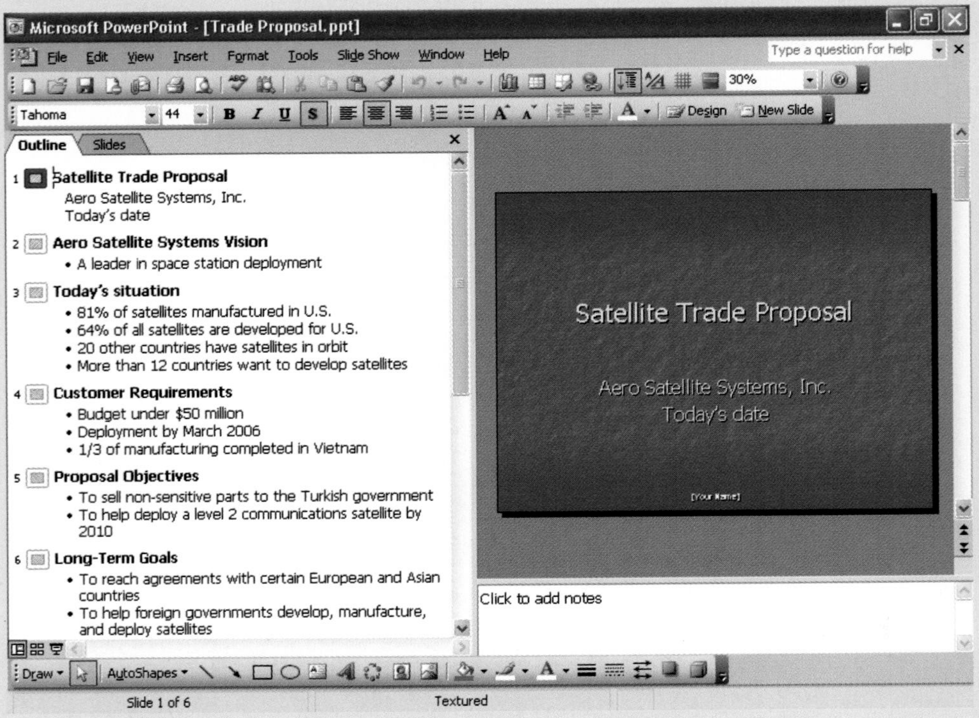

UNIT
C
PowerPoint 2003

Modifying a Presentation

OBJECTIVES

- Open an existing presentation
- Draw and modify an object
- Edit drawn objects
- Align and group objects
- Add and arrange text
- Format text
- Import text from Microsoft Word
- Customize the color scheme and background

If you have a SAM user profile, you may have access to hands-on instruction, practice, and assessment of the skills covered in this unit. Log in to your SAM account and go to your assignments page to see what your instructor has assigned.

After you create the basic outline of your presentation and enter text, you need to add images to your slides to help you communicate your message effectively. In this unit, you open an existing presentation; draw and modify objects; add, arrange, and format text; and work with the color scheme. You continue your work on the eMedia marketing presentation by drawing and modifying objects from the AutoShapes menu. You then edit the text and change the color scheme to create a professional look for the presentation.

UNIT C
PowerPoint 2003

Opening an Existing Presentation

Sometimes the easiest way to create a new presentation is by changing an existing one. Revising a presentation means that you do not have to re-create slides that already exist and that you can use them again. You simply open the file you want to change, then use the Save As command to save a copy of the file with a new name. Whenever you open an existing presentation in this book, you will save a copy of it with a new name—this keeps the original file intact. Saving a copy does not affect the original file. You are ready to add some visual elements to your presentation, so you open the presentation you have been working on and save it with a new name.

STEPS

QUICK TIP
To open the file without opening a copy, click the Open hyperlink under Open in the Getting Started task pane, or click the Open button on the Standard toolbar.

1. **Start PowerPoint, then click the Create a new presentation hyperlink in the Open section in the Getting Started task pane**
   The New Presentation task pane opens.
2. **Click the From existing presentation hyperlink in the New section in the New Presentation task pane**
   The New from Existing Presentation dialog box opens.
3. **Click the Look in list arrow, locate the drive and folder where your Data Files are stored, click the Views button list arrow on the dialog box toolbar, then click Preview**
   A list of your Data Files appears in the dialog box.
4. **If it is not selected, click PPT C-1.ppt**
   The first slide of the selected presentation appears in the preview box on the right side of the dialog box. See Figure C-1.
5. **Click Create New**
   A copy of the PPT C-1.ppt presentation file opens in Normal view. The presentation title bar displays the temporary filename "Presentation2".

QUICK TIP
If the file is not yet named, you can click the Save button to open the Save As dialog box.

6. **Click File on the menu bar, then click Save As**
   The Save As dialog box opens.
7. **Make sure the Save in list box shows the drive and folder where your Data Files are stored, verify that the current filename in the File name text box is selected, then type eMediaC**
8. **Click Save to close the Save As dialog box and save the file**
   The file is saved with the name eMediaC.

TROUBLE
If you have another PowerPoint presentation open and it appears next to this presentation, close it, then repeat Step 9.

9. **Click the Slide Design button on the Formatting toolbar, click Window on the menu bar, then click Arrange All**
   See Figure C-2. You can work with the task pane opened or closed. Many of the figures in this book show only the window that contains the Slide and notes panes and the Slides and Outline tabs.

FIGURE C-1: New from Existing Presentation dialog box

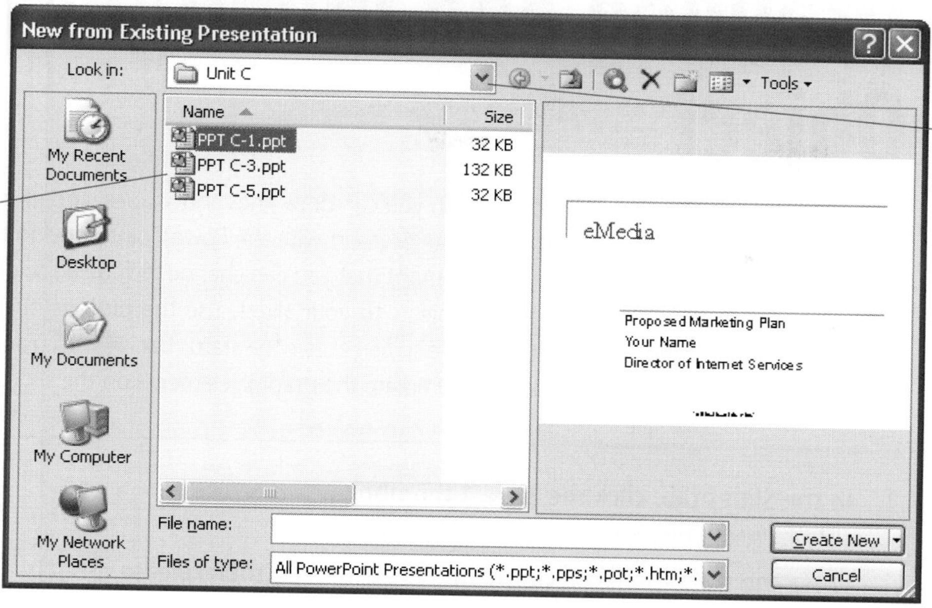

Your list of folders and files may be different

Look in list arrow

FIGURE C-2: First slide of the eMedia presentation

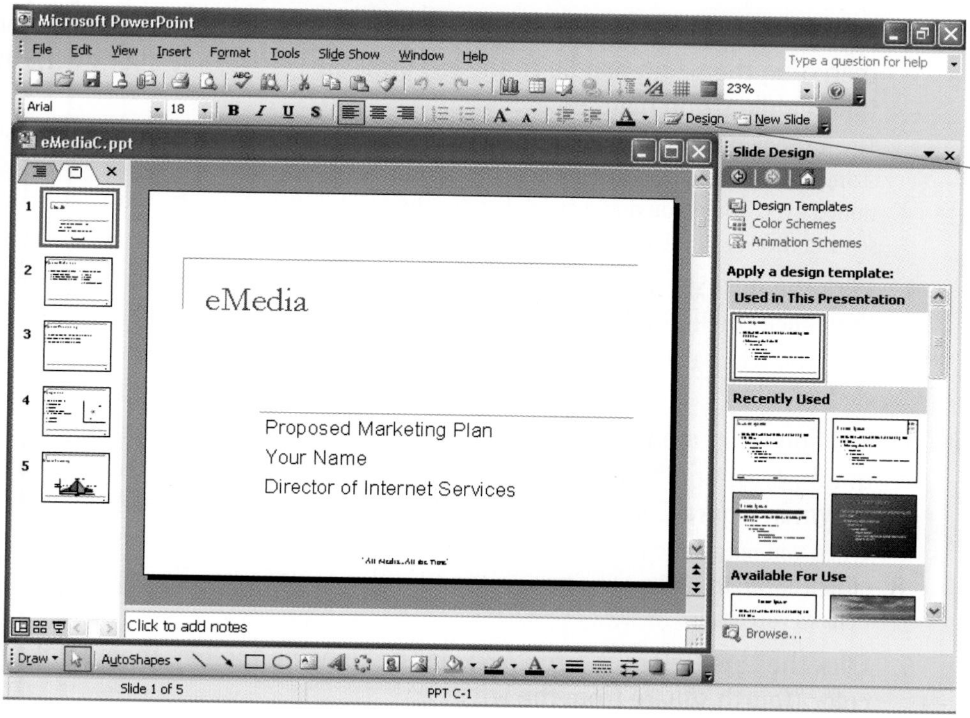

Slide Design button

Clues to Use

Setting permissions

In PowerPoint 2003, you can set specific access permissions for people who review or edit your work, so you have better control over your content. For example, you may want to give a user permission to edit or change your presentation but not allow them to print it. You can also restrict a user by permitting them to view the presentation, without the ability to edit or print the presentation, or you can give the user full access or control of the presentation. To set user access permissions, click the Permission button on the Standard toolbar. To use this feature, you have to first install the Windows Rights Management software.

UNIT C

PowerPoint 2003

Drawing and Modifying an Object

Using the drawing commands in PowerPoint, you can draw lines and shapes, and insert objects to enhance your presentation. The objects that you create or insert with the PowerPoint drawing tools can be modified to meet your design needs. The graphic attributes that you can change include fill color, line color, line style, shadow, and 3-D effects. To add drawn objects to your slides, use the buttons on the Drawing toolbar, which is typically docked at the bottom of the screen above the status bar. You decide to draw more objects on Slide 4 of your presentation to complete the graphic elements on the slide.

STEPS

1. **In the Slides tab, click the Slide 4 thumbnail**
   Slide 4, titled "Competition", appears in the Slide pane.
2. **Press and hold [Shift], click the body text object, then release [Shift]**
   A dotted selection box with small circles called **sizing handles** appears around the text object. If you click a text object without pressing [Shift], a selection box composed of slanted lines appears, indicating that the object is active and ready to accept text, but it is not selected. When an object is selected, you can change its size, shape, or attributes by dragging one of the sizing handles.

TROUBLE
If you are not satisfied with the size of the text object, resize it again.

3. **Position the pointer over the right, middle sizing handle, the pointer changes to ⟷, then drag the sizing handle to the left until the vertical line aligns with the top and bottom middle sizing handles**
   The text object is about half its original size, as shown in Figure C-3. When you position the pointer over a sizing handle, it changes to ⟷. It points in different directions depending on which sizing handle it is positioned over. When you drag a sizing handle, the pointer changes to +, and a dotted outline appears, representing the size of the text object.
4. **Click the AutoShapes button AutoShapes on the Drawing toolbar, point to Block Arrows, then click the Right Arrow button (first row, first column)**
   After you select a shape from the AutoShapes menu and move the pointer over the slide, the pointer changes to +.

TROUBLE
If your arrow object is not approximately the same size as the one shown in Figure C-4, press [Shift] and drag one of the corner sizing handles to resize the object.

5. **Position + in the blank area of the slide to the right of the text object and below the graph, press and hold [Shift], drag down and to the right to create an arrow object, as shown in Figure C-4, release [Shift], then release the mouse button**
   When you release the mouse button, an arrow object appears on the slide, filled with the default color and outlined with the default line style. Pressing [Shift] while you create the object maintains the object's proportions as you change its size.
6. **Click the Line Color list arrow on the Drawing toolbar, then point to the dark green color (fourth square from the left)**
   A ScreenTip appears identifying this color as the Follow Title Text Scheme Color.
7. **Click the dark green color**
   PowerPoint applies the green color to the selected arrow object's outline.
8. **Click the Fill Color list arrow on the Drawing toolbar, then click the white color (first square on the left, the Follow Background Scheme Color)**
   PowerPoint fills the selected arrow object with white.
9. **Click the Save button on the Standard toolbar to save your changes**

FIGURE C-3: Resizing a text object

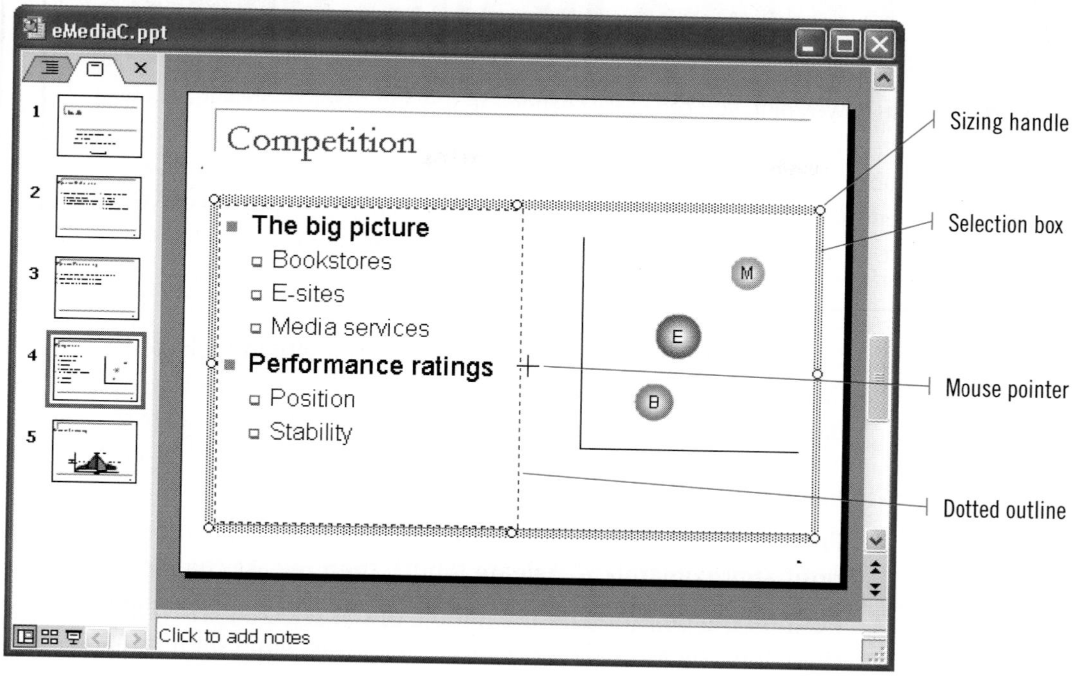

FIGURE C-4: Arrow object on slide

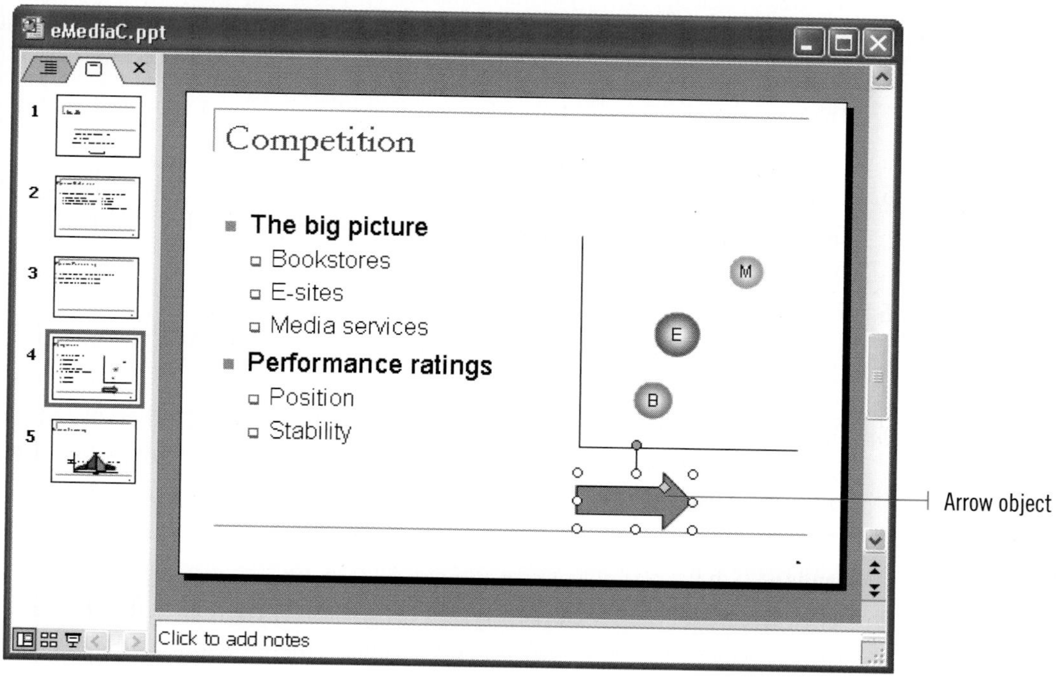

PowerPoint 2003

Clues to Use

Understanding PowerPoint objects

In PowerPoint, you often work with multiple objects on the same slide. These may be text objects or graphic objects, such as drawn objects, clip art, or charts. To help you organize objects on a slide, you can align, group, and stack the objects using the Align or Distribute, Group, and Order commands on the Draw menu on the Drawing toolbar. When you align objects, you place their edges (or their centers) on the same plane. For example, you might want to align two squares vertically (one above the other) so that their left edges are in a straight vertical line. When you group objects, you combine two or more objects into one object. It's often helpful to group objects into one when you have finished positioning them on the slide. When you stack objects, you determine their order, that is, which ones are in front and which are in back. You can use the stacking order of objects to overlap them to create different effects.

UNIT
C
PowerPoint 2003

Editing Drawn Objects

In PowerPoint, you can easily change the size and shape of objects on a slide. You can alter the appearance of any object by dragging the sizing handles to adjust its dimensions. You can add text to most PowerPoint objects and you can move or copy objects. You want two arrows on Slide 4 that are the same shape and size. You first change the shape of the arrow object you've already drawn, and then you make a copy of it. Finally, you rotate one arrow to complete the graphic element.

STEPS

1. **Click the arrow object to select it, if it is not already selected**
   In addition to sizing handles, two other handles appear on the selected object. You use the **adjustment handle**—a small yellow diamond—to change the appearance of an object. The adjustment handle appears next to the most prominent feature of the object, like the head of an arrow in this case. You use the **rotate handle**—a small green circle—to rotate the object.

2. **Press and hold [Shift], drag the right, middle sizing handle on the arrow object to the right approximately ½", release [Shift], then release the mouse button**

3. **Position the pointer over the middle of the selected arrow object so that it changes to , then drag the arrow object so that the arrow aligns with the horizontal axis of the chart as shown in Figure C-5**
   A dotted outline appears as you move the arrow object to help you position it. PowerPoint uses a hidden grid to align objects; it forces objects to "snap" to the grid lines. Make any adjustments to the arrow object position.

4. **Position over the arrow object, then press and hold [Ctrl]**
   The pointer changes to , indicating that PowerPoint makes a copy of the arrow object when you drag the mouse.

5. **Holding [Ctrl], drag the arrow object to the left until the dotted lines indicate that the arrow object copy is in a blank area of the slide, release the mouse button, then release [Ctrl]**
   An identical copy of the arrow object appears on the slide.

6. **Type Price**
   The text appears in the center of the selected arrow object. The text is now part of the object, so if you move or rotate the object, the text moves with it.

7. **Position the pointer over the rotate handle of the selected arrow object so that it changes to , then drag the rotate handle counterclockwise until the arrow head is pointing straight up**
   If you need to make any adjustments to the arrow object, drag the rotate handle again. Compare your screen with Figure C-6.

8. **Click the other arrow object, type Performance, then click in a blank area of the slide**
   Clicking a blank area of the slide deselects all objects that are selected.

9. **Click the Save button on the Standard toolbar to save your changes**

TROUBLE

If you have trouble aligning the object in this step, press and hold [Alt] to turn off the snap to grid feature, then drag the object.

QUICK TIP

Rulers can help you align objects. To display the rulers, position the pointer in a blank area of the slide, right-click, then click Ruler on the shortcut menu.

QUICK TIP

You can also use the Rotate or Flip commands on the Draw button on the Drawing toolbar to rotate or flip objects 90 degrees.

FIGURE C-5: Slide showing resized arrow object

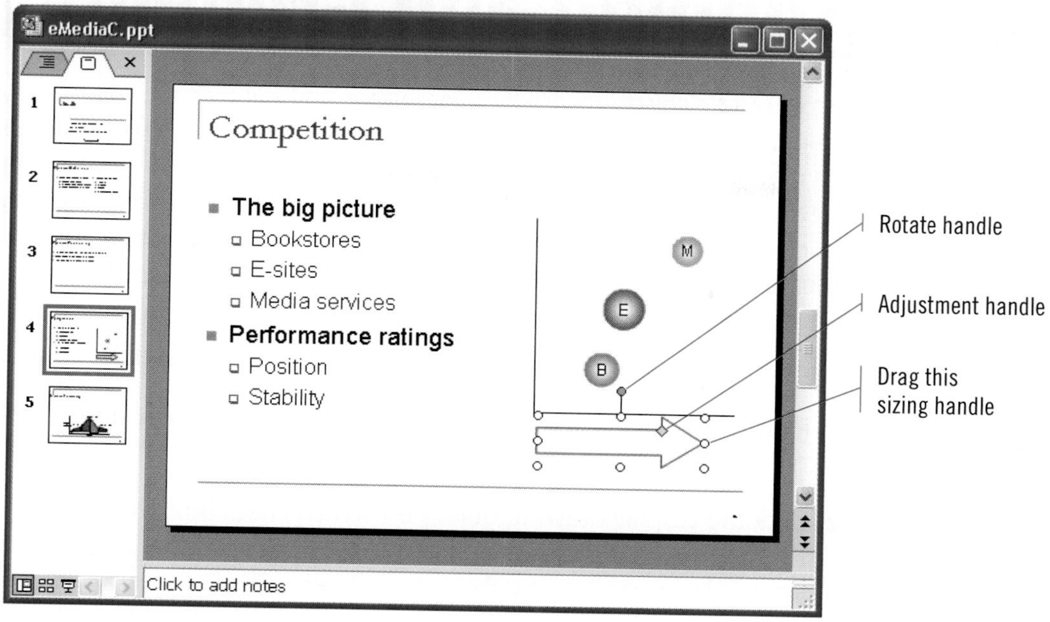

FIGURE C-6: Slide showing duplicated arrow object

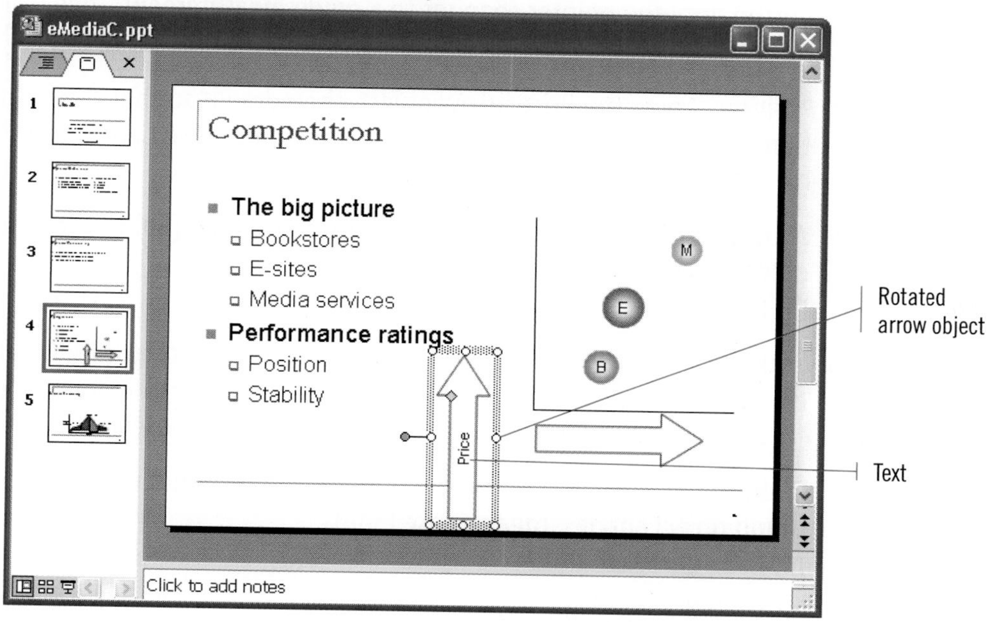

Clues to Use

More ways to change objects

You can layer objects over one another by changing their stacking order, or you can change the appearance of an object by making it three-dimensional or by applying a shadow effect. To change the stacking order of an object, select the object, click the Draw button on the Drawing toolbar, point to Order, then click one of the menu commands shown in Figure C-7. To make an object three-dimensional, select it, click the 3-D Style button on the Drawing toolbar, then click one of the buttons on the shortcut menu shown in Figure C-8. To add a shadow to an object, select it, click the Shadow Style button on the Drawing toolbar, then click one of the buttons on the shortcut menu shown in Figure C-9.

FIGURE C-7: Order menu

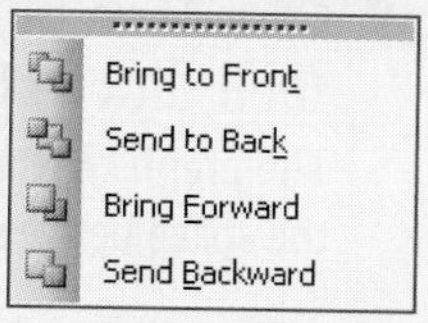

FIGURE C-8: 3-D Style menu

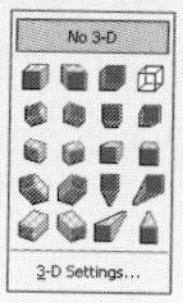

FIGURE C-9: Shadow Style menu

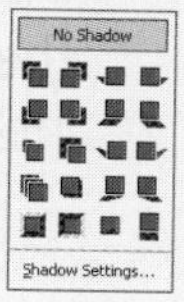

UNIT C

PowerPoint 2003

Aligning and Grouping Objects

After you create objects, modify their appearance, and edit their size and shape, you can position them on the slide, align them, distribute them, and then group them. The Align command arranges objects relative to each other by snapping the selected objects to a hidden grid of evenly spaced vertical and horizontal lines. The Distribute command evenly distributes the space horizontally or vertically between selected objects. The Group command groups objects into one object, which makes retaining their relative position easy while editing and moving them. You are ready to position and group the arrow objects on Slide 4 and then align and distribute some other objects with which you have been working.

STEPS

QUICK TIP

To add a new guide to the slide, press [Ctrl], then drag an existing guide. The original guide remains in place as you move the new guide. Drag a guide off the slide to delete it.

TROUBLE

Make sure you position the pointer over a section of the arrow object without text.

1. **Right-click a blank area of the slide, then click Grid and Guides on the shortcut menu**
   The Grid and Guides dialog box opens.
2. **Click the Display drawing guides on screen check box, then click OK**
   The PowerPoint guides appear as dotted lines on the slide. (The dotted lines may be very faint on your screen.) The guides intersect at the center of the slide. They help you position the arrow object.
3. **Position the pointer over the vertical guide in a blank area of the slide, press and hold the mouse button until the pointer changes to a guide measurement, then drag the guide to the right until the guide measurement box reads approximately 1.00**
4. **Position the pointer over the Price arrow object, then drag it so that the right edge of the selection box touches the vertical guide as shown in Figure C-10**
   The arrow object attaches or "snaps" to the vertical guide.
5. **With the Price arrow object selected, press and hold [Shift], click the Performance arrow object, then release [Shift]**
   The two objects are now selected.
6. **Click the Draw button on the Drawing toolbar, then click Group**
   The arrow objects group to form one object without losing their individual attributes. Notice the sizing handles and rotate handle now appear on the outer edge of the grouped object, not around each individual object.
7. **In the Slides tab, click the Slide 5 thumbnail, press and hold [Shift], click each of the five graph object shapes, then release [Shift]**
   The five graph object shapes are selected.
8. **Click Draw, then point to Align or Distribute**
   A menu of alignment and distribution options appears. The top three options align objects vertically; the next three options align objects horizontally; and the last three options evenly distribute the space between objects.
9. **Click Align Bottom, click Draw, point to Align or Distribute, click Distribute Horizontally, then click a blank area of the slide**
   The graph objects are now aligned horizontally along their bottom edges and are distributed evenly so that the space between each object is equal. Compare your screen with Figure C-11.
10. **Right-click a blank area of the slide, click Grid and Guides on the shortcut menu, click the Display drawing guides on screen check box, click OK, then click the Save button on the Standard toolbar to save your changes**
    The guides are no longer displayed on the slide.

FIGURE C-10: Repositioned arrow object

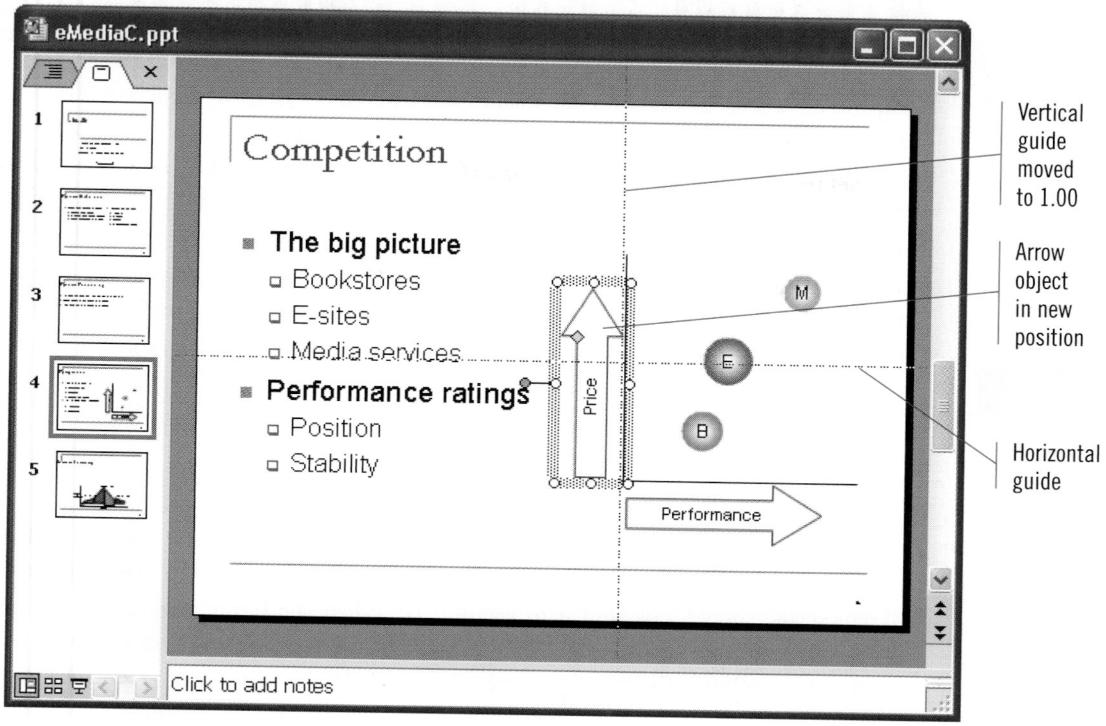

FIGURE C-11: Aligned and distributed graph objects

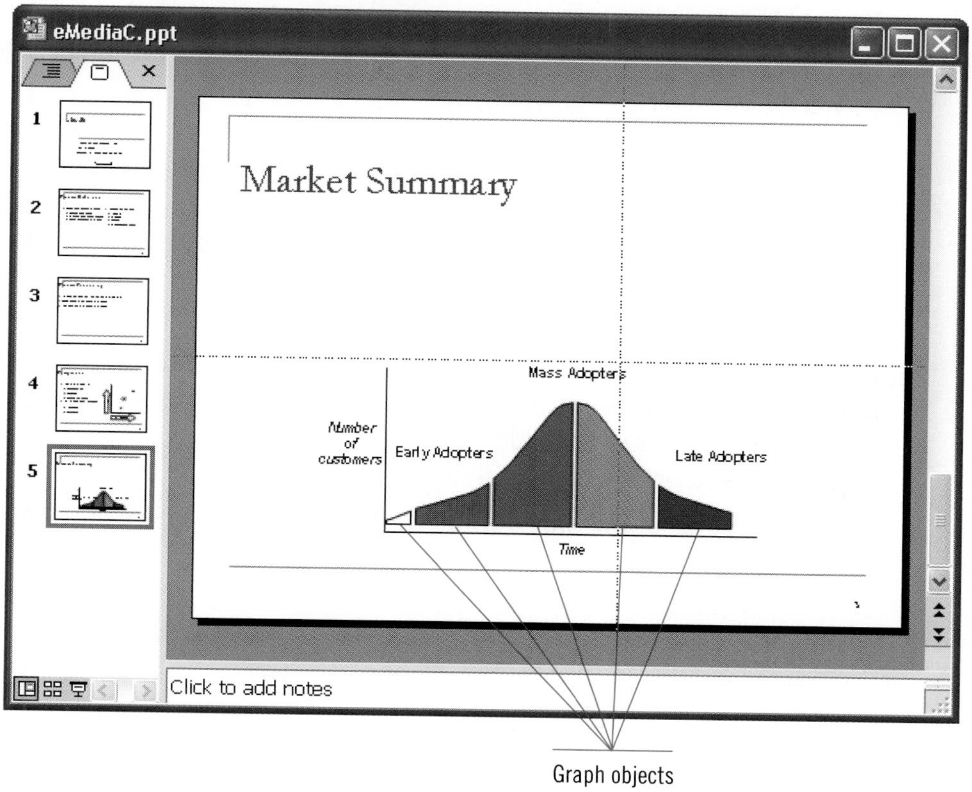

UNIT C
PowerPoint 2003

Adding and Arranging Text

Using the advanced text-editing capabilities of PowerPoint, you can easily type, insert, or rearrange text. The PowerPoint slide layouts allow you to enter text in prearranged text placeholders. If these text placeholders don't provide the flexibility you need, you can use the Text Box button on the Drawing toolbar to create your own text objects. With the Text Box button, you can create two types of text objects: a text label, used for a small phrase where text doesn't automatically wrap to the next line inside the box; and a word processing box, used for a sentence or paragraph where the text wraps inside the boundaries of the box. You decide that Slide 5 needs a little more information to make it complete. Use the Text Box button to create a word processing box to enter information about the graph chart that is on the slide.

STEPS

1. **Click the Text Box button on the Drawing toolbar**
   The pointer changes to ↓.

> **QUICK TIP**
> To create a text label in which text doesn't wrap, click , position ↓ where you want to place the text, then click once and enter the text.

2. **Position ↓ near the left side of the slide, above the top of the chart, then drag down and toward the right side of the slide about an inch and a half to create a word processing box**
   Your screen should look similar to Figure C-12. When you begin dragging, an outline of the text object appears, indicating how large a text object you are drawing. After you release the mouse button, an insertion point appears inside the text object, ready to accept text.
3. **Type Changes in market, costs, share, pricing, and competition**
   Notice that the text object increases in size as your text wraps inside the text object. There is a mistake in the text. It should read "market share".
4. **Double-click the word share to select it**
5. **Position the pointer on top of the selected word and press and hold the mouse button**
   The pointer changes to .

> **QUICK TIP**
> You also can use the Cut and Paste buttons on the Standard toolbar or the Cut and Paste commands on the Edit menu to move a word.

6. **Drag the word share to the right of the word market in the text object, then release the mouse button**
   A dotted insertion line appears as you drag, indicating where PowerPoint places the word when you release the mouse button. The word "share" moves next to the word "market". Moving the word "share" leaves an extra comma, which you need to delete.
7. **Position I to the right of one of the commas after the word "costs", then press [Backspace]**
   One of the commas is deleted.
8. **Drag the right-middle sizing handle of the text object to the right until the word "costs" moves to the top line of the text object, position over the text object border, then drag it to the center of the slide**
   Your screen should look similar to Figure C-13.
9. **Click a blank area of the slide outside the text object, then click the Save button on the Standard toolbar to save your changes**

FIGURE C-12: Word processing box ready to accept text

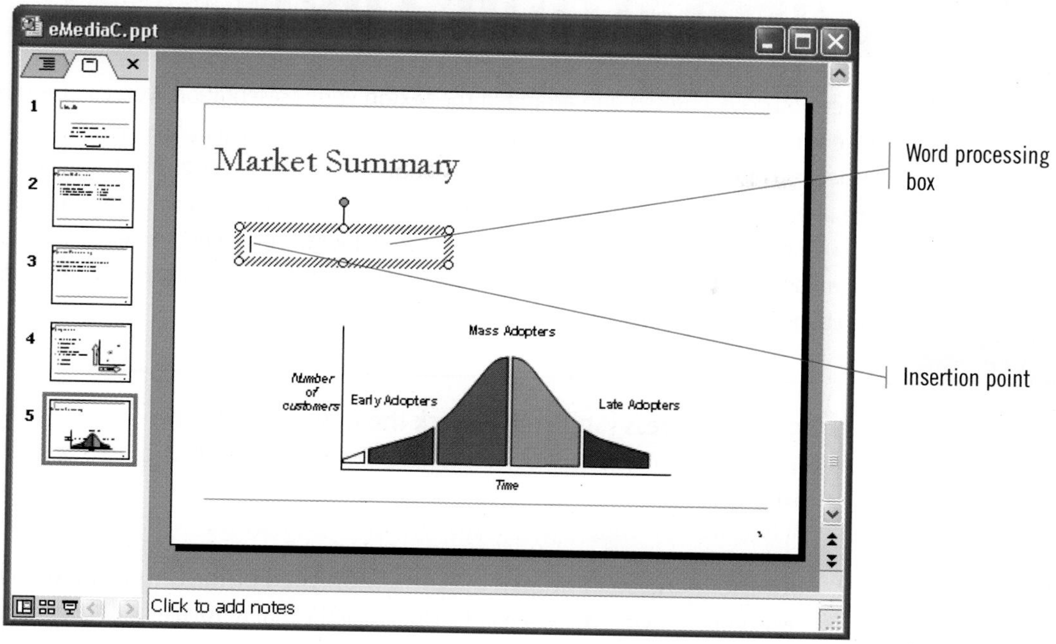

FIGURE C-13: Text added to the word processing box

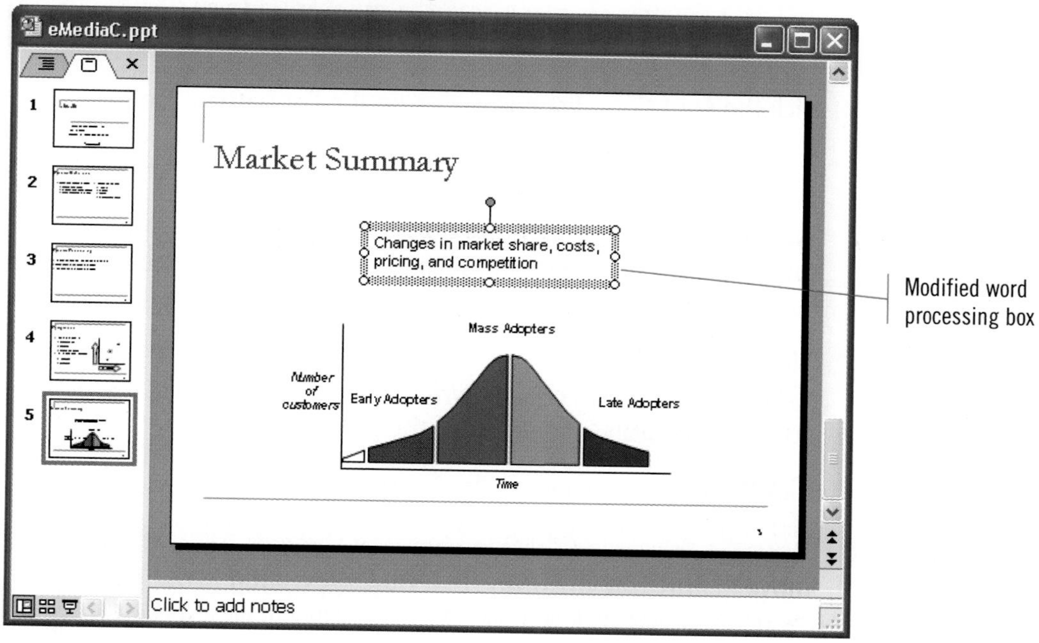

PowerPoint 2003

Clues to Use

Review a presentation

You can send a copy of a presentation over the Internet to others for them to review, edit, and add comments. To send your presentation out for review, you can use Microsoft Outlook, which automatically tracks changes made by reviewers, or you can use any other compatible e-mail program. To send a presentation to reviewers using Outlook, click File on the menu bar, point to Send To, then click Mail Recipient (for Review). Outlook opens and automatically creates a "Review Request" e-mail with the PowerPoint presentation attached to it for you to send to reviewers. Reviewers can use any version of PowerPoint to review, edit, and comment on their copy of your presentation. Once a reviewer is finished with the presentation and sends it back to you, you can combine their changes and comments with your original presentation using the PowerPoint Compare and Merge Presentations feature. When you do this, the Revisions task pane opens with commands that allow you to accept or reject reviewers' changes.

UNIT C

PowerPoint 2003

Formatting Text

Once you have entered and arranged the text in your presentation, you can modify the way the text looks to emphasize your message. Important text needs to be highlighted in some way to distinguish it from other text or objects on the slide. Less important information does not need to be emphasized. For example, if you have two text objects on the same slide, you could draw attention to one text object by changing its color or size. To change the way text looks, you need to select it, then choose a Formatting command. In this lesson, you use some of the commands on the Formatting and Drawing toolbars to change the way the new text object looks on Slide 5.

STEPS

1. **On Slide 5, press [Shift], then click the new text object**
   The entire text object is selected. Any changes you make affect all the text in the selected text object. Changing the text's size and appearance helps emphasize it. When a text object is already selected because you have been entering text in it, you can select the entire text object by clicking on its border with .

QUICK TIP
You can also click the Font Size list arrow 18 on the Formatting toolbar, then click the font size you want from the list.

2. **Click the Increase Font Size button on the Formatting toolbar twice**
   The text increases in size to 24 points. The size of the font is listed in the Font Size text box on the Formatting toolbar.

3. **Click the Italic button on the Formatting toolbar**
   The text changes from normal to italic text. The Italic and Bold buttons are toggle buttons, which you click to turn the attribute on or off.

QUICK TIP
The Font Color button can also be found on the Drawing toolbar.

4. **Click the Font Color list arrow on the Formatting toolbar**
   The Font Color menu appears, showing the eight colors used in the current presentation and the More Colors command, which lets you choose additional colors.

5. **Click More Colors to open the Colors dialog box, then click the teal cell in the upper-left corner of the color hexagon, second from the left, as shown in Figure C-14**
   The Current color and the New color appear in the box in the lower-right corner of the dialog box.

6. **Click OK**
   The text in the text object changes to teal, and the teal color is added as the ninth color in the set of colors used in the presentation.

7. **Click the Font list arrow on the Formatting toolbar**
   A list of available fonts opens with Arial, the font used in the text object, selected in the list.

8. **Click the down scroll arrow, then click Times New Roman**
   The Times New Roman font replaces the original font in the text object.

9. **Click the Center button on the Formatting toolbar, then resize the text object so that the word "costs" is on the top line in the text object**
   The text is aligned in the center of the text object and is contained on two lines.

10. **Drag the text object so it is centered over the chart, click a blank area of the slide outside the text object to deselect it, then click the Save button on the Standard toolbar**
    Compare your screen to Figure C-15.

FIGURE C-14: Colors dialog box

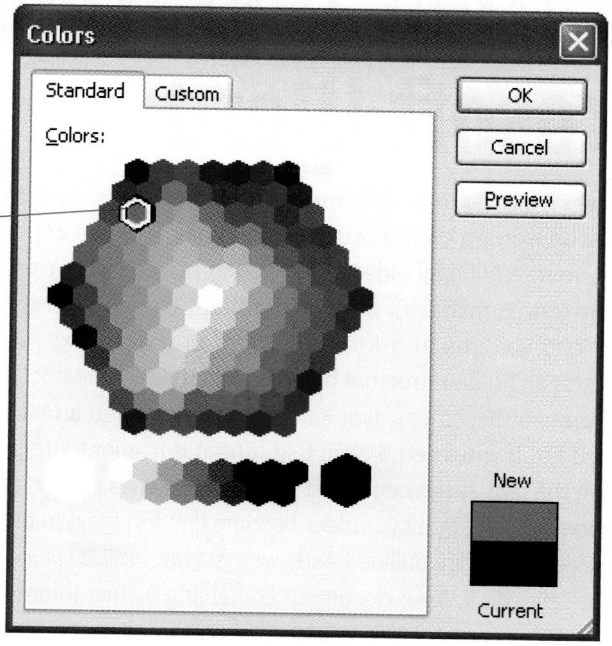

Select this color

FIGURE C-15: Slide showing formatted text object

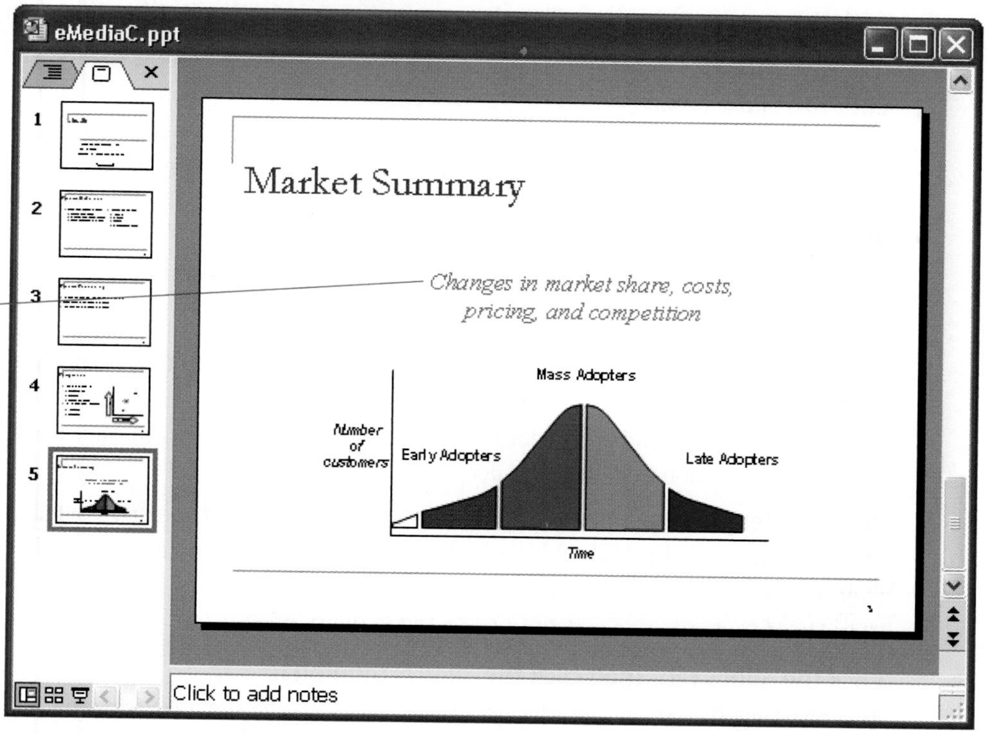

Formatted text

Clues to Use

Replacing text and attributes

As you review your presentation, you may decide to replace certain words throughout the entire presentation. You can automatically modify words, sentences, text case, and periods. To replace specific words or sentences, click Edit on the menu bar, then click Replace. To automatically add or remove periods from title or body text and to automatically change the case of title or body text, click Tools on the menu bar, click Options, click the Spelling and Style tab, then click Style Options to open the Style Options dialog box. Specify the options you want on the Case and End Punctuation tab. The options on the Visual Clarity tab in the Style Options dialog box control the legibility of bulleted text items on the slides.

PowerPoint 2003

UNIT C

PowerPoint 2003

Importing Text from Microsoft Word

PowerPoint makes it easy to insert information from other sources, such as Microsoft Word, into a presentation. If you have an existing Word document or outline, you can import it into PowerPoint to create a new presentation or insert additional slides in an existing presentation. Documents saved in Microsoft Word format (.doc), Rich Text Format (.rtf), plain text format (.txt), and HTML format (.htm) can be inserted into a presentation. When you import a Microsoft Word or a Rich Text Format document into a presentation, PowerPoint creates an outline structure based on the styles in the document. For example, a Heading 1 style in the Word document becomes a slide title in PowerPoint and a Heading 2 style becomes the first level of text in a bulleted list. If you insert a plain text format document into a presentation, PowerPoint creates an outline based on the tabs at the beginning of the document's paragraphs. Paragraphs without tabs become slide titles; paragraphs with one tab indent become first-level text in bulleted lists; paragraphs with two tabs become second-level text in bulleted lists; and so on. One of your colleagues from the Sales Department has sent you a Word document containing further information that you need for your presentation. You insert this document into your presentation.

STEPS

1. **Click the Outline tab, then click the up scroll arrow in the Outline tab until the Slide 4 slide title appears**

2. **Click the Slide 4 icon**

   Slide 4 appears in the Slide pane. Each time you click a slide icon in the Outline tab, the slide title and text are highlighted indicating the slide is selected. Before you insert information into a presentation, you must first designate where you want the information to be placed. In this case, the Word document is inserted after Slide 4, the selected slide.

3. **Click Insert on the menu bar, then click Slides from Outline**

   The Insert Outline dialog box opens.

4. **Locate the Word document PPT C-2.doc in the drive and folder where your Data Files are stored, then click Insert**

   Three new slides (5, 6, and 7) are added to the presentation. See Figure C-16. Slide 5 is selected showing you where the information from the Word document begins.

5. **Read the text for the new Slide 5 in the Slide pane, click the down scroll arrow in the Outline tab until the Slide 8 icon is displayed, click the Slide 6 icon in the Outline tab, then review the text on that slide**

   Slide 6 is selected; you can see the text for Slide 7 in the Outline tab.

6. **Click the Slides tab, then click the Slide 7 thumbnail**

   After reviewing the text on this slide, you realize that someone else is covering this information in another presentation.

7. **Right-click the Slide 7 thumbnail, then click Delete Slide on the shortcut menu**

   Slide 7 is deleted from the presentation. The last slide in the presentation, Market Summary, now appears in the Slide pane. Compare your screen to Figure C-17.

8. **Click the Save button on the Standard toolbar to save your changes**

FIGURE C-16: Outline tab showing imported text

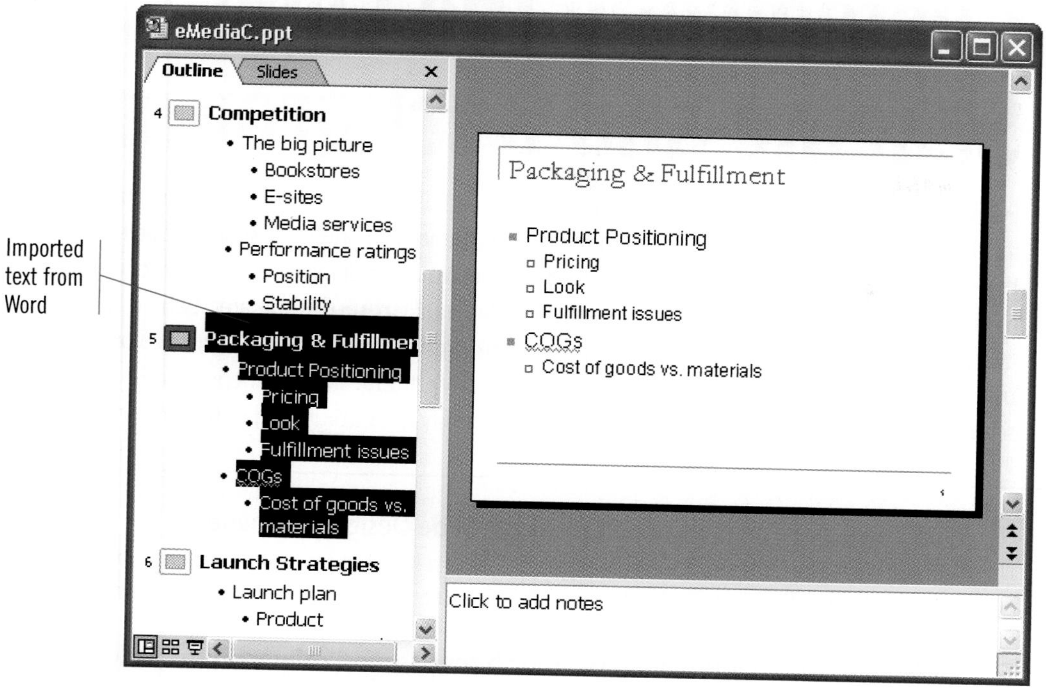

FIGURE C-17: Presentation after deleting slide

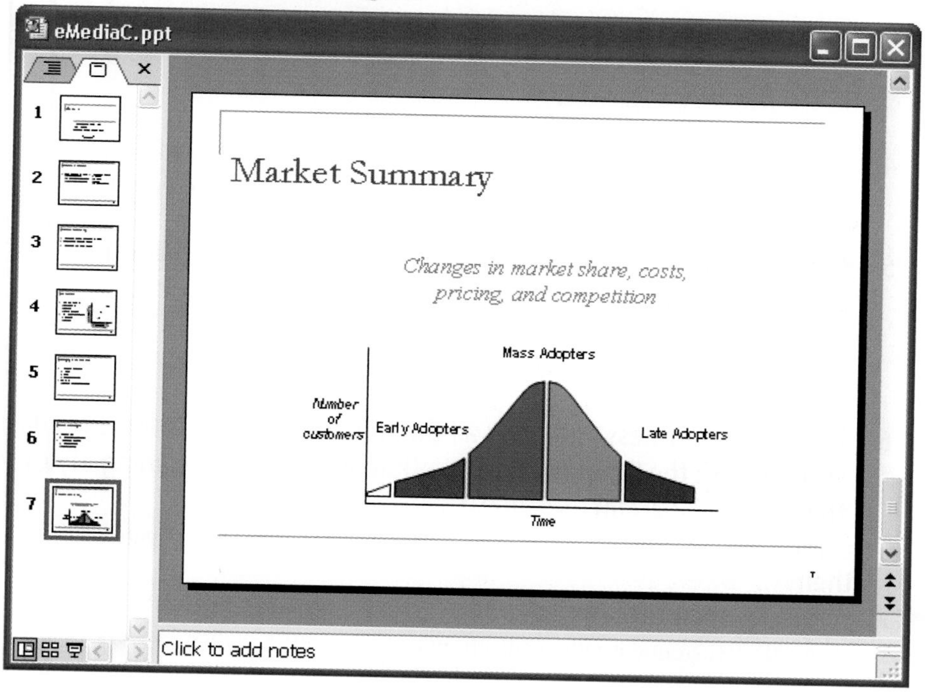

PowerPoint 2003

Clues to Use

Inserting slides from other presentations

To insert slides into the current presentation, click Insert on the menu bar, then click Slides from Files. Click Browse in the Slide Finder dialog box, then locate the presentation from which you want to copy slides. In the Select slides section, select the slide(s) you want to insert, click Insert, then click Close. The new slides automatically take on the design of the current presentation. If both presentations are open, you can copy the slides from one presentation to another. Change the view of each presentation to Slide Sorter view, select the desired slides, then copy and paste them (or use drag and drop) into the desired presentation. You can then rearrange the slides in Slide Sorter view if necessary.

UNIT
C
PowerPoint 2003

Customizing the Color Scheme and Background

Every PowerPoint presentation has a **color scheme**, a set of eight coordinated colors that determine the colors for the slide elements in your presentation: slide background, text and lines, shadows, title text, fills, accents, and hyperlinks. The design template that is applied to a presentation determines its color scheme. See Table C-1 for a description of the slide color scheme elements. The **background** is the area behind the text and graphics. Every design template in PowerPoint—even the blank presentation template—has a color scheme that you can use or modify. You can change the background color and appearance independently of changing the color scheme. You change the color scheme and modify the background of the presentation.

STEPS

1. **Click the Color Schemes hyperlink in the Slide Design task pane**
   The current, or default, color scheme is selected with a blue border as shown in Figure C-18. Additional color schemes designed specifically for the applied design template (in this case, the Edge template) are also shown.

2. **Click the color scheme icon in the fourth row, second column in the Slide Design task pane**
   The new color scheme is applied to all the slides in the presentation. In this case, the new color scheme changes the color of the slide graphics and title text, but the bulleted text and background remain the same.

3. **Click Format on the menu bar, then click Background**
   The Background dialog box opens.

4. **In the Background fill section, click the list arrow below the preview of the slide, click Fill Effects, then click the Gradient tab, if it is not already selected**

5. **Click the One color option button in the Colors section, click the Color 1 list arrow, then click the olive green color (the Follow Accent Scheme Color)**
   The green color fills the Color 1 list arrow and the four variant colors preview in the Variants section, showing that the background is shaded with green.

6. **Drag the Brightness scroll box all the way to the right (toward Light) in the Colors section, click the Diagonal down option button in the Shading Styles section, then click the lower-left variant**
   The four variant previews change shading. Compare your screen to Figure C-19.

7. **Click OK, then click Apply to All**
   The slide background is now shaded from green to white and then green again.

8. **Click the Slide Sorter View button, click the Zoom list arrow on the Standard toolbar, then click 50%**
   The final presentation appears in Slide Sorter view. Compare your screen to Figure C-20.

9. **Add your name as a footer on the notes and handouts, print the slides as handouts (4 slides per page), click the Save button, close the presentation, then exit PowerPoint**

QUICK TIP

To apply a new color scheme to only selected slides, select the slides on the Slides tab or in Slide Sorter view, point to the color scheme in the Slide Design task pane, click the list arrow that appears, then click Apply to Selected Slides.

QUICK TIP

If you click the Preset option button, you can choose from a variety of predesigned backgrounds. You can also add other backgrounds by clicking one of the other tabs in the Fill Effects dialog box.

QUICK TIP

You can also apply a shaded background to an AutoShape by right-clicking the object, then clicking Format Autoshape in the shortcut menu.

FIGURE C-18: Slide Design task pane

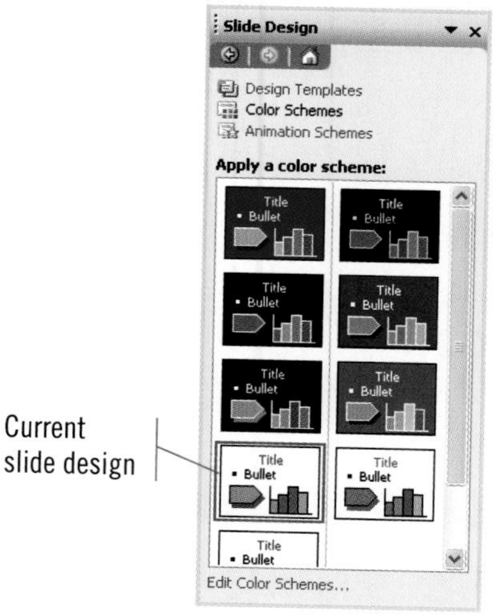

FIGURE C-19: Completed Fill Effects dialog box

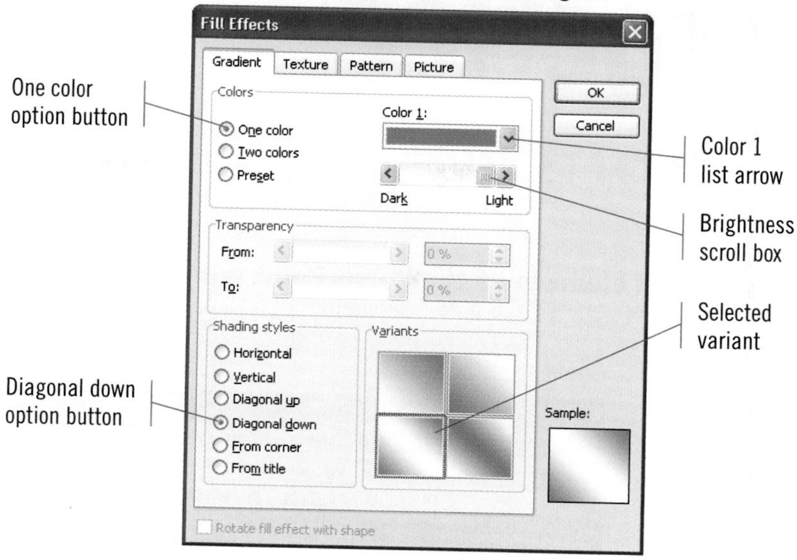

FIGURE C-20: Final presentation in Slide Sorter view

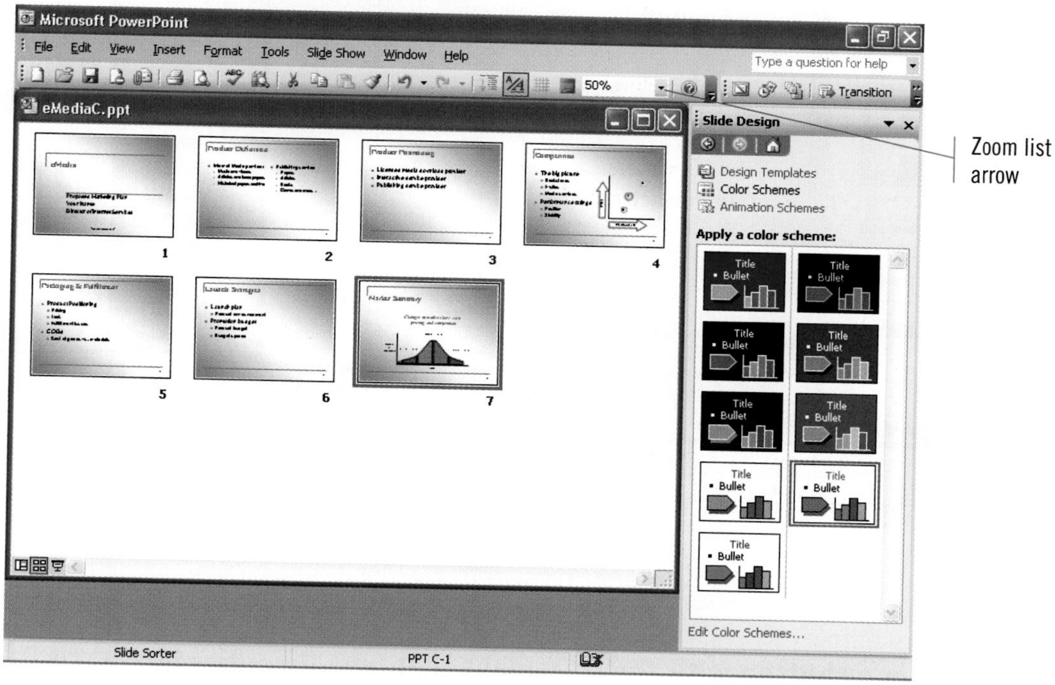

TABLE C-1: Color scheme elements

scheme element	description
Background color	Color of the slide's canvas or background
Text and lines color	Used for text and drawn lines; contrasts with the background color
Shadows color	Color of the shadow of the text or other object; generally a darker shade of the background color
Title text color	Used for slide title; like the text and line colors, contrasts with the background color
Fills color	Contrasts with both the background and the text and line colors
Accent colors	Colors used for other objects on slides, such as bullets
Accent and hyperlink colors	Colors used for accent objects and for hyperlinks you insert
Accent and followed hyperlink color	Color used for accent objects and for hyperlinks after they have been clicked

Practice

▼ CONCEPTS REVIEW

Label each element of the PowerPoint window shown in Figure C-21.

FIGURE C-21

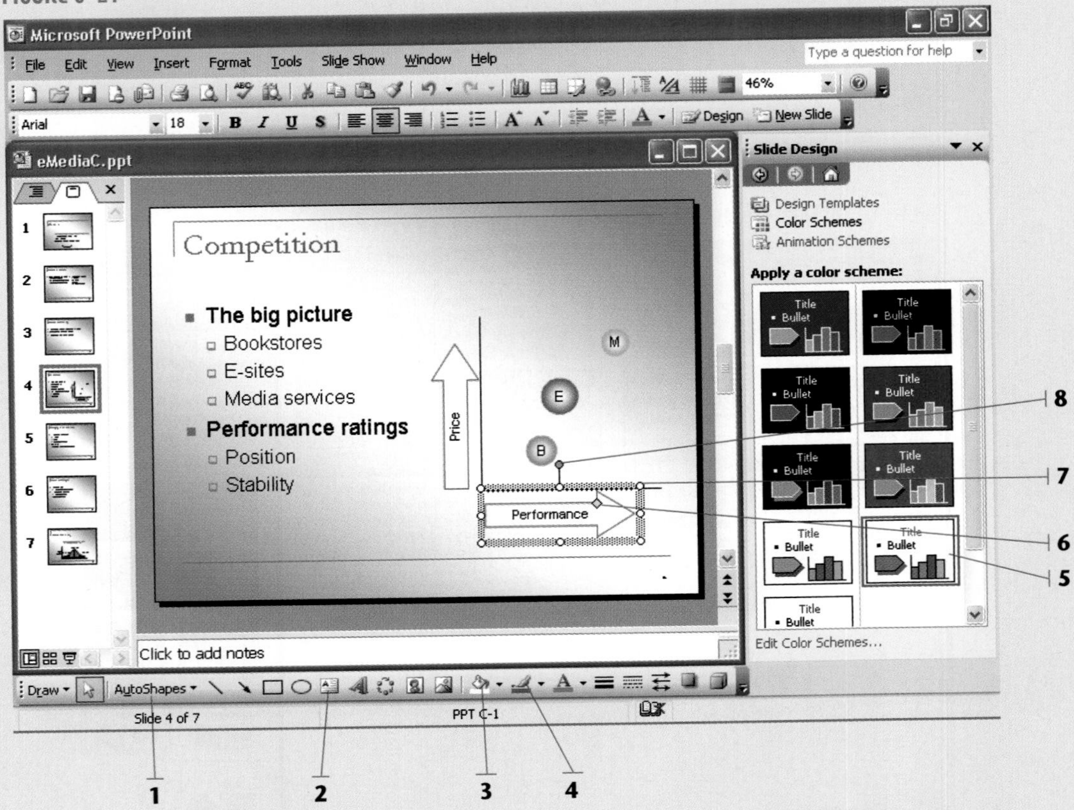

Match each term or button with the statement that best describes it.

9. Sizing handle
10. Guide
11. Text label
12. Color scheme
13. Background

a. A text object for a word or small phrase
b. A dotted line that helps you position objects
c. The area behind the text and graphics of a slide
d. Used to change the size and shape of an object
e. A set of eight coordinated colors

Select the best answer from the list of choices.

14. What is the easiest way to line objects along their tops on a slide?

a. Group the objects together

b. Use PowerPoint anchor lines

c. Place the objects on the edge of the slide

d. Use the Align Top command

15. What does *not* happen when you group objects?

a. Sizing handles appear around the grouped object.

b. Objects are grouped together as a single object.

c. Objects lose their individual characteristics.

d. The grouped objects have a rotate handle.

16. What is *not* true about guides?

a. You can drag a guide off the slide to delete it.

b. A PowerPoint guide is a dotted line.

c. Slides can have only one vertical and one horizontal guide.

d. You can press [Ctrl] and drag a guide to create a new one.

17. What is *not* true about a presentation color scheme?

a. Every presentation has a color scheme.

b. There are eight colors to every color scheme.

c. You can't change the background color without changing the color scheme.

d. The color scheme determines the colors of a slide.

18. How do you change the size of a PowerPoint object?

a. Click the Resize button.

b. Drag a sizing handle.

c. Drag the rotate handle.

d. You can't change the size of a PowerPoint object.

19. What would you use to position objects at a specific place on a slide?

a. PowerPoint lines

b. PowerPoint anchor lines

c. PowerPoint placeholders

d. PowerPoint guides and rulers

20. PowerPoint objects can be:

a. Grouped and aligned.

b. Converted to pictures.

c. Distributed evenly.

d. Both A and C.

21. What is a slide background?

a. The slide grid

b. The area behind text and graphics

c. A picture

d. The pasteboard off the slide

22. What does the adjustment handle do?

a. Changes the angle adjustment of an object

b. Changes the appearance of an object

c. Adjusts the position of an object

d. Adjusts the size of an object

▼ SKILLS REVIEW

1. Open an existing presentation.

a. Start PowerPoint.

b. Open the file **PPT C-3.ppt** from the drive and folder where your Data Files are stored.

c. Save it as **Product Report.ppt** to the drive and folder where your Data Files are stored.

2. Draw and modify an object.

a. Click Slide 4 in the Slides tab, insert the Left-Right-Up Arrow AutoShape from the Block Arrows category on the AutoShapes menu to the blank area on the slide.

b. Open the Line Color menu, click More Line Colors, then click the black color cell in the Colors dialog box to make the line color black.

c. Change the fill color to light green (the Follow Accent Scheme Color).

d. Rotate the arrow object so that the middle arrowhead points to the right. (*Hint*: 90° to the right.)

e. Use the arrows' sizing handles to adjust the size of the object until it matches Figure C-22.

f. Move the arrow object on the slide so that it is in the center of the blank space on the slide.

g. Deselect the arrow object, then save your changes.

FIGURE C-22

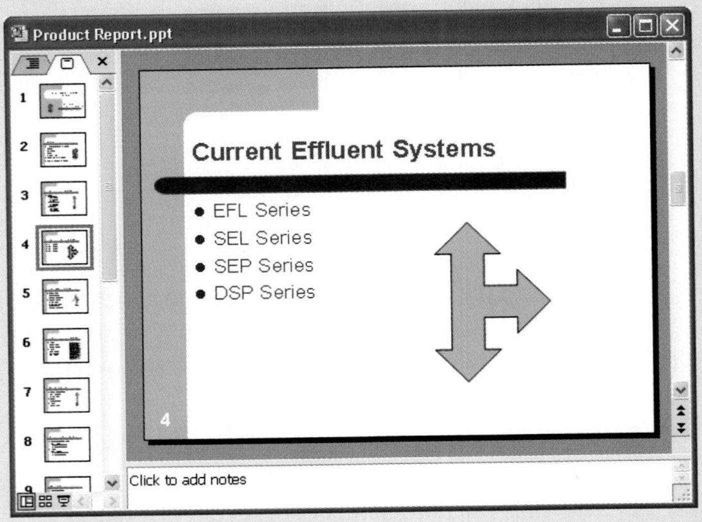

3. Edit drawn objects.

a. Select Slide 9, resize the arrow object so it is about ½" shorter. (*Hint*: You might want to resize the bulleted list text object so it does not interfere with your work.)

b. Drag the arrow object next to the left side of the box.

c. Use the adjustment handle to lengthen the arrow object's head about ¼", then insert the text **Satisfaction**. Enlarge the arrow object so that all the text fits inside it, if necessary.

d. Make two copies of the arrow object and arrange them to the left of the first one so that they are pointing in succession toward the box.

e. Drag to select the word **Satisfaction** on the middle arrow object, then type the word **Growth**.

f. Replace the word **Satisfaction** on the left arrow object with the word **Products**.

g. Insert the word **Success** in the cube object.

h. Change the text font for each of the objects to Arial italic. Enlarge the cube as necessary so the word **Success** fits in it.

i. Save your changes.

4. Align and group objects.

a. Align the middles of the four objects, then horizontally distribute the objects.

b. Group the arrow objects and the cube together.

c. Display the guides, then move the vertical guide left so the box displays 4.17; move the horizontal guide down to display 3.08.

d. Align the grouped object so its lower-left sizing handle snaps to where the guides intersect. (*Hint*: If your object does not snap to the guides, open the Grid and Guides dialog box, and make sure the Snap objects to grid check box is checked.)

e. Hide the guides, then save your changes. Compare your screen with Figure C-23.

FIGURE C-23

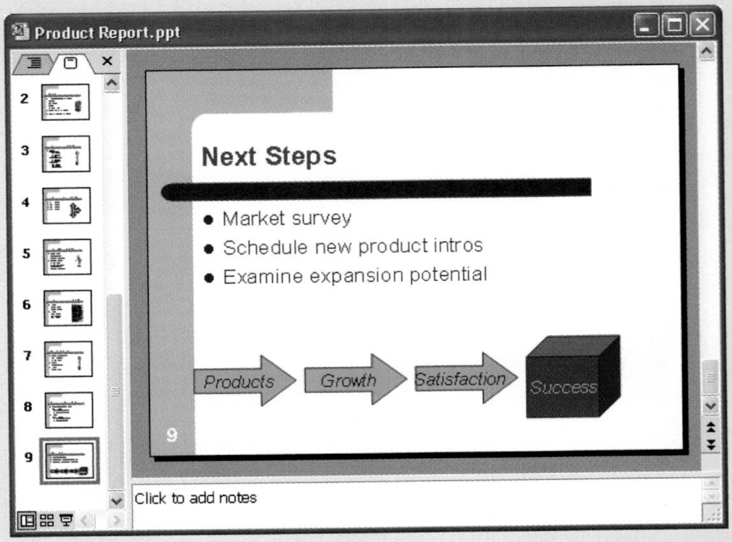

5. **Add and arrange text.**
   a. Add the text **Next steps** as a fourth item to the body text box on Slide 2.
   b. Near the bottom of the slide, below the graphic, create a word processing box about 3" wide, and in it enter the text: **The Future of Water Systems and Pumps.**
   c. Drag the word **Pumps** to the right of the word **Water**.
   d. Delete the word **and** and then the letter **s** on the word Pumps. The text object should now read, The Future of Water Pump Systems.
   e. Adjust the size of the text object to fit the text, then move the text object so that it is directly under the graphic.
   f. Save your changes.

6. **Format text.**
   a. Select the text object so that formatting commands apply to all the text in the object.
   b. Change the font color to the dark green color (the Follow Title Text Scheme Color), increase the font size to 24 points, then, if necessary, resize the word processing box so the text fits on one line.
   c. Change the text style to Italic, then align the words to the center of the text object.
   d. Click Slide 9 in the Slides tab, select the text in the cube, then change the font color to a light fluorescent green. (*Hint*: Use the Colors dialog box.)
   e. Click Slide 1 in the Slides tab, select the top title text font (Hildebrand Water Systems), then change the font size to 44.
   f. Deselect the text object, then save your changes.

7. **Import text from Microsoft Word.**
   a. Click Slide 9 in the Slides tab.
   b. Import the Word file PPT C-4.doc. Check the formatting of each of the three new slides—slides 10, 11, and 12.
   c. In the Slides tab, drag Slide 8 below Slide 11.
   d. In the Slides tab, delete Slide 9, Market Surveys.
   e. Save your changes.

8. **Customize the color scheme and background.**
   a. Open the Slide Design task pane and click the Color Schemes hyperlink.
   b. Apply the top right color scheme in the list to all the slides.
   c. Open the Background dialog box, then open the Fill Effects dialog box.
   d. On the Gradient tab, select the One color option, click the Color 1 list arrow, then click the yellow color.
   e. Drag the Brightness scroll box almost all the way to the right, select the From corner shading style and the lower-right variant.
   f. Apply this background to all slides.
   g. Add your name as a footer to the notes and handouts.
   h. Save your changes, then print the slides as handouts (4 slides per page).
   i. Close the file and exit PowerPoint.

UNIT D

PowerPoint 2003

Inserting Clip Art

PowerPoint has ready access to many professionally designed images, called **clip art**, that you can place in your presentation. Using clip art is the easiest and fastest way to enhance a presentation. In Microsoft Office, clip art and other media files, including photographs, movies, and sounds, are stored in a file index system called the Microsoft Clip Organizer. The Clip Organizer sorts the clip art into groups, including My Collections, Office Collections, and Web Collections. The Office Collections group holds all the media files that come with Microsoft Office. You can customize the Clip Organizer by adding clips to a collection, moving clips from one collection to another, or creating a new collection. As with drawing objects, you can modify clip art images by changing their shape, size, fill, or shading. Clip art is available from many sources outside the Clip Organizer, including the Microsoft Office Online Web site and collections on CD-ROMs. Add a picture from the Clip Organizer to one of the slides and then adjust its size and placement.

STEPS

1. **Start PowerPoint, open the presentation PPT D-1.ppt from the drive and folder where your Data Files are stored, save it as eMediaD, click View on the menu bar, click Task Pane, click Window on the menu bar, then click Arrange All**
2. **Click Slide 8 in the Slides tab, then click the Insert Clip Art button on the Drawing toolbar**
   The Clip Art task pane opens. Each clip in the Clip Organizer is identified by descriptive keywords. At the top of the task pane in the Search for text box, you enter a keyword to search for clips that meet that description. You can search for a clip in a specific collection or in all collections. You can search for a clip that is a specific media type, such as clip art, photographs, movies, or sounds. At the bottom of the task pane, you can click one of the hyperlinks to organize clips, locate other pieces of clip art at the Office Online Web site, or read tips on how to find clip art.
3. **Select any text in the Search for text box, type plans, then click Go**
   PowerPoint searches for clips identified by the keyword "plans".
4. **Scroll down in the Clip Art task pane, then click the clip art thumbnail shown in Figure D-1**
   The clip art object appears in the center of the slide and the Picture toolbar opens. If you don't have the clip art picture shown in Figure D-1 in your Clip Organizer, select a similar picture.
5. **Place the pointer over the lower-right sizing handle, then drag the handle down and to the right about ½"**
   The clip art object proportionally increases in size.
6. **Click the Line Style button on the Picture toolbar, then click the 6pt solid line style**
   The clip art now has a 6-point border. It appears to be framed.
7. **Drag the clip art object to the right of the text object as shown in Figure D-2**
   The new clip art object appears next to the text object. Compare your screen to Figure D-2.
8. **Click a blank area of the slide, then click the Save button on the Standard toolbar to save your changes**

QUICK TIP

Apply any of the "content" slide layouts except the Blank layout, then click the Insert Clip Art button in the Content placeholder to insert a piece of clip art.

QUICK TIP

You can also use the keyboard arrow keys or the Nudge command on the Draw menu button to reposition any selected object by small increments.

FIGURE D-1: Screen showing Clip Art task pane

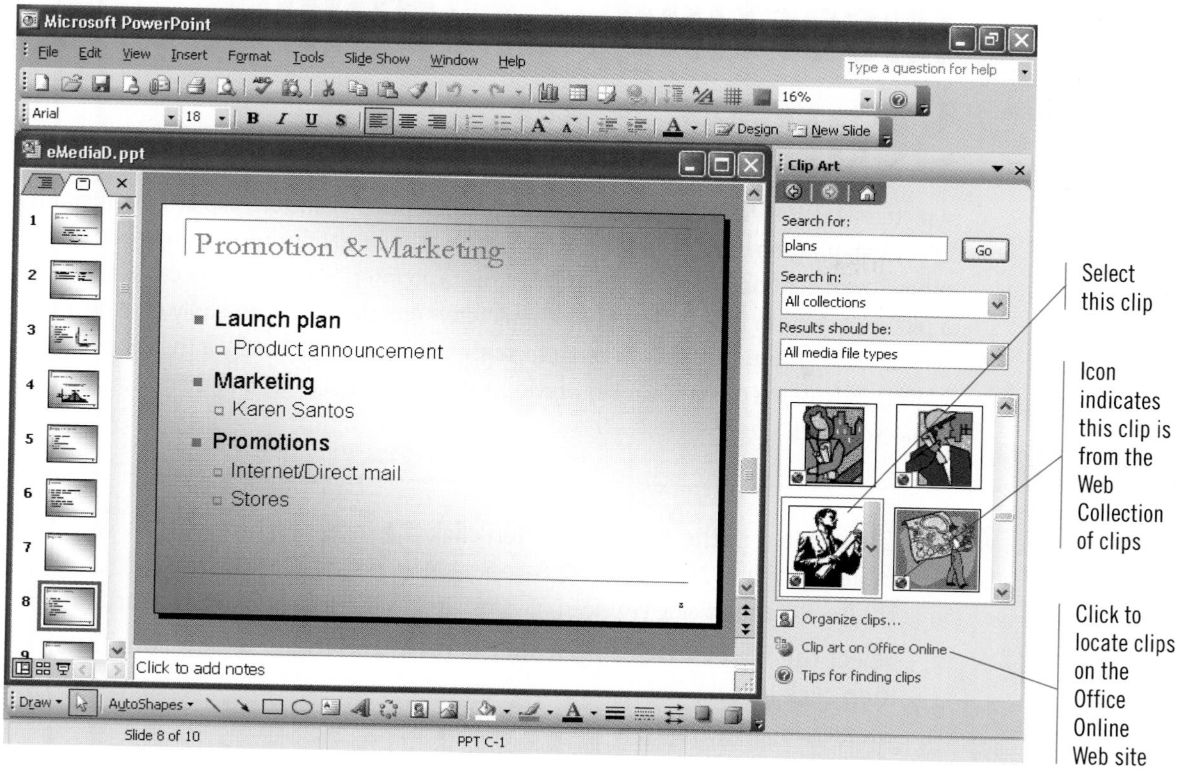

FIGURE D-2: Slide with clip art object resized and repositioned

PowerPoint 2003

Clues to Use

Find more clips online

If you can't find the clips you need in the Clip Organizer, you can easily download and use clips from the Clip Art and Media Web page in the Microsoft Office Online Web site. To get clips from the Clip Art and Media Web page, click the Clip art on Office Online hyperlink at the bottom of the Clip Art task pane. This will launch your Web browser and automatically connect you to the Microsoft Office Online Web site. You can search the site by keyword or browse by media type category. Each clip you download is automatically inserted into the Clip Organizer Web Collections folder and appears in the Clip Art task pane.

UNIT
D
PowerPoint 2003

Inserting, Cropping, and Scaling a Picture

A picture in PowerPoint is a scanned photograph, a piece of line art, clip art, or other artwork that is created in another program and inserted into a PowerPoint presentation. You can insert 18 types of pictures. As with other PowerPoint objects, you can move or resize an inserted picture. You can also crop pictures. **Cropping** a picture means to hide a portion of the picture. Although you can easily change a picture's size by dragging a corner sizing handle, you can also **scale** it to change its size by a specific percentage. In this lesson, you insert a picture that has previously been saved to a file, and then you crop and scale it and adjust its background.

STEPS

QUICK TIP
You can also insert a picture by clicking the Insert Picture button on any of the Content slide layout placeholders.

1. **Click Slide 6 in the Slides tab, then click the Insert Picture button on the Drawing toolbar**
   The Insert Picture dialog box opens. By default, the My Pictures folder is selected.
2. **Select the file PPT D-2.bmp from the drive and folder where your Data Files are stored, then click Insert**
   The picture appears in the center of the slide, and the Picture toolbar opens.
3. **Drag the picture to the right of the text object**
   The picture would fit better on the slide if it didn't show the boxes on the left side of the picture.

TROUBLE
If the Picture toolbar is in the way, drag it by its title bar.

4. **Click the Crop button on the Picture toolbar, then place the pointer over the left-middle sizing handle of the picture**
   The pointer changes to ⊣. When the Crop button is active, the sizing handles appear as straight black lines.
5. **Press and hold [Alt], then drag the left edge of the picture to the right until the dotted line indicating the left edge of the picture has cut out the boxes, as shown in Figure D-3, then click**
   Pressing [Alt] while dragging or drawing an object in PowerPoint overrides the automatic snap-to-grid setting. Now the picture needs to be enlarged and positioned into place.
6. **Click the Format Picture button on the Picture toolbar, click the Size tab in the Format Picture dialog box, make sure the Lock aspect ratio check box has a check mark, click the Height up arrow in the Scale section until the Height and Width percentages reach 175%, then click OK**
   When you are scaling a picture and Lock aspect ratio is selected, the ratio of height to width remains the same. The white background is distracting.

QUICK TIP
You cannot change the colors in a bit-mapped (.bmp) object in PowerPoint, but you can change the background colors of the object.

7. **With the picture still selected, click the Set Transparent Color button on the Picture toolbar, the pointer changes to , then click the white background in the picture**
   The white background is no longer visible, and the picture contrasts well with the background.
8. **Drag the picture to center it in the blank area to the right of the text object on the slide, click a blank area on the slide to deselect it, then save your changes**
   See Figure D-4.

FIGURE D-3: Using the cropping pointer to crop a picture

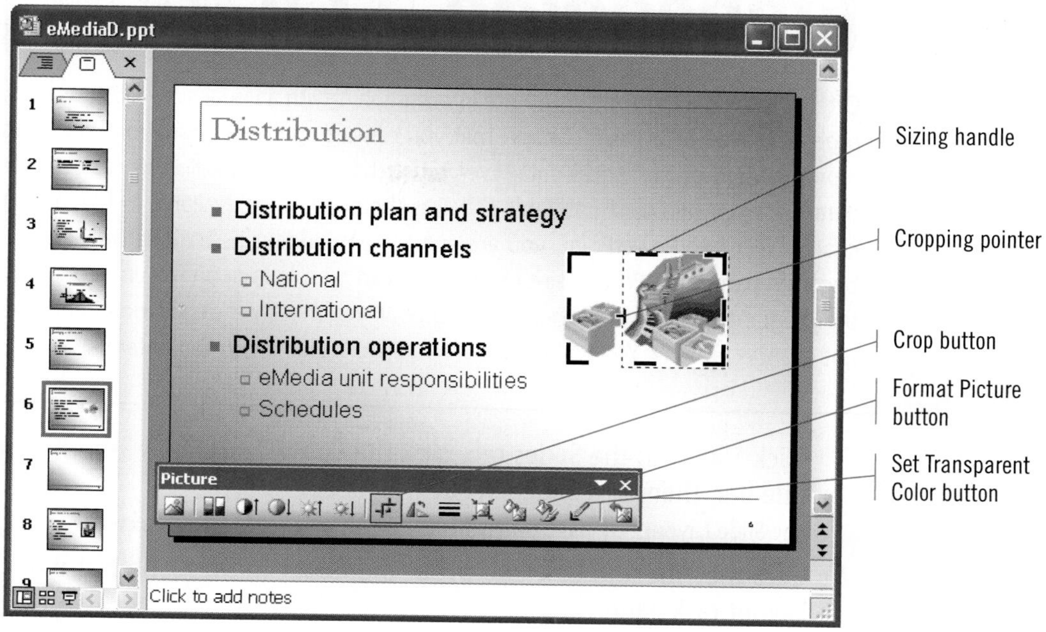

FIGURE D-4: Cropped and resized picture

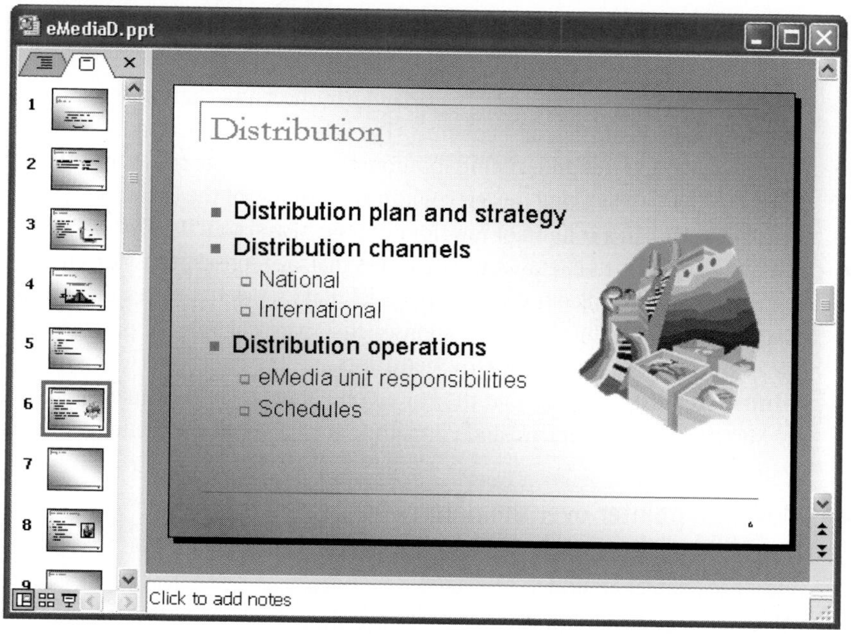

Clues to Use

Using graphics in PowerPoint

You can insert pictures with a variety of graphics file **formats**, or file types, in PowerPoint. Most of the clip art that comes with PowerPoint is in Windows metafile format and has the .wmf file extension. You can change the colors in a .wmf graphic object by selecting it, then clicking the Recolor Picture button on the Picture toolbar. You can then replace each color in the graphic with another color. A graphic in .wmf format can be ungrouped into its separate PowerPoint objects, then edited with any of the PowerPoint drawing tools. You cannot recolor or ungroup pictures (files with the .bmp or .tif extension). The clip art you inserted in the last lesson is in .wmf format, and the picture you inserted in this lesson is in .bmp format.

You can also save PowerPoint slides as graphics and later use them in other presentations, in graphics programs, and on Web pages. Display the slide you want to save, then click Save As from the File menu. In the Save As dialog box, click the Save as type list arrow, and scroll to the desired graphics format. Name the file, click OK, then click the desired option when the alert box appears asking if you want to save all the slides or only the current slide.

UNIT

D

PowerPoint 2003

Embedding a Chart

Often, the best way to communicate information is with a visual aid such as a chart. PowerPoint comes with a program called **Microsoft Graph** that you can use to create charts for your slides. A **chart** is the graphical representation of numerical data. Every chart has a corresponding **datasheet** that contains the numerical data displayed by the chart. Table D-1 lists the chart types available in Microsoft Graph. When you insert a chart object into PowerPoint, you are actually embedding it. **Embedding** an object means that the object becomes part of the PowerPoint file, but you can double-click on the embedded object to display the tools of the program in which the object was created. If you modify the embedded object, the original object file does not change. You embed a chart on Slide 9 that shows the potential revenue of the eMedia product.

STEPS

1. **Click Slide 9 in the Slides tab, click the Other Task Panes list arrow ▼ on the task pane title bar, then click Slide Layout**
   The Slide Layout task pane opens with the Title and Text layout selected.
2. **Click the Title and Content layout thumbnail in the Content Layouts section of the Slide Layout task pane**
   Remember to use the ScreenTips to help locate the correct slide layout. A content placeholder appears on the slide. Six buttons are in the middle of the placeholder. Each of these buttons represents a different object, such as a table, picture, or chart, which you can apply to your slide.
3. **Click the Insert Chart button in the content placeholder**
   Microsoft Graph opens and embeds a default datasheet and chart into the slide, as shown in Figure D-5. The datasheet consists of rows and columns. The intersection of a row and a column is called a **cell**. Cells are referred to by their row and column location; for example, the cell at the intersection of column A and row 1 is called cell A1. Cells along the left column and top row of the datasheet typically contain **data labels** that identify the data in a column or row; for example, "East" and "1st Qtr" are data labels. Cells below and to the right of the data labels contain the data values that are represented in the chart. Each column and row of data in the datasheet is called a **data series**. Each data series has corresponding **data series markers** in the chart, which are graphical representations such as bars, columns, or pie wedges. The gray boxes along the left side of the datasheet are called **row headings** and the gray boxes along the top of the datasheet are called **column headings**. Notice that the PowerPoint Standard and Formatting toolbars have been replaced with the Microsoft Graph Standard and Formatting toolbars, and the menu bar has changed to include Microsoft Graph commands.
4. **Move the pointer over the datasheet**
   The pointer changes to ✚. Cell A1 is the **active cell**, which means that it is selected. The active cell has a thick black border around it.
5. **Click cell B3, which contains the value 46.9**
   Cell B3 is now the active cell.
6. **Click a blank area on the slide to exit Graph, then click again to deselect the chart object**
   The chart closes and the PowerPoint menu bar and toolbars appear.
7. **Save your changes**

QUICK TIP

You can also add a chart to a slide by clicking the Insert Chart button on the Standard toolbar.

QUICK TIP

When Data and Chart are on the menu bar, you are working in Graph. Click outside the chart object to return to PowerPoint.

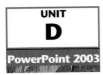

FIGURE D-5: Microsoft Graph datasheet and chart in PowerPoint

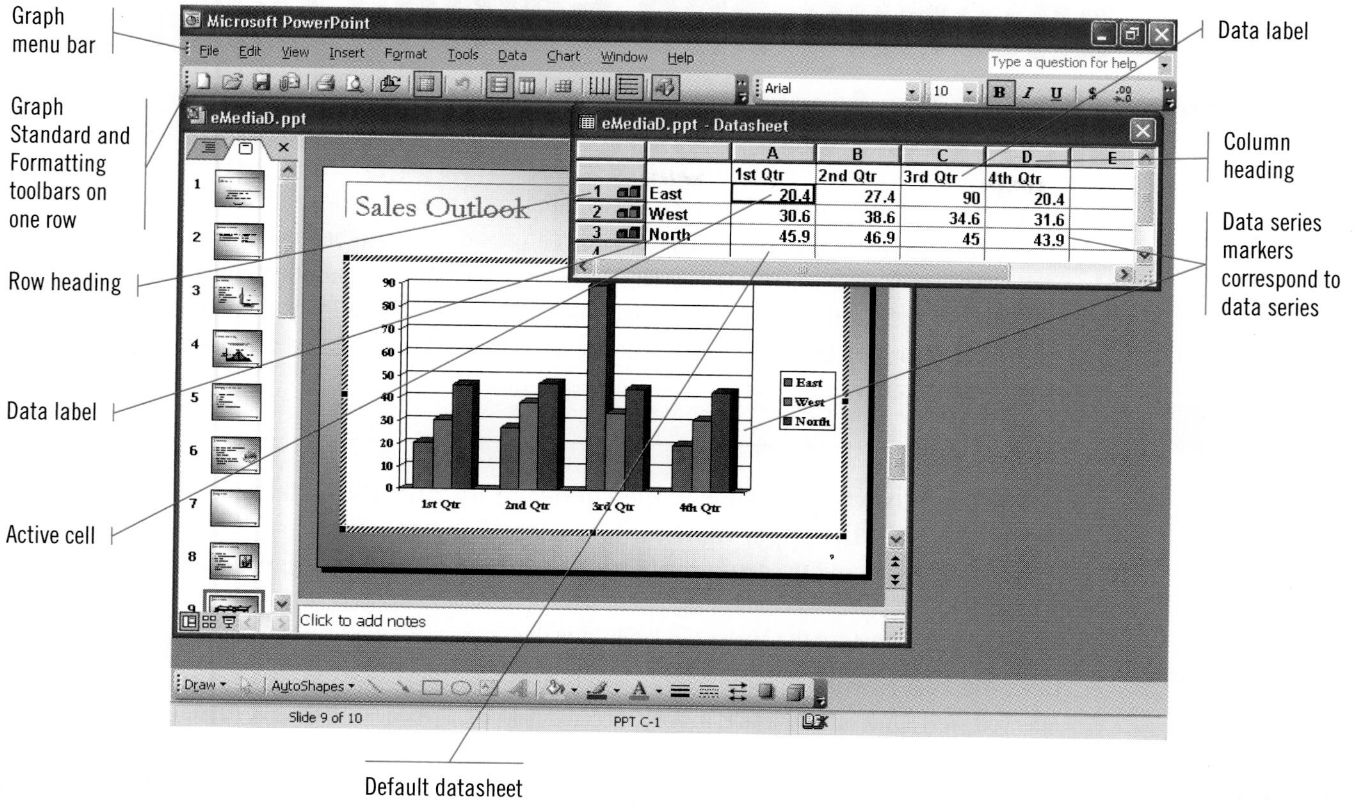

TABLE D-1: Microsoft Graph chart types

chart type	looks like	use to
Column		Track values over time or across categories
Bar		Compare values in categories or over time
Line		Track values over time
Pie		Compare individual values to the whole
XY (Scatter)		Compare pairs of values
Area		Show contribution of each data series to the total over time
Doughnut		Compare individual values to the whole with multiple series
Radar		Show changes in values in relation to a center point
Surface		Show value trends across two dimensions
Bubble		Indicate relative size of data points
Stock		Show stock market information or scientific data
Cylinder		
Cone		Track values over time or across categories
Pyramid		

UNIT D

PowerPoint 2003

Entering and Editing Data in the Datasheet

After you embed the default chart into your presentation, you need to replace the data labels and numeric data with the correct information. If you have data in a spreadsheet or other source, you can import it into Microsoft Graph; otherwise you can type your own information into the datasheet. As you enter data in the cells or make changes to data labels in the datasheet, the chart automatically changes to reflect the new entries. You have been asked to create a chart showing the projected revenue figures for the first year of eMedia operation.

STEPS

1. **Double-click the chart on Slide 9, then, if necessary, drag the Datasheet title bar to move the datasheet to the upper-right corner of the Slide pane**
   The chart is selected and the datasheet opens. The column data labels representing the quarters are correct, but the row data labels need adjusting, and the numeric data needs to be replaced with eMedia's projected quarterly sales figures for the Media and Publishing divisions.

QUICK TIP

Double-click the column divider lines between the column headings to automatically resize the column width to accommodate the widest entry.

2. **Click the East row label, type Media, then press [Enter]**
   After you press [Enter], the data label in Row 2 becomes selected. Pressing [Enter] in the datasheet moves the active cell down one cell; pressing [Tab] in the datasheet moves the active cell to the right one cell.

3. **Type Publish, then press [Tab]**
   Cell A2 becomes active. Notice in the chart, behind the datasheet, that the data labels you typed are now in the legend to the right of the chart. The information in Row 3 of the datasheet is not needed.

4. **Click the row heading for Row 3, then press [Delete]**
   Clicking the row heading for Row 3 selects the entire row. The default information in Row 3 of the datasheet is deleted and the columns in the chart adjust accordingly. The quarters appear along the horizontal axis, the values appear along the vertical axis in the chart.

5. **Click cell A1, type 17,000, press [Enter], type 14,500, press [Tab], then press [↑] to move to cell B1**
   Notice that the height of each column in the chart, as well as the values along the vertical axis, adjust to reflect the numbers you typed. The vertical axis is also called the **Value axis**. The horizontal axis is called the **Category axis**.

6. **Enter the rest of the numbers shown in Figure D-6 to complete the datasheet, then press [Enter]**
   The chart currently shows the columns grouped by quarter, and the legend represents the rows in the datasheet. The icons in the row headings indicate that the row labels appear in the legend. It would be more effective if the column data appeared in the legend so you could compare quarterly earnings for each eMedia product.

TROUBLE

If you don't see the By Column button, click the Toolbar Options button on the Standard toolbar to view buttons that are not visible on your toolbar.

7. **Click the By Column button on the Standard toolbar**
   The division labels are now on the Category axis of the chart, and the quarters are listed in the legend. The groups of data markers (the columns) now represent the projected revenue for each product by quarter. Notice that the small column chart icons that used to be in the row headings in the datasheet have now moved to the column headings, indicating that the series are now in columns.

8. **Click a blank area on the slide, click again to deselect the chart object, compare your chart to Figure D-7, then save the presentation**
   The datasheet closes, allowing you to see your entire chart. This chart layout clearly shows eMedia's projected revenue for the first year it's in operation.

FIGURE D-6: Datasheet showing eMedia's projected revenue

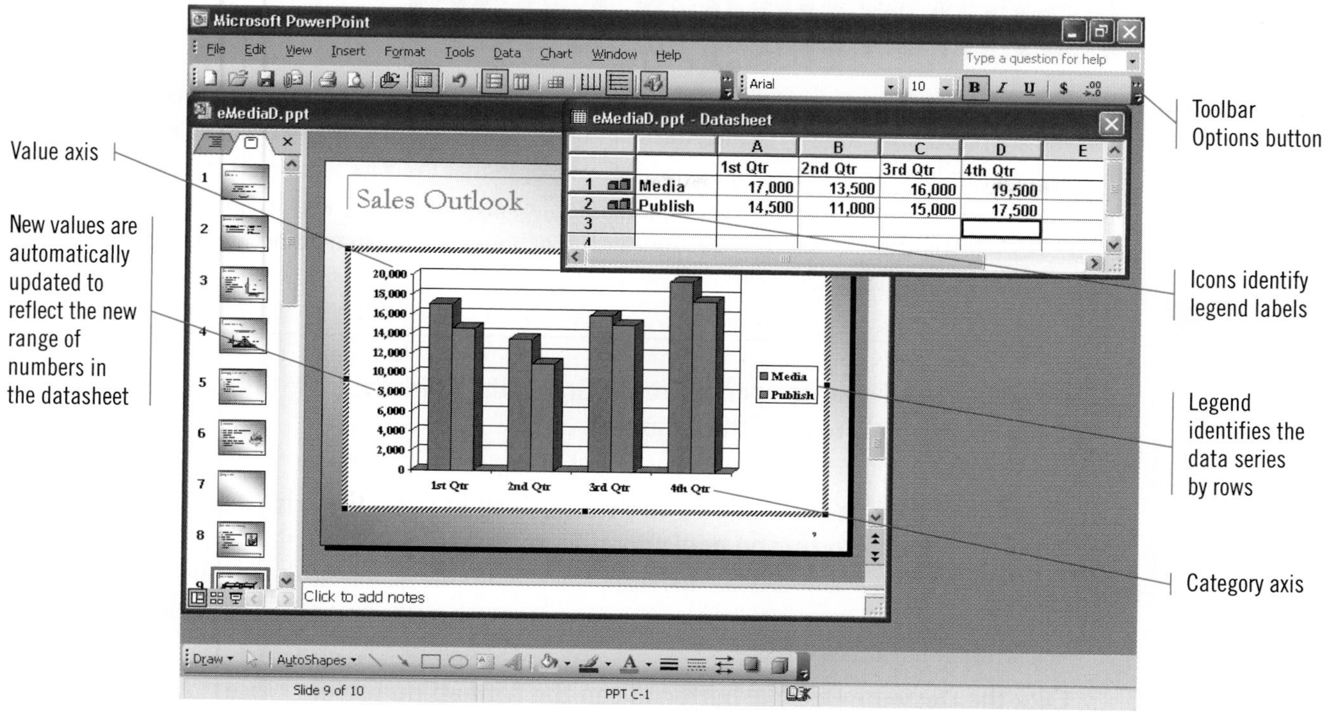

FIGURE D-7: Chart showing data grouped by division

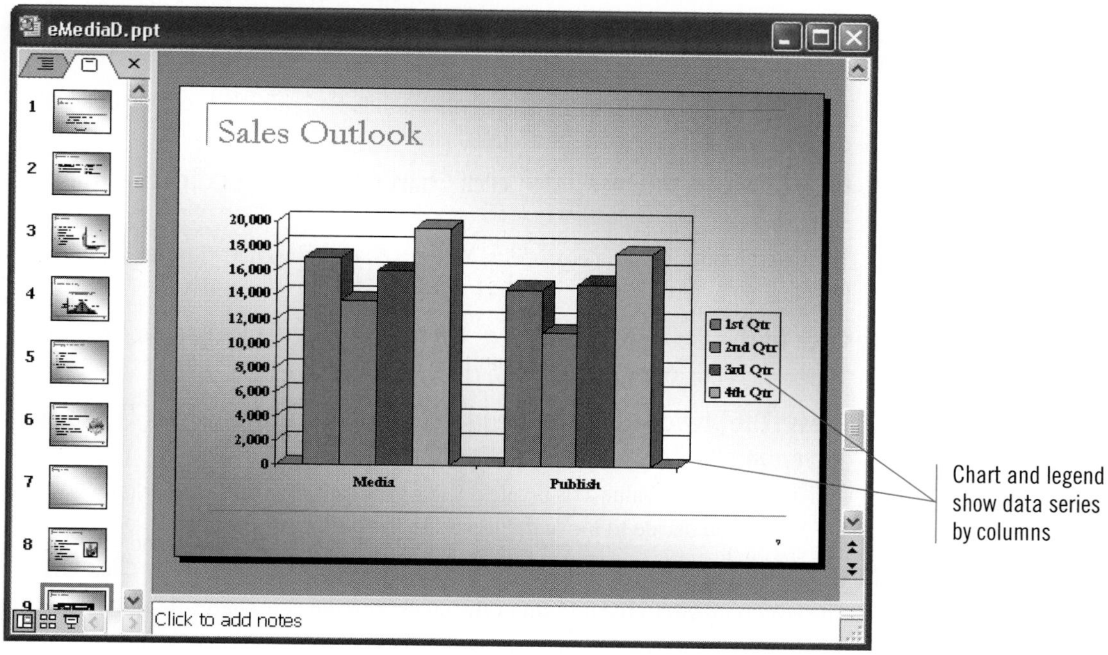

Clues to Use

Series in Rows vs. Series in Columns

If you have difficulty visualizing the difference between the Series in Rows and the Series in Columns commands on the Data menu, think about what is represented in the legend. **Series in Rows** means that the information in the datasheet rows will be on the Value or vertical axis and is the information shown in the legend, and the column labels will be on the Category or horizontal axis. **Series in Columns** means that the information in the columns becomes the information shown on the Value axis and in the legend, and the row labels will be on the horizontal or Category axis. Microsoft Graph places a small chart icon representing the chart type on the axis items that are currently represented by the chart series items, for example, bars, columns, or lines.

UNIT D

PowerPoint 2003

Formatting a Chart

Microsoft Graph lets you change the appearance of the chart to emphasize certain aspects of the information you are presenting. You can change the chart type (for example pie, column, bar, or line), create titles, format the chart labels, move the legend, add arrows, or format the data series markers. Like other objects in PowerPoint, you can change the fill color, pattern, line style and color, and style of most elements in a chart. You want to improve the appearance of your chart by formatting the Value and Category axes and by inserting a title.

STEPS

1. **Double-click the chart to open Microsoft Graph, then click the Close button in the Datasheet window to close the datasheet**
   The Microsoft Graph menu and toolbars remain at the top of the window.
2. **Click one of the revenue numbers on the Value axis to select the axis, then click the Currency Style button on the Formatting toolbar**
   Before you can format any object on the chart, you need to select it. The numbers on the Value axis appear with dollar signs and two decimal places. You don't need to show the two decimal places because all the values are whole numbers.
3. **Click the Decrease Decimal button on the Formatting toolbar twice**
   The numbers on the Value axis now have dollar signs and show only whole numbers. See Figure D-8. The division names on the Category axis would be easier to see if they were larger.
4. **Click one of the division names on the Category axis, click the Font Size list arrow on the Formatting toolbar, then click 20**
   The font size changes from 18 points to 20 points for both labels on the Category axis. The chart would be easier to read if it had a title and axis labels.
5. **Click Chart on the menu bar, click Chart Options, then click the Titles tab, if it is not already selected**
   The Chart Options dialog box opens. You can change the chart title, axes, gridlines, legend, data labels, and the data table.
6. **Click in the Chart title text box, then type eMedia Projected Revenue**
   The preview box shows you how the chart looks with the title.
7. **Press [Tab] twice to move the insertion point to the Value (Z) axis text box, then type Revenue**
   In a 3-D chart, the Value axis is called the Z-axis, and the depth axis, which you don't usually work with, is the Y-axis. You decide to move the legend to the bottom of the chart.
8. **Click the Legend tab, click the Bottom option button, then click OK**
   The legend moves to the bottom of the chart, and the new chart title and axis title appear on the chart. The axis title would look better and take up less space if it were rotated 90 degrees.
9. **Right-click the Revenue label on the Value axis, click Format Axis Title, click the Alignment tab, drag the red diamond in the Orientation section counterclockwise to a vertical position so that the spin box reads 90 degrees, click OK, then click a blank area of the slide**
   Graph closes and the PowerPoint toolbars and menu bar appear.
10. **Drag the chart to the center of the slide, click a blank area of the slide, then save your changes**
    Compare your screen to Figure D-9.

TROUBLE

If you don't see $ or on the Formatting toolbar, click a Toolbar Options button on a toolbar to locate buttons that are not visible on your toolbar.

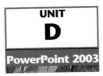

FIGURE D-8: Chart showing applied Currency style to data

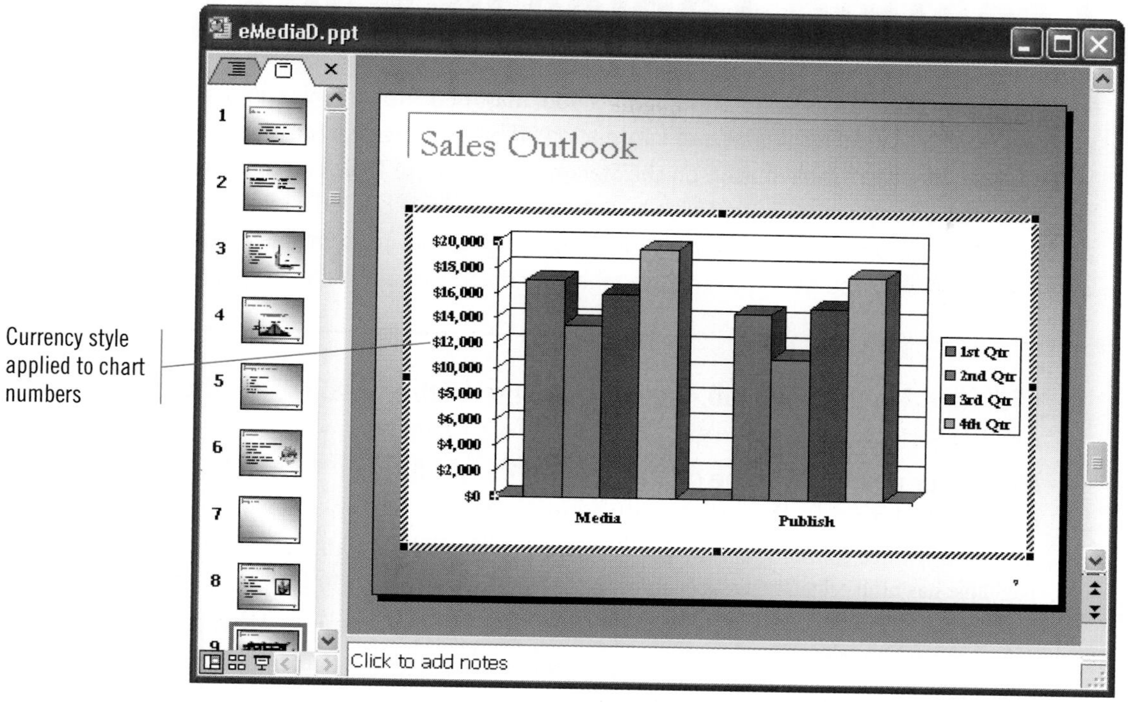

FIGURE D-9: Slide showing formatted chart

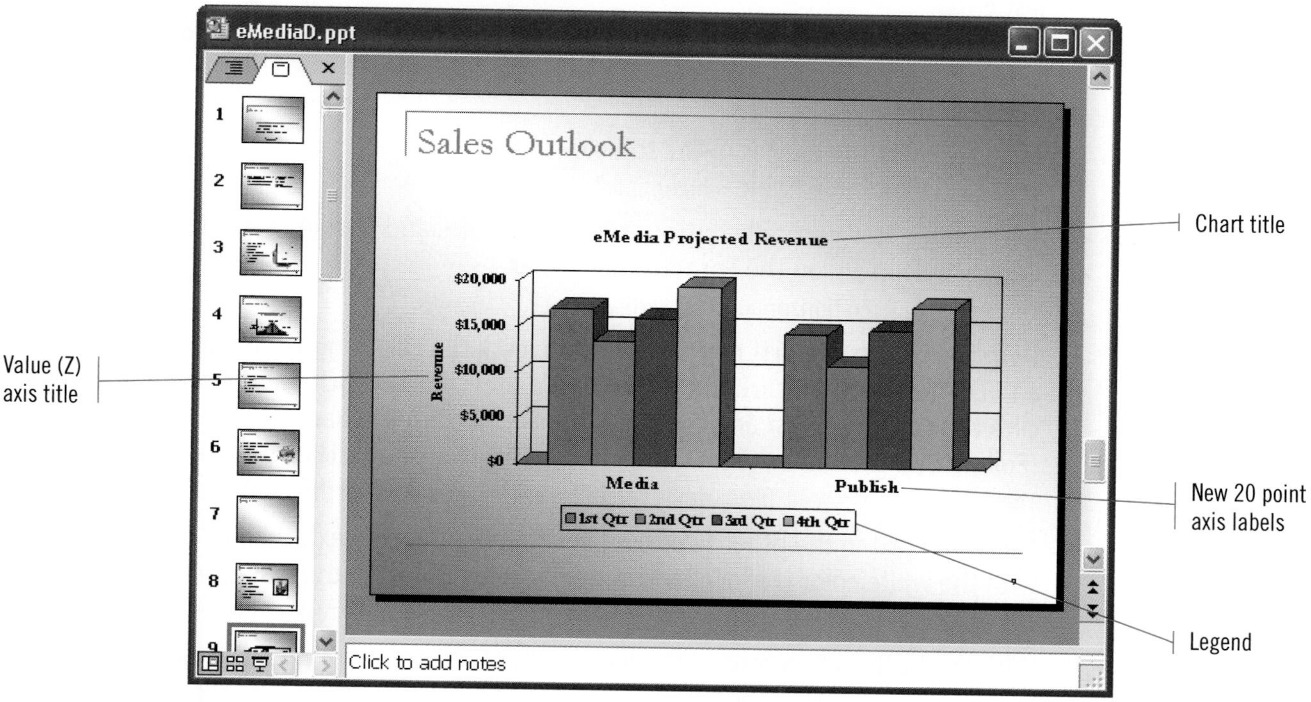

Clues to Use

Customizing data series in charts

You can easily customize the look of any chart in Microsoft Graph. Click the chart to select it, then double-click any data series element (a column, for example) to open the Format Data Series dialog box. Use the tabs to change the element's fill color, border, shape, or data label. You can even use the same fill effects you apply to a presentation background. In 3-D charts, you can change the chart depth as well as the distances between series.

UNIT
D
PowerPoint 2003

Creating Tables in PowerPoint

As you create your PowerPoint presentation, you may need to organize information into rows and columns. A table is ideal for this type of information. There are three ways to create a table in PowerPoint, you can click the Insert Table button on the Standard toolbar, the Table command on the Insert menu, or the Table icon on any of the content slide layouts. Once you have created a table, you can use the buttons on the Tables and Borders toolbar or on the Formatting toolbar to format the table to best present the information. You decide to create a table describing eMedia's different pricing plans.

STEPS

1. **Click Slide 7 in the Slides tab, then click the Insert Table button on the Standard toolbar**
   A grid appears that allows you to specify the number of columns and rows you want in your table.
2. **Move your pointer over the grid to select a 3 × 3 cell area ("3 × 3 Table" appears at the bottom of the grid), then click your mouse button**
   A table with three columns and three rows appears on the slide, and the Tables and Borders toolbar opens. The table has nine cells. The first cell in the table is selected and ready to accept text.
3. **Type Basic, press [Tab], type Standard, press [Tab], type Premium, then press [Tab]**
   The text you typed appears in the top three cells of the table. Pressing [Tab] moves the insertion point to the next cell. Pressing [Enter] moves the insertion point to the next line in the cell.
4. **Enter the rest of the table information shown in Figure D-10, do not press [Tab] after the last entry**
   Pressing [Tab] when the insertion point is in the cell in the last column and last row in a table creates a new row and places the insertion point in the cell in the first column of that row. The table would look better if it were formatted.
5. **Drag to select the entries in the top row of the table**
   The text in the first row becomes highlighted.
6. **Click the Center Vertically button on the Tables and Borders toolbar, then click the Center button on the Formatting toolbar**
   The text is centered horizontally and vertically.
7. **With the text in the first row still selected, click the Fill Color list arrow on the Tables and Borders toolbar, click the red color (Follow Title Text Scheme Color) in the first row, click the Font Color list arrow on the Formatting toolbar, click the white color (Follow Background Scheme Color) in the first row, then click a blank area of the slide**
   The cells in the top row are filled with the color red and the font color for the text in the cells is white.
8. **Select the text in the other two rows, vertically center the text, then fill these two rows with the white color (Follow Background Scheme Color) in the first row of the Fill Color list**
   The table would look better if the last two rows were a little farther away from the cell edges.
9. **With the bottom two rows still selected, click Format on the menu bar, click Table, click the Text Box tab, click the Left up arrow until it reads .25, click OK, click a blank area of the slide, then save the presentation**
   The Tables and Borders toolbar closes and the table is no longer selected. Compare your screen with Figure D-11.

TROUBLE
If the Tables and Borders toolbar does not open, click View on the menu bar, point to Toolbars, then click Tables and Borders. If the toolbar obscures part of the table, drag it out of the way.

QUICK TIP
You can change the height or width of any table cell by dragging its top or side borders.

QUICK TIP
You can use the Format Table dialog box to apply a diagonal line through any table cell. Click the Borders tab, then click a diagonal line button.

FIGURE D-10: The new table before formatting

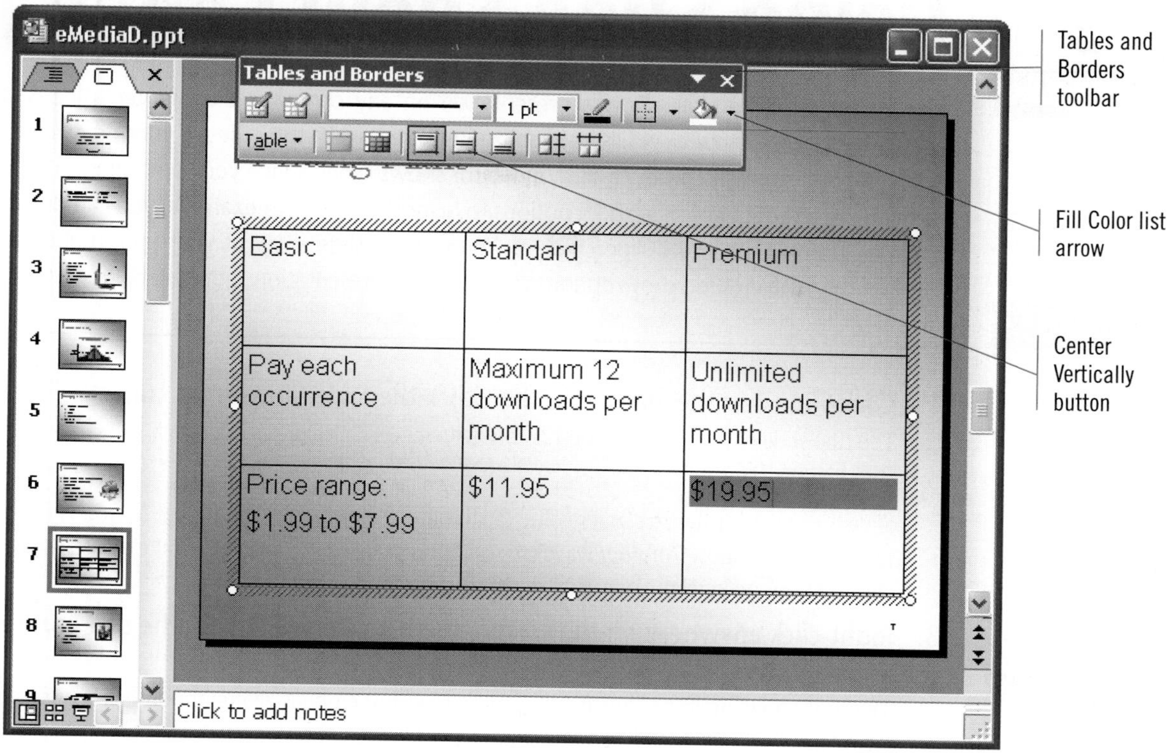

FIGURE D-11: Formatted table

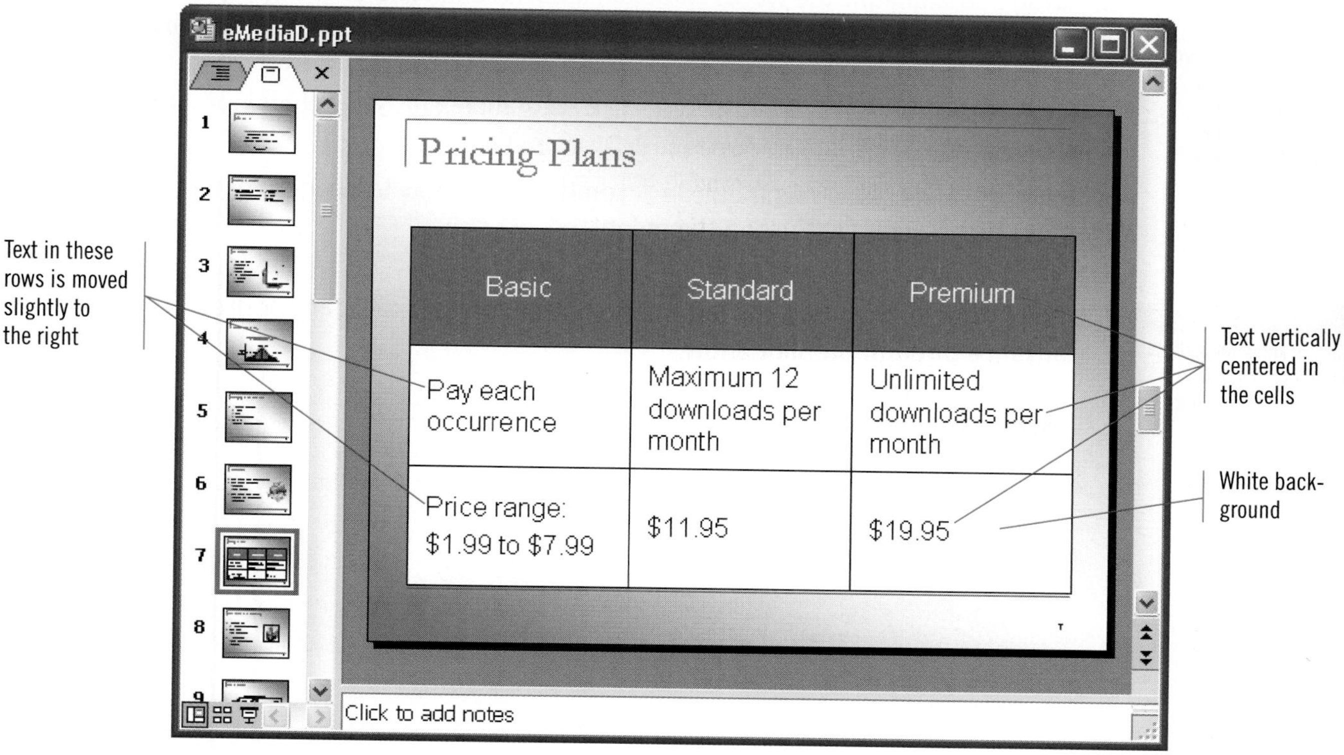

UNIT D

PowerPoint 2003

Using Slide Show Commands

With PowerPoint, you can show a presentation on any compatible computer using Slide Show view. As you've seen, Slide Show view fills your computer screen with the slides of your presentation, showing them one at a time, similarly to how a slide projector shows slides. Once your presentation is in Slide Show view, you can use a number of slide show options to tailor the show. For example, you can draw on, or **annotate**, slides or jump to a specific slide. You run the slide show of your presentation and practice using some of the custom slide show options to make your presentation more effective.

STEPS

1. **Click Slide 1 in the Slides tab, then click the Slide Show from current slide button**
   The first slide of the presentation fills the screen.
2. **Press [Spacebar]**
   Slide 2 appears on the screen. Pressing [Spacebar] or clicking the left mouse button is the easiest way to move through a slide show. Another way is to use the keys listed in Table D-2. You can also use the Slide Show shortcut menu for on-screen navigation during a slide show.
3. **Right-click anywhere on the screen, point to Go to Slide on the shortcut menu, then click 6 Distribution**
   The slide show jumps to Slide 6. You can highlight or emphasize major points in your presentation by annotating the slide during a slide show using one of PowerPoint's annotation tools.
4. **Move the mouse across the screen to display the Slide Show toolbar, click the Pen Options menu button, then click Highlighter**
   The pointer changes to .
5. **Drag to highlight the words National, International, and Schedules**
   Compare your screen to Figure D-12. While the annotation tool is visible, mouse clicks do not advance the slide show; however, you can still move to the next slide by pressing [Spacebar] or [Enter].
6. **Click on the Slide Show toolbar, click Erase All Ink on Slide, then press [Ctrl][A]**
   The annotations on Slide 6 are erased and the pointer returns to .
7. **Click the Slide Show menu button on the Slide Show toolbar, point to Go to Slide, then click 9 Sales Outlook on the menu**
   Slide 9 appears.
8. **Press [Home], then click the left mouse button, press [Spacebar], or press [Enter] to advance through the slide show**
   After the black slide that indicates the end of the slide show appears, the next click ends the slide show and returns you to Normal view.

QUICK TIP
The Slide Show menu buttons are transparent and will change to match the background color on the slide.

QUICK TIP
You have the option of saving annotations you create while in Slide Show view when you end or quit the slide show.

QUICK TIP
If you know the slide number of a slide you want to jump to during a slide show, type the number, then press [Enter].

FIGURE D-12: Slide 6 in Slide Show view with highlight annotations

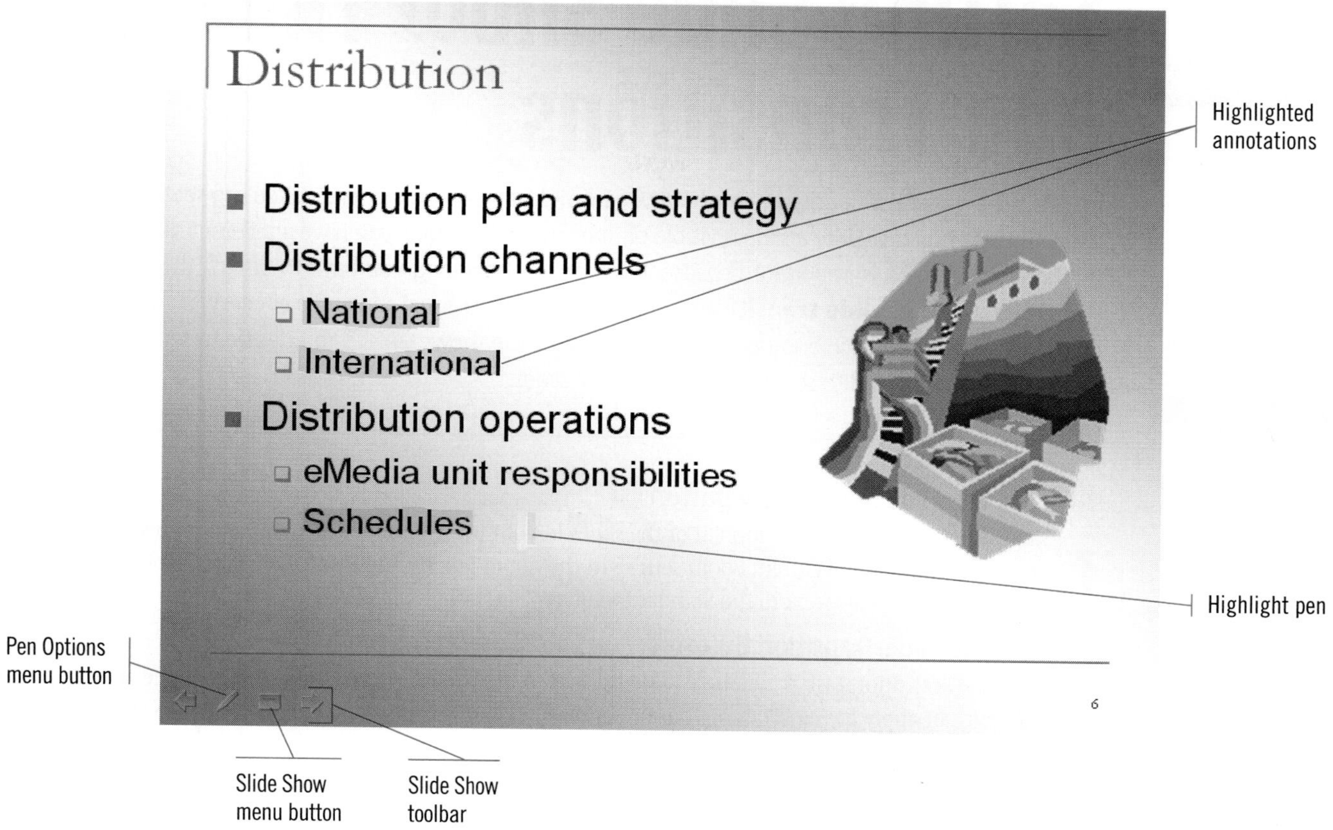

TABLE D-2: Basic Slide Show keyboard controls

control	description
[Enter], [Spacebar], [PgDn], [N], [down arrow key], or [right arrow key]	Advances to the next slide
[E]	Erases the annotation drawing
[Home], [End]	Moves to the first or last slide in the slide show
[H]	Displays a hidden slide
[up arrow key] or [PgUp]	Returns to the previous slide
[W]	Changes the screen to white; press again to return
[S]	Pauses the slide show; press again to continue
[B]	Changes the screen to black; press again to return
[Ctrl][M]	Shows or hides annotations on the slide
[Ctrl][A]	Changes pointer to
[Esc]	Stops the slide show

UNIT D

PowerPoint 2003

Setting Slide Show Timings and Transitions

In a slide show, you can specify when and how each slide appears on the screen. You can set the **slide timing**, which is the amount of time a slide is visible on the screen. Each slide can have a different slide timing. Setting the right slide timing is important because it determines how long you have to discuss the material on each slide. You can also set **slide transitions**, which are the special visual and audio effects you apply to a slide that determine how it moves in and out of view during the slide show. You decide to set a 10 second slide timing for each slide and to set transitions for all the slides.

STEPS

1. **Click the Slide Sorter View button**

   Slide Sorter view shows a thumbnail of the slides in your presentation. The number of slides you see on your screen depends on the current zoom setting in the Zoom box on the Standard toolbar. Notice that the Slide Sorter toolbar appears next to the Standard toolbar.

2. **Click the Slide Transition button on the Slide Sorter toolbar**

   The Slide Transition task pane opens. The list box at the top of the task pane contains the slide transitions that you can apply to the slides of your presentation. Use the Modify transition section to change the speed of slide transitions. You can also add a sound to a slide so that it plays during a slide show. Use the Advance slide section to determine how slides progress during a slide show—either manually or with a slide timing.

3. **Make sure the On mouse click check box is selected in the Advance slide section, click the Automatically after check box to select it, drag to select the number in the Automatically after text box, type 10, then click Apply to All Slides**

   The timing between slides is 10 seconds which appears under each slide in Slide Sorter view. When you run the slide show, each slide will remain on the screen for 10 seconds. You can override a slide's timing and speed up the slide show by pressing [Spacebar], [Enter], or clicking the left mouse button.

4. **Scroll down the list of transitions at the top of the task pane, click Wheel Clockwise, 8 Spokes, then click Apply to All Slides**

   All of the slides now have the Wheel Clockwise transition applied to them as indicated by the transition icon under each slide. You can apply a transition to one slide or to all of the slides in your presentation. The selected slide, Slide 1, displays the slide transition immediately after you apply the transition to all the slides. See Figure D-13. The slide transition would have more impact if it were slowed down.

5. **Click the Speed list arrow in the Modify transition section in the task pane, click Medium, then click Apply to All Slides**

6. **Scroll down the Slide Sorter view pane, click Slide 10, click the Sound list arrow in the Modify transition section in the task pane, scroll down the list, then click Chime**

   The sound plays when you apply the sound to the slide. The sound will now play when Slide 10 appears during the slide show.

7. **Press [Home], click the Slide Show button in the Slide Transition task pane, then watch the slide show advance automatically**

8. **When you hear the chime and see the black slide at the end of the slide show, press [Spacebar]**

   The slide show ends and returns to Slide Sorter view with Slide 1 selected.

TROUBLE

If you don't see the Slide Transition button, click a Toolbar Options button on the Slide Sorter toolbar to locate buttons that are not visible on your toolbar.

QUICK TIP

Click the transition icon under any slide to see its transition play.

QUICK TIP

To end a slide show, press [Esc] or click End Show on the Slide Show menu.

FIGURE D-13: Screen showing Slide Transition task pane

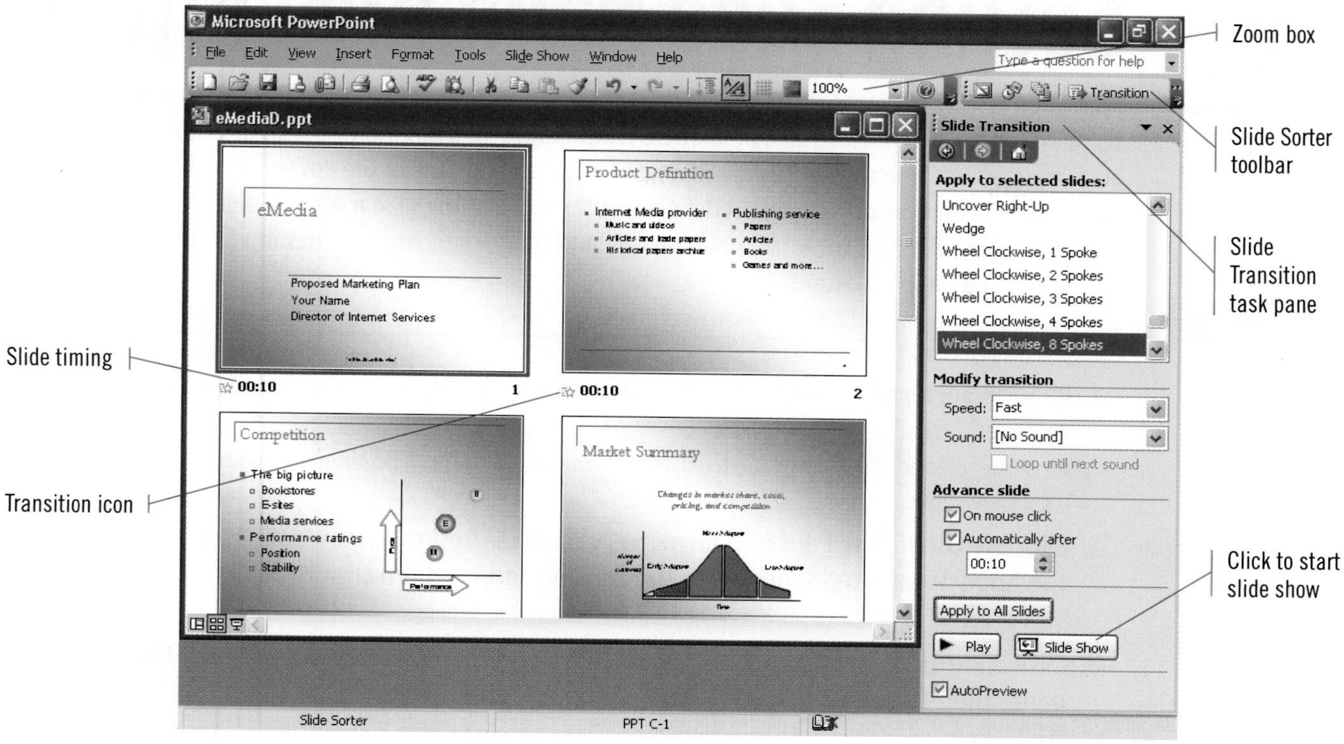

PowerPoint 2003

Clues to Use

Rehearsing slide show timing

You can set different slide timings for each slide. For example, you can have the title slide appear for 20 seconds, the second slide for 3 minutes, and so on. You can set timings by clicking the Rehearse Timings button on the Slide Sorter toolbar or by choosing the Rehearse Timings command on the Slide Show menu. The Rehearsal toolbar shown in Figure D-14 opens. It contains buttons to pause between slides and to advance to the next slide. After opening the Rehearsal toolbar, practice giving your presentation. PowerPoint keeps track of how long each slide appears and sets the timing accordingly. You can view your rehearsed timings in Slide Sorter view. The next time you run the slide show, you can use the timings you rehearsed.

FIGURE D-14: Rehearsal toolbar

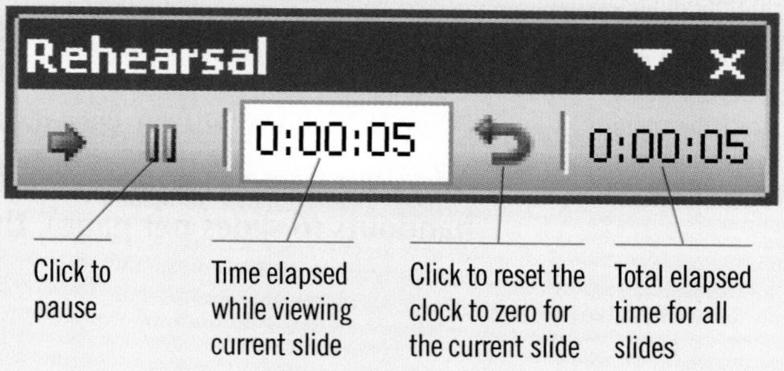

UNIT D
PowerPoint 2003

Setting Slide Animation Effects

Animation effects let you control how the graphics and main points in your presentation appear on the screen during a slide show. You can animate text, images, or even individual chart elements, or you can add sound effects. You can set custom animation effects or use one of the PowerPoint animation schemes. An **animation scheme** is a set of predefined visual effects for the slide transition, title text, and bullet text of a slide. You want to animate the text and graphics of several slides in your presentation using PowerPoint animation schemes.

STEPS

1. **In Slide Sorter view, click Slide 2, press and hold [Ctrl], click Slides 3, 5, 6, and 8, then release [Ctrl]**

   All of the selected slides have bulleted lists on them. The bullets can be animated to appear one at a time during a slide show.

2. **Click the Other Task Panes list arrow ▼, click Slide Design – Animation Schemes, scroll down the Apply to selected slides list to the Exciting section, then click Neutron**

   Each of the selected slides previews the Neutron animation scheme.

3. **Click Slide 1, click the Slide Show button on the Slide Design – Animation Schemes task pane, then press [Esc] when you see the black slide**

   The Neutron animation scheme is displayed on the selected slides. You can also animate objects on a slide by setting custom animations. To set custom animation effects, the slide you want to animate must be in Slide view.

4. **Double-click Slide 3 in Slide Sorter view, click Slide Show on the menu bar, then click Custom Animation**

   The Custom Animation task pane opens. Objects that are already animated appear in the Custom Animation task pane list in the order in which they will be animated. **Animation tags** on the slide label the order in which elements are animated during a slide show.

5. **Click the grouped arrow object on the slide to select it, then click the Add Effect button in the Custom Animation task pane**

   A menu of animation effects appears.

6. **Point to Entrance, then click More Effects**

   The Add Entrance Effect dialog box opens. All of the effects in this dialog box allow an object to enter the slide using a special effect.

7. **Scroll down to the Exciting section, click Pinwheel, then click OK**

   The arrow object now has the pinwheel effect applied to it as shown in Figure D-15.

8. **Run the Slide Show from Slide 1**

   The special effects make the presentation more interesting to view.

9. **Click the Slide Sorter View button, click the Zoom list arrow on the Standard toolbar, then click 50%**

   Figure D-16 shows the completed presentation in Slide Sorter view at 50% zoom.

10. **Add your name as a footer on the notes and handouts, save your presentation, print it as handouts (6 slides per page), then close the presentation and exit PowerPoint**

QUICK TIP

Keep in mind that the animation effects you choose give a certain "flavor" to your presentation. They can be serious and business-like or humorous. Choose appropriate effects for your presentation content and audience.

QUICK TIP

If you want the parts of a grouped object to animate individually, then you must ungroup them first.

QUICK TIP

To change the order in which objects are animated on the slide, select the object you want to change in the Custom Animation list in the task pane, then click the appropriate Re-Order arrow below the list.

FIGURE D-15: Screen with Custom Animation task pane open

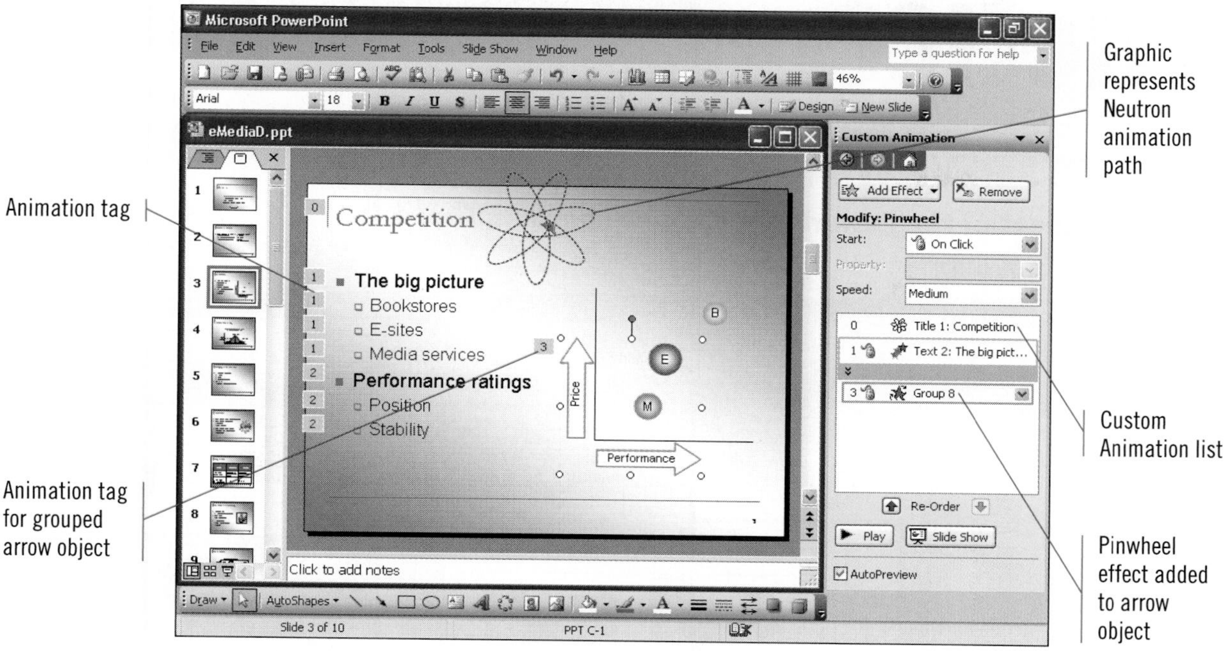

FIGURE D-16: Completed presentation in Slide Sorter view

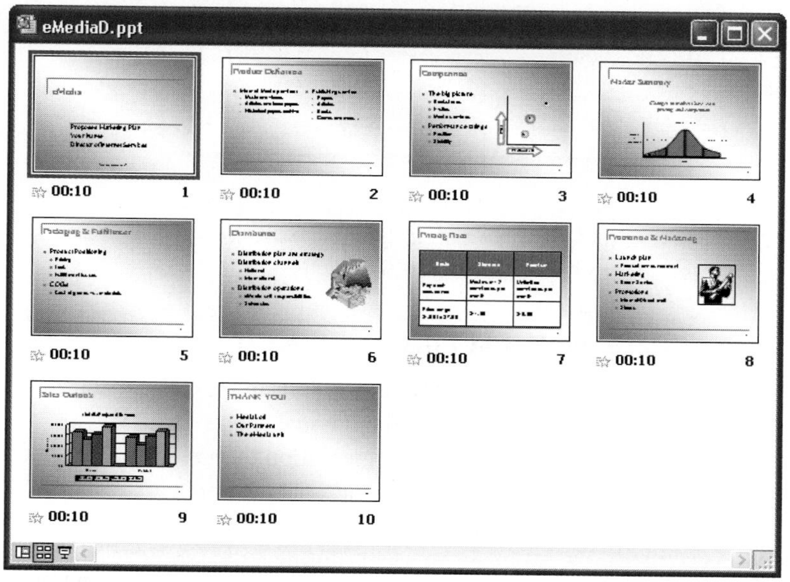

Clues to Use

Presentation checklist

You should always rehearse your slide show. If possible, rehearse your presentation in the room and with the computer that you will use. Use the following checklist to prepare for the slide show:

- Is **PowerPoint** or **PowerPoint Viewer** installed on the computer?
- Is your **presentation file** on the hard drive of the computer you will be using? Try putting a shortcut for the file on the desktop. Do you have a backup copy of your presentation file on a floppy disk?
- Is the **projection device** working correctly? Can the slides be seen from the back of the room?
- Do you know how to control **room lighting** so that the audience can see both your slides and their handouts and notes? You may want to designate someone to control the lights if the controls are not close to you.
- Will the **computer** be situated so you can advance and annotate the slides yourself? If not, designate someone to advance them for you.
- Do you have enough copies of your **handouts**? Bring extras. Decide when to hand them out, or whether you prefer to have them waiting at the audience members' seats when they enter.

Practice

▼ CONCEPTS REVIEW

Label each element of the PowerPoint window shown in Figure D-17.

FIGURE D-17

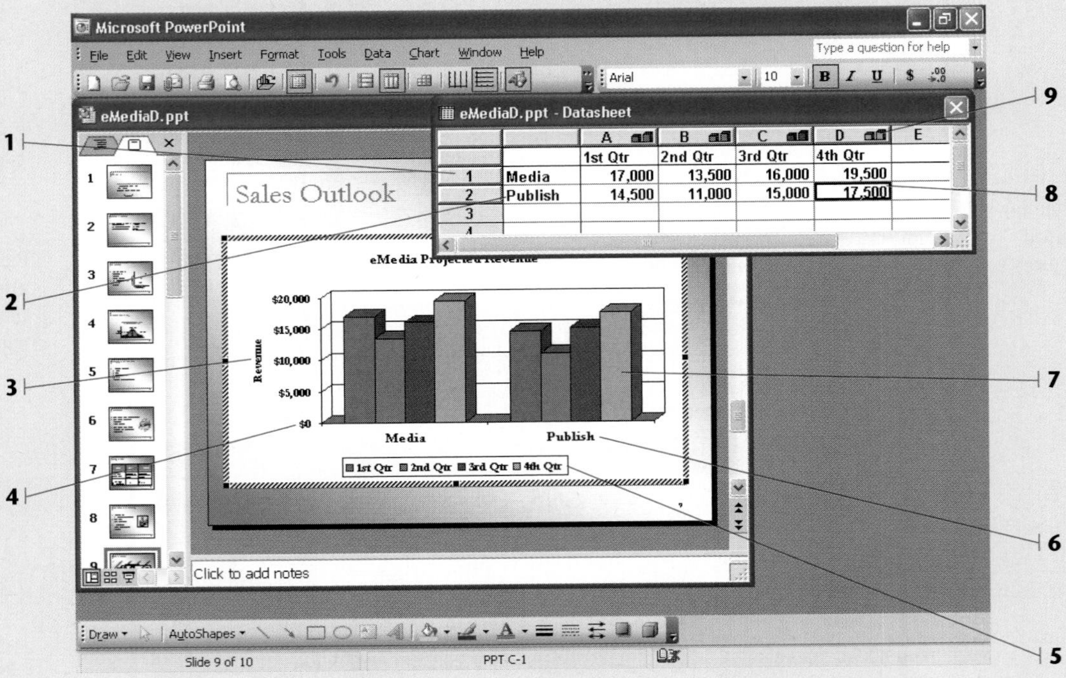

Match each term with the statement that best describes it.

10. Annotate
11. Data series markers
12. Crop
13. Datasheet
14. Chart
15. Animation scheme

a. Graphical representations of numerical data
b. A set of predefined visual effects
c. A graphical representation of numerical data
d. Where the numerical data is stored for a chart
e. To hide a portion of a picture
f. To draw on a slide during a slide show

Select the best answer from the list of choices.

16. When you want an object to become a part of a PowerPoint file you:
- **a.** Annotate the object.
- **b.** Embed the object.
- **c.** Crop the object.
- **d.** Scale the object.

17. Professionally designed images that you can place in your presentation are called:
- **a.** Thumbnails.
- **b.** Pictures.
- **c.** Clip art.
- **d.** AutoShapes.

18. Cropping is essentially the same as:
- **a.** Hiding.
- **b.** Deleting.
- **c.** Resizing.
- **d.** Scaling.

19. What are you doing when you drag a sizing handle of an object?
- **a.** Moving
- **b.** Scaling
- **c.** Hiding
- **d.** Deleting

20. **What does pressing [Alt] while dragging an object's sizing handle do?**
   - **a.** Overrides the automatic snap-to-grid setting
   - **b.** Constrains the proportions of the object
   - **c.** Deletes that portion of the object
   - **d.** Scales the object larger or smaller
21. **What is a chart in PowerPoint?**
   - **a.** A datasheet that contains numerical data
   - **b.** A table you create with the Diagram button
   - **c.** A graphical representation of numerical data
   - **d.** An organizational chart
22. **Where is the numerical data for a chart found?**
   - **a.** The data series markers
   - **b.** The slide
   - **c.** The chart
   - **d.** The datasheet
23. **Which axis is the vertical axis?**
   - **a.** Value axis
   - **b.** Category axis
   - **c.** Legend axis
   - **d.** Horizontal axis

▼ SKILLS REVIEW

1. **Insert clip art.**
   - **a.** Open the presentation PPT D-3.ppt from the drive and folder where your Data Files are stored, then save it as **Year End Report**.
   - **b.** Go to Slide 2, search for clip art using the keyword CD, then insert the clip on the slide.
   - **c.** On the Picture tab of the Format Picture dialog box, click the Color list arrow, then click Grayscale.
   - **d.** Drag the graphic so the top of the graphic aligns with the body text box and is centered in the blank area on the right of the slide, then save your changes.
2. **Insert, crop, and scale a picture.**
   - **a.** Go to Slide 6 and insert the picture file PPT D-4.jpg.
   - **b.** Crop about ¾" off the top of the picture.
   - **c.** Drag the picture so its top is aligned with the top line of text.
   - **d.** Scale the picture to 65%, then using the Color button on the picture toolbar change the picture to grayscale.
   - **e.** Reposition the graphic, then save your changes.
3. **Embed a chart.**
   - **a.** Go to Slide 3, 2005 CD Sales by Quarter, and apply the Title and Content layout.
   - **b.** Start Microsoft Graph.
   - **c.** Deselect the chart object and save your changes.
4. **Enter and edit data in the datasheet.**
   - **a.** Open Graph again.
   - **b.** Enter the information shown in Table D-4 into the datasheet.
   - **c.** Delete any unused rows of default data.
   - **d.** Place the data series in columns.
   - **e.** Save your changes.

TABLE D-4

	1st Qtr	2nd Qtr	3rd Qtr	4th Qtr
East Div.	405	340	390	320
West Div.	280	320	380	250

5. **Format a chart.**
   - **a.** Close the datasheet but leave Graph running.
   - **b.** Change the region names font on the Category axis to 20 point and regular font style (no bold).
   - **c.** Apply the Currency Style with no decimals to the values on the Value axis.
   - **d.** Insert the chart title **Division Sales**.
   - **e.** Add the title **Thousands** to the Value axis, then change the alignment of this label to vertical.
   - **f.** Change the legend text font to 16-point Arial font and regular font style (no bold).
   - **g.** Exit Graph and save your changes.
6. **Create a table.**
   - **a.** Insert a new slide after Slide 2 using the Title and Content slide layout.
   - **b.** Add the slide title **CD Sales by Type**.
   - **c.** Click the Insert Table button in the placeholder, then insert a table with two columns and five rows.
   - **d.** Enter **Type** in the first cell and **Sales** in the second cell in the first row.
   - **e.** In the first column, enter the following: **Rock**, **Rap**, **New Age**, and **Country**.

▼ SKILLS REVIEW (CONTINUED)

f. In the second column, enter sales figures: **20,000**, **35,000**, **55,650**, and **80,000** for each CD type.
g. Format the table using fills, horizontal and vertical alignment, and other features.
h. Save your changes.

7. Use slide show commands.

a. Begin the slide show at Slide 1, then proceed through the slide show to Slide 3.
b. On Slide 3, use the Ballpoint pen to draw straight-line annotations under each type of music.
c. Erase the pen annotations, then change the pointer back to an arrow.
d. Go to 5 Summary slide using the Slide Show menu button on the Slide Show toolbar, then using the Highlighter, highlight all of the points on the slide.
e. Press [End] to move to the last slide. Don't save any changes.
f. Return to Normal view.

8. Set slide show timings and transitions.

a. Switch to Slide Sorter view, then open the Slide Transition task pane.
b. Specify that all slides should advance after eight seconds.
c. Apply the Newsflash transition effect to all slides.
d. View the slide show to verify the transitions are correct, then save your changes.

9. Set slide animation effects.

a. Switch to Normal view, then open the Custom Animation task pane.
b. Switch to Slide 5, apply the (Entrance) Fly In animation effect to the bulleted list.
c. Go to Slide 2, apply the (Emphasis) Shimmer animation effect to the text object. (*Hint*: Look in the Moderate section after clicking More effects.)
d. Apply the (Exit) Faded Zoom animation effect to the graphic on Slide 2. (*Hint*: Look in the Subtle section after clicking More effects.)
e. Run the slide show from the beginning to check the animation effects.
f. Add your name as a footer to the notes and handouts, then print the presentation as handouts (4 slides per page).
g. Save your changes, close the presentation, and exit PowerPoint.

▼ INDEPENDENT CHALLENGE 1

You are a financial management consultant for Northwest Investments, located in Tacoma, Washington. One of your responsibilities is to create standardized presentations on different financial investments for use on the company Web site. In this challenge, you enhance the look of the slides by adding and formatting objects and adding animation effects and transitions.

a. Open the file PPT D-5.ppt from the drive and folder where your Data Files are stored, and save it as **Web Seminar1**.
b. Add your name as the footer on all slides and handouts.
c. Apply the Title and Chart layout to Slide 6, and enter the data in Table D-5 into the datasheet.
d. Format the chart. Add titles as necessary.

TABLE D-5

	1 year	3 year	5 year	10 year
Bonds	4.2%	5.2%	7.9%	9.4%
Stocks	4.5%	6.3%	9.8%	10.6%
Mutual Funds	6.1%	6.3%	7.4%	8.1%

Advanced Challenge Exercise

ACE

- Double-click one of the 10 year data series markers to select the data series.
- On the Data Labels tab, click the Series name check box.
- On the Patterns tab, click the red color in the Area section.

e. Add an appropriate clip art item to Slide 2, then format as necessary.
f. On Slide 4, use the Align and Group commands to organize the shapes.
g. Spell check the presentation, then save it.
h. View the slide show, evaluate your presentation, and add a template of your choice. Make changes if necessary.
i. Set animation effects, slide transitions, and slide timings, keeping in mind that your audience includes potential investors who need the information you are presenting to make decisions about where to put their hard-earned money.
j. View the slide show again.
k. Print the slides as handouts (6 slides per page), then close the presentation, and exit PowerPoint.

▼ INDEPENDENT CHALLENGE 2

You are the manager of the Indiana University Student Employment Office. Work-study students staff the office; new students start every semester. Create a presentation that you can use to train them.

a. Plan and create the slide presentation. As you plan your outline, make sure you include slides that will help explain to the work-study staff the main features of the office, including its employment database, library of company directories, seminars on employment search strategies, interviewing techniques, and resume development, as well as its student consulting and resume bulk-mailing services. Add more slides with more content if you wish.

b. Use an appropriate design template.

c. Add clip art and photographs available in the Clip Organizer to help create visual interest.

d. Save the presentation as **Indiana USEO** to the drive and folder where your Data Files are stored. View the slide show and evaluate the contents of your presentation. Make any necessary adjustments.

e. Add transitions, special effects, and timings to the presentation. Remember that your audience is university students who need to assimilate a lot of information in order to perform well in their new jobs. View the slide show again to evaluate the effects you added.

f. Add your name as a footer to slides and handouts. Spell check, save, and print the presentation as handouts (4 slides per page).

g. Close the presentation and exit PowerPoint.

▼ INDEPENDENT CHALLENGE 3

You are the managing development engineer at SportDesign, Inc, an international sports product design company located in Ottawa, Ontario, Canada. SportDesign designs and manufactures items such as bike helmets, bike racks, and kayak paddles, and markets these items primarily to countries in North America and Western Europe. You need to create a quarterly presentation that outlines the progress of the company's newest technologies, and present it.

a. Plan and create a slide show presentation that includes two new technologies.

b. Use an appropriate design template.

c. Add one chart and one table in the presentation that shows details (such as performance results, testing criteria, etc.) about the new technologies.

d. Include at least two slides that explain how the new technologies will appeal specifically to individual countries in the European and North American markets.

e. Set slide transitions, animation effects, and slide timings. View the slide show to evaluate the effects you added.

Advanced Challenge Exercise

- Click the Rehearse Timings button on the Slide Sorter toolbar.
- Set slide timings for each slide in the presentation.
- Save new slide timings.

f. Add your name as a footer to the handouts. Save the presentation as **SportDesign** to the drive and folder where your Data Files are stored.

g. Print the presentation as handouts (4 slides per page), then close the presentation and exit PowerPoint.

E-QUEST

▼ INDEPENDENT CHALLENGE 4

You work for IRAssets, a small retirement investment firm. You have been asked to complete a retirement investing presentation started by your boss. Most of the information has already been entered into the PowerPoint presentation; you just need to add a template and a table to complete the presentation. To find the data for the table, you need to use the Web to locate certain information.

You'll need to find the following information on the Web:

- Data for a table that compares the traditional IRA with the Roth IRA.
- Data for a table that compares at least two other retirement plans.

▼ INDEPENDENT CHALLENGE 4 (CONTINUED)

a. Open the file PPT D-6.ppt from the drive and folder where your Data Files are stored and save it as **Retirement**.
b. Connect to the Internet, then use a search engine to locate Web sites that have information on retirement plans.
c. Review at least two Web sites that contain information about retirement plans. Print the Home pages of the Web sites you use to gather data for your presentation.
d. Apply the Title and Table layout to Slide 7, then enter the data you found that compares the IRA retirement plans.
e. Apply the Title and Table layout to Slide 8, then enter the data you found that compares the other retirement plans.
f. Apply a template to the presentation, then customize the slide background and the color scheme.
g. Format the Autoshape objects on Slides 4 and 5.
h. Use text formatting to help emphasize important points, then add your name as a footer to the handouts.
i. Add slide transitions, slide timings, and animation effects.
j. Spell check the presentation, view the slide show, save the final version, then print the handouts.
k. Close the presentation and exit PowerPoint.

▼ VISUAL WORKSHOP

Create a slide with a chart that looks like the slide in Figure D-18. Add your name as a footer on the slide. Save the presentation as **2006 Expenses** to the drive and folder where your Data Files are stored.

FIGURE D-18

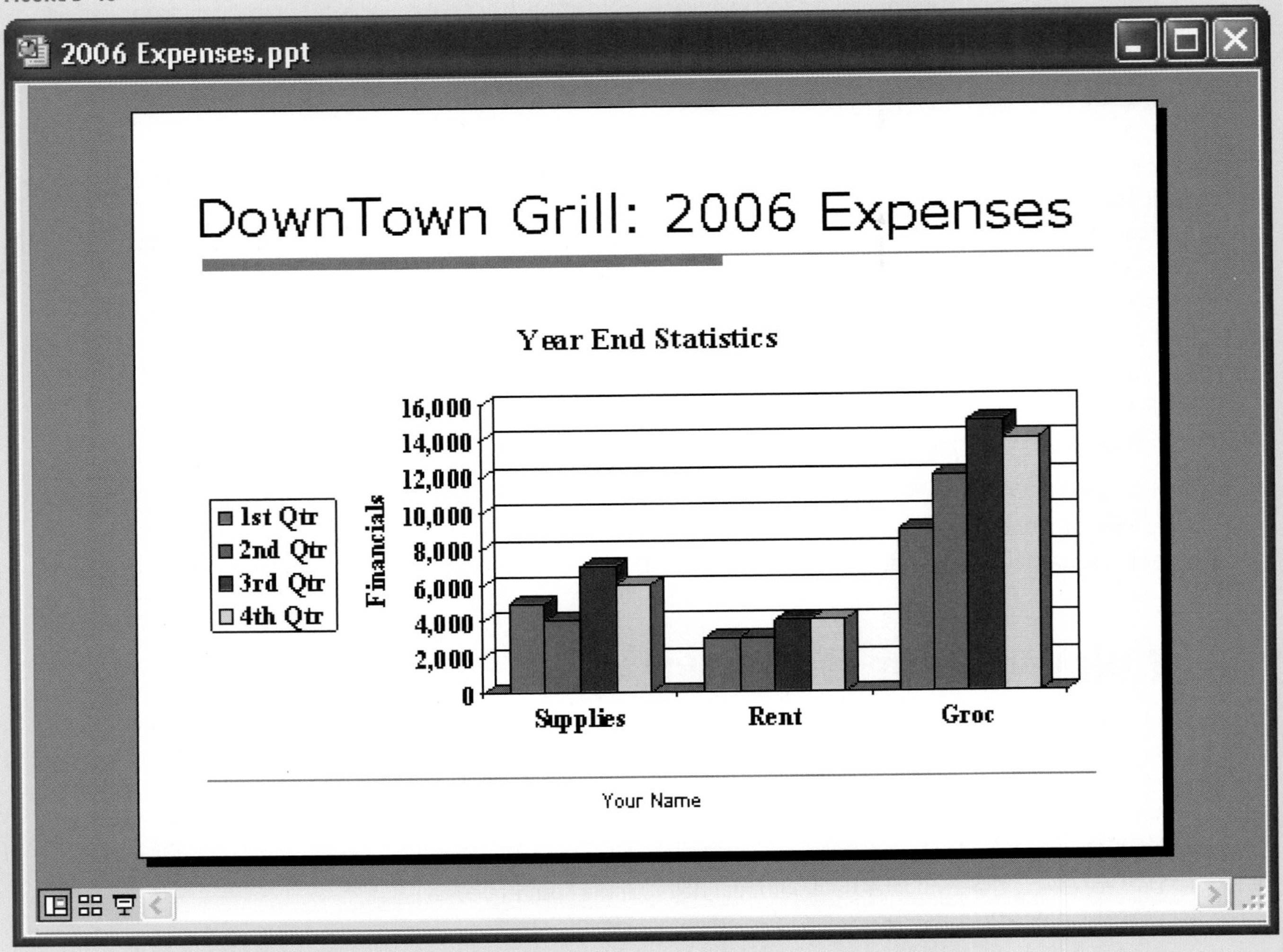

UNIT
E
PowerPoint 2003

Customizing a Presentation

OBJECTIVES

- Understand PowerPoint masters
- Format master text
- Change master text indents
- Adjust text objects
- Use advanced drawing tools
- Use advanced formatting tools
- Insert and format WordArt
- Create a template

If you have a SAM user profile, you may have access to hands-on instruction, practice, and assessment of the skills covered in this unit. Log in to your SAM account and go to your assignments page to see what your instructor has assigned.

Design features such as text spacing and color are some of the most important qualities of a professional-looking presentation. It is important to make design elements consistent throughout a presentation to hold the reader's attention and to avoid confusion. PowerPoint helps you achieve the look you want by providing ways of customizing and enhancing your slides, notes pages, and handouts. Maria Abbott is MediaLoft's general sales manager. You are her assistant, and you have been working on a marketing presentation for a new Internet product that you will give later in the month. After receiving some initial feedback from a couple of coworkers, you revise the presentation by customizing the slide format and enhancing the graphics. You then create a presentation template so you and other coworkers at MediaLoft can create additional presentations with a similar look.

UNIT
E
PowerPoint 2003

Understanding PowerPoint Masters

Each presentation in PowerPoint uses **Master views** to store information about the design template. This information includes font styles, text placeholder position and size, and color scheme. Design elements that you place in Slide Master view appear on every slide in the presentation. For example, you could insert a company logo in the upper-right corner of the slide master and that logo would then appear on every slide in your presentation. There are three Master views: Slide Master view, Handout Master view, and Notes Master view. Changes made to the slide master are reflected on all the slides, changes made to the notes master are reflected in the Notes Page view, and changes made to the handout master are reflected when you print your presentation using one of the Handout print options. Slide Master view actually has two master slides: one for the slide master and one for the title master. These two masters are called a **slide-title master pair**. Table E-1 describes the Slide Master View toolbar buttons. You want to make a few changes and add an optional design template to the presentation, so you open your presentation and examine the slide master.

STEPS

QUICK TIP
You can press and hold [Shift] and click the Normal View button to display the slide master.

QUICK TIP
A slide master is preserved by default when you insert, paste, or drag a design template into Slide Master view or when you add a new design template in Slide Master view. A preserved slide master is identified by a push pin icon.

QUICK TIP
Click the second slide master thumbnail to display the title master.

1. **Start PowerPoint, open the presentation PPT E-1.ppt from the drive and folder where your Data Files are stored, then save the presentation as eMediaE**
   The title slide of the presentation appears.

2. **Click View, point to Master, then click Slide Master**
   The presentation's Slide Master view appears, showing the title master in the Slide pane. The slide-title master pair appears as thumbnails to the left of the Slide pane. The title master controls the title, subtitle, and footer placeholders for any slide in the presentation with the Title Slide layout. You can add more than one design template to the same presentation.

3. **Click the Slide Design button on the Formatting toolbar, scroll down through the design templates, click the Compass design template list arrow in the Slide Design task pane in the Available For Use section, then click Add Design**
   There are now two slide-title master pairs to the left of the Slide pane indicating that there are two design templates available in this presentation. You can apply a different template for different audiences or situations. You can also use multiple templates in one presentation at the same time.

4. **Click the first slide master thumbnail**
   The slide master for the first presentation design template appears. It contains a **Master title placeholder** and a **Master text placeholder**, as shown in Figure E-1. These placeholders control the format for each title text object and body text object for each slide in the presentation that doesn't have the Title Slide layout. Figure E-2 shows Slide 6 of the presentation. Examine Figures E-1 and E-2 to better understand the relationship between the slide master and the slide.

   - The Master title placeholder, labeled "Title Area for AutoLayouts", indicates the position of the title text object and its font size, style, and color. Compare this to the slide title shown in Figure E-2.
   - The Master text placeholder, labeled "Object Area for AutoLayouts", determines the characteristics of the body text objects on all the slides in the presentation. Compare the colors and fonts of each bullet level in the body text objects of both figures.
   - You can resize and move Master title and text placeholders as you would any placeholder in PowerPoint.
   - The slide master can contain background objects, such as AutoShapes, clip art, or pictures, that appear on every slide in the presentation behind the text and objects on the slides.

FIGURE E-1: Slide Master

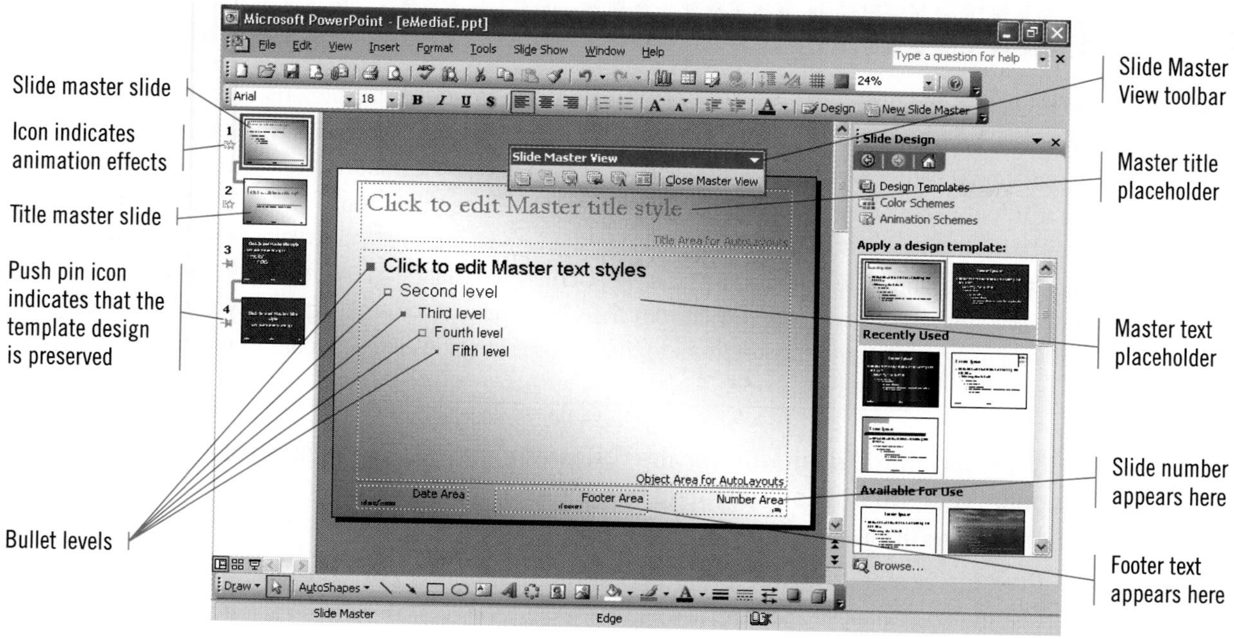

FIGURE E-2: Slide 6 in Normal view

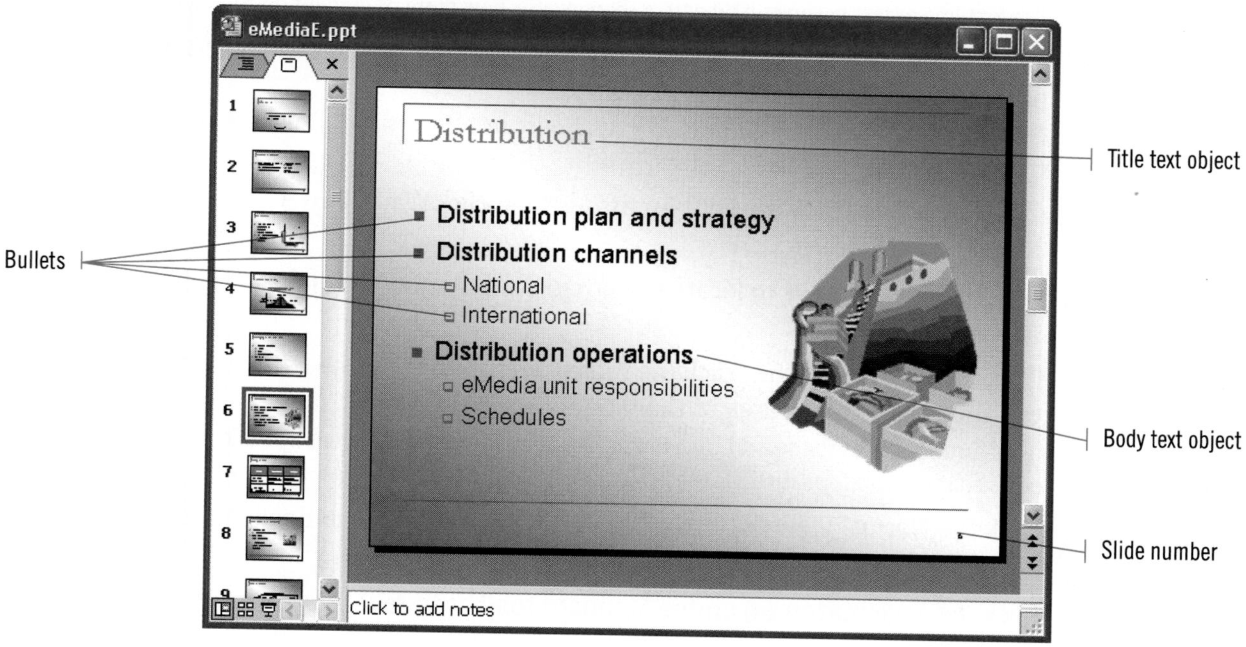

TABLE E-1: Slide Master View toolbar buttons

button	button name	function
	Insert New Slide Master	Inserts a new blank slide master thumbnail below the current slide-title master pair
	Insert New Title Master	Inserts a new blank title master thumbnail below the current slide-title master pair
	Delete Master	Deletes a slide master thumbnail or a title master thumbnail from the presentation
	Preserve Master	Prevents a slide-title master pair from being accidentally deleted
	Rename Master	Provides a text box in which a new master name can be typed
	Master Layout	Opens the Master Layout dialog box; Master placeholders can be deleted and restored

UNIT E

PowerPoint 2003

Formatting Master Text

To ensure that you don't use a mixture of fonts and styles throughout the presentation, you can format text in a Master view. Changes made in a Master view are applied to the whole presentation. For example, if your presentation is part of a marketing campaign for a travel tour to the Middle East, you may decide to switch the title text font of the entire presentation from the standard Times New Roman font to a script font. You format text in the Master view the same way you format text in any of the other PowerPoint views. You can change text color, style, size, and bullet type in the Master view. When you change a bullet type, you can use a character bullet symbol from a font, a picture bullet from the Clip Organizer, or an image that you scan in. You decide to make a few formatting changes to the Master text placeholder of your presentation.

STEPS

1. **Make sure the slide master for the first presentation design template appears in the Slide pane, click Window on the menu bar, then click Arrange All**

   This ensures that your screen matches the figures in this book.

2. **Click Click to edit Master text styles in the first line of text in the Master text placeholder**

   Clicking anywhere in a Master view selects the entire line of text.

3. **Click the Bold button on the Formatting toolbar, then click the Shadow button on the Formatting toolbar**

   The first line of text becomes bold with a shadow; it is now more prominent on the slide.

4. **Right-click Second level in the Master text placeholder, then click Bullets and Numbering on the shortcut menu**

   The Bullets and Numbering dialog box opens. Notice that there is also a Numbered tab that you can use to create sequentially numbered or lettered bullets.

5. **Click Customize, click the Font list arrow, then click Wingdings 3**

   The available bullet choices change.

6. **Click the scroll arrows to locate the arrow symbol shown in Figure E-3, click the arrow symbol, then click OK**

7. **Click the Color list arrow, click the red color (fourth from the left in the top row), click OK, then click a blank area of the slide**

   A red arrow replaces the second-level bullet. The second-level bullet is more visible now that the bullet symbol is changed and formatted.

8. **Click the Normal View button, then click the Slide 5 thumbnail in the Slides tab**

   Compare your screen to Figure E-4.

9. **Click the Save button on the Standard toolbar to save your changes**

QUICK TIP

To insert a picture bullet, click Picture in the Bullets and Numbering dialog box, then click the desired bullet. You may need access to the Office CD to use picture bullets.

QUICK TIP

A bullet looks best if it is smaller than the text it identifies. Click the Size arrows in the Bullets and Numbering dialog box to specify the percentage of the text size you want the bullet to be.

FIGURE E-3: Symbol dialog box

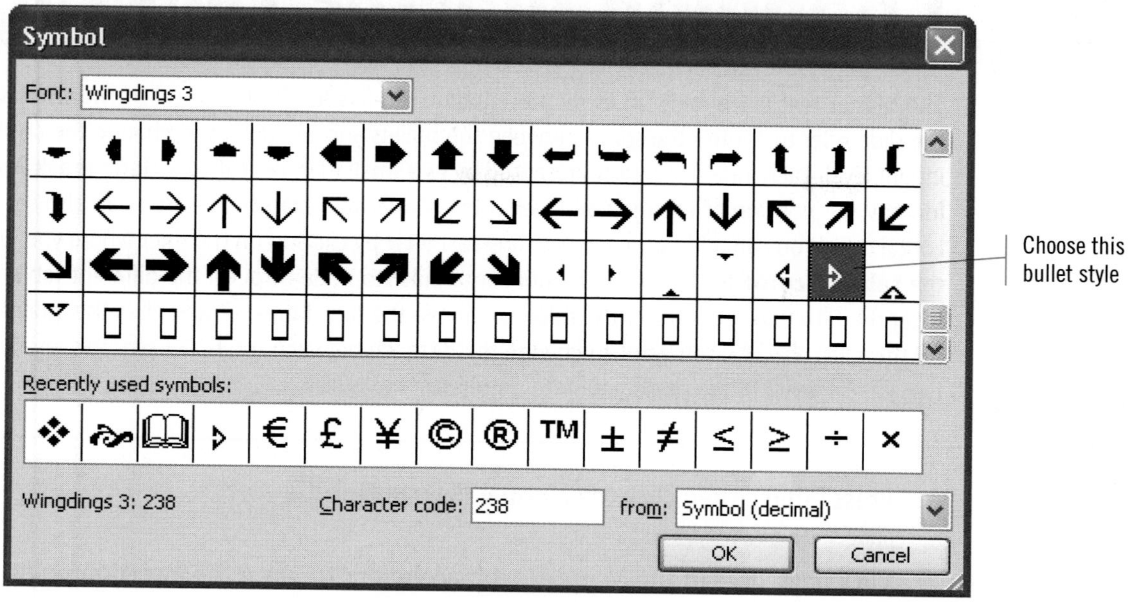

FIGURE E-4: Slide 5 with modified text and bullet styles

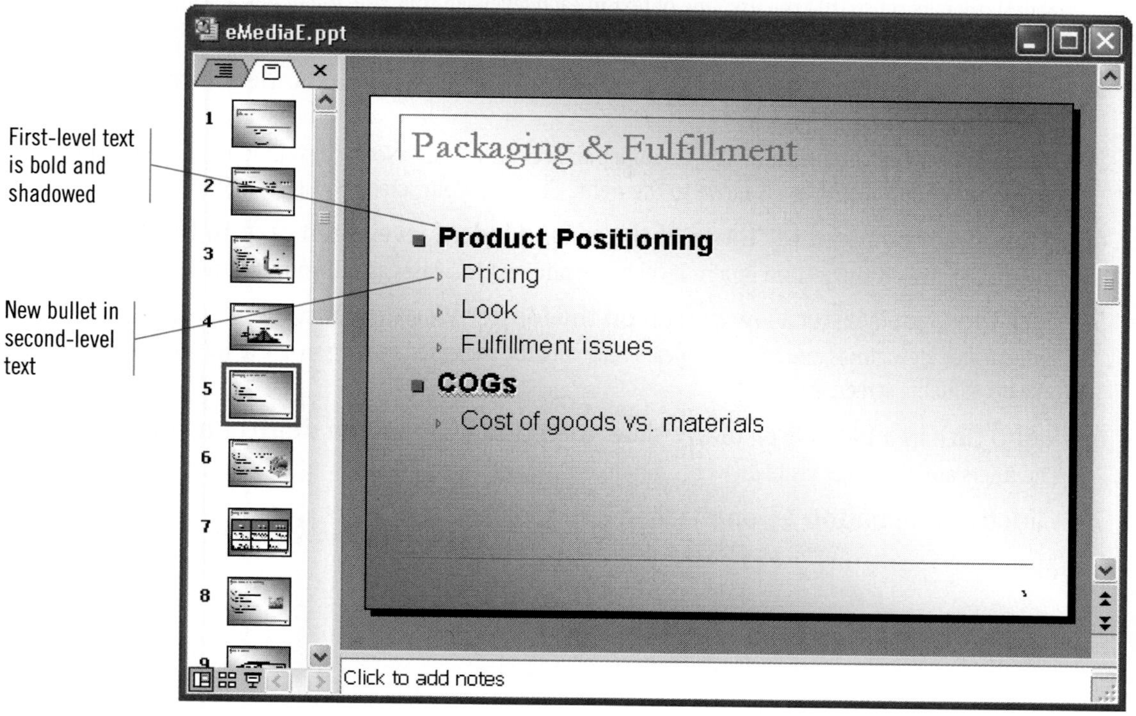

Clues to Use

Exceptions to the slide master

If you change the format of text on a slide and then apply a different template to the presentation, the slide that you formatted retains the text formatting changes you made. These format changes that differ from the slide master are known as exceptions. Exceptions can only be changed on the individual slides where they occur. For example, you might change the font and size of a particular text object on a slide to make it stand out and then decide later to add a different template to your presentation. The text you formatted before you applied the template is an exception and it is unaffected by the new template. Another way to override the slide master is to remove the master graphics on one or more slides. You might want to do this to get a clearer view of your slide text. Click Format on the menu bar, click Background, then click the Omit background graphics from master check box to select it.

UNIT E

PowerPoint 2003

Changing Master Text Indents

The Master text placeholder in every presentation has five levels of text, called **indent levels**. You can use the slide ruler to control the space between the bullets and the text or to change the position of the whole indent level. Each indent level is represented by two small triangles called **indent markers** on the ruler that identify the position of each indent level in the Master text placeholder. You can also set tabs on the horizontal ruler. You can add tab markers to any text level by clicking on the ruler where you want the tab. Click the **tab indicator** to the left of the horizontal ruler to cycle through the different tab alignment options. Drag the tab marker down off the ruler to remove the tab. Table E-2 describes the indent and tab markers on the ruler. You want to change the distance between the bullet symbols and the text in the first two indent levels of the presentation to emphasize the bullets.

STEPS

1. **Press [Shift], then click the Normal View button**

   Slide Master view appears.

2. **Click anywhere in the Master text placeholder to place the insertion point, click View on the menu bar, then click Ruler**

   The horizontal and vertical slide rulers for the Master text placeholder appear. The indent markers on the horizontal ruler are set so that the first line of text in each level—in this case, the bullet—begins to the left of subsequent lines of text. This is called a **hanging indent**.

3. **Position the pointer over the left indent marker of the first indent level, then drag to the ½" mark on the ruler**

   The space between the first-indent level bullet and text increases. Notice also that all of the indent markers for the other four indent levels move to the right. Compare your screen to Figure E-5.

4. **Position the pointer over the of the second indent level, then drag to the 1⅛" mark**

   The space between the second indent level bullet and text increases as shown in Figure E-6.

5. **Click the Close Master View button on the Master View toolbar**

   Slide Master view closes and Slide 5 appears, showing the increased indents in the body text object. The rulers take up valuable screen area.

6. **Right-click in a blank area of the slide, then click Ruler on the shortcut menu**

   The rulers are no longer visible.

7. **Click the Save button on the Standard toolbar**

TROUBLE

If your rulers are already visible, skip Step 2.

TROUBLE

If you accidentally drag an indent marker past the ½" mark, click the Undo button to restore the indent levels to their original position.

TABLE E-2: Indent and Tab Markers

symbol	name	function
	First line indent marker	Controls the position of the first line of text in an indent level
	Left indent marker	Controls the position of subsequent lines of text in an indent level
	Left tab stop	Aligns tab text on the left
	Right tab stop	Aligns tab text on the right
	Center tab stop	Aligns tab text in the center
	Decimal tab stop	Aligns tab text on a decimal point

FIGURE E-5: Slide Master with first-level, left indent marker moved

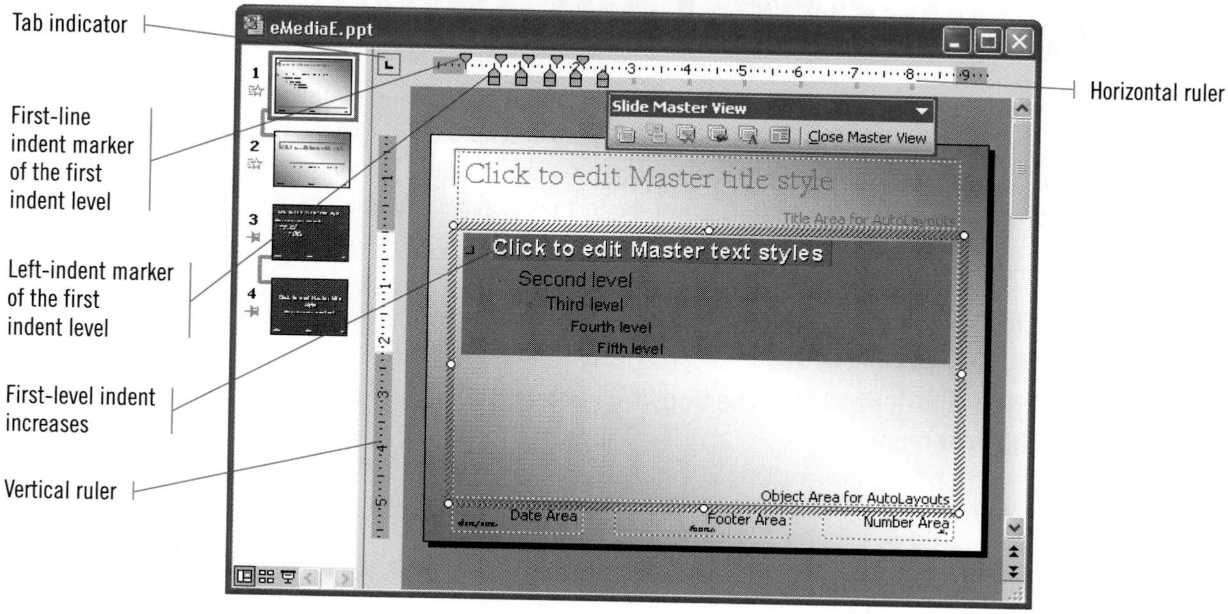

FIGURE E-6: Slide Master with second-level, left indent marker moved

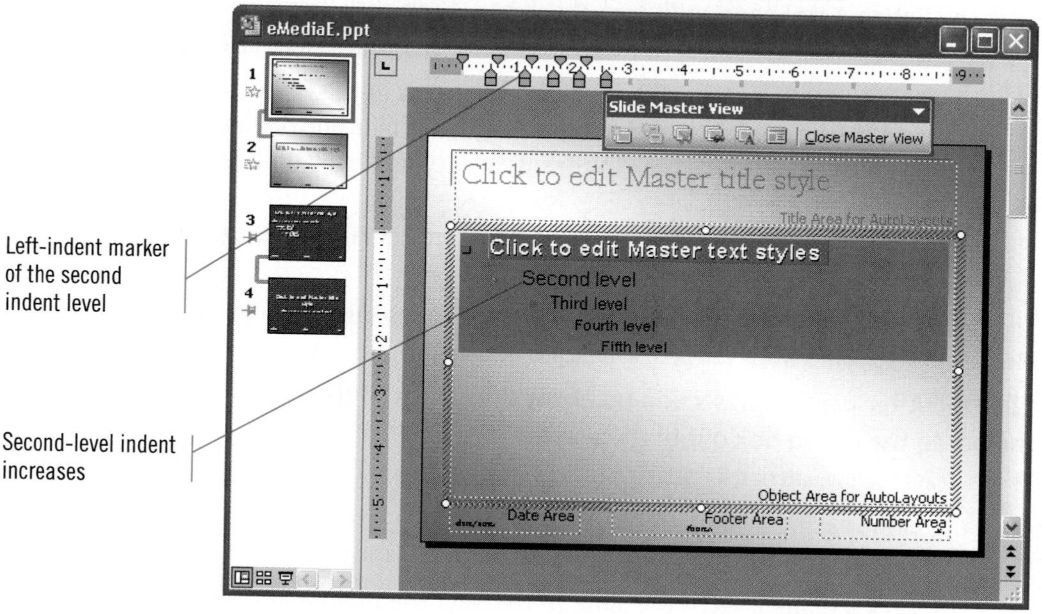

Clues to Use

Restoring the master layout

If a master placeholder is missing or deleted from a master view, you can click the Master Layout button on the Slide Master View toolbar to reapply the placeholder. Clicking the Master Layout button opens the Master Layout dialog box, as shown in Figure E-7. Click the placeholder check box to reapply the placeholder. Each master view has its own Master Layout dialog box.

FIGURE E-7: Master Layout dialog box

UNIT
E
PowerPoint 2003

Adjusting Text Objects

You have complete control over the placement of your text on PowerPoint slides. With the **text anchor** feature, you can adjust text position within text objects or shapes to achieve the best look. If you want your text to fill more or less of the slide, you can adjust the spacing between lines of text, called **leading** (rhymes with "wedding"). You decide to adjust the text position and line spacing of the text object on Slide 11.

STEPS

1. **Click the Slide 11 thumbnail in the Slides tab**
   Slide 11 appears in the slide pane.
2. **Press [Shift], right-click the body text object, then click Format Placeholder on the shortcut menu**
   Pressing [Shift] when clicking a text object ensures that the entire text object is selected. The Format AutoShape dialog box opens. The text would look better centered in the text box.
3. **Click the Text Box tab, click the Text anchor point list arrow, click Middle Centered, then click Preview**
   Compare your Format AutoShape dialog box to Figure E-8. The text moves to the middle center of the text object. To make it easier to select, resize the text object.
4. **Click the Resize AutoShape to fit text check box, then click Preview**
   The text object shrinks to fit the text. The text object would look better with a fill color behind the text.
5. **Click the Colors and Lines tab, click the Color list arrow in the Fill section, click the teal color (second from right in row below Automatic Fill Color button, labeled Follow Accent and Hyperlink Scheme Color), click the Transparency up arrow until 60% appears, then click OK**
   The text object is filled with a teal color. The bulleted lines are a little too close together.
6. **Click Format on the menu bar, then click Line Spacing**
   The Line Spacing dialog box opens. Line spacing can be measured in lines or points. Change the measurement method to points when you need a more precise line spacing measurement.
7. **Click the After paragraph section up arrow four times so that 0.2 appears, click Preview, then drag the dialog box out of the way**
   The space, or leading, after each paragraph bulleted item increases. The text is easier to read.
8. **Click the Line spacing section up arrow until 2 appears, then click Preview**
   Compare your Line Spacing dialog box to Figure E-9. The line spacing between the text lines increases.
9. **Click OK, click a blank area of the slide to deselect the main text object, then save your changes**
   Compare your screen to Figure E-10.

TROUBLE

If the Format AutoShape dialog box prevents you from seeing the slide, drag it out of the way.

QUICK TIP

You can also drag the Transparency scroll box to the desired percentage.

Clues to Use

Changing margins around text in shapes

You can also use the Text Anchor Point command to change the margins around a text object to form a shape that suits the text better. Right-click the shape, click Format Placeholder, click the Text Box tab, then adjust the Internal margin settings. Click Preview to see your changes before you apply them to the shape.

FIGURE E-8: Format AutoShape dialog box

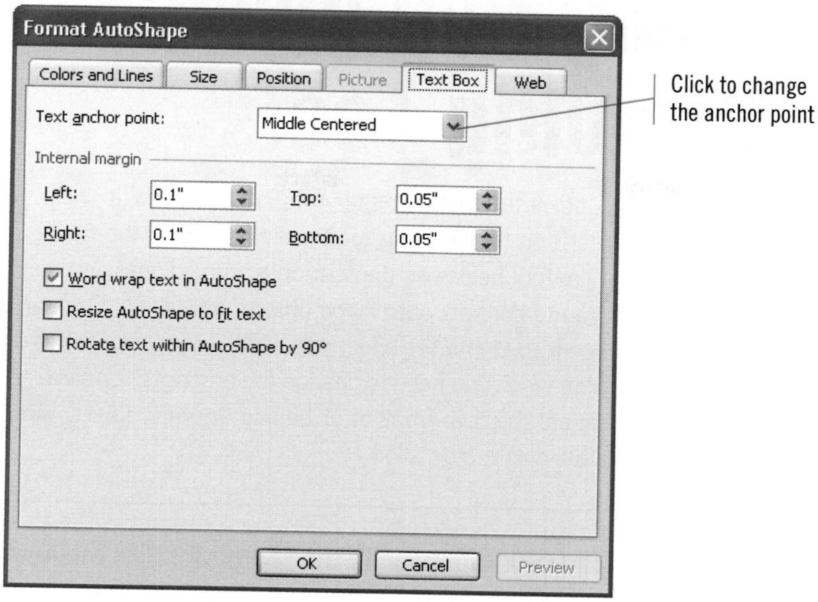

FIGURE E-9: Line Spacing dialog box

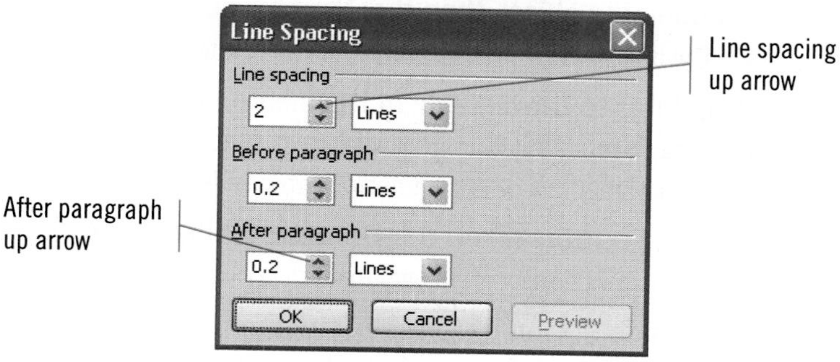

FIGURE E-10: Slide showing formatted body text object

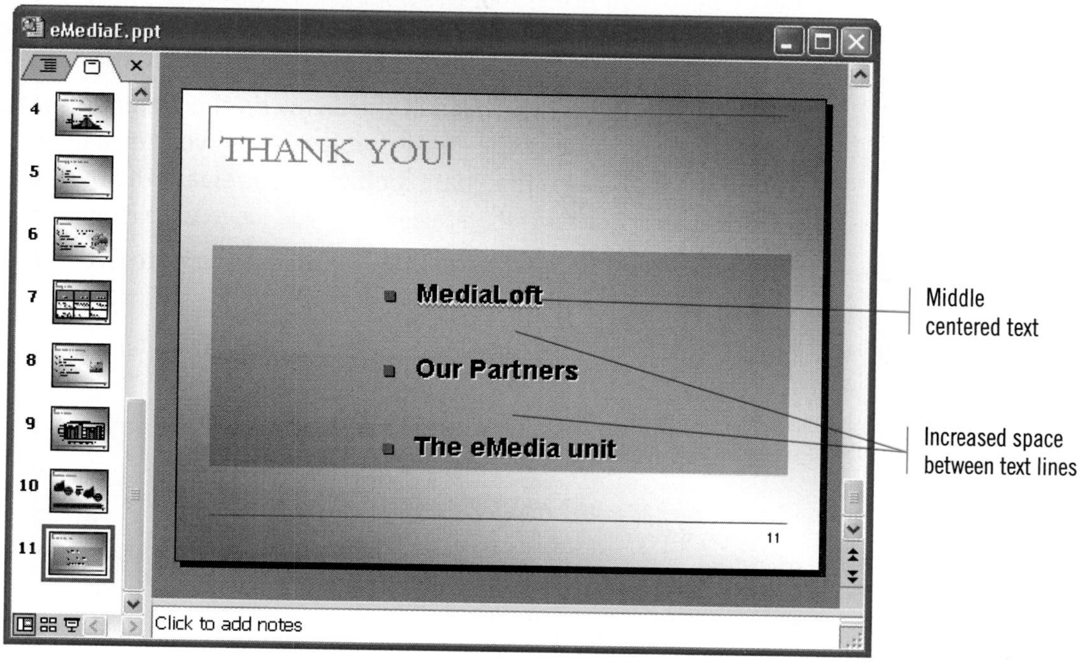

PowerPoint 2003

UNIT
E
PowerPoint 2003

Using Advanced Drawing Tools

PowerPoint has powerful tools on the AutoShapes menu to help you draw all types of shapes. The AutoShapes menu is on the Drawing toolbar. For example, the Curve tool allows you to create a free-form curved line, the Arc tool helps you draw smooth, curved lines and pie-shaped wedges, and the Connector line tool allows you to connect AutoShape objects with a line. Once you have drawn a shape, you can format and rearrange it to create the effect you want. As you work with different objects in PowerPoint there may be an occasion when you need to change the order of the objects to achieve a desired result. The Order command moves an object in front of or behind another object. The Connector line tool works great to complete a diagram on Slide 10.

STEPS

1. **Click the Slide 10 thumbnail in the Slides tab, click the AutoShapes menu button on the Drawing toolbar, point to Connectors, then click the Straight Arrow Connector button**
   The pointer changes to +.
2. **Move the + pointer to the right side of the Phase 2 object until it changes to ⌖ and blue dots appear around the object, then click the blue dot on the right side of the Phase 2 object**
   See Figure E-11. The blue dots are anchor points for the connector arrow.
3. **Move the + pointer to the left side of the diamond object when you see the left blue dot inside the pointer, then click the ⌖ pointer to place the right side of the connector arrow**
   A red circle appears at either end of the connector arrow, indicating that the arrow connects the two objects.
4. **Click the Line Style button on the Drawing toolbar, then click the 2¼ pt line style**
   The line style of the arrow connector changes to a thicker weight.
5. **Click the Arrow Style button on the Drawing toolbar, click More Arrows, then click the Colors and Lines tab in the Format AutoShape dialog box**
   The arrow would look better with a more distinct shape.
6. **Click the End size list arrow in the Arrows section, click the Arrow R Size 8 button (second button, last row), then click OK**
   The style of the arrow on the connector line changes to a more distinct style.
7. **Place the + pointer over the head of the arrow on the diamond shape, drag the connector arrow to the left side of the Phase 3 object, when you see a blue dot inside the ⌖ pointer on the left side of the Phase 3 object then release the mouse button**
   The arrow connector crosses over the diamond shape and connects the Phase 2 and Phase 3 objects.
8. **Click the Draw menu button on the Drawing toolbar, point to Order, then click Send to Back**
   The arrow connector line moves behind the diamond shape.
9. **Click in a blank area of the slide, then save the presentation**
   Compare your screen to Figure E-12.

TROUBLE

If a green box appears at either end of the line, drag the green square until the blue connection point on the object appears.

QUICK TIP

To change the default attributes of an AutoShape, format the AutoShape, select it, click the menu button on the Drawing toolbar, then click Set AutoShape Defaults.

FIGURE E-11: Slide showing Connector anchor points

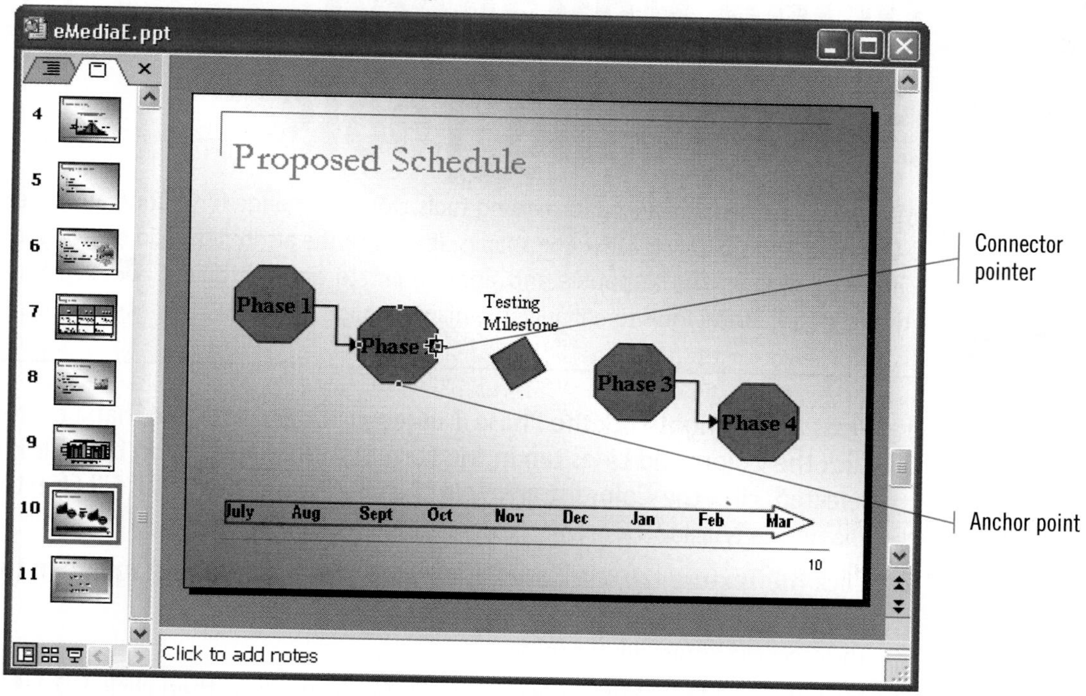

FIGURE E-12: Slide showing formatted connector arrow

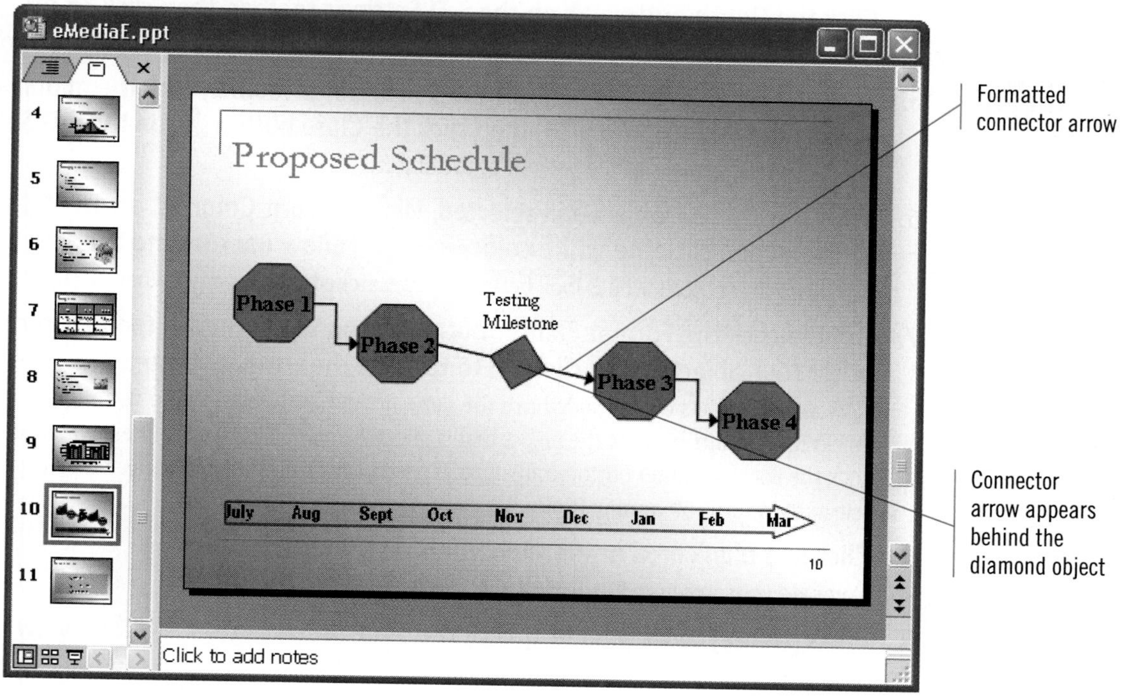

Clues to Use

Drawing a freeform shape

A freeform shape can consist of straight lines, freehand (or curved) lines, or a combination of the two. To draw a freeform shape, click the AutoShapes menu button, point to Lines, then click the Freeform button. Drag the pointer to draw the desired shape (the pointer changes to a pencil as you draw), then double-click when you are done. To draw a straight line with the Freeform tool, click where you want to begin the line, drag the pointer, then double-click to deactivate the Freeform tool. To edit a freeform object, right-click the object, then click Edit Points on the shortcut menu.

UNIT
E
PowerPoint 2003

Using Advanced Formatting Tools

With the PowerPoint advanced formatting tools, you can change formatting attributes such as fill texture, 3-D effects, and shadow for text and shapes. If you like the attributes of an object, you can use the Format Painter to pick up the attributes and apply them to another object. You decide to use the advanced formatting tools to enhance the diagram Slide 10.

STEPS

1. **Press [Shift], right-click the Phase 1 object, click Format AutoShape on the shortcut menu, click the Colors and Lines tab in the Format AutoShape dialog box if it is not already selected, click the Color list arrow in the Fill section, then click Fill Effects**

   The Fill Effects dialog box opens.

2. **Click the Texture tab, click the Paper bag thumbnail (second square in the fifth row), click OK, then click OK again**

   The paper bag texture fills the shape.

3. **Click the 3-D Style button on the Drawing toolbar, then click 3-D Settings**

   The 3-D Settings toolbar appears.

4. **Click the Depth button on the 3-D Settings toolbar, then click 36 pt**

   A 3-D effect is applied and the depth of the 3-D effect lengthens from the default of 0 points to 36 points.

5. **Click the Direction button on the 3-D Settings toolbar, click the middle effect in the top row, as shown in Figure E-13, then click the Close button on the 3-D Settings toolbar**

   The 3-D effect changes to the bottom of the object.

6. **With the Phase 1 object still selected, click the Font Color list arrow on the Drawing toolbar, then click the white color (labeled Follow Background Scheme Color)**

   The other four objects would look better if they matched the formatted Phase 1 object.

7. **Double-click the Format Painter button on the Standard toolbar, click each of the other four objects, then click to turn off the Format Painter**

   Now all the objects on the slide have the same fill and 3D effects. When you use the Format Painter tool, it "picks up" the attributes of the object that is selected and copies them to the next object that you click. If you click the Format Painter button only once, it pastes the attributes of the selected object to the next object you select, then turns off automatically.

8. **Click in a blank area of the slide, then save your changes**

   Compare your screen to Figure E-14.

9. **Press [Home] to view Slide 1, click the Slide Show button, then view the presentation**

QUICK TIP

The name of the texture appears below the samples.

QUICK TIP

When you click , you can click one of the 3-D styles on the shortcut menu. The default 3-D style is Style 1, the first style in the first row.

FIGURE E-13: Slide showing formatted 3-D object

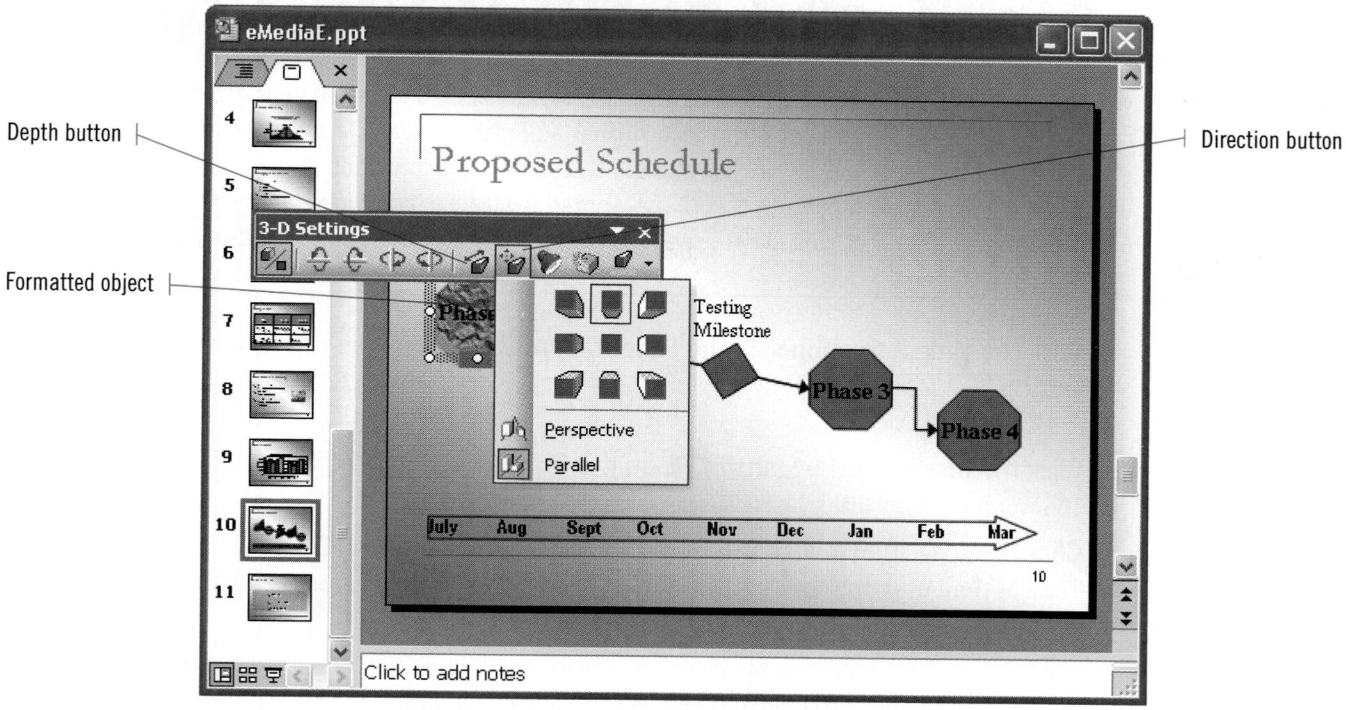

FIGURE E-14: Slide showing formatted objects

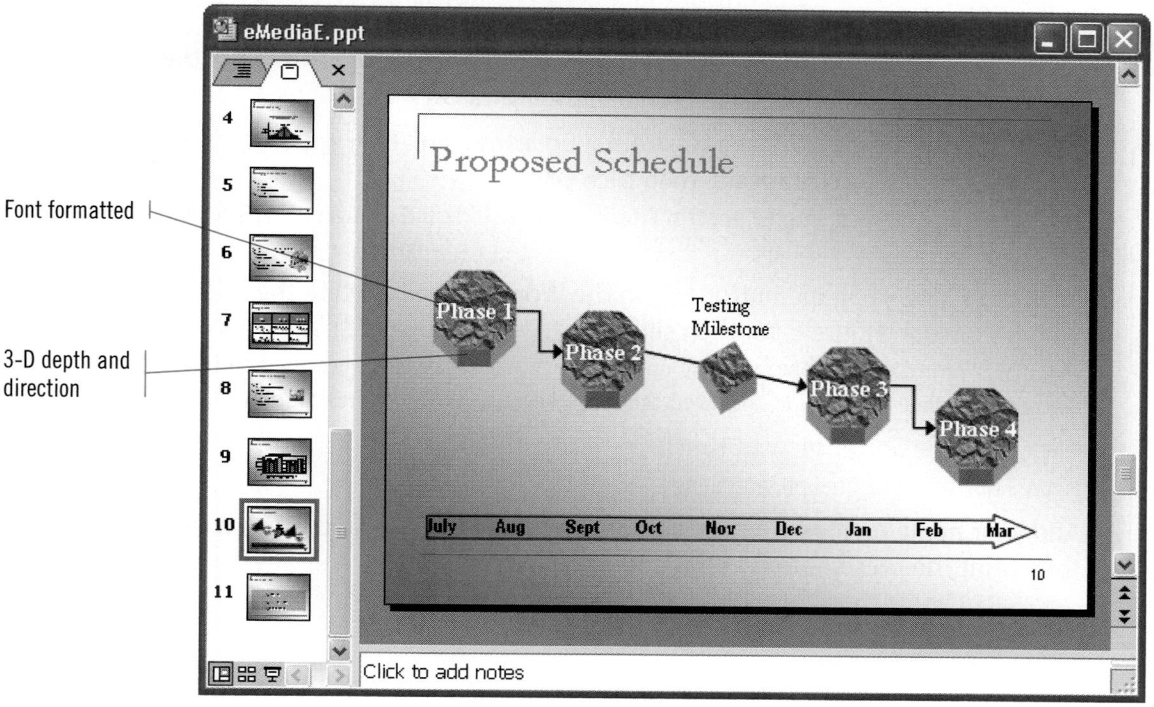

PowerPoint 2003

Clues to Use

Applying a color scheme to another presentation

If you develop a custom color scheme that you like, you can use the Format Painter tool to apply it to another presentation. To apply a color scheme from one presentation to another, open each presentation in Slide Sorter view, then use the Arrange All command on the Windows menu to arrange the Presentation windows side by side. Select a slide in the presentation with the color scheme you want to copy, double-click the Format Painter button on the Standard toolbar, then click each slide that you want to change in the other presentation.

Insert and Format WordArt

When you want to be artistic with text in PowerPoint, you can insert and format WordArt. Using WordArt you can apply a number of special effects to text, such as a predefined shape, a special shadow, or a stretched effect. A WordArt object is a drawn object and can be changed and formatted like any object that you create using the AutoShapes menu button. Use WordArt to create a simple logo for the new eMedia product. Because you want every slide to display the new WordArt object, you put the object on the Slide Master.

STEPS

1. **Click the** Slide 2 thumbnail **in the Slides tab, press [Shift], then click the** Normal View **button** ▣

 Slide Master view appears.

2. **Click the** Insert WordArt button ◢ **on the Drawing toolbar**

 The WordArt Gallery dialog box opens displaying all of the WordArt styles.

3. **Click the style shown in Figure E-15, then click** OK

 The Edit WordArt Text dialog box opens. The default font for the text is Times New Roman 36 pt.

4. **Type** eMedia, **then click** OK

 The WordArt object appears in the shape you selected using the default font in the middle of the slide. The WordArt toolbar, which you can use to format the WordArt object, also appears.

5. **Click the** Format WordArt button ▨ **on the WordArt toolbar**

 The Format WordArt dialog box opens. The Colors and Lines tab is selected.

6. **Click the** Color list arrow, **click** Fill Effects, **click the** Color 1 list arrow, **click the** red color **(labeled Follow Title Text Scheme Color), then click** OK

TROUBLE
If you can't choose the exact position settings listed in this step, select settings that are close.

7. **Click the** Position tab, **click the** Horizontal up arrow **until** 8.46 **appears, click the** Vertical down arrow **until** 0.26 **appears, then click** OK

 The WordArt object moves to the upper-right corner of the slide and changes color. The object would look a little better with a different shape.

8. **Click the** WordArt Shape button ▲ **on the WordArt toolbar, click the** Triangle Down shape **shown in Figure E-16, then click** ▣

 The new WordArt object appears in the upper-right corner of the slide. Because you inserted the WordArt object on the slide master slide, the object appears on every slide in the presentation, except the title slide.

9. **Click the** Slide Sorter View button ▦

 Figure E-17 shows the final presentation.

10. **Add your name to Slide 1 and as a footer to the notes and handouts, save your changes, then print the presentation as handouts (4 per page)**

FIGURE E-15: WordArt Gallery dialog box

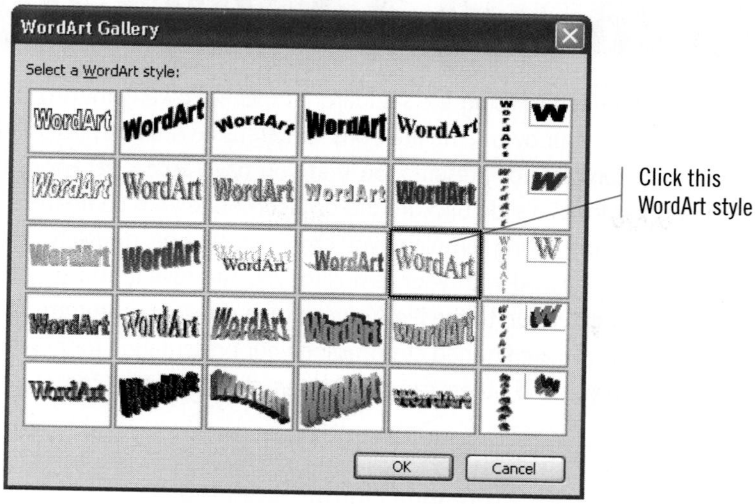

FIGURE E-16: WordArt Shape button

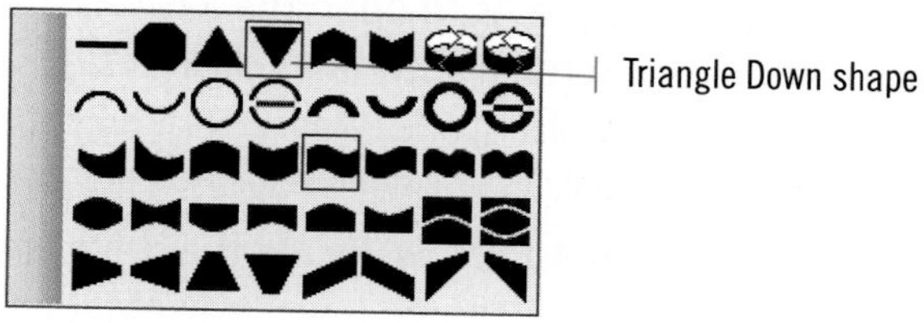

FIGURE E-17: Completed presentation in Slide Sorter view

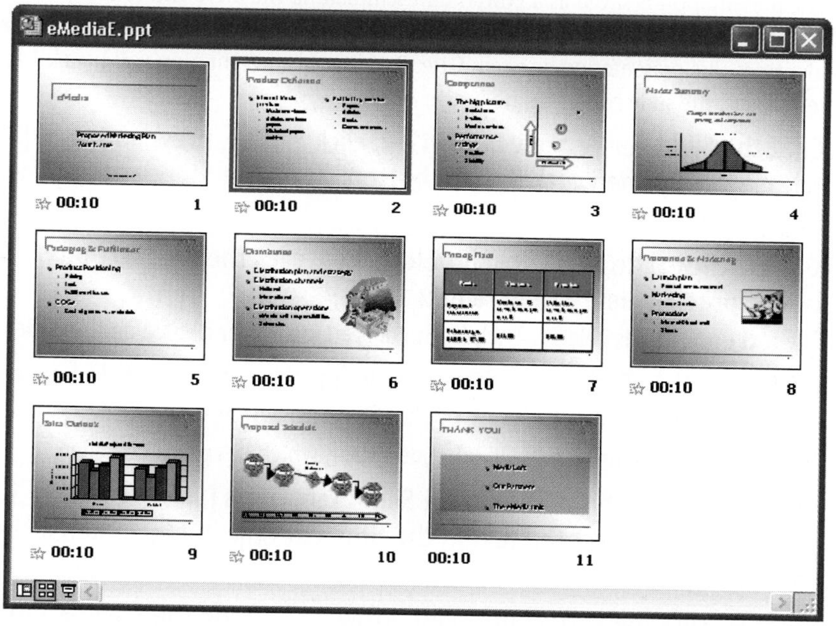

Clues to Use

Using the Style Checker

To help you correct common design mistakes, the Style Checker feature in PowerPoint reviews your presentation for typical errors such as incorrect font sizes, use of too many fonts, extra words, errors in punctuation, and other readability problems. When you activate the Style Checker, PowerPoint checks your presentation for style inconsistencies and flags potential problem areas with a lightbulb. If you see the lightbulb, click it to see a list of suggested options for handling the problem or improving the presentation. To use the Style Checker, click Tools on the menu bar, click Options, click the Spelling and Style tab, then click the Check style checkbox.

UNIT E

PowerPoint 2003

Creating a Template

You are not limited to using the standard templates PowerPoint provides or the ones you find on the Web. You can create your own template from scratch using a blank presentation, or you can modify any existing PowerPoint template or presentation that you have access to. For example, you might want to use your company's color as a slide background or incorporate your company's logo on the slides of a presentation. If you modify an existing template, you can keep, change, or delete any color, graphic, or font as necessary. When you are finished with your template, you can save it as a special template file in PowerPoint, which adds the .pot extension to the file. You can then use your customized template as a basis for new presentations. You are finished customizing your presentation for now. You want to save the presentation as a template so you and others can use this template for future company presentations.

STEPS

1. **Click the Slide 2 thumbnail in the Slides tab**
   Slide 2 appears in the Slide pane.
2. **Click File, click Save As to open the Save As dialog box, click the Save as type list arrow, click the down scroll arrow, then click Design Template (*.pot)**
   Because this is a template, PowerPoint automatically opens the Templates folder on your hard drive as shown in Figure E-18. Templates saved in this folder appear in the Slide Design task pane in PowerPoint.
3. **Click the Save in list arrow, locate the drive and folder where your Data Files are stored, drag to select the filename (currently eMediaE.pot) in the File name list box, type eMedia Template, then click Save**
   The presentation is saved as a PowerPoint template to the drive and folder where your Data Files are stored, and it appears in the PowerPoint window. Notice the .pot extension on the filename in the title bar, which identifies this presentation as a template. Because this presentation will be used as a template for other presentations, the slide content is no longer needed.
4. **Click the Slide Sorter View button, click Slide 3, press and hold [Shift], click Slide 11, release [Shift], then click the Cut button on the Standard toolbar**
   Slides 3 through 11 are deleted.
5. **Double-click Slide 2, press and hold [Shift], click the title text box, click both body text boxes, press [Delete], then release [Shift]**
   The text on Slide 2 is deleted. The placeholders are no longer needed on this slide.
6. **Click the Other Task Panes list arrow on the task pane title bar, click Slide Layout, then click the Blank content layout in the Content Layouts section**
   The slide layout changes to the Blank slide layout, which has no placeholders.
7. **Click the Slide 1 thumbnail in the Slides tab, press [Shift], click the Subtitle text object, press [Delete], select the text in the title text object, type eMedia Template, then save your changes**
8. **Click, click the Zoom button list arrow 100% on the Standard toolbar, then click 100%**
   Figure E-19 shows the final template presentation in Slide Sorter view.
9. **Save your changes, print the template presentation as handouts (2 per page), close the presentation, then exit PowerPoint**

FIGURE E-18: Save As dialog box showing Templates folder

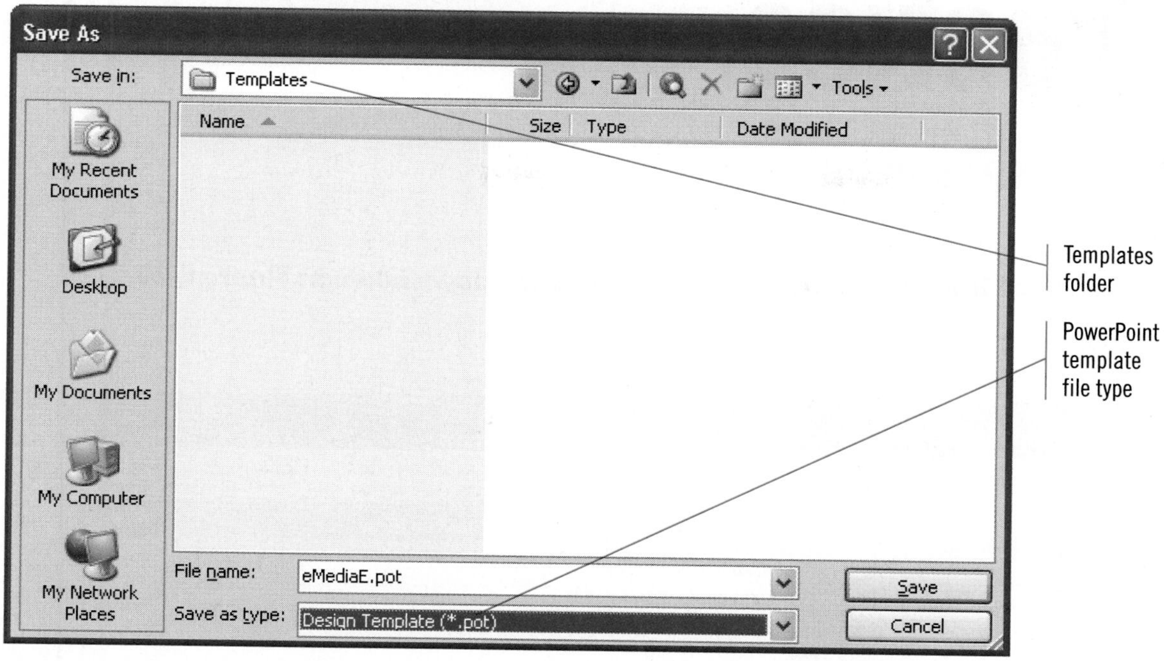

FIGURE E-19: Completed template presentation in Slide Sorter view

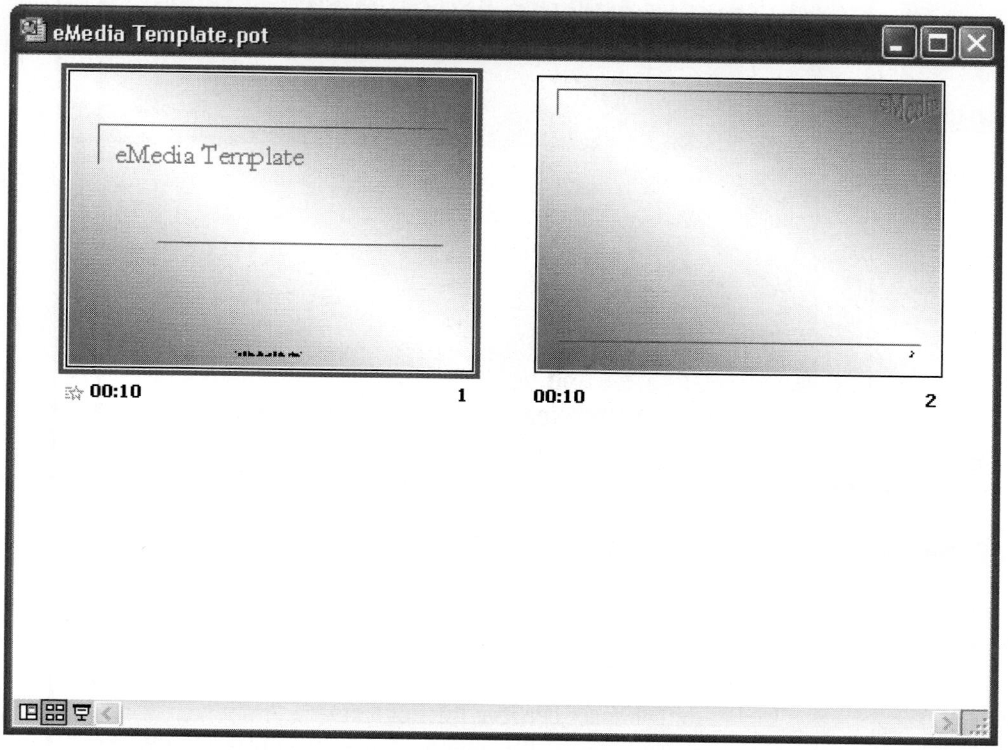

Clues to Use

Applying a template from another presentation

When you apply a design template from another presentation, you automatically apply the master layouts, fonts, and colors over the existing presentation's design template. To apply a template from another presentation, open the Slide Design task pane, then click the Browse hyperlink at the bottom of the pane. In the Apply Design Template dialog box, click All PowerPoint Files in the Files of type list box, then use the Look in list arrow to navigate to the presentation whose design you want to apply. (It does not have to be a template.) Click the presentation or template name, then click Apply.

PowerPoint 2003

Practice

▼ CONCEPTS REVIEW

Label each of the elements of the PowerPoint window shown in Figure E-20.

FIGURE E-20

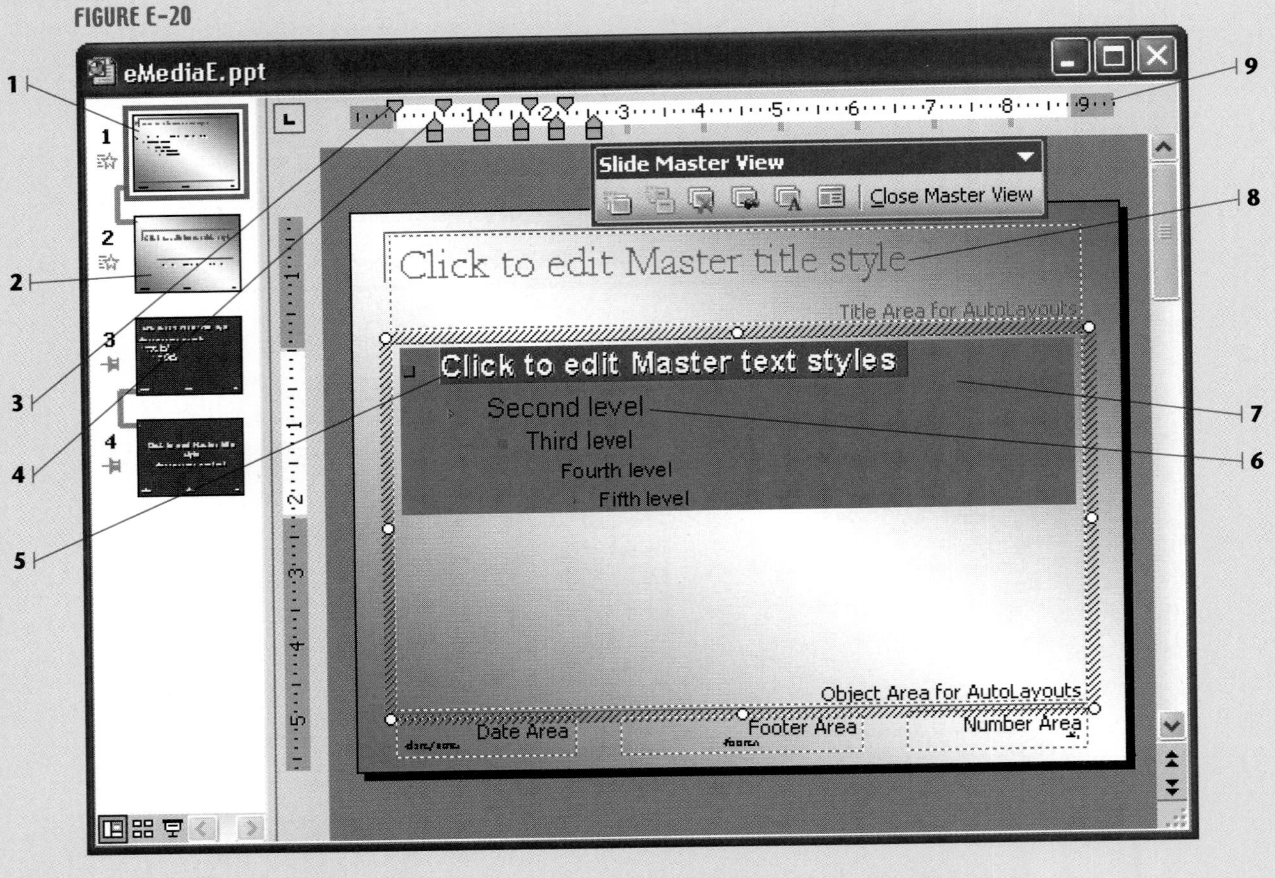

Match each of the terms with the statement that best describes its function.

10. Slide-title master pair
11. First line indent marker
12. Indent levels
13. Exception
14. Leading
15. Hanging indent

a. Controls the position of the first line of text in an indent level
b. The first line of text begins to the left of subsequent lines of text
c. The slide master and title master slides shown in Slide Master view
d. The space between lines of text
e. The five levels of text in a master text placeholder
f. A format change that is different from the slide master

Select the best answer from the list of choices.

16. What does the Slide Master view do in PowerPoint?

- **a.** Places figures that are used on the slides of the presentation.
- **b.** Stores information about the design template, text placeholders, and the color scheme.
- **c.** Saves a presentation to the Web.
- **d.** Previews a presentation before printing.

17. A background item on the slide master:

- **a.** Changes all views of your presentation.
- **b.** Is visible when you print handouts.
- **c.** Is a simple way to place an object on every slide of your presentation.
- **d.** Does not affect the slides of your presentation.

18. The small triangles that represent the position of each indent level in a text placeholder are:

- **a.** Indent markers.
- **b.** Indent levels.
- **c.** Ruler marks.
- **d.** Tabs.

19. Text anchor allows you to adjust the:

- **a.** Vertical space between lines of text.
- **b.** The distance between text objects.
- **c.** The diagonal space between letters.
- **d.** Text position within a text object.

20. The Format Painter button:

- **a.** Allows you to change the type of AutoShape.
- **b.** Is the feature you use to paint objects in PowerPoint.
- **c.** Changes the order of AutoShapes on a slide.
- **d.** Picks up and applies formatting attributes from one object or slide to another.

21. In PowerPoint, tabs:

- **a.** Have symbols for top and bottom tabs.
- **b.** Determine the location of margins.
- **c.** Can be aligned on the left, right, or center of a character or on a decimal.
- **d.** Can be only left- or center-aligned.

▼ SKILLS REVIEW

1. Format Master text.

- **a.** Start PowerPoint and open the presentation PPT E-2.ppt, then save it as **BookSource Report** to the drive and folder where your Data Files are stored.
- **b.** Go to Slide 2, switch to Slide Master view, then make the first-level bulleted item in the Master text placeholder bold.
- **c.** Change the bullet symbol of the first-level bullet to a character bullet. In Wingdings, select Character code 38, the seventh bullet from the left in the first row.
- **d.** Use the Bullets and Numbering dialog box to set the size of the bullet to 75% of the text.
- **e.** Change the bullet color to the yellow color (far-right color).
- **f.** Change the bullet symbol color of the second indent level to dark blue (third from left).
- **g.** Take the shadow attribute off the second-level bulleted item and change its font to Arial.
- **h.** Save the presentation.

2. Change Master text indents.
   a. Display the rulers.
   b. Move the left indent marker of the first-level bullet to just beyond the ½" mark and the second-level bullet to 1⅛".
   c. Hide the rulers, then save the presentation. Compare your screen to Figure E-21.
   d. Switch to Normal view.

FIGURE E-21

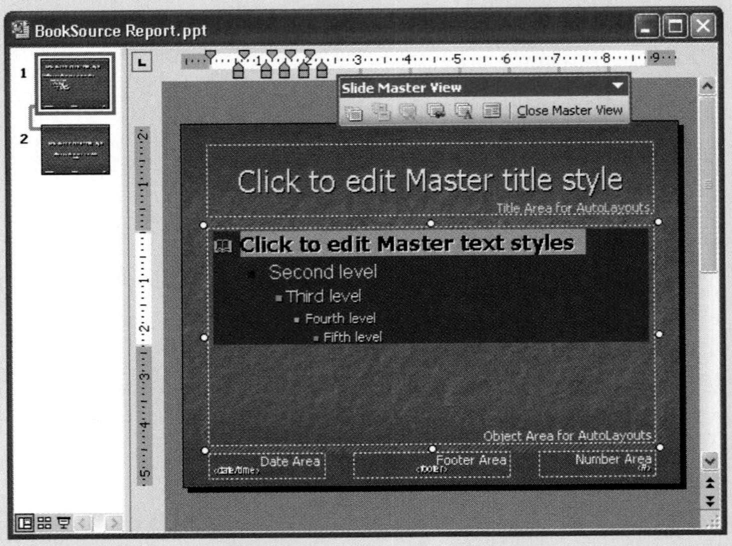

3. Adjust text objects.
   a. Press [Shift], right-click anywhere in the body text object on Slide 2, then click Format Placeholder on the shortcut menu.
   b. Click the Text Box tab.
   c. Set the text anchor point to Top Centered.
   d. Adjust the internal margin on the left and right sides to 0.5 and preview your change.
   e. Select the Resize AutoShape to fit text check box, preview it, and click OK.
   f. Select the entire text object. (*Hint*: Press [Shift] while clicking the object.)
   g. Change the line spacing to 0.75 lines, preview it, then click OK.
   h. Move the text object up and to the left about ½".
   i. Save your changes.

4. Use advanced drawing tools.
   a. Go to Slide 4.
   b. Use the Elbow Connector to connect the left corner of the Warehouse diamond to the top corner of the Regional Warehouse diamond.
   c. Use the Straight Connector to connect the right side of the Regional Warehouse diamond to the left side of the Individual Stores diamond.
   d. Use the Elbow Connector to connect the top corner of the Individual Stores diamond to the right corner of the Warehouse diamond.
   e. Select all three of the connector lines, make them 3 points wide, then deselect them.
   f. Change the dash style of the connector line connecting the Regional Warehouse diamond to the Individual Stores diamond to the Square Dot, dashed line style.
   g. Change the arrow style of the two elbow connector lines to Arrow Style 10.
   h. Deselect all objects, then save your changes.

5. Use advanced formatting tools.
   a. Go to Slide 1.
   b. Select the entire text object in the lower-right corner of the slide.
   c. Use the Texture tab in the Fill Effects dialog box to apply the White Marble texture to the object. (*Hint*: Read the description of the selected texture in the box under the textures.)
   d. Change the font to 20 pt. Arial.
   e. Double-click the Format Painter to pick up the format of the selected text box on the title slide and apply it to each of the diamond objects on Slide 4, then deselect the Format Painter and all objects.
   f. Use the 3-D Style button to apply 3-D Style 7 to the objects on Slide 4.
   g. Click the 3-D Color list arrow on the 3-D Settings toolbar, then click the blue color (Follow Accent Scheme Color).
   h. Deselect all objects, close the 3-D Settings toolbar, then save your changes.

▼ SKILLS REVIEW (CONTINUED)

6. Insert and format WordArt.

- **a.** Go to Slide 5.
- **b.** Create a new slide, then apply the Blank slide layout to the new slide.
- **c.** Create a WordArt object. In the WordArt Gallery dialog box, select the fifth style in the third column.
- **d.** Type the text, **Moving Toward Excellence**.
- **e.** Drag the bottom right sizing handle of the WordArt object at least an inch.
- **f.** Change the shape of the WordArt object to the Curve Down shape.
- **g.** Drag the WordArt object to the middle of the slide, then save your changes.
- **h.** View the presentation in Slide Sorter view.
- **i.** Add your name to the notes and handouts footer, print the presentation as Handouts, six slides per page.

7. Create a template.

- **a.** Open the Save As dialog box, then save the presentation as a Design Template (*.pot), named **BookSource Template** to the drive and folder where your Data Files are stored.
- **b.** Delete Slides 3, 4, 5, and 6, delete all the text in the text objects on Slide 2, then delete the clip art on Slide 2.
- **c.** Go to Slide 1, delete the text in the Subtitle text object, then type **BookSource Template** in the title text object in place of the current text.
- **d.** Save the presentation template, then print the presentation as handouts, two slides per page.
- **e.** Close the presentation and exit PowerPoint.

▼ INDEPENDENT CHALLENGE 1

You are the finance director at ZIPPO Records in Los Angeles, CA. ZIPPO Records specializes in alternative music, Rap, and Hip Hop. As a growing record company, your business is looking for investment capital to expand its business markets and increase sales. It is your responsibility to develop the outline and basic look for a standard presentation that the president can present to various investors.

You will complete an outline and choose a custom background for the presentation. You'll need to create a presentation consisting of at least six slides. Assume the following about ZIPPO Records:

- ZIPPO Records has been in business for 12 years.
- ZIPPO Records currently has 32 recording contracts. ZIPPO wants to double that during the next two years.
- ZIPPO Records has five superstar recording groups, including the groups Jam It and The Skunk.

- **a.** Open the file PPT E-3.ppt from the drive and folder where your Data Files are stored, then save it as **ZIPPO** to the location where your Data Files are stored.
- **b.** Enter text into the title and main text placeholders of the slides.
- **c.** Format the Master text placeholder by changing master text indents and bullet styles.
- **d.** Add clip art and format the presentation using PowerPoint formatting tools.
- **e.** Use advanced drawing and formatting tools to create a unique look.
- **f.** Create one slide that has at least two AutoShapes connected by connectors.
- **g.** Include WordArt in one slide.
- **h.** Add your name to the notes and handouts footer, save the presentation, then print the slides of your final presentation as handouts in pure black and white.
- **i.** View the presentation in Slide Show view, then close the presentation and exit PowerPoint.

▼ INDEPENDENT CHALLENGE 2

You are the owner of Down Under Catering in Brisbane, Queensland, Australia. You have built your business on private parties, wedding receptions, and special events over the last five years. To expand, you decide to cater to the business community by offering executive meals and business luncheons. Use PowerPoint to develop a presentation that you can use to gain corporate catering accounts.

Create an outline and modify the look of a presentation. You will create your own material to complete the slides of the presentation. Assume the following about Down Under:

- Down Under Catering has 15 full-time employees and 20 part-time or on-call staff.
- Down Under Catering handles catering jobs up to 500 people.
- Down Under Catering is a full-service catering business providing cost estimates, setup, complete preparation, service personnel, and cleanup.

a. Open the file PPT E-4.ppt from the drive and folder where your Data Files are stored, then save it as **DUCatering**.
b. Switch to the Outline tab and create a presentation outline. Add your name to the notes and handout footer.
c. Customize your presentation by formatting the Slide Master.
d. Search PowerPoint clip art and add a koala bear to both the slide master and the title master. Format the clip art as necessary.
e. Use the PowerPoint advanced drawing and formatting tools to give your presentation a unique look. Be sure to use 3-D effects, and Fill Effects.
f. Switch to the last slide and change the text anchor and line spacing to create the best look.
g. Add and format a WordArt object.
h. Add transitions and animation effects.
i. Save and print the presentation as handouts, two slides per page.
j. View the presentation in Slide Show view.

Advanced Challenge Exercise

ACE

- Save this presentation as a template, name the template **Catering Template**, then save it to the drive and folder where your Data Files are stored.
- Delete all the slides except the first slide and the last slide.
- Add two additional design templates (title-master pairs) to the template.
- Print the slides of your final template.

k. Close the presentation template and exit PowerPoint.

▼ INDEPENDENT CHALLENGE 3

You are a computer game designer for eNetGames, an Internet interactive game developer. One of your jobs is to develop new interactive game concepts and present the information at a company meeting. Develop a 10- to 15-slide presentation that promotes two of the new interactive games concepts you've developed. Use PowerPoint clip art and shapes to enhance your slides. Use a PowerPoint template, design one of your own, or copy one from another presentation. Use the following game ideas in your presentation or create two of your own.

- **Space Raiders** is an interactive game that puts you in one of four different futuristic situations, where you are a space law enforcement officer trying to prevent an evil villain from destroying Earth.
- **SUB Command** is an adventure game in which you are a submarine commander during the Cold War trying to prevent a nuclear holocaust between the United States and the Soviet Union. Assume that there are four different game scenarios.

Create your own information, but assume the following:

- The product is designed for adults and children ages 13 and up.
- The cost of product development is estimated to be $300,000.
- Development time is three months.

a. Open a new presentation and save it as **eNetGames** to the drive and folder where your Data Files are stored.
b. Plan the story line of how the software was developed using five or more slides. Plan the beginning and ending slides. What do you want your audience to know about the product idea?

▼ INDEPENDENT CHALLENGE 3 (CONTINUED)

c. Use clip art and shapes to enhance the presentation. Change the bullet and text formatting in the Master text and title placeholders to fit the subject matter.

d. Use advanced drawing and formatting tools to create a unique look.

e. Add your name to the notes and handouts footer, then save the presentation.

Advanced Challenge Exercise

ACE

- Open the Slide Design task pane, click Browse at the bottom of the task pane, then locate where your Data Files are stored for this unit.
- Locate the file eMedia Template.pot, then click Apply.
- Click Yes in the dialog box that opens to place all of the templates in the presentation.
- Go to the Slide Master view, locate the eMedia logo on the slide master slide, then delete it.

f. Print the final presentation as handouts in pure black and white.

g. View the presentation Slide Show view, close the presentation, and exit PowerPoint.

E-QUEST

▼ INDEPENDENT CHALLENGE 4

You are the travel coordinator for Mediaquest Inc., a large graphic multimedia development company in Seattle, WA. One of the benefits Mediaquest offers its employees is the option to vacation at a destination planned by the company. Your job is to find a reasonable vacation spot and then negotiate with travel companies for reduced group rates that are charged to Mediaquest employees if they choose to utilize the benefit. Once you negotiate a contract with a travel organization, you create a brief presentation that outlines the vacation benefit packages for the employees.

Plan and create an 8- to 10-slide presentation that details the vacation package for the current year. Develop your own content, but assume the following:

- The vacation package is a 7-day Alaskan cruise or a 7-day Mexican cruise.
- Air travel originates from the Seattle/Tacoma Airport (SeaTac).
- Cruises can be booked on one of two different cruise lines.
- The price is 30% off the listed price based on double occupancy.
- Mediaquest employees can book a cruise anytime during the current year.

You'll need to find the following information on the Web:

- Price and schedule information. (*Hint*: Remember the price you list in the presentation is 30% lower than the listed price you find on the Internet.)
- A list of ships with a brief description of at least one ship from each cruise line.
- Ports of call for one Mexican cruise and one Alaskan cruise.

a. Open a new presentation, and save it as **Mediaquest** to the location where your Data Files are stored.

b. Add your name as the footer on all slides and handouts.

c. Connect to the Internet, then use a search engine to locate Web sites that have information on Mexican and Alaskan cruises.

d. Review at least two Web sites that contain information about Mexican cruises and Alaskan cruises. Print the Home pages of the Web sites you use to gather data for your presentation.

e. Decide on two cruise lines to use in your presentation, then create slides that present the information.

f. Use clip art and shapes to enhance the presentation. Change the bullet and text formatting in the Master text and title placeholders to fit the subject matter.

g. Apply a template to the presentation and customize the slide background appropriately.

h. Use advanced drawing and formatting tools to create a unique look.

i. Use text formatting as necessary to make text visible and help emphasize important points.

j. Spell check the presentation, view the final presentation in Slide Show view, then save the final version.

k. Print the slides and handouts, then close the presentation and exit PowerPoint.

▼ VISUAL WORKSHOP

Create two slides that look like the examples in Figures E-22 and E-23. Be sure to use connector lines. Add your name to the handout footer, then save the presentation as **Product**. Print the Slide view of the presentation. Submit the final presentation as printed handouts.

FIGURE E-22

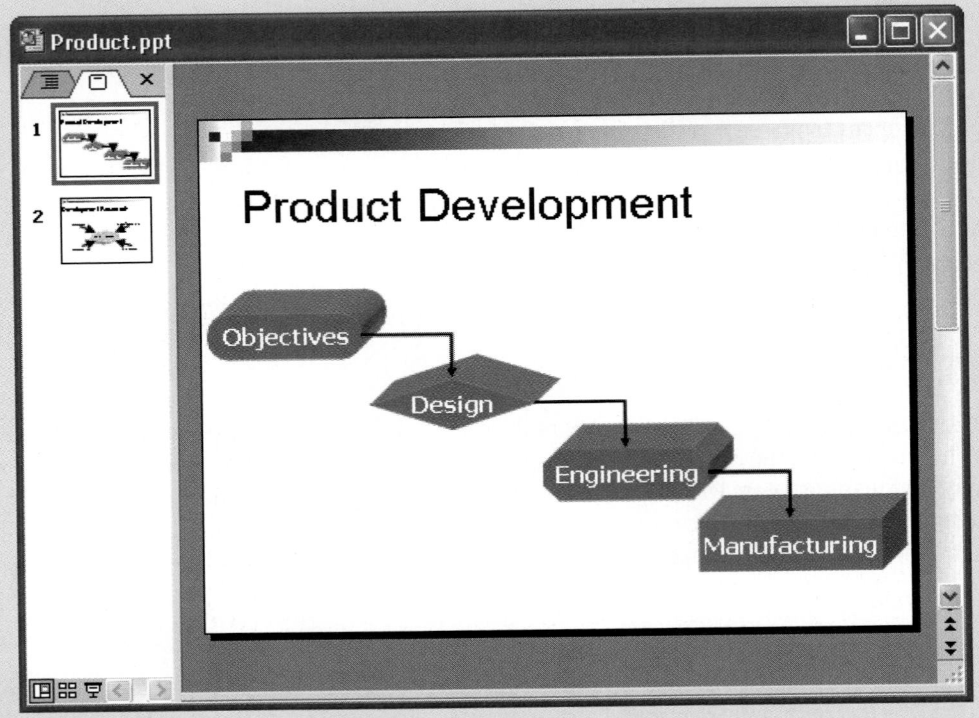

FIGURE E-23

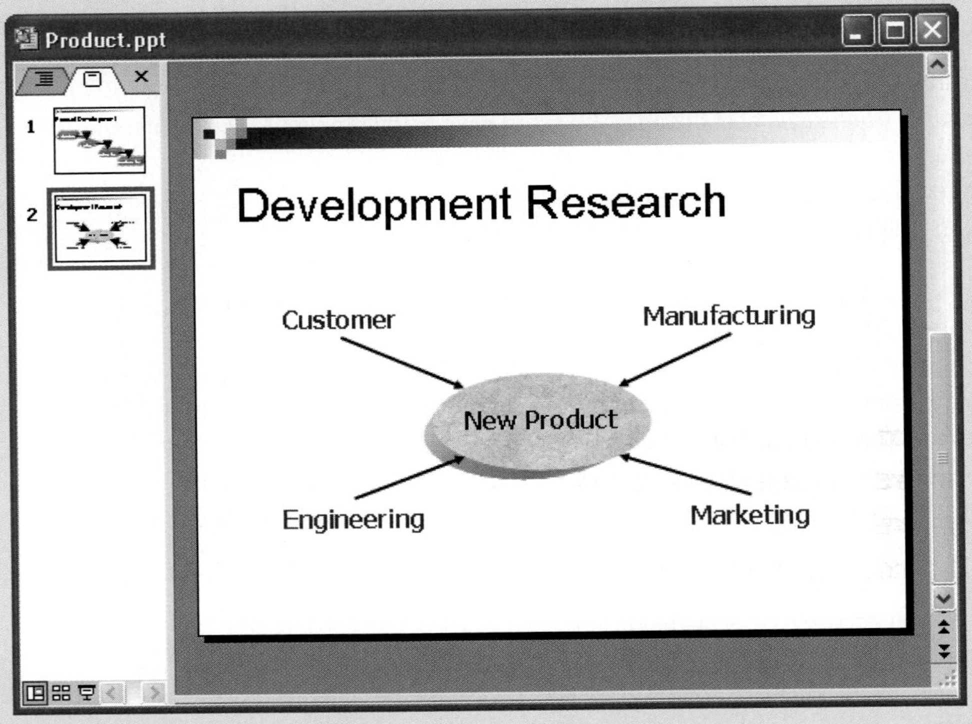

UNIT F

PowerPoint 2003

Enhancing Charts

OBJECTIVES

- Insert data from a file into a datasheet
- Format a datasheet
- Change the chart type
- Change chart options
- Work with chart elements
- Animate charts and add sound
- Embed an organization chart
- Modify an organization chart

If you have a SAM user profile, you may have access to hands-on instruction, practice, and assessment of the skills covered in this unit. Log in to your SAM account and go to your assignments page to see what your instructor has assigned.

A PowerPoint presentation is first and foremost a visual communication tool. Slides that deliver information with relevant graphics have a more lasting impact than slides with plain text. Graphs and charts often communicate information more effectively than words alone. Microsoft Graph and Microsoft Organization Chart are built-in PowerPoint programs that allow you to easily create and embed graphs and charts in your presentation. In this unit, you update the data and enhance the appearance of a Microsoft Graph chart and then you create and format an organization chart showing the management structure of the eMedia division.

UNIT F

PowerPoint 2003

Inserting Data from a File into a Datasheet

With Microsoft Graph, you can enter your own data into a datasheet using the keyboard, or you can import existing data from a spreadsheet file that was created in a program like Microsoft Excel. The Accounting Department just gave you an updated sales projection spreadsheet in an Excel file. You need to insert this updated data into the chart on Slide 11 of the eMedia presentation. To do this, you open Microsoft Graph and import the data from Excel into the presentation.

STEPS

1. **Start PowerPoint, open the presentation PPT F-1.ppt from the drive and folder where your Data Files are stored, then save the presentation as eMediaF**
2. **Click View on the menu bar, click Task Pane, click Window on the menu bar, then click Arrange All**

   Your screen now matches the figures in this book.
3. **Click the Slide 11 thumbnail in the Slides tab, then double-click the chart object on the slide in the Slide pane**

   When you double-click an embedded object in PowerPoint, the object opens in the program in which the object was created. The Graph chart and datasheet open and the Graph menu bar and toolbars are now displayed. You can replace the data in the Graph datasheet with data that is in an Excel worksheet.
4. **Click the Dept. cell in the datasheet (first cell, first column)**

   Clicking a cell identifies where the imported data begins in the datasheet.
5. **Click the Import File button on the Graph Standard toolbar**

   The Import File dialog box opens.
6. **Navigate to the drive and folder where your Data Files are stored, click PPT F-2.xls, then click Open**

   Excel files have an .xls file extension. The Import Data Options dialog box opens. Because you want to import the entire sheet and overwrite the existing cells, all the options are correctly specified.
7. **Click OK**

   The chart changes to reflect the new data you imported into the datasheet. Compare your screen to Figure F-1. Notice the column headings, the gray boxes along the top of the datasheet, now show lettered headings. The row headings, the gray boxes along the left side of the datasheet, now show numbered headings. Spreadsheets identify columns with letters and rows with numbers.
8. **Double-click the column D column heading**

   The data in column D is grayed out, indicating that it is excluded from the datasheet and will not appear in the chart. See Figure F-2.
9. **Click the Save button on the Graph Standard toolbar**

TROUBLE

If you don't see on the Standard toolbar, click a Toolbar Options button on a toolbar to locate buttons that are not visible on your toolbar.

QUICK TIP

To include data that you've previously excluded, double-click the control box again.

FIGURE F-1: Datasheet showing imported data

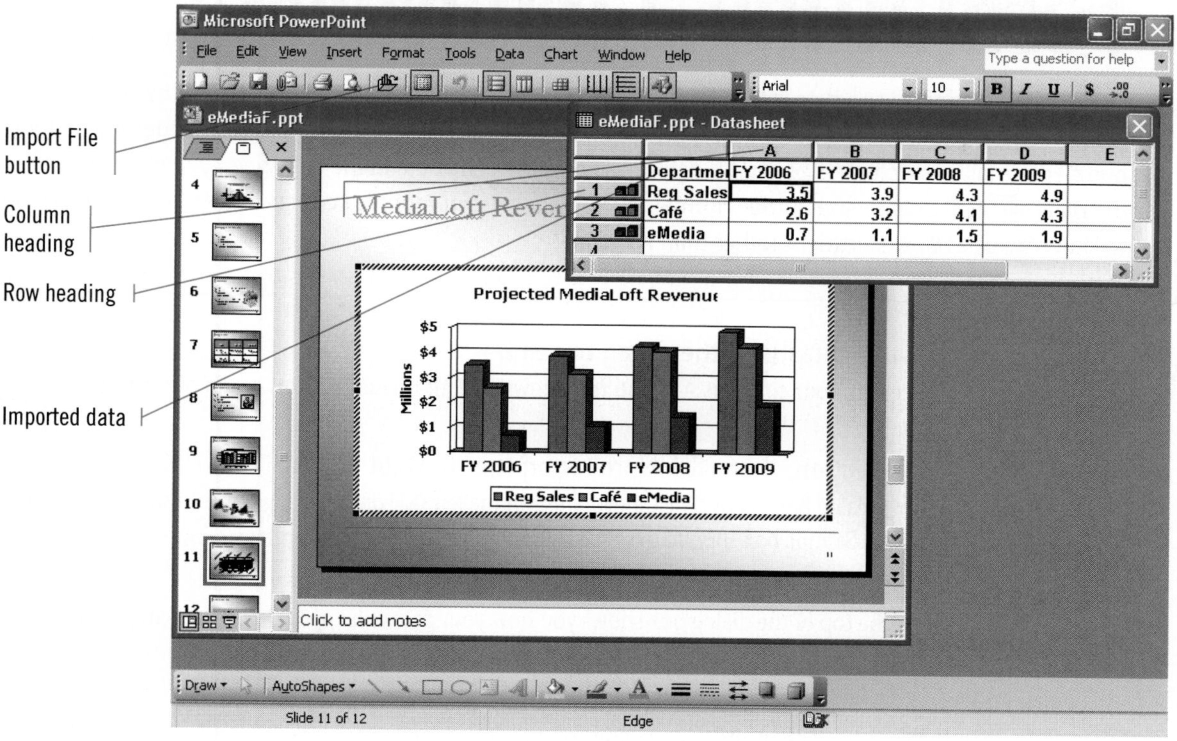

FIGURE F-2: Datasheet showing excluded column

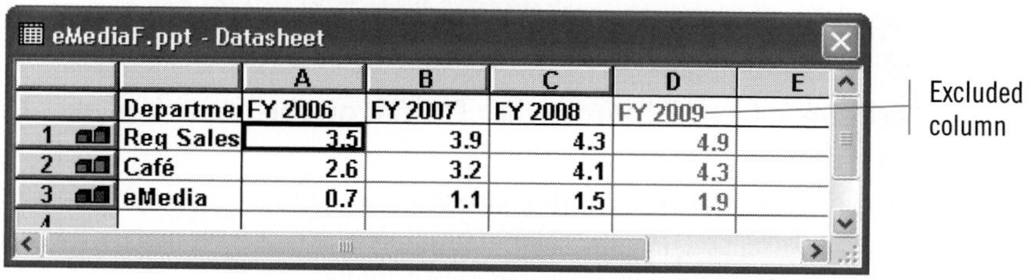

Clues to Use

Data series and data series markers

Each column or row of data in the datasheet is called a data series. Each data series has corresponding data series markers in the chart, which are graphical representations such as bars, columns, or pie wedges. Figure F-3 shows how each number in the eMedia data series appears in the chart. Notice the correlation between the data in the third row of the datasheet and the data series markers in the chart.

FIGURE F-3: Graph chart and datasheet

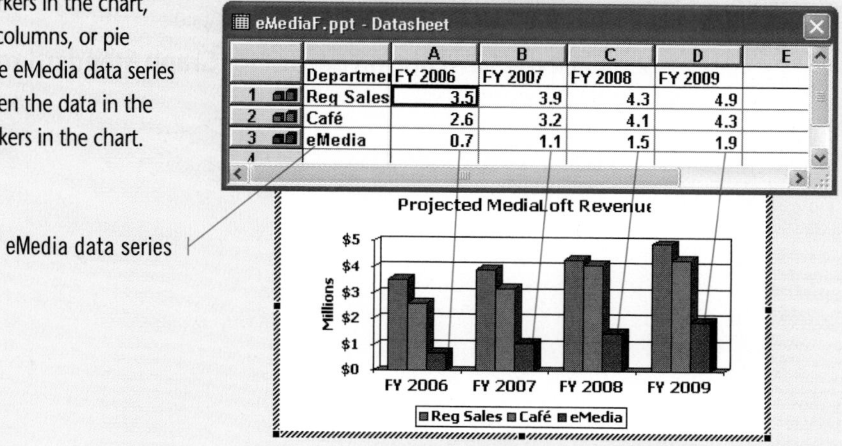

UNIT F

PowerPoint 2003

Formatting a Datasheet

Once you've imported the data from another file, it can be helpful to modify and format the datasheet to make your data easier to view and use. With Graph, you can make simple formatting changes to the font, number format, and column size in your datasheet. To format the data in the datasheet, you must first select the data. Change the number format to show the sales numbers as currency, then change the chart to show the sales by department rather than by year.

STEPS

1. **Click cell A1 in the datasheet, then drag to cell D3**
   You selected the cells in four columns A-D and three rows 1-3. All the data in this group of continuous cells, or range, is selected.
2. **Right-click the selection, then click Number on the shortcut menu**
   The Format Number dialog box opens. The Category list on the left side of the dialog box indicates the available format categories. The Sample box shows an example of the currently selected format.
3. **Click Currency in the Category list**
   The Sample box at the top of the dialog box shows you how your data will appear in the currency format with a dollar sign and two decimal places. See Figure F-4.
4. **Click OK**
   The data in the datasheet and in the chart change to the currency format. The numbers represent millions of dollars, so the number of digits after the decimal place needs to be adjusted.
5. **Click Format on the menu bar, click Number, click the Decimal places down arrow once to display 1, click OK, then click anywhere in the datasheet**
   The datasheet columns can be adjusted to better fit the data.
6. **Click the Select All button, click Format on the menu bar, click Column Width, then click Best Fit**
   The datasheet looks better with the columns containing the numbers narrowed and the first column wide enough to accommodate the column heading. The Best Fit command automatically resizes the selected column widths to fit the widest label in each column.
7. **Click any cell in the datasheet, then click the By Column button on the Graph Standard toolbar**
   The chart is more helpful showing the sales figures along the Value axis, in a series by column. The icons now appear in the column headings in the datasheet to indicate that the fiscal year in the columns is now graphed in the chart. The column headings now appear in the legend. Compare your datasheet to Figure F-5.
8. **Click the Close button in the datasheet**
   The datasheet closes, but Graph is still open.
9. **Click the Save button on the Graph Standard toolbar**

QUICK TIP

To quickly change the number format to Currency, click the Currency Style button $ on the Graph Formatting toolbar.

QUICK TIP

To quickly adjust the column width to fit the widest cell of data in a column, double-click the border to the right of the column heading box.

FIGURE F-4: Format Number dialog box

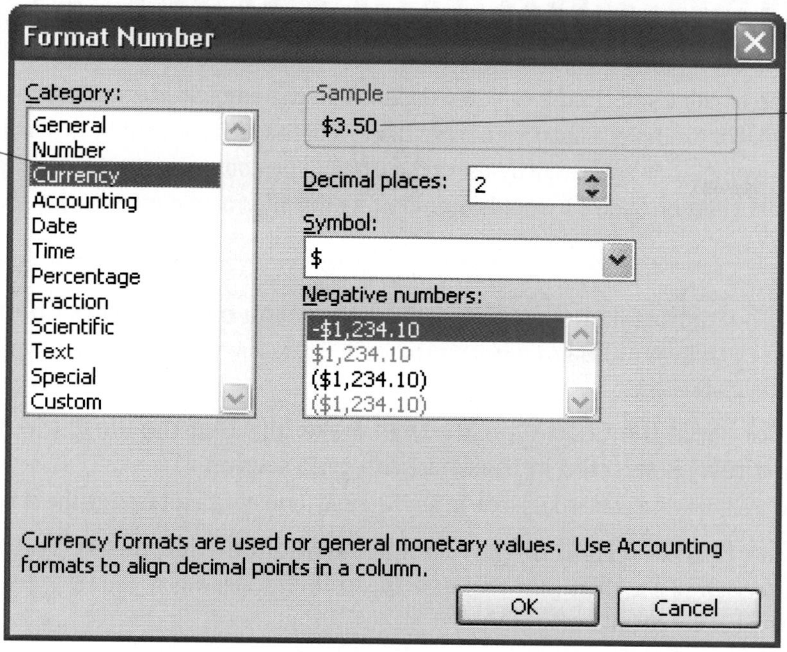

FIGURE F-5: Datasheet showing formatted data

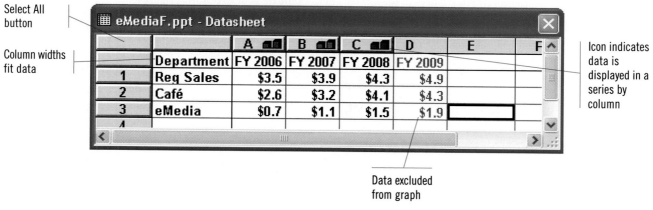

PowerPoint 2003

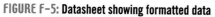

Clues to Use

Formatting datasheets and charts

You can format data in both datasheets and in charts created by Graph. Sometimes it's easier to view the numbers in the datasheet after they have been formatted; other times, you may want to manipulate the numbers after they have been placed into a chart to get a better picture. After you've formatted the data in the datasheet, the formatting changes will be reflected in the chart; however, formatting changes made to the data in the chart will not be reflected in the datasheet.

UNIT F

PowerPoint 2003

Changing the Chart Type

The type of chart you choose typically depends on the amount of information you have and how it's best depicted. For example, a chart with more than six data series does not fit well in a pie chart. You can change a chart type quickly and easily by using the Chart Type command on the Chart menu. You decide that a bar chart on Slide 11 would communicate the information more clearly than a column chart.

STEPS

1. **With Graph still open, click Chart on the menu bar, then click Chart Type**
   The Chart Type dialog box opens, as shown in Figure F-6. The current chart type is a clustered column chart with a 3-D effect.
2. **Click Bar in the Chart type list, then make sure that the Clustered Bar subtype (first chart, first row) is selected in the Chart sub-type section**
   To see how your data would look in any selected format without closing the dialog box, you can preview it.
3. **Click Press and Hold to View Sample and hold the left mouse button**
   A preview of the chart with your data appears in the area where the sub-types had been listed. This chart would look better if it were 3-D.
4. **Release the left mouse button, then click the Clustered Bar with a 3-D visual effect sub-type in the Chart sub-type section (first chart, second row)**
   The box below the sub-type section shows that you have selected a clustered bar with a 3-D visual effect.
5. **Click Press and Hold to View Sample and hold the left mouse button**
   The preview shows a 3-D version of the column chart.
6. **Release the left mouse button, then click OK**
   The chart type changes to the 3-D bar chart. Compare your screen with Figure F-7.
7. **Click the Save button on the Graph Standard toolbar**

QUICK TIP

To quickly change the chart type, click the Chart Type button on the Graph Standard toolbar.

FIGURE F-6: Chart Type dialog box

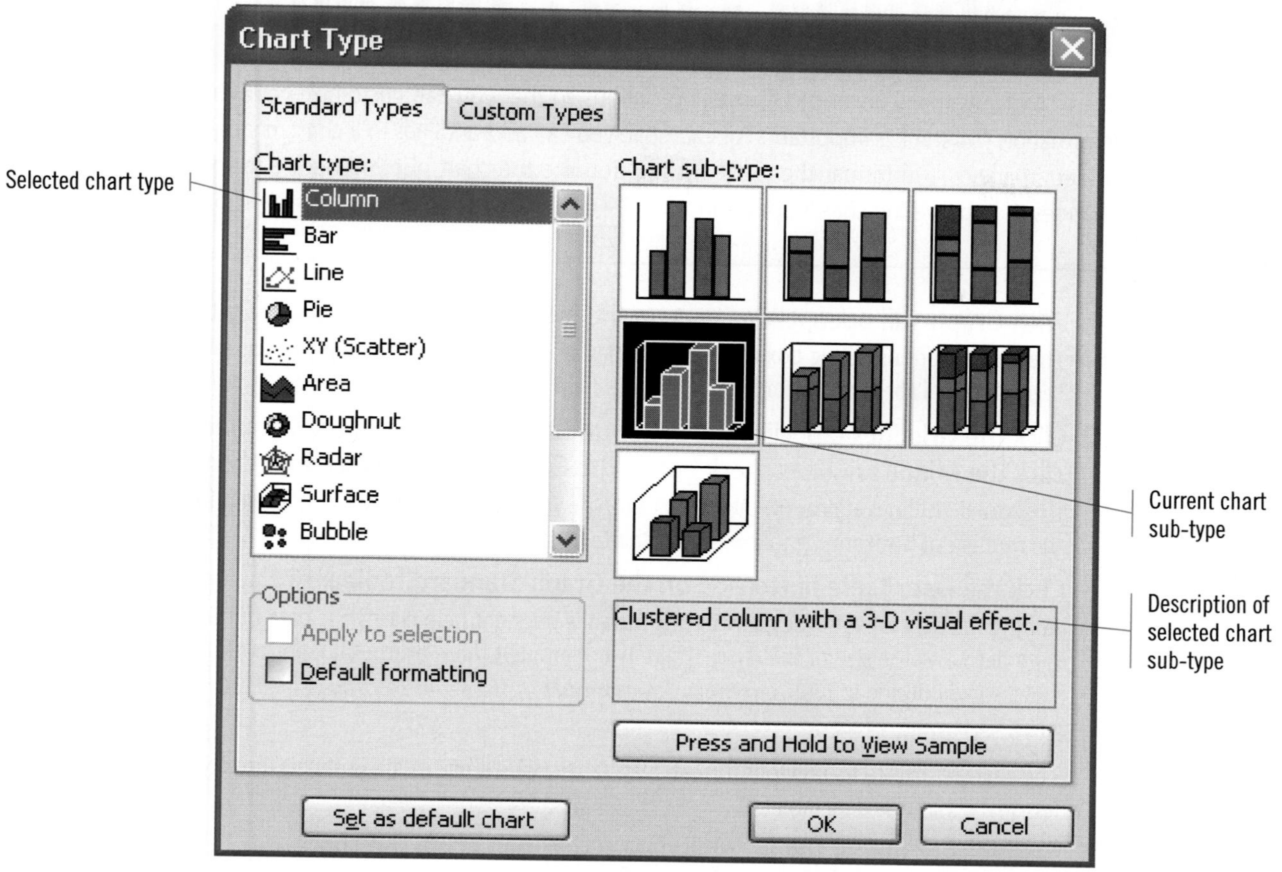

FIGURE F-7: Chart as new bar chart type

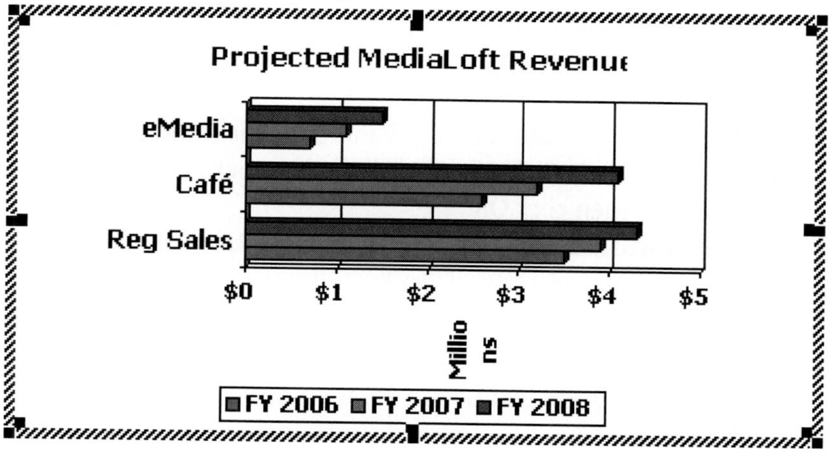

Clues to Use

Customized chart types

There are two ways to create customized chart types: you can use PowerPoint custom types or customize your own. To use PowerPoint custom types, click the Custom Types tab in the Chart Type dialog box. You will see more chart types such as Floating Bars and Area Blocks. To customize your own, click any chart series element (such as a bar) in the chart window, click Format on the menu bar, then click Selected Data Series to open the Format Chart dialog box. Use the Patterns, Shape, Data Labels, or Options tabs to customize the color, shape, or appearance of the selected element. You can reuse the chart type you have created through customization. To make your customized chart a type in the Chart Type dialog box, click the User-defined option button, click Add, then assign a name to it and click OK. To use it later, click the User-defined option button in the Chart Type dialog box and then click the name of the chart you added.

UNIT F

PowerPoint 2003

Changing Chart Options

Graph provides many advanced formatting options so that you can customize your chart to emphasize the information you think is important. For example, you can add gridlines to a chart, change the color or pattern of data markers, and format the axes. You like the chart but you decide to make some formatting changes to improve the chart's appearance.

STEPS

QUICK TIP

To quickly add major gridlines, click the Category Axis Gridlines button on the Standard toolbar.

TROUBLE

If the incorrect dialog box opens, you double-clicked the wrong chart element or double-clicked too slowly. Close the dialog box, then double-click the correct chart element.

1. **With Graph still open, click Chart on the menu bar, then click Chart Options**
   The Chart Options dialog box opens. The Titles tab is selected. The dialog box has tabs for Axes, Gridlines, Legend, Data Labels, and Data Table. Gridlines help separate and clarify data series markers.
2. **Click the Gridlines tab, click the Major gridlines check box in the Category (X) axis section, click the Minor gridlines check box in the Category (X) axis section, then click OK**
   Horizontal gridlines appear on the chart. Compare your screen to Figure F-8. Adding minor gridlines increases the number of horizontal gridlines in the chart.
3. **Click the Data Table button on the Graph Standard toolbar**
   Adding the data table to the chart in this instance does not help clarify the data in the chart and it dramatically decreases the size of the chart. There is not enough room on the slide for both the chart and the data table, so you decide to return to the previous format.
4. **Click again**
   The chart returns to its previous format. Data labels, which place data numbers directly on the chart, take up less space than the data table.
5. **Double-click one of the FY 2008 data series markers in the chart**
   The Format Data Series dialog box opens.
6. **Click the Data Labels tab, click the Value check box to select it, then click OK**
   The FY 2008 values from the datasheet appear to the right of the columns, as shown in Figure F-9. Adding data labels to one of the data series makes the series easier to identify. You can also change the way the numbers appear on the horizontal axis.
7. **Right-click one of the values on the Value axis, click Format Axis on the shortcut menu to open the Format Axis dialog box, click the Number tab, click the Decimal places up arrow until 1 appears, then click OK**
   After the Format Axis dialog box closes, the values on the Value axis display one decimal point. The labels on the Category axis would look better if they were oriented at an angle.
8. **Right-click any of the labels on the Category axis, click Format Axis on the shortcut menu, click the Alignment tab, drag the red diamond in the Orientation section counterclockwise to set the Degrees text box to 15, then click OK**
   The labels on the Category axis are oriented at a 15-degree angle. The Category axis title would look better if it were rotated to a horizontal position.
9. **Right-click the Millions axis title, click Format Axis Title on the shortcut menu, click the Alignment tab if it is not already selected, drag the red diamond in the Orientation section clockwise to set the Degrees text box to 0, then click OK**
10. **Click a blank area of the slide twice, then save your presentation**
    Compare your screen to Figure F-10.

FIGURE F-8: Chart with new gridlines

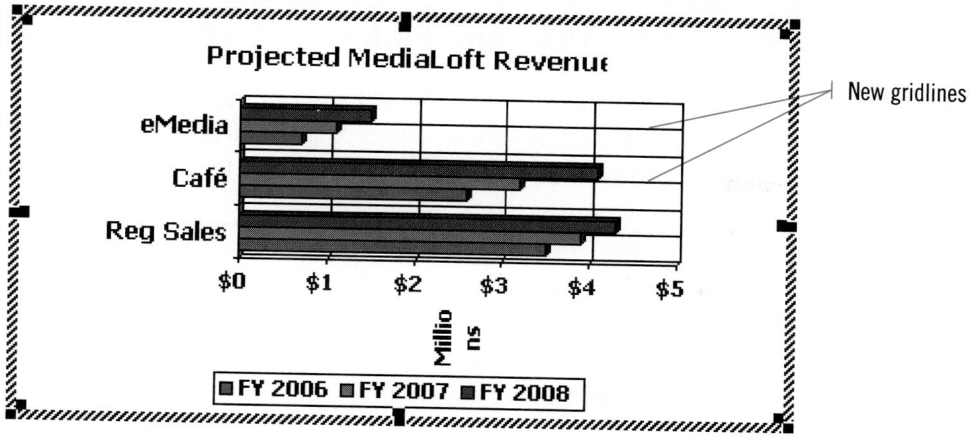

FIGURE F-9: Chart showing data labels

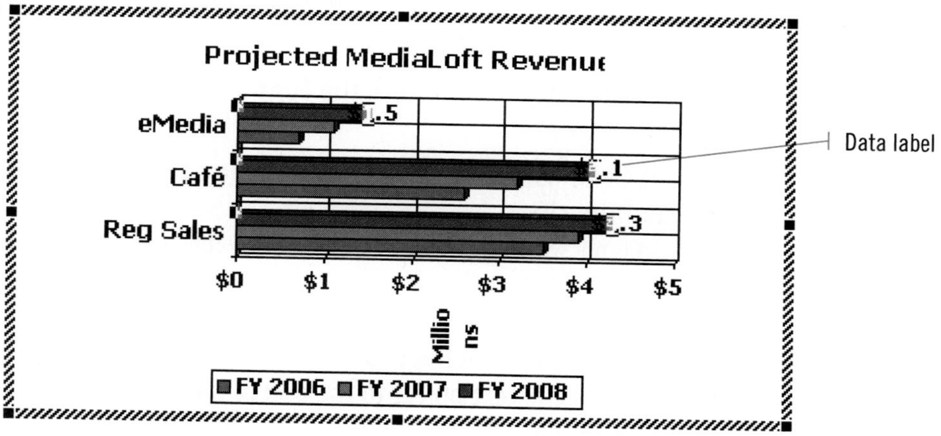

FIGURE F-10: Modified chart

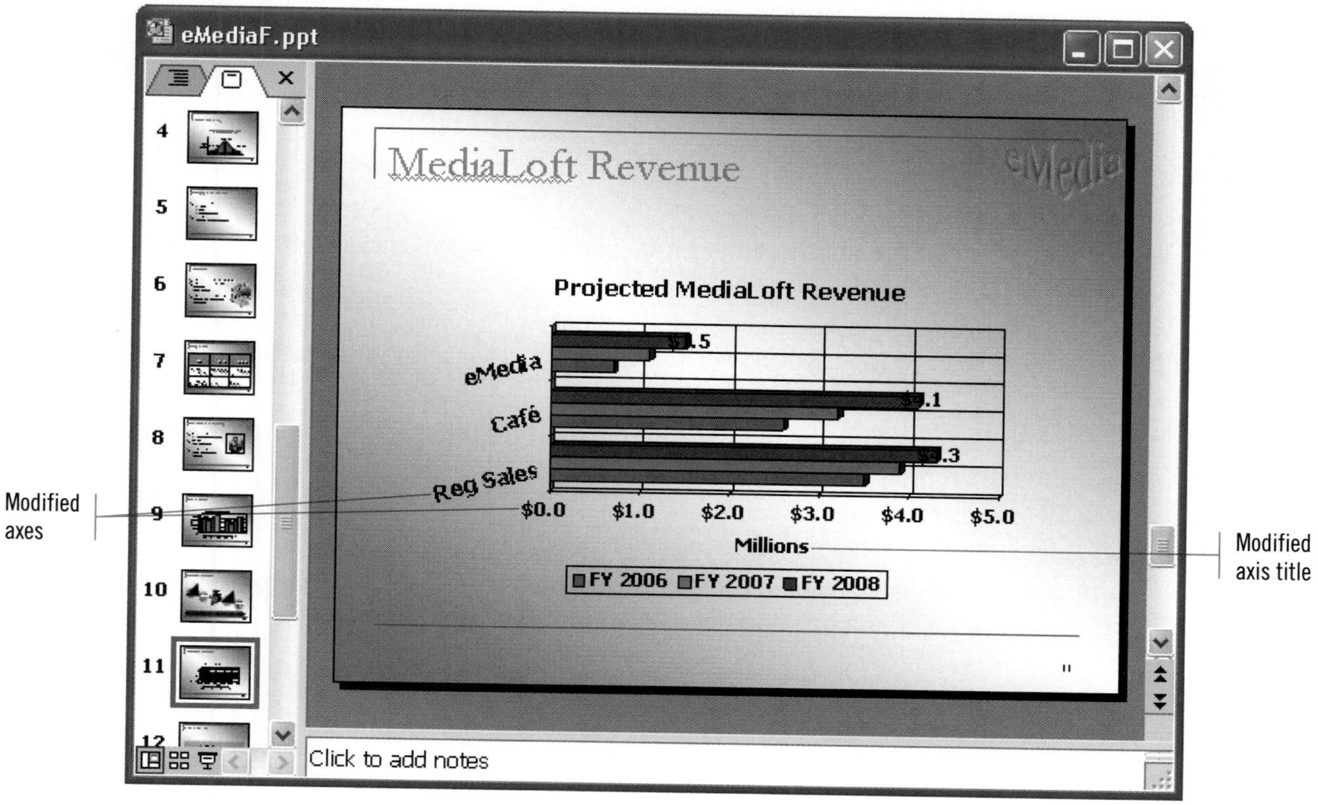

UNIT
F
PowerPoint 2003

Working with Chart Elements

Chart elements are objects you can add and format to help highlight certain information in your chart. Chart elements include legends, arrows, shapes or lines, text objects, and chart titles. You decide to add a text object and an arrow object to draw attention to the strong expected sales in the café in 2008.

STEPS

TROUBLE

If the Drawing toolbar is not visible, click View on the menu bar, point to Toolbars, then click Drawing.

TROUBLE

If the text box no longer accommodates all the text, drag a sizing handle to make it larger.

QUICK TIP

To quickly change the color of the arrow, click the Line Color button on the Drawing toolbar. To change the weight of the line, click the Line Style button on the Drawing toolbar.

QUICK TIP

To edit a comment, right-click the comment icon, click Edit Comment, then change the text.

1. **Double-click the Graph chart object, then click the Text Box button on the Drawing toolbar**

   Graph opens and the Drawing toolbar is displayed on the screen. The pointer changes to + when it is positioned in the chart area.

2. **Position + to the right of the eMedia FY 2008 data marker, drag to create a text box, then type Exceeds Goal!**

   The default size of the text, 8 point, is too small, so you change the color and size of the text to make it easier to read.

3. **Drag I over the text to select it, click the Font Size list arrow on the Formatting toolbar, then click 18**

4. **Click the Font Color list arrow on the Drawing toolbar, click the Red color, then click a blank area of the chart**

   If the text object is not where you want it, position the pointer over the edge of the text object, then drag it to another position in the chart. Compare your screen to Figure F-11. Arrows can help connect text objects to data markers in a chart.

5. **Click the Arrow button on the Drawing toolbar, position + under the word "Goal," then drag an arrow from the text object to the end of the Café FY 2008 data marker**

   Arrows can be formatted so they are more prominent, or fit a design theme.

6. **Click the Arrow Style button on the Drawing toolbar, click More Arrows, then click the Color list arrow in the Line section**

7. **Click the Red color (first column, third row), click the Weight up arrow until 2 pt appears, then click OK**

   You are satisfied with the way the chart looks for now. It is your intention to send this presentation out for review when you complete your work, so you decide to write a comment to the reviewer who looks over the sales numbers in this chart.

8. **Click a blank area of the slide, click a blank area again, click Insert on the menu bar, then click Comment**

   A new comment icon and text box appear in the upper-left corner of the slide ready to accept text. The comment icon has the initials of the user, you, and a number. Comments are numbered sequentially; this is comment 1. The Reviewing toolbar also appears below the Standard toolbar.

9. **Type Please review the numbers in this chart for accuracy, click outside the comment text box, then drag the comment icon to the right of the chart title**

   You can drag a comment icon anywhere on the slide as well as edit the comment. Usually, you want to place the comment icon near the slide item on which you are commenting.

10. **Right-click the Reviewing toolbar, click Reviewing, then save your presentation**

    Compare your screen to Figure F-12.

FIGURE F-11: Chart showing new text object

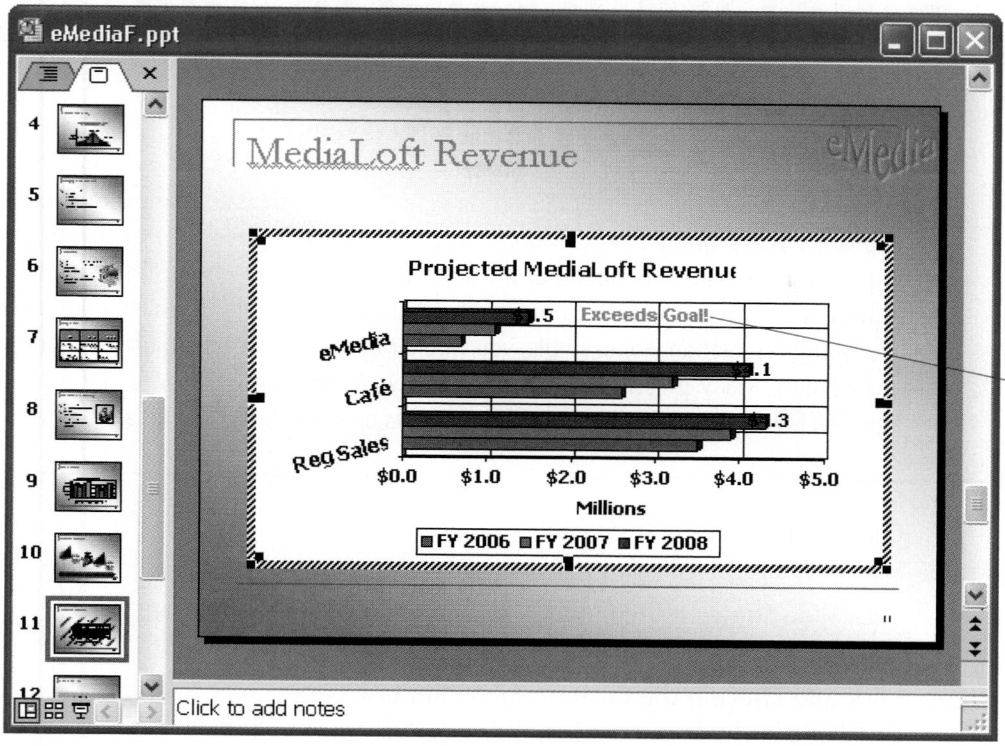

FIGURE F-12: Chart showing added chart elements and comment icon

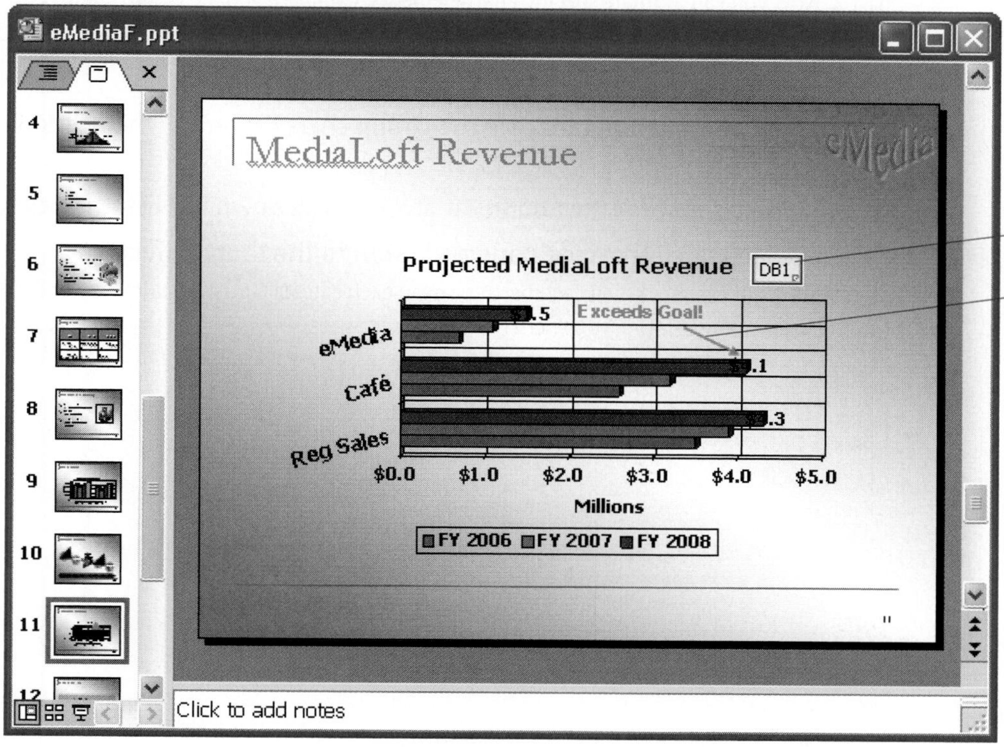

PowerPoint 2003

Clues to Use

Moving and sizing chart elements

To move a chart element, such as an arrow or the legend, you must first select the object to view its sizing handles, then drag the object to its new location. Make sure that the pointer is over the object's border when you drag it, not over a sizing handle. To change the size of a chart element, click the object to view its sizing handles, then drag a sizing handle.

UNIT F

PowerPoint 2003

Animating Charts and Adding Sounds

Just as you can animate bullets and graphics on slides, you can animate chart elements. You can have chart bars appear by series, groups, or individually. You can choose to have the legend and grid animated. You can also control the order and timing of the animations. Sound effects, including applause, a drum roll, a typewriter, and an explosion, can accompany the chart animation. Be sure to choose sounds that are appropriate for your presentation. For example, you would not use the screeching brakes sound in a serious financial presentation. Many presentations are effective with no sound effects to distract from the speaker's message. You decide to animate the elements on your chart and add a sound effect.

STEPS

1. **Click the chart once to select it**
   Make sure you do not double-click the chart.
2. **Click Slide Show on the menu bar, then click Custom Animation**
   The Custom Animation task pane opens.
3. **Click Add Effect in the Custom Animation task pane, point to Entrance, click More Effects, click Fade in the Subtle section of the Add Entrance Effect dialog box, then click OK**
   The Fade animation effect is added to the chart, and the chart is added to the Effects list in the task pane as Chart 2. Now you can animate specific chart elements. Compare your screen to Figure F-13.
4. **Click the Chart 2 list arrow in the task pane, then click Effect Options**
   The Fade dialog box opens.
5. **Click the Chart Animation tab, click the Group chart list arrow, then click By element in category**
6. **Click the Effect tab, click the Sound list arrow, scroll down the list, then click Push**
7. **Click OK, then watch the Slide pane and listen to the sound effect**
   The chart grid appears first, then each bar appears in each category, accompanied by the Push sound. Compare your screen to Figure F-14.

QUICK TIP

If you want the animated chart elements to appear automatically, click the Timing tab in the Fade dialog box, then set the appropriate options.

TROUBLE

If you do not hear the Push sound as each bar appears, then your computer might not have a sound card, or if it does, the volume may be turned down.

FIGURE F-13: Screen showing Custom Animation task pane

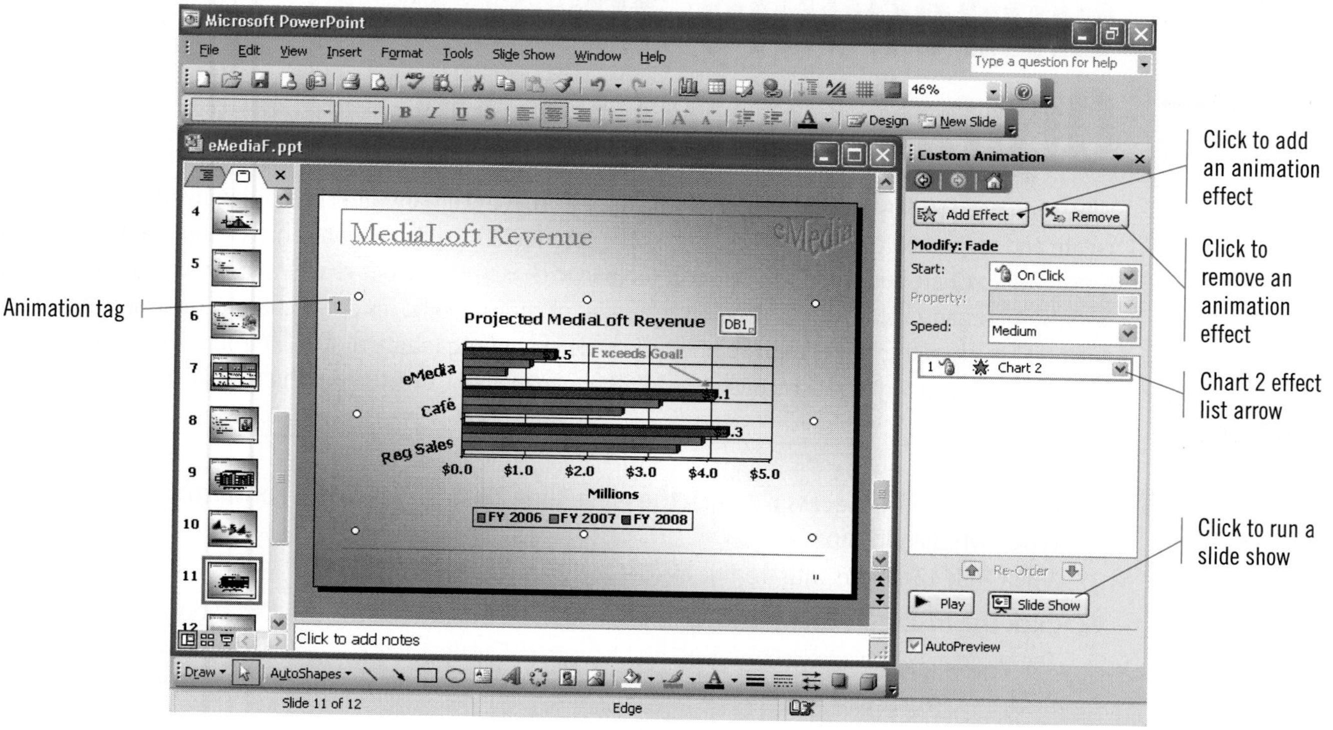

FIGURE F-14: Slide showing animated Graph chart

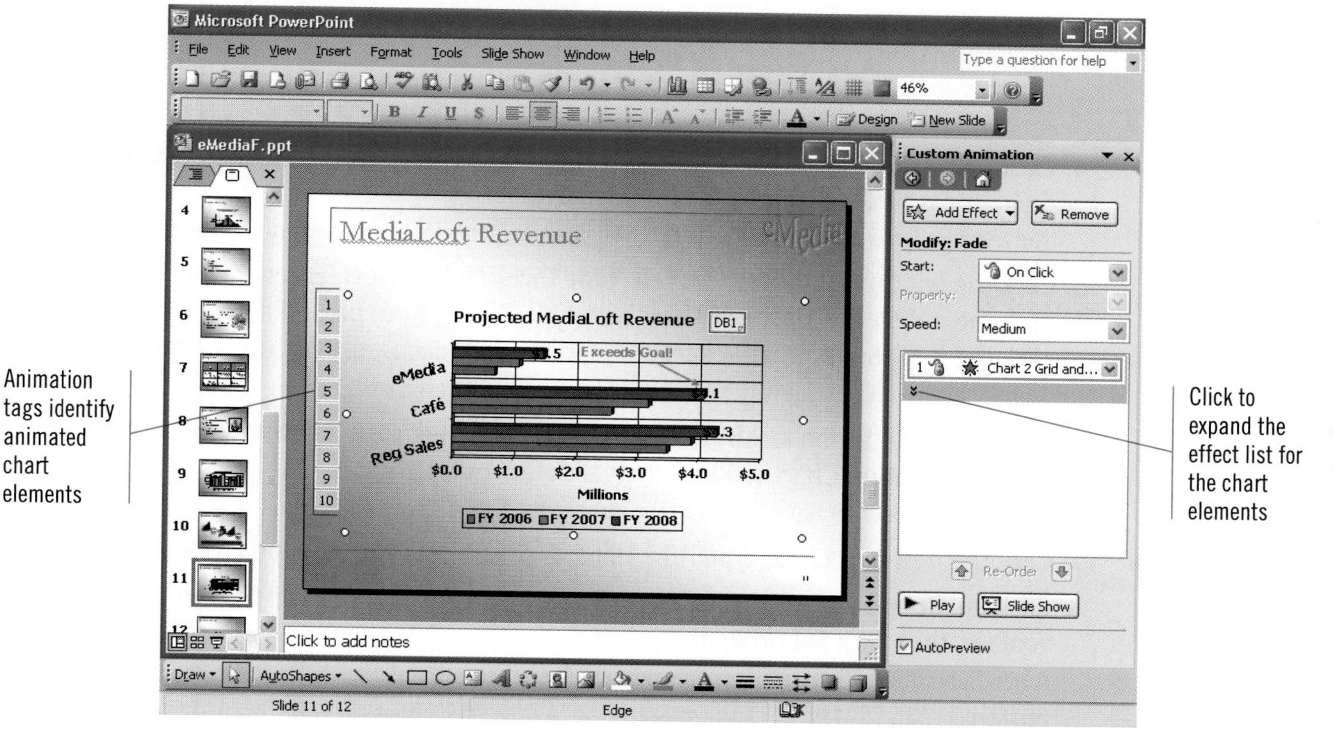

Clues to Use

Adding voice narrations

If your computer has a sound card and a microphone, you can record a voice narration that plays with your slide show. To record a narration, click Slide Show on the menu bar, then click Record Narration. If you want the recording to be linked to the presentation, click the Link narrations in check box. If you do not select this option, the recording will be embedded in the presentation. If the Record Narration command is not available, then you do not have the necessary hardware.

UNIT
F
PowerPoint 2003

Embedding an Organization Chart

When you need to illustrate a hierarchical structure, such as the organization of a company or group, you can create and embed an organization chart in your presentation. To do so, you can click the Insert Diagram or Organization Chart button on the Drawing toolbar or change the layout of your slide to one of the Content layouts. An organization chart is made up of a series of connected boxes called chart boxes in which you can enter text, such as the names and job titles of people in your organization. You now turn your attention to creating an organization chart showing the management structure for the eMedia group.

STEPS

TROUBLE
If the text you type doesn't appear as the slide title, click in the title placeholder, then type it again.

1. **Go to Slide 11 if necessary, click the New Slide button on the Formatting toolbar, then type eMedia Division**
   A new Slide 12 appears with the title eMedia Division.
2. **Click the Insert Diagram or Organization Chart button on the Drawing toolbar**
   The Diagram Gallery dialog box opens. In the Diagram Gallery dialog box, you have the option to insert one of six diagrams. See Table F-1 for information on how to use the different diagrams. The Organization Chart option is selected.
3. **Click OK**
   An organization chart appears on the slide with the Organization Chart toolbar. See Figure F-15. The default organization chart contains four placeholder chart boxes. The chart box at the top of the window is a Manager chart box and the three chart boxes below it are Subordinate chart boxes. To enter text in a chart box, select the chart box and then type.
4. **Click the Manager chart box (top chart box) if it is not already selected, type Recina Sipin, press [Enter], then type Manager**
   The text is entered into the text box. The spell checker identifies the name as not in the dictionary.
5. **Click the left Subordinate chart box, type Clark Pham, press [Enter], type Development, click the middle Subordinate chart box, type Robert Koo, press [Enter], type Marketing, click the right Subordinate chart box, type Sarina Jacobs, press [Enter], then type Sales**
   Additional chart boxes can be added to the default organization chart.
6. **Verify that the Sarina Jacobs chart box is still selected, click the Insert Shape list arrow on the Organization Chart toolbar, then click Coworker**
   A new Coworker chart box is added to the right of the Sarina Jacobs chart box.

QUICK TIP
Each chart box you add automatically decreases the size of all the chart boxes and their text so that the entire organization chart will fit on the slide.

7. **Click the new chart box, type Amy Hilliard, press [Enter], then type Production**
8. **Click the Robert Koo chart box, click the Insert Shape list arrow on the Organization Chart toolbar, then click Subordinate**
   A new Subordinate chart box appears under the Robert Koo chart box.
9. **Click the new chart box, type Sean Janis, press [Enter], then type Technology**
10. **Click a blank area of the slide to deselect the chart, then save your changes**
    Compare your screen to Figure F-16.

FIGURE F-15: Default organization chart

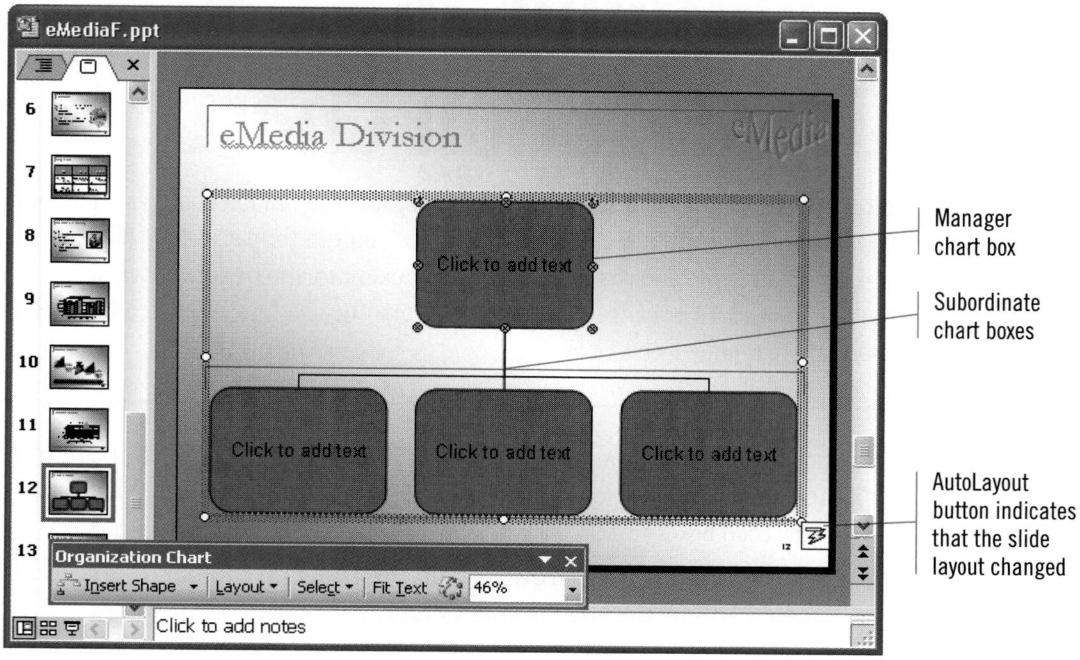

FIGURE F-16: Organization chart showing new chart boxes

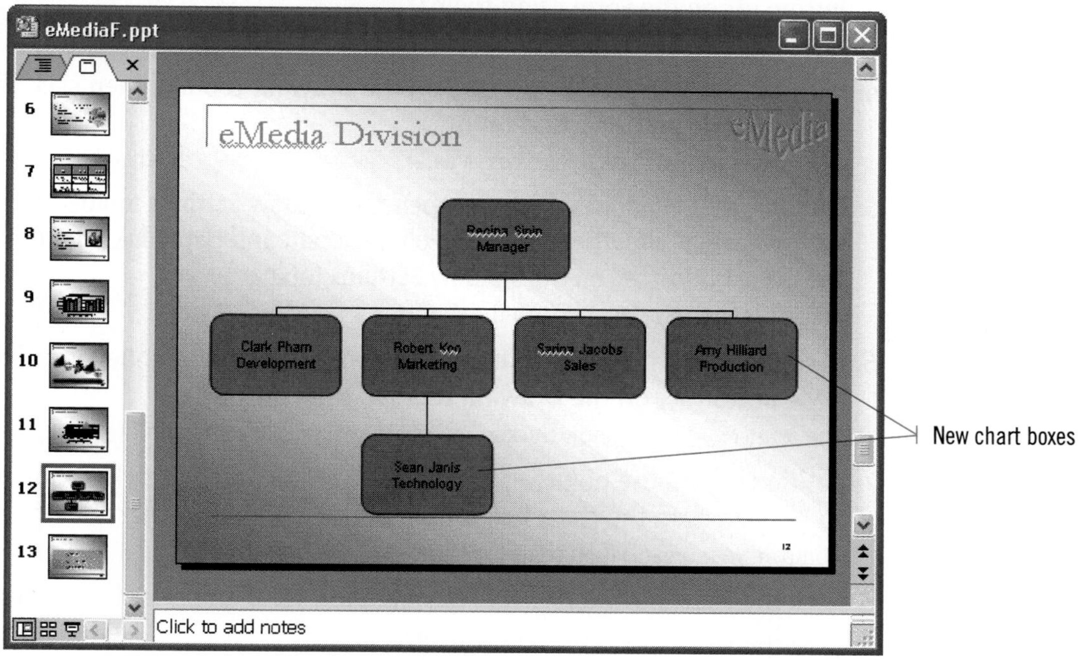

TABLE F-1: Diagram Gallery dialog box

diagram icon	diagram name	diagram used to show
	Organization Chart	hierarchical relationships
	Cycle Diagram	a process with a continuous cycle
	Radial Diagram	relationships with a core element
	Pyramid Diagram	foundational relationships
	Venn Diagram	overlap between elements
	Target Diagram	steps toward a goal

Modifying an Organization Chart

After you add all the chart boxes you need for your organization chart, you can format the chart boxes and connecting lines. Attributes of a chart box that you can format include fill color, line color, line style, font size, color, and type and shadow style. Chart boxes can also be rearranged within the organization chart as desired. To enhance the slide, you format the chart boxes and connecting lines of the organization chart and rearrange a chart box.

STEPS

1. **Click the Recina Sipin chart box, click the Select button on the Organization Chart toolbar, then click Branch**
   All the chart boxes are selected and ready to be formatted.
2. **Click the Fill Color list arrow on the Drawing toolbar, then click the olive green color (labeled Follow Accent Scheme Color)**
   The fill color of the chart boxes changes to olive green.
3. **Click the Font list arrow on the Formatting toolbar, click Arial Black, then click the Shadow button on the Formatting toolbar**
   Compare your screen to Figure F-17.
4. **Click the Shadow Style button on the Drawing toolbar, then click Shadow Style 6 (second style in the second row)**
   A shadow is applied to each chart box. A darker shadow might make the chart boxes stand out more on the slide.
5. **Click, click Shadow Settings to open the Shadow Settings toolbar, click the Shadow Color list arrow, click the teal color (Follow Accent and Hyperlink Scheme Color), then click the Close button on the Shadow Settings toolbar**
   Thicker connecting lines between the chart boxes would look better.
6. **Click Select on the Organization Chart toolbar, click All Connecting Lines, click the Line Style button on the Drawing toolbar, then click 3 pt**
   The connector lines are now thicker. You can move chart boxes within the chart.
7. **Position the mouse pointer over the edge of the Sean Janis chart box so that it changes to, then drag the chart box on top of the Clark Pham chart box**
   Compare your organization chart to Figure F-18.
8. **Click the Slide Show button to view Slide 12, then press [Esc] to end the slide show**
9. **Click the Slide Sorter View button**
   Compare your screen to Figure F-19. Slides 11 and 12 are the only slides you modified in this unit.
10. **Click the Normal View button, add your name to Slide 1 and as a footer to the notes and handouts, save your presentation, print the presentation as handouts (6 slides per page), then close the presentation and exit PowerPoint**

QUICK TIP

Only chart boxes at the end of a branch can be moved to another position in the organization chart.

FIGURE F-17: Organization chart showing formatted chart boxes

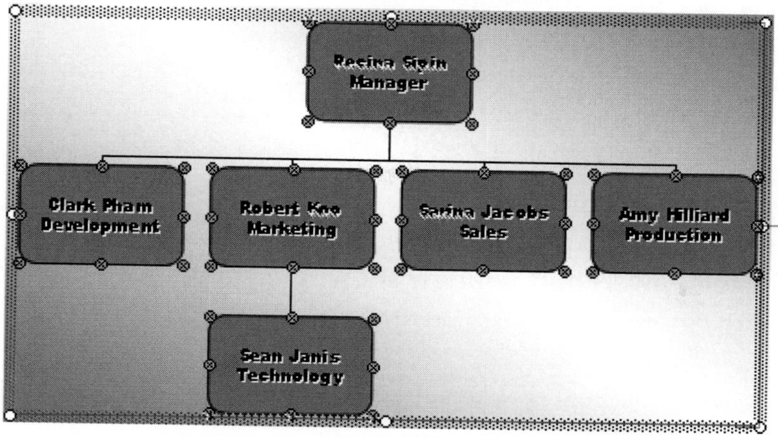

FIGURE F-18: Organization chart showing rearranged chart box

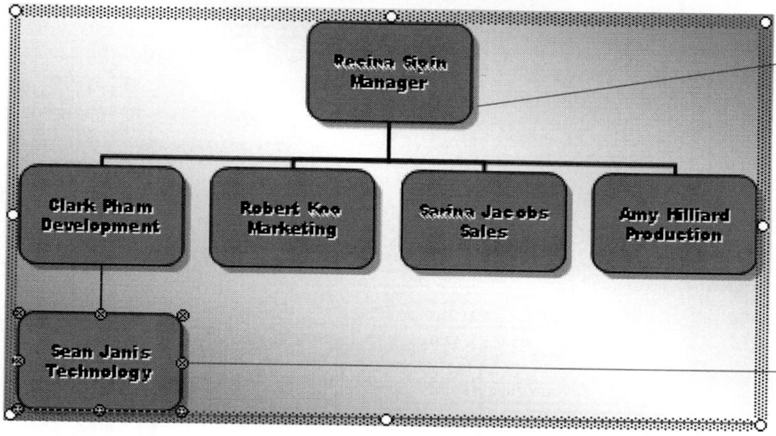

FIGURE F-19: Final presentation in Slide Sorter view

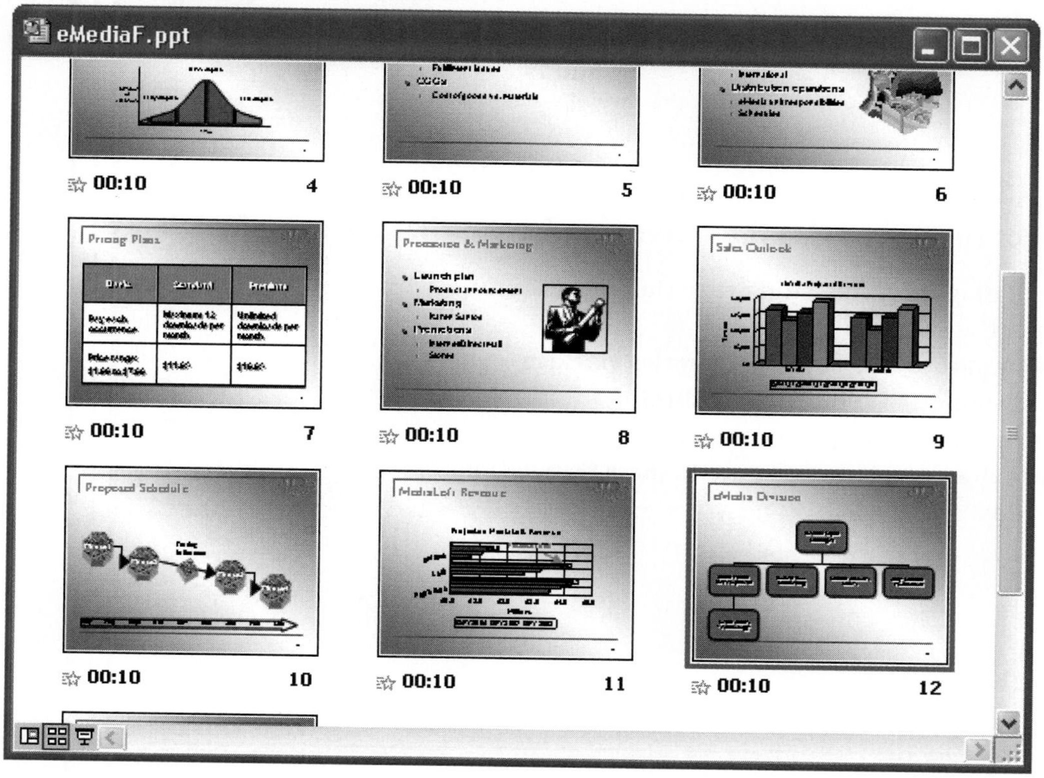

Practice

▼ CONCEPTS REVIEW

Label each element of the PowerPoint window shown in Figure F-20.

FIGURE F-20

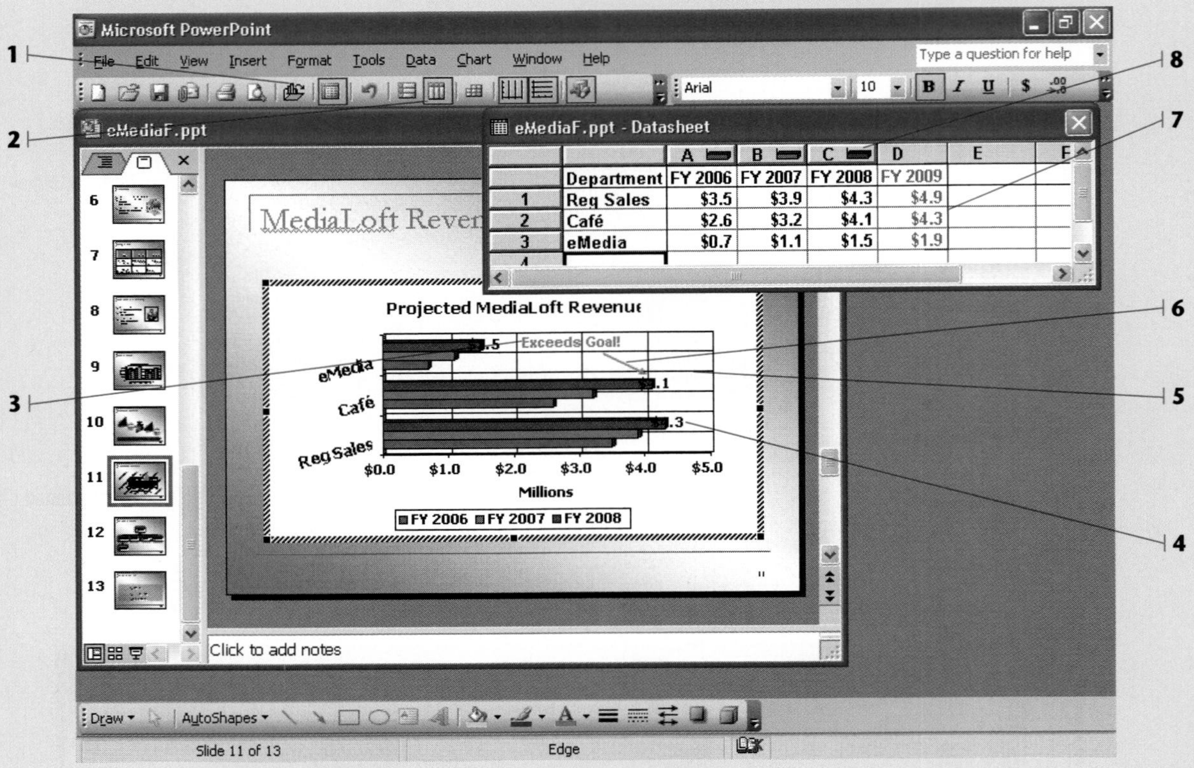

Match each of the terms with the statement that best describes its function.

9. **The type of diagram you would use to show relationships with a core element**
10. **Lines that separate and clarify data series markers**
11. **A group of connected cells in a datasheet**
12. **Graphical representation of a data series**
13. **The type of diagram you would use to show foundational relationships**

a. Pyramid
b. Gridlines
c. Data series markers
d. Radial
e. Range

Select the best answer from the list of choices.

14. What does it mean when data is grayed out in the datasheet?
- **a.** The data is excluded from the datasheet.
- **b.** The data is excluded from the chart.
- **c.** The data has been accidentally deleted.
- **d.** The data appears only in the chart.

15. What is a data series?
- **a.** A graphical representation of a data series marker.
- **b.** A range of data.
- **c.** All of the data elements in a chart.
- **d.** A column or row of data.

16. Which of the following is not true about chart types?
- **a.** A chart with eight data series would fit well in a pie chart.
- **b.** The type of chart you choose usually depends on the amount of data.
- **c.** You can create a custom chart type using the Custom Types tab in the Chart Type dialog box.
- **d.** Examples of custom chart types include area blocks, floating bars, and outdoor bars.

17. Which is not true about animation sound effects?
- **a.** Most presentations are ineffective without some sort of animation sound.
- **b.** A sound effect can distract from the speaker's message.
- **c.** Animation sound effects include a drum roll and an explosion.
- **d.** A sound effect can accompany a chart animation.

18. What is the chart or diagram called that is made up of connected chart boxes?
- **a.** Venn diagram.
- **b.** Organization chart.
- **c.** Graph chart.
- **d.** Target diagram.

19. Based on what you know of organization charts, which of the following data would best fit in an organization chart?
- **a.** Spreadsheet data.
- **b.** A company's annual financial numbers.
- **c.** A company's database mailing list.
- **d.** A company's division structure.

20. What do chart gridlines help you do?
- **a.** Combine data series markers.
- **b.** Separate and clarify data series markers.
- **c.** See chart elements, such as text or lines.
- **d.** Change the chart type.

PowerPoint 2003

▼ SKILLS REVIEW

1. Insert data from a file into a datasheet.
- **a.** Start PowerPoint, open the presentation PPT F-3.ppt, then save it as **London Publishing** to the drive and folder where your Data Files are stored.
- **b.** Select Slide 3, then open Microsoft Graph.
- **c.** Click the upper-left cell in the datasheet, then import Sheet1 of the Excel file PPT F-4 .xls from the drive and folder where your Data Files are stored into the Graph datasheet.
- **d.** Exclude the Mystery column from the chart, then save the chart.

2. Format a datasheet.
- **a.** Select the range of cells from cell A1 to cell D5.
- **b.** Format the datasheet numbers with Currency format.

▼ SKILLS REVIEW (CONTINUED)

c. Change the format of the datasheet numbers so that they have no decimal places. (*Hint*: Click the Decrease Decimal button on the Standard toolbar twice.)

d. Adjust the column width for all the columns to Best Fit. Compare your datasheet with Figure F-21.

e. Close the datasheet.

f. Save the chart.

FIGURE F-21

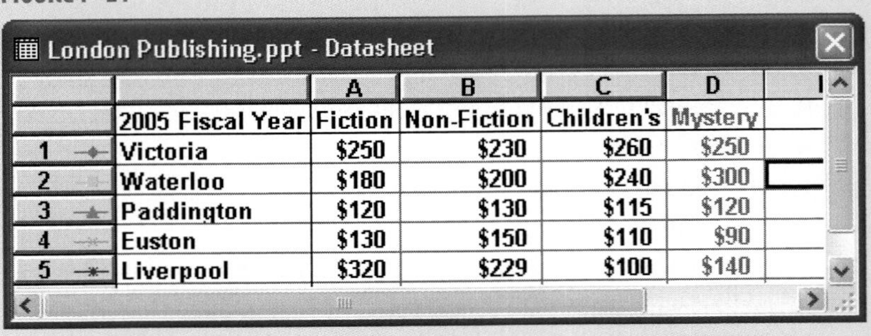

London Publishing.ppt - Datasheet

		A	B	C	D
	2005 Fiscal Year	Fiction	Non-Fiction	Children's	Mystery
1	Victoria	$250	$230	$260	$250
2	Waterloo	$180	$200	$240	$300
3	Paddington	$120	$130	$115	$120
4	Euston	$130	$150	$110	$90
5	Liverpool	$320	$229	$100	$140

3. Change the chart's type.

a. Change the chart type to a clustered 3-D column chart.

b. Change the chart to a line chart with markers displayed at each data value, preview it, then accept it.

c. Save the chart.

4. Change chart options.

a. Show major gridlines on both the x and the y axes.

b. Add a title to the y axis that reads **Thousands**.

c. Save your changes.

5. Work with chart elements.

a. Add a text box object in the upper-right corner of the chart for Liverpool Fiction sales.

b. Add the text **A Record!** to the text box.

c. Change the font size of the text to 22 point and the font to Times New Roman.

d. Change the color of the text to blue.

e. Add a blue arrow pointing from the text box to the appropriate data point.

f. Format the arrow line as 3 point.

g. Compare your chart with Figure F-22 and adjust the text box and arrow positions as necessary.

h. Click a blank area of the slide, then save your changes.

FIGURE F-22

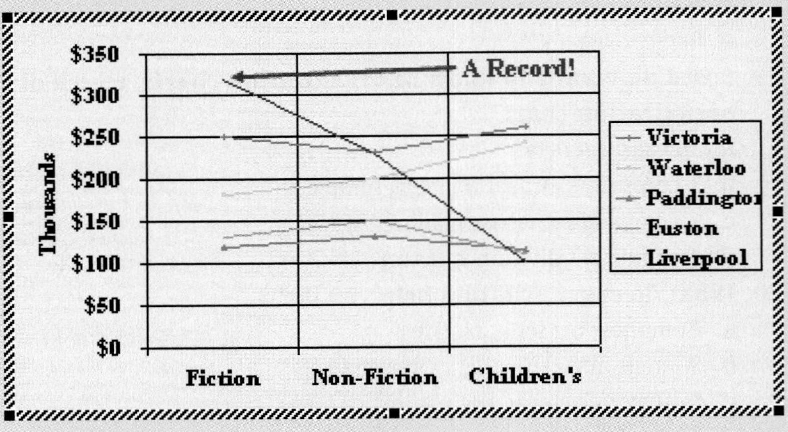

6. Animate charts and add sounds.

a. Animate the chart with the Entrance Fade effect.

b. Animate the chart elements so they are introduced by series.

c. Add the Arrow sound effect to the animation.

d. In the Custom Animation task pane, click the Speed list arrow and change the speed to Fast.

e. Preview the animation.

f. Check the animation in Slide Show view, then save the presentation.

7. Embed an organization chart.

a. Select Slide 4.

b. Add an organization chart to the slide.

c. At the top level, type **Sarah Wiley** as **Division Manager**.

d. In the Subordinate chart boxes, type the following names and titles:

Janice Britt, Distribution Manager
Robert Sarhi, Purchasing Manager
Evelyn Storey, Circulation Manager

▼ SKILLS REVIEW (CONTINUED)

e. Change the fill color for all the chart boxes to a light blue color.
f. Change the line color for all the chart boxes to a dark purple color, then save your changes.

8. Modify an organization chart.

a. Add an assistant chart box to the Sarah Wiley chart box.
b. Drag the organization chart sizing handles to make the chart as big as possible.
c. Enter **Kris Courter** as her **Special Assistant**.
d. Add two Subordinate boxes to the Evelyn Storey chart box, and enter the following:
Perry Jones, Purchase Orders
Lynette Groshem, Financial Assistant
e. Drag the Perry Jones chart box and the Lynette Groshem chart box so they are under the Robert Sarhi chart box.
f. Select the Sarah Wiley chart box and change the font to 16 point.
g. Format all the other chart boxes using the formatting characteristics from the Sarah Wiley chart box. (*Hint*: Use the Format Painter button.)
h. Format the connecting lines to 3 point.
i. Select Slide 1, then view the presentation in Slide Show view.
j. Reduce the font size for all the text in the chart to 12 point. (*Hint:* Select the chart, then click the Decrease Font Size button on the Formatting toolbar twice.)
k. Add your name to the notes and handouts footer.
l. Save your changes, print the presentation as handouts (3 slides per page), then close the presentation and exit PowerPoint.

▼ INDEPENDENT CHALLENGE 1

You work for Ryers Associates, a business consulting company that helps small- and medium-sized businesses organize or restructure themselves to be more efficient and profitable. You are one of six senior consultants who works directly with clients. To prepare for an upcoming meeting with executives at ComSystems, a mobile phone communications company, you create a brief presentation outlining Ryers' typical investigative and reporting techniques, past results versus the competition, and the company's business philosophy.

The following is a sample of the type of work you perform as part of your duties at Ryers: You usually investigate a client's business practices for two weeks and analyze all relevant records. Once the initial investigation stage is complete, you submit a client recommendation report to your boss that describes the known problem areas, the consequences of the problems, the reasons for the problems, the recommended solutions, the anticipated results for each solution, the anticipated cost to the client for each solution, and Ryers' final professional recommendation. After your boss approves the client recommendation report, you prepare a full report for the client. If the client approves the plan, you develop a maintenance schedule (usually one year or less) to make sure the plan is implemented correctly.

a. Open the file PPT F-5.ppt from the drive and folder where your Data Files are stored, then save it as **Ryers Presentation**.
b. Think about the results you want to see, the information you need, and how you want to communicate the message. Sketch how you want your presentation to look.
c. Create charts on Slides 3 and 4 using one of the charts available in the Diagram Gallery. Use the information provided in this Independent Challenge to show the various stages of investigation and reporting.
d. Create a Graph chart on Slide 5 that shows how Ryers compares with two competitors. For example, you might illustrate the satisfaction level of Ryers clients compared to its competitors' clients or Ryers' consumer rating.
e. Format the chart and add additional chart elements using the skills learned in this unit.

Advanced Challenge Exercise

ACE

- Change the chart type of the chart on Slide 5 to a cylinder with a 3-D Column with a cylindrical shape sub-type.
- Open the Format Axis dialog box for the Value axis, open the Scale tab, then change the Major unit from the default setting.
- Change the Maximum scale on the Scale tab to a number that displays the values on the chart well.

▼ INDEPENDENT CHALLENGE 1 (CONTINUED)

f. Format the text on the slides. Modify the master views to achieve the look you want.

g. Spell check and save your presentation.

h. Add your name as a footer to the slides and handouts, print the slides of the presentation, then submit your presentation plan and printouts.

i. View the presentation in Slide Show view, close the presentation, and exit PowerPoint.

▼ INDEPENDENT CHALLENGE 2

This year, you have been selected by your peers to receive a national teaching award for the educational program that you created for disabled children in your home state of Vermont. In accepting this award, you have the opportunity to give a presentation describing your program's results since its introduction. You will give the presentation at an educator's convention in Washington, DC.

Plan and create a slide presentation describing your results. Create your own data, but assume the following:

- Over the last three years, 3,548 children in 251 classrooms throughout Vermont have participated in your program.
- Children enrolled in your program have shown at least a 7% improvement in skills for every year the program has been in effect.
- Children ages 4 through 12 have participated in the program.
- Money to fund the program comes from the National Education Association (NEA) and the State of Vermont Public School Department. The money goes to each participating school district in the state.
- Funding per child is $2,867 per school year. Funding per child in a regular classroom is $3,950 per year.

a. Think about the results you want to see, the information you need to create the slide presentation, and how your message should be communicated.

b. Create a presentation using a chart from the Diagram Gallery to build some of your slides. Think about how you can effectively show information in a chart.

c. Format the charts using PowerPoint's formatting features.

d. Use clip art, shapes, and a shaded background to enhance the presentation. Change the bullet and text formatting in the Master text and title placeholders to fit the subject matter.

e. Spell check and save the presentation as **Award** to the drive and folder where your Data Files are stored.

f. Add your name as a footer to the slides and handouts, then print the final slide presentation.

g. View the presentation in Slide Show view, close the presentation, and exit PowerPoint.

▼ INDEPENDENT CHALLENGE 3

MedTech Industries is a large company that develops and produces technical medical equipment and machines for operating and emergency rooms throughout the United States. You are the business manager, and one of your assignments is to prepare a presentation for the stockholders on the profitability and efficiency of each division in the company.

Plan and create a slide presentation that shows all the divisions and divisional managers of the company. Also, graphically show how each division performed in relation to its previous year's performance. Create your own content, but assume the following:

- The company has seven divisions: Administration, Accounting, Sales and Marketing, Research and Development, Product Testing, Product Development, and Manufacturing.
- Three divisions increased productivity by at least 15%.
- The presentation will be given in a boardroom using a projector.

a. Think about the results you want to see, the information you need to create the slide presentation, what type of message you want to communicate, and the target audience.

b. Use Outline view to create the content of your presentation.

c. Create a Graph chart, then insert the Excel file PPT F-6.xls into the datasheet.

▼ INDEPENDENT CHALLENGE 3 (CONTINUED)

Advanced Challenge Exercise

- Add one of the following entrance animation effects for the Graph chart: Blinds, Box, Diamond, or Fade.
- Change the effect options of the animation effect in the Chart Animation tab so that the data series markers of the chart appear by element, by category.
- In the Chart Animation tab deselect the Animate grid and legend check box.
- On the Custom Animation task pane change the Direction to Vertical and the Speed to Fast.

d. Create organization charts to help present the information you want to communicate.
e. Use clip art, pictures, or a shaded background to enhance the presentation, and format the content.
f. Save the presentation as **MedTech Industries** to the drive and folder where your Data Files are stored.
g. Add your name as a footer to the slides and handouts, then print the final slide presentation.
h. View the presentation in Slide Show view, close the presentation and exit PowerPoint.

▼ INDEPENDENT CHALLENGE 4

You are a PC game analyst for Potus Inc., a computer software research company. One of your responsibilities every quarter is to create a brief presentation that identifies the top three computer games based on industry and consumer reviews. In your presentation, you include charts that help define the data you compile.

Develop your own content, but assume the following:

- Each game has at least one defined mission or task.
- Consumer satisfaction of each game is identified on a scale of 1.0 to 10.0.
- There are three categories of games: Adventure, Action, and Strategy.

You'll need to find the following information on the Web:

- Consumer or industry reviews of three PC computer games.
- A description of each game, including the story line of the game or individual mission.
- The price of each game.

a. Open a new presentation, and save it as **3 Qrtr Review** to the drive and folder where your Data Files are stored.
b. Add your name as the footer on all slides and handouts.
c. Connect to the Internet, then use a search engine to locate Web sites that have information on PC computer games.
d. Review at least two Web sites that contain information about computer games. Print the Home pages of the Web sites you use to gather data for your presentation.
e. Using PowerPoint, create an outline of your presentation. It should contain between eight and 10 slides, including a title slide.
f. Include at least one chart that identifies consumer satisfaction numbers that you develop.
g. Create a diagram or organization chart that briefly explains the story line of one of the games.
h. Create a table that lists the price of each game.
i. Enhance the presentation with clip art or other graphics, an appropriate template and/or background, or other items that improve the look of the presentation.
j. Change the master views, if necessary, to fit your presentation.
k. Spell check, save the presentation, then view the presentation in Slide Show view.
l. Print the slides of the presentation as handouts (4 slides per page).
m. Close the presentation and exit PowerPoint.

▼ VISUAL WORKSHOP

Create two slides that look like the examples in Figures F-23 and F-24. Save the presentation as **Eastern Products**. Add your name as a footer on the slides, then save and print the presentation slides.

FIGURE F-23

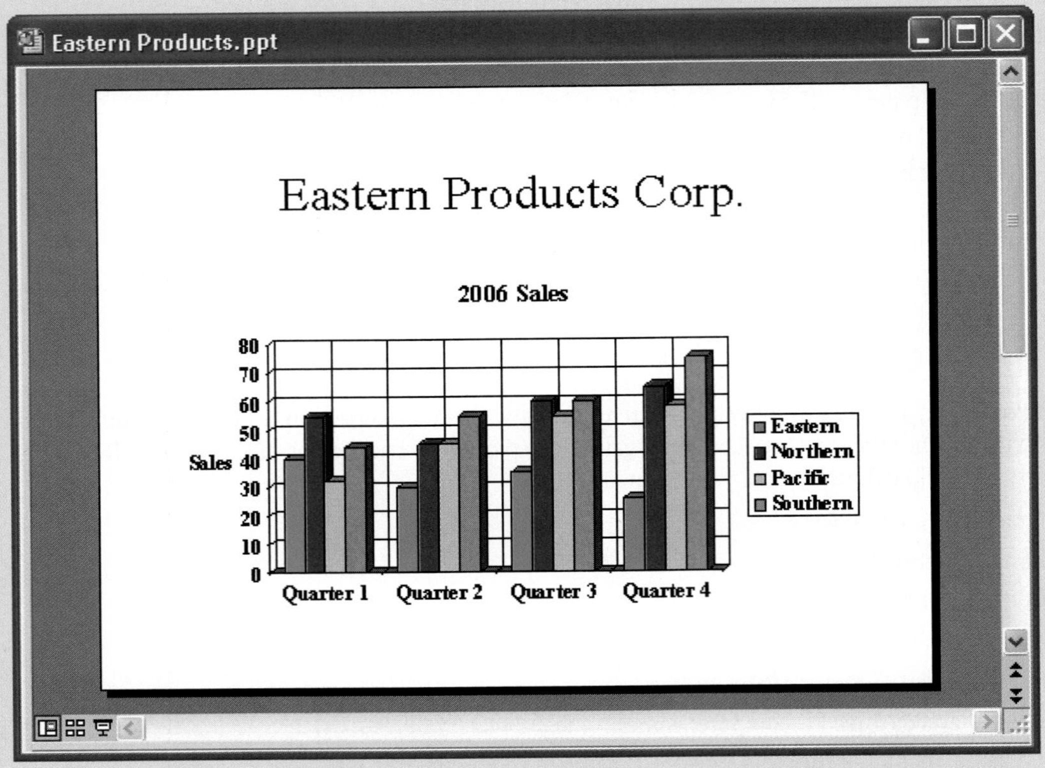

FIGURE F-24

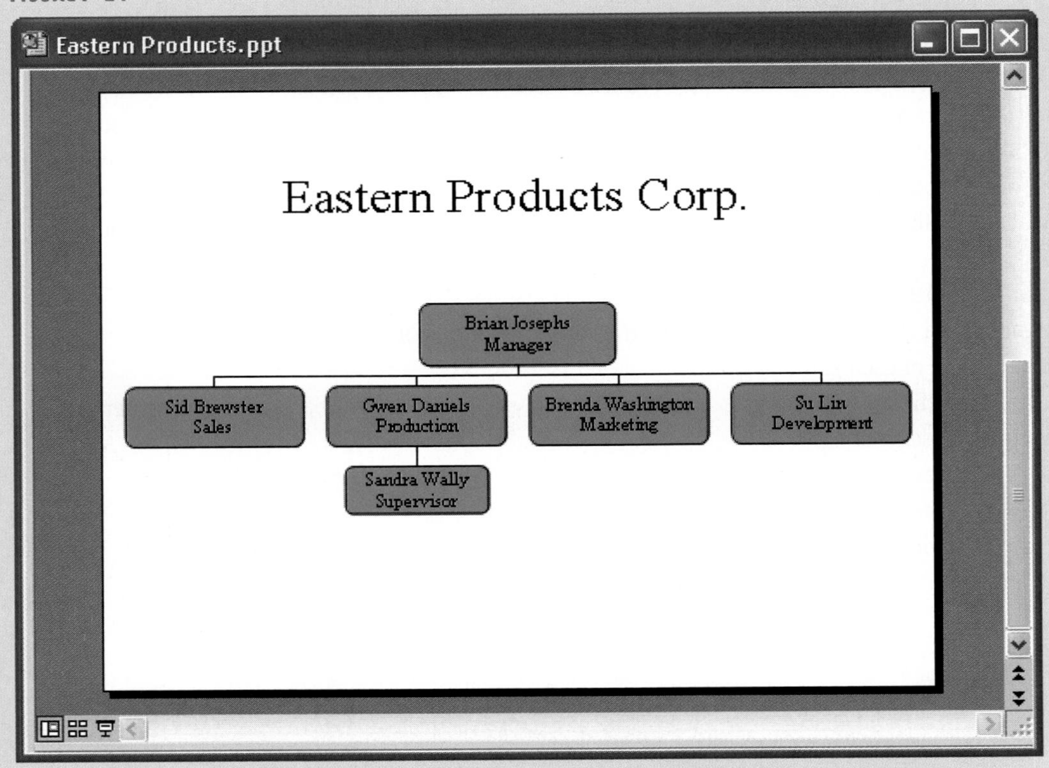

UNIT
G
PowerPoint 2003

Working with Embedded and Linked Objects and Hyperlinks

OBJECTIVES

- Embed a picture
- Embed an Excel chart
- Link an Excel worksheet
- Update a linked Excel worksheet
- Insert an animated GIF file
- Insert a sound
- Insert a hyperlink
- Create a photo album

If you have a SAM user profile, you may have access to hands-on instruction, practice, and assessment of the skills covered in this unit. Log in to your SAM account and go to your assignments page to see what your instructor has assigned.

PowerPoint offers many ways to add graphic elements to a presentation. In this unit, you will learn how to embed and link objects. Embedded and linked objects are created in another program and then either stored in or linked to the PowerPoint presentation. In this unit, Maria Abbott asks you to create a brief presentation that outlines MediaLoft's Video Department using embedded and linked objects. She will use the slide presentation you create in a company meeting next week at MediaLoft's headquarters.

UNIT
G
PowerPoint 2003

Embedding a Picture

You can embed more than 20 types of pictures, including JPEG File Interchange Format (**.jpg**), Windows Bitmap (**.bmp**), and Graphics Interchange Format (**.gif**) using the Insert Picture command. Frequently, a presentation's color scheme will not match the colors in pictures, especially photographs. In order to make the picture look good in the presentation, you may need to adjust the slide's color scheme, recolor the picture, or change the presentation's template. You want to embed a photograph on Slide 2 of the presentation you are working on for Maria. After you embed the picture you adjust the slide's color scheme to make the photograph look better.

STEPS

1. **Start PowerPoint, open the presentation PPT G-1.ppt from the drive and folder where your Data Files are stored, save the presentation as Video Report, click View on the menu bar, click Task Pane, click Window on the menu bar, then click Arrange All**

TROUBLE
If the Picture toolbar is in the way, move the toolbar to another part of the screen.

2. **Click Slide 2 in the Slides tab, click the Insert Picture button on the Drawing toolbar, select the file PPT G-2.jpg from the drive and folder where your Data Files are stored, then click Insert**

   A picture with a travel theme appears in the center of the slide and the Picture toolbar opens.

3. **Resize and drag the picture to match Figure G-1**

   A different slide background color would provide a better contrast for this picture.

4. **Click the Slide Design button on the Formatting toolbar, then click the Color Schemes hyperlink in the Slide Design task pane**

   The Slide Design task pane opens, showing the available color schemes. There are nine standard color schemes from which to choose.

5. **Click each color scheme list arrow, then click Apply to Selected Slides to preview each of the color schemes for Slide 2**

   You can evaluate each color scheme as it is applied to the presentation. The color scheme in the first row and first column matches best with the picture colors.

TROUBLE
If you click Apply to All Slides by mistake, click the Undo button, then repeat Step 6.

6. **Click the blue color scheme list arrow (first row, first column), then click Apply to Selected Slides**

   Make sure you do not click Apply to All Slides or click the color scheme box, which is the same as applying the color scheme to all of the slides. The color scheme for Slide 2 changes to a blue background.

7. **Click a blank area of the slide, compare your screen to Figure G-2, then click the Save button on the Standard toolbar**

FIGURE G-1: Slide showing embedded picture

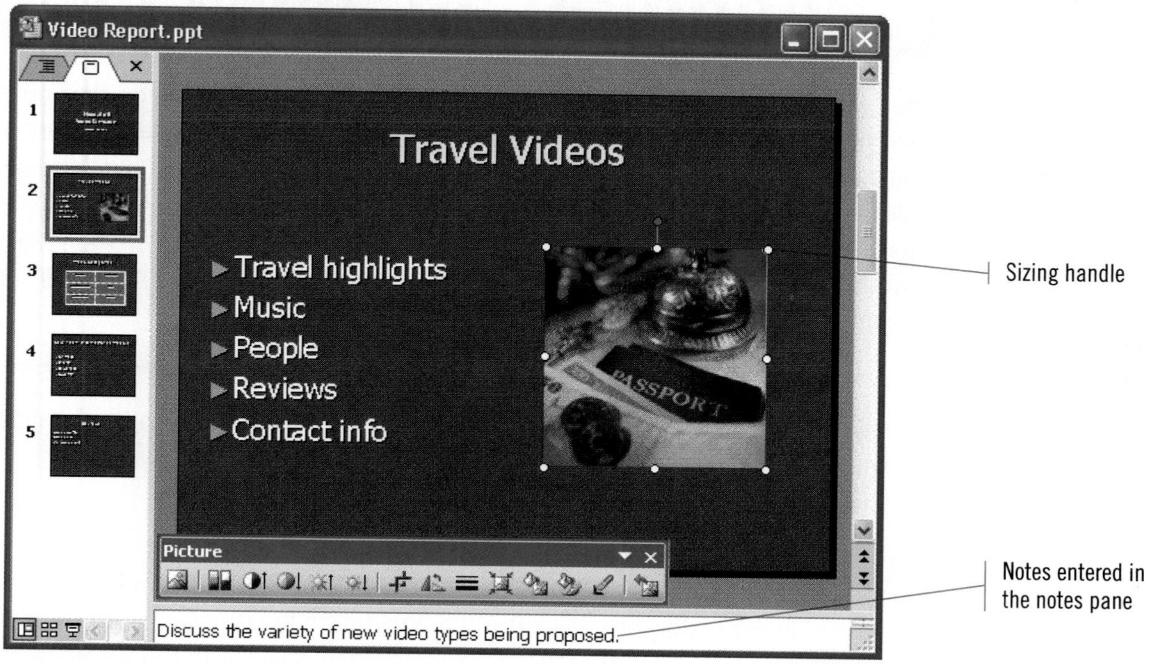

FIGURE G-2: Slide showing new color scheme

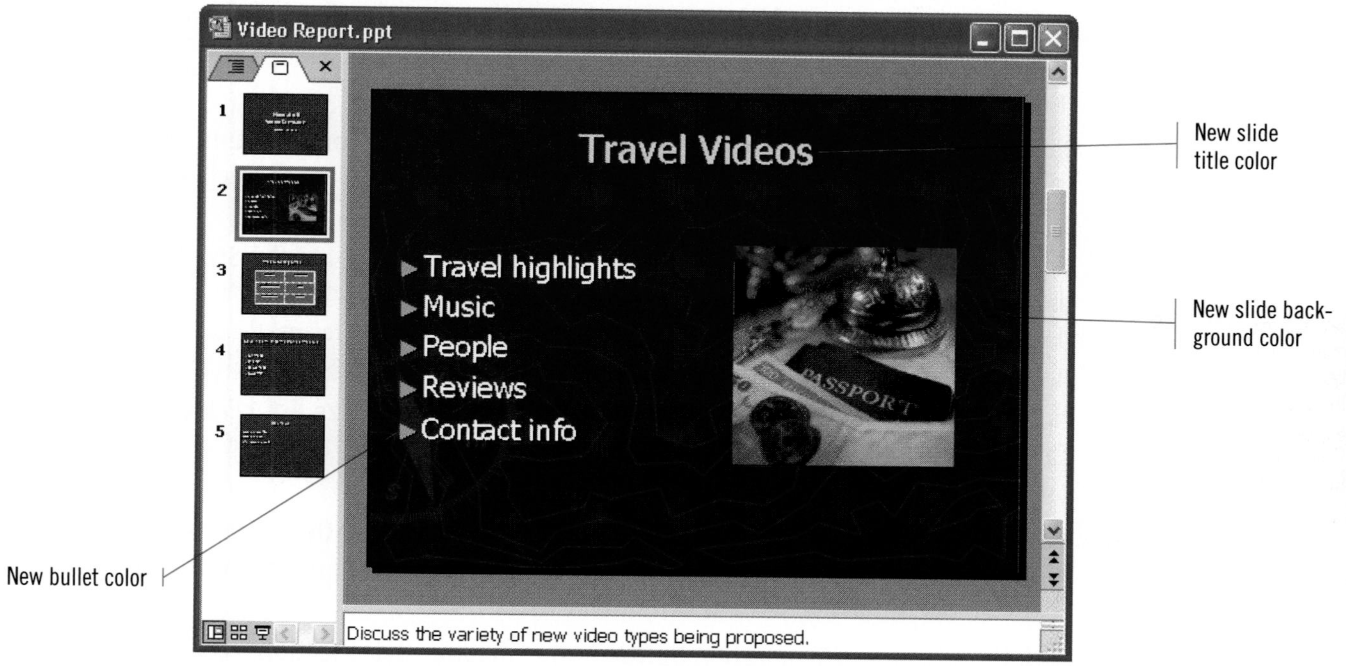

Clues to Use

Exporting a presentation

Sometimes it's helpful to use a word processing program like Word to create detailed speaker's notes or handouts. You might also want to create a Word document based on the outline of your PowerPoint presentation. To export a presentation to Word, click File on the menu bar, point to Send to, then click Microsoft Office Word. The Send to Microsoft Office Word dialog box opens and provides you with a number of document layout options from which to choose. Select a layout, click OK, and a new Word document opens with your embedded presentation or outline, using the layout you selected. To include text you enter in the notes pane of your slides, select one of the Notes layouts. If you want to export just the text of your presentation, you can save it as an outline in rich text format (.rtf format). You can view RTF documents in any word processing program. To do this, click File on the menu bar, click Save As, click Outline/RTF in the Save as type list box, then click Save.

UNIT G

PowerPoint 2003

Embedding an Excel Chart

When a chart is the best way to present information on a slide, you can create a chart using Microsoft Graph from within PowerPoint; however, for large amounts of data, it's easier to create a chart using a spreadsheet program like Excel. Then you can embed the chart file in your PowerPoint presentation and edit it using Excel tools. Excel is the chart file's **source program**, the program in which the file was created. PowerPoint is the **destination program**, the file into which the chart is embedded. Maria created an Excel chart showing MediaLoft's quarterly video sales. She wants you to include this chart in the presentation, so you embed it in a new slide.

STEPS

1. **Click Slide 3 in the Slides tab, click the New Slide button on the Formatting toolbar, then click the Title Only layout in the Slide Layout task pane**
   The new Slide 4 is selected and appears in the Slide pane.
2. **Type Quarterly Sales in the title placeholder**
3. **Click Insert on the menu bar, click Object, click the Create from file option button in the Insert Object dialog box, click Browse, locate the file PPT G-3.xls in the drive and folder where your Data Files are stored, click OK, then click OK in the Insert Object dialog box**
   The chart containing the quarterly sales data appears on the slide. The text labels on the chart are too small to read. Because the chart is embedded, you can edit the chart using Excel formatting tools.
4. **Double-click the chart to open Microsoft Excel**
   The Excel menu bar and Excel toolbars now appear on the screen.
5. **Right-click the Chart Title, click Format Chart Title on the shortcut menu, click the Font tab in the Format Chart Title dialog box, click 28 in the Size list, then click OK**
   The chart title is larger and more legible.
6. **Right-click the Value Axis Title, click Format Axis Title, click 24 in the Size list, click OK, click the Legend, then press [F4]**
   The axis title and legend are now larger and easier to read. Pressing [F4] repeats the last formatting action in Excel.
7. **Right-click the Value Axis, click Format Axis, click 22 in the Size list, click OK, click the Category Axis, then press [F4]**
   Compare your screen to Figure G-3.
8. **Double-click the chart area to the right of the chart title, click the Patterns tab in the Format Chart Area dialog box, click Fill Effects, click the Preset option button, click the Preset colors list arrow, scroll down, then click Silver**
9. **Click the Diagonal down option button in the Shading styles section, click OK, then click OK in the Format Chart Area dialog box**
   The chart background becomes a shaded silver color.
10. **Click outside the chart to exit Excel, click a blank area of the slide to deselect the chart object, then save the presentation**
    Compare your screen to Figure G-4.

TROUBLE

If the Chart toolbar appears in the middle of your screen, drag it to the top of the screen.

QUICK TIP

You can see if you selected the correct object on the graph because the name of the selected object appears in the Chart Objects box on the Chart toolbar.

FIGURE G-3: Embedded chart with formatted text

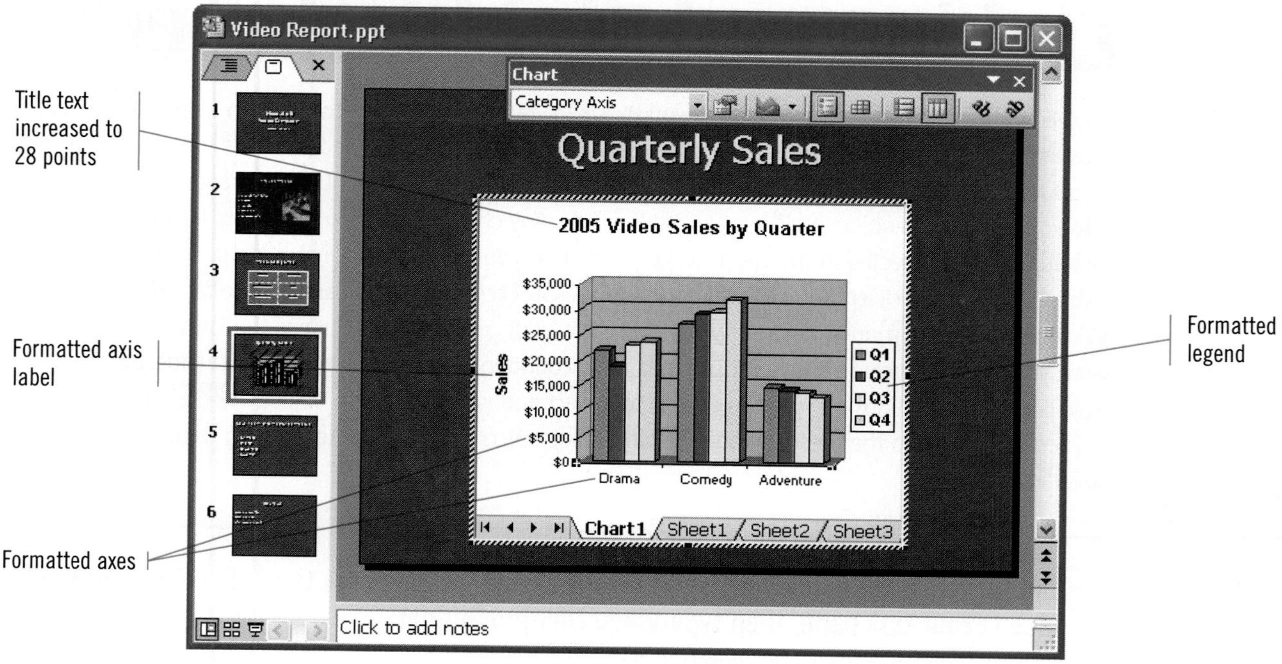

FIGURE G-4: Embedded chart with silver background

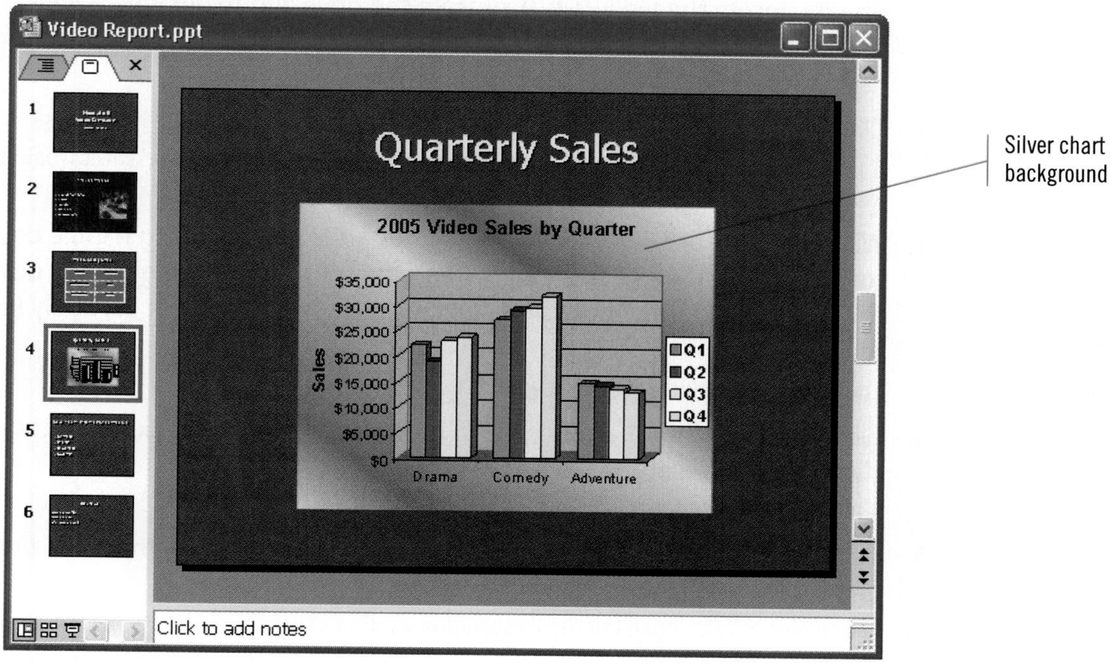

Clues to Use

Embedding a worksheet

You can embed all or part of an Excel worksheet in a PowerPoint slide. To embed an entire worksheet, go to the slide where you want to place the worksheet. Click Insert on the menu bar, then click Object. The Insert object dialog box opens. Click the Create from file option button, click Browse, locate and double-click the spreadsheet filename, then click OK. The worksheet is embedded in the slide. Double-click it to edit it using Excel commands as needed to work with the worksheet. To insert only a portion of a worksheet, open the Excel workbook and copy the cells you want to include in your presentation. Leave Excel and the source worksheet open, open the PowerPoint presentation, click Edit on the menu bar, then click Paste Special. To paste the cells as a worksheet object that you can edit in Excel, click Microsoft Excel Worksheet Object in the Paste Special dialog box, and then click OK.

Linking an Excel Worksheet

Another way to connect objects like Excel worksheets to your presentation is to establish a **link**, or connection, between the source file and the PowerPoint presentation. Unlike an embedded object, a linked object is stored in its source file, not on the slide, so when you link an object to a PowerPoint slide, a representation (picture) of the object, not the object itself, appears on the slide. Any changes made to the source file of a linked object are automatically reflected in the linked representation in your PowerPoint presentation. Some of the objects that you can link to PowerPoint include movies, Microsoft Excel worksheets, and PowerPoint slides from other presentations. Use linking when you want to be sure your presentation contains the latest information and when you want to include an object, such as an accounting spreadsheet, that may change over time. See Table G-1 for suggestions on when to embed an object and when to link an object. You need to link an Excel worksheet to the presentation. The worksheet was created by the Accounting Department manager earlier in the year.

STEPS

QUICK TIP

If you plan to do the steps in this unit again, be sure to make and use a copy of the Excel file PPT G-4.xls.

1. **Click the New Slide button on the Formatting toolbar, click the Title Only layout in the Slide Layout task pane, then type Video Division Budget**

   The new Slide 5 is selected and appears in the Slide pane.

2. **Click Insert on the menu bar, click Object, click the Create from file option button, click Browse, locate the file PPT G-4.xls from the drive and folder where your Data Files are stored, click OK, then click the Link check box to select it**

   Compare your screen to Figure G-5.

3. **Click OK in the Insert Object dialog box**

   A very small image of the linked worksheet appears on the slide. The worksheet would be easier to see if it were larger and had a background fill color.

4. **With the worksheet still selected, drag the bottom-right sizing handle down to the right toward the right edge of the slide, drag the bottom-left sizing handle down to the left toward the left edge of the slide, then position the worksheet vertically in the middle of the slide**

   The worksheet should be about as wide as the slide.

5. **Click the Fill Color list arrow on the Drawing toolbar, click the Automatic box, then click a blank area of the slide**

   A purple background fill color appears behind the worksheet, as shown in Figure G-6.

6. **Click the Save button on the Standard toolbar, then click the Close button in the presentation title bar**

   PowerPoint remains open but the Presentation window closes.

TABLE G-1: Embedding Versus Linking

situation	action
When you are the only user of an object and you want the object to be a part of your presentation	Embed
When you want to access the object in its source application, even if the original file is not available	Embed
When you want to update the object manually while working in PowerPoint	Embed
When you always want the latest information in your object	Link
When the object's source file is shared on a network or when other users have access to the file and can change it	Link
When you want to keep your presentation file size small	Link

FIGURE G-5: Insert Object dialog box ready to link an object

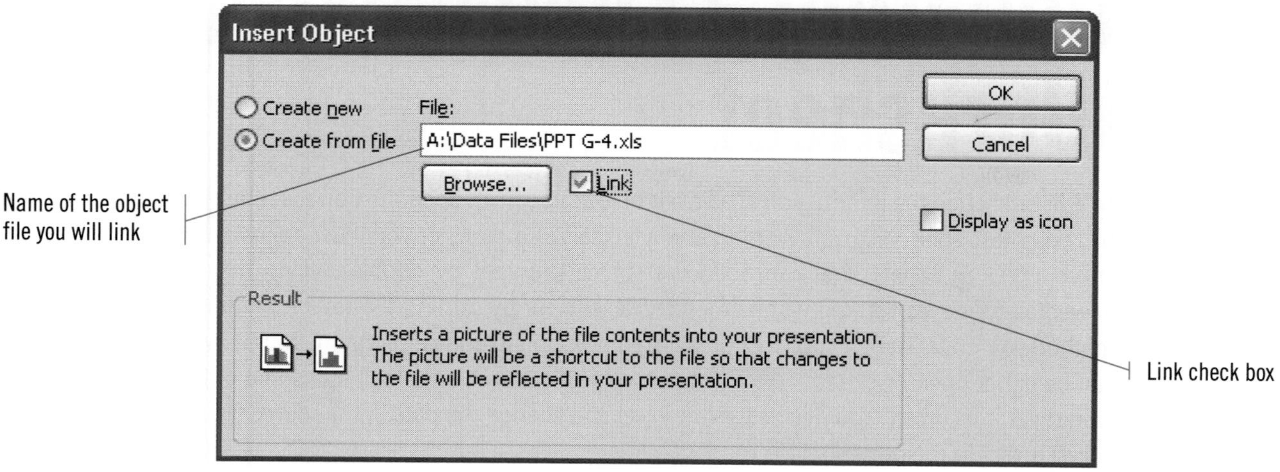

FIGURE G-6: Linked worksheet with background fill color

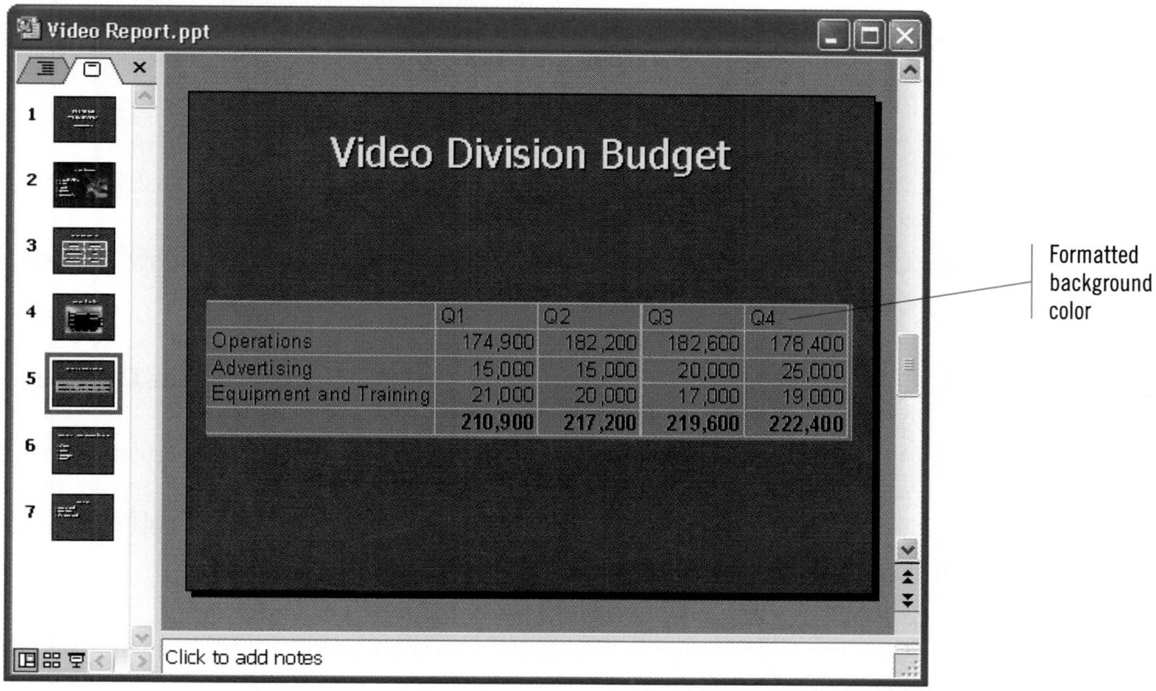

Clues to Use

Linking objects using Paste Special

You can also link an object or selected information from another program to PowerPoint by copying and pasting. This technique is useful when you want to link part of a worksheet rather than the entire file. For example, you may want to link a worksheet from a Microsoft Excel workbook that contains both a worksheet and a chart. To link just the worksheet, open the Microsoft Excel workbook file that contains the worksheet, select the worksheet, then copy it to the Clipboard. Leaving Excel and the source worksheet open, open the PowerPoint presentation, click Edit on the menu bar, click Paste Special, click the Paste link option button, then click OK.

UNIT G
PowerPoint 2003

Updating a Linked Excel Worksheet

To edit or change the information in a linked object, you must open the object's source program. For example, you must open Microsoft Word to edit a linked Word table, or you must open Microsoft Excel to edit a linked Excel worksheet. You can open the source program by double-clicking the linked object in the PowerPoint slide, as you did with embedded objects, or by starting the source program directly using any method you prefer. When you work on a linked object in its source program, your PowerPoint presentation can be either open or closed. You have just received an e-mail that some of the data in the Excel worksheet is incorrect. You decide to start Excel and change the data in the source file and then update the linked object in the presentation.

STEPS

1. **Click the Start button on the taskbar, point to All Programs, point to Microsoft Office, then click Microsoft Office Excel 2003**

   The Microsoft Excel program opens.

> **QUICK TIP**
> To edit or open a linked object in your presentation, the object's source program and source file must be available on your computer or network.

2. **Click File on the menu bar, click Open, select the file PPT G-4.xls from the drive and folder where your Data Files are stored, then click Open**

   The PPT G-4.xls worksheet opens.

3. **Click cell B3, type 22000, click cell C3, type 18000, then press [Enter]**

   The Q1 and Q2 totals are automatically recalculated. The Q1 total now reads 217,900 instead of 210,900 and the Q2 total reads 220,200 instead of 217,200.

4. **Click the Close button in the Microsoft Excel program window, then click Yes to save the changes**

   Microsoft Excel closes and the PowerPoint window opens.

> **QUICK TIP**
> The destination file can remain open when you update links. After you change the source file and switch back to the presentation file, the linked object is updated.

5. **Click in the PowerPoint program window to activate it, click the Open button on the Standard toolbar, click the file Video Report, then click Open**

   A Microsoft Office PowerPoint alert box opens, telling you that the Video Report presentation contains links and asking if you want to update them. See Figure G-7. This message appears whenever you open a PowerPoint presentation that contains linked objects that have been changed.

6. **Click Update Links**

   The worksheet in the presentation slide is now updated with the new data.

7. **Click the Slide Design button on the Formatting toolbar, click Window on the menu bar, click Arrange All, then click Slide 5 in the Slides tab**

   Compare your screen to Figure G-8. The linked Excel worksheet shows the new totals for Q1 and Q2. The changes you made in Excel were automatically entered in this linked copy when you updated the links.

8. **Click the Save button on the Standard toolbar**

FIGURE G-7: Alert box to update links

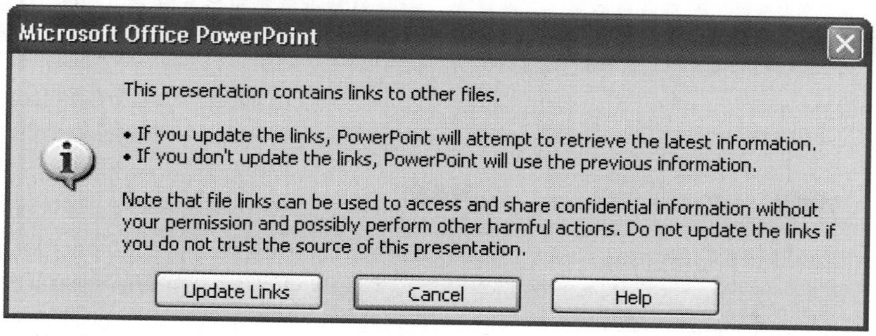

FIGURE G-8: Slide with updated, linked worksheet

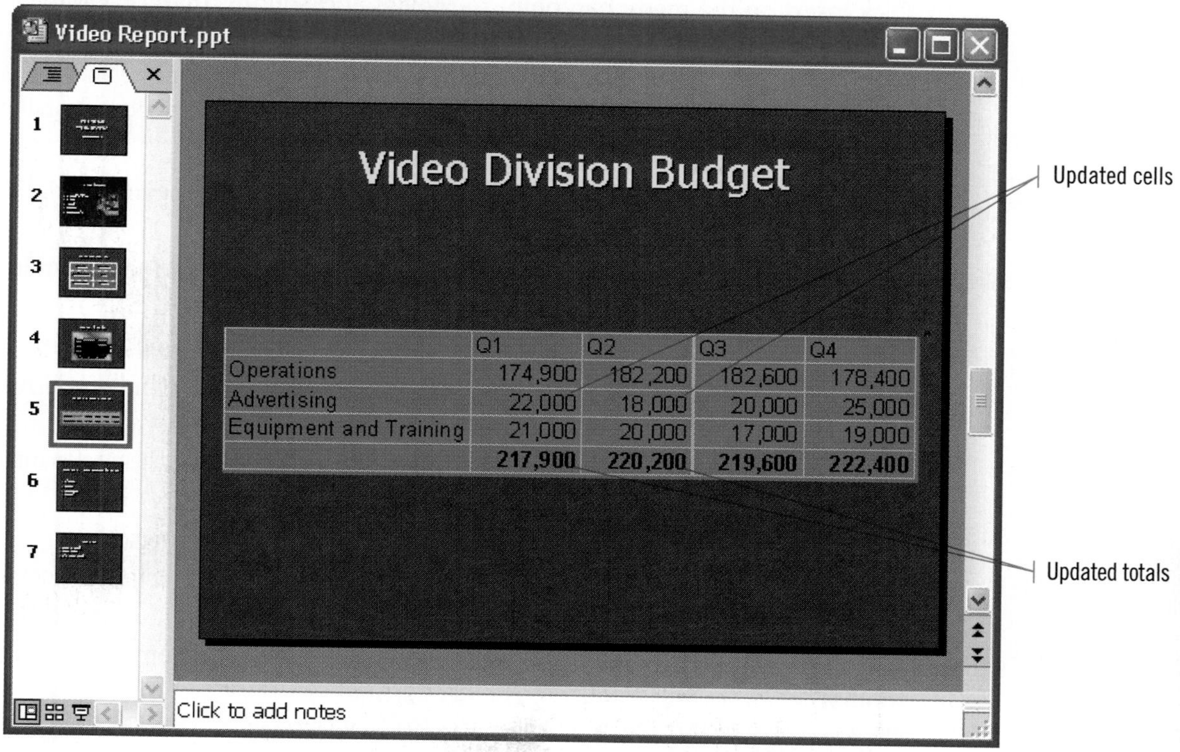

PowerPoint 2003

Clues to Use

Using the Links dialog box

You can use the Links dialog box to update a link, open a linked object's source program, change a linked object's source program, break a link, and determine if links are updated automatically or manually. To open the Links dialog box, click Edit on the menu bar, click Links, then click the link you want. The Links dialog box opens, as shown in Figure G-9. If the Manual option button is selected, the links in the target file will not be updated unless you select the link in this dialog box and click Update Now.

FIGURE G-9: Links dialog box

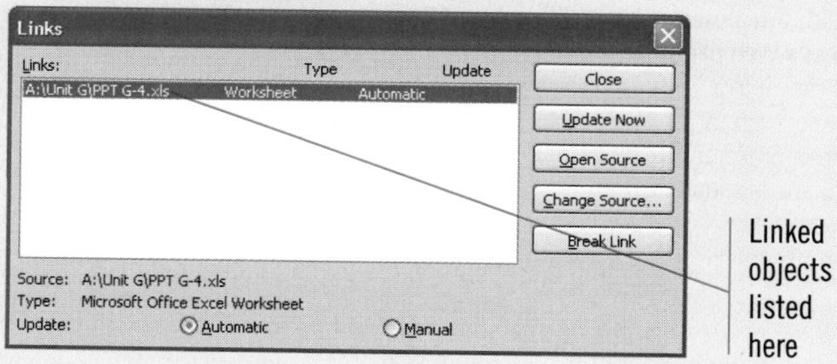

UNIT
G
PowerPoint 2003

Inserting an Animated GIF File

In your presentations, you may want to use special effects to illustrate a point or capture the attention of your audience. You can do this by inserting an animation or a movie. An **animation** contains multiple images that stream together or move when you run a slide show to give the illusion of motion. Animations are stored as Graphics Interchange Format (GIF) files. PowerPoint comes with a number of animated GIFs, which are stored in the Microsoft Clip Organizer. The **Clip Organizer** contains various drawings, photographs, clip art, sounds, animated GIFs, and movies that you can insert into your presentation. A **movie** is live action captured in digital format by a movie camera. You continue to develop your presentation by embedding an animated GIF file in a slide about international videos.

STEPS

1. **Click Slide 6 in the Slides tab**
2. **Click Insert on the menu bar, point to Movies and Sounds, then click Movie from Clip Organizer**
   The Clip Art task pane opens and displays all the animated GIFs available for you to use. If you don't want to view all the animation clips in the Clip Art task pane, you can narrow the results that it displays.
3. **Type travel in the Search for text box, then click Go**
   All the clips that have a travel attribute appear in the Clip Art task pane. The animation clip you want is near the bottom of the list.
4. **Click the down scroll arrow until you see the GIF file of the bridge shown in Figure G-10, then click the GIF file image**
   The animated GIF appears in the center of the slide and the Picture toolbar opens.
5. **Resize the image so it is approximately the same height as the bulleted list, then drag the image so it's directly across from the bulleted list**
   If a GIF image is too dark or too light, or if its colors don't match the color scheme, you can format the image using the commands on the Picture toolbar.
6. **Click the Color button on the Picture toolbar, then click Grayscale**
   The animated GIF's colors are changed to shades of gray, which makes the animation look a little better with the presentation's color scheme, but the animation looks too dark now.
7. **Click , click Automatic, then click the More Brightness button once on the Picture toolbar**
   The animated GIF changes back to color and is slightly brightened.
8. **Click the Less Contrast button on the Picture toolbar twice, then click in a blank area of the slide**
   The animated GIF has less contrast. Compare your screen with Figure G-11. The animation won't begin unless you view it in Slide Show view.
9. **Click the Slide Show button , watch the animation, press [Esc], then click the Save button on the Standard toolbar**

TROUBLE

If you do not see the GIF file in Figure G-10, choose a different GIF or ask your instructor or technical support person for help.

QUICK TIP

An animated GIF file will also play if you publish the presentation as a Web page and view it in a browser such as Internet Explorer or Netscape Navigator.

FIGURE G-10: Clip Organizer showing animated GIF files

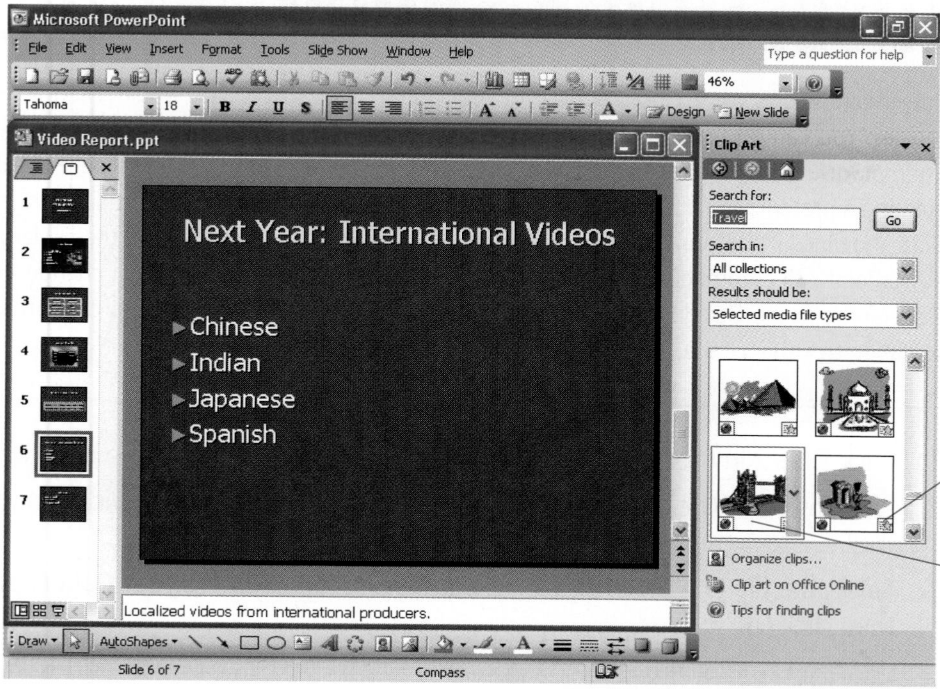

FIGURE G-11: Animated GIF in Normal view

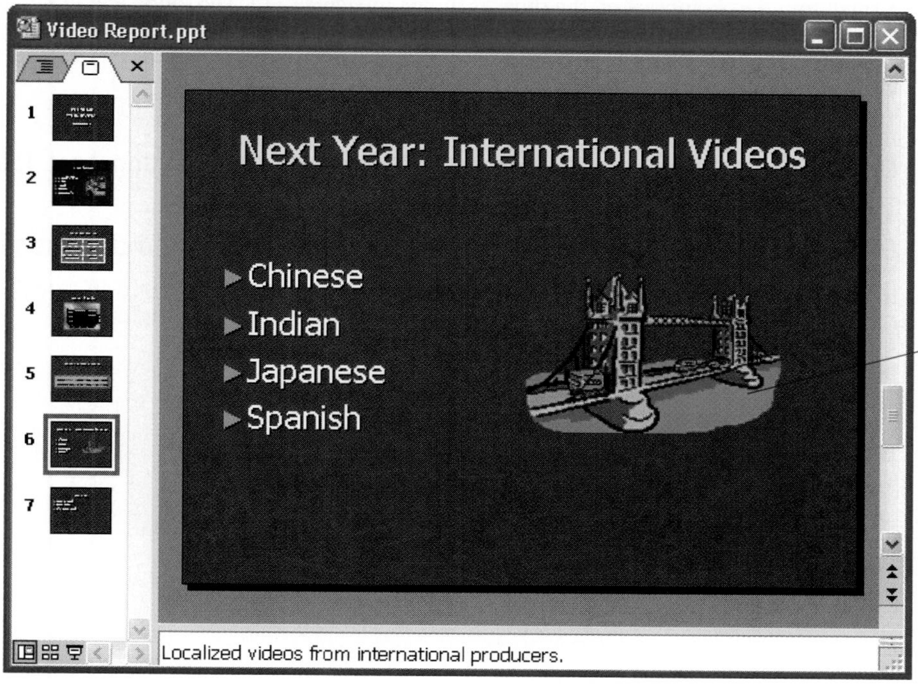

PowerPoint 2003

Clues to Use

Inserting movies

You can insert movies from the Clip Organizer, the Microsoft Web site, or from disk files. To insert a movie from a disk, click Insert on the menu bar, point to Movies and Sounds, then click Movie from File. Navigate to the location of the movie you want, then insert it. If you're using the Clip Art task pane, search for the file you want, then insert it. After you insert a movie, you can edit it using the Picture toolbar. You can also open the Custom Animation task pane and apply an effect to the movie. From the Custom Animation task pane, you can indicate whether to continue the slide show or to stop playing the clip.

Inserting a Sound

PowerPoint allows you to insert sounds in your presentation just as you would insert animated GIF files or movies. You can add sounds to your presentation from files on a disk, the Microsoft Clip Organizer, the Internet, or a location on a network. Use sound to enhance the message of a slide. For example, if you are creating a presentation about a raft tour of the Colorado River, you might insert a rushing water sound on a slide showing a photograph of people rafting. If you try to insert a sound that is larger than 100 KB, PowerPoint will automatically link the sound file to your presentation. You can change this setting on the General tab in the Options dialog box. You insert a sound of a camera click on Slide 2 of the presentation to enhance the picture on the slide.

STEPS

1. **Click Slide 2 in the Slides tab**
2. **Click Insert on the menu bar, point to Movies and Sounds, then click Sound from File**
   The Insert Sound dialog box opens.
3. **Select the file PPT G-5.wav from the drive and folder where your Data Files are stored, then click OK**
   A dialog box opens asking if you want the sound to play automatically or if you want it to play only when you click the icon during the slide show.

TROUBLE
The sound icon you see may be different from the one illustrated in Figure G-12 depending on your sound card software.

4. **Click Automatically**
   A small sound icon appears on the slide, as shown in Figure G-12. The sound will play automatically during a slide show.
5. **Click Format on the menu bar, click Picture, then click the Size tab**
   The Size tab opens in the Format Picture dialog box.
6. **Double-click the number in the Height text box in the Scale section, type 150, then click OK**
   The sound icon enlarges to 150% of its original size.
7. **Drag the sound icon to the lower-right corner of the slide, then click the slide background to deselect the icon**
   Compare your screen to Figure G-13.

TROUBLE
If you do not hear a sound, your computer may not have a sound card installed. See your instructor or technical support person for help.

8. **Double-click the sound icon**
   The sound of the shutter on a camera clicking plays out of your computer's speakers.
9. **Click the Save button on the Standard toolbar**

FIGURE G-12: Slide showing small sound icon

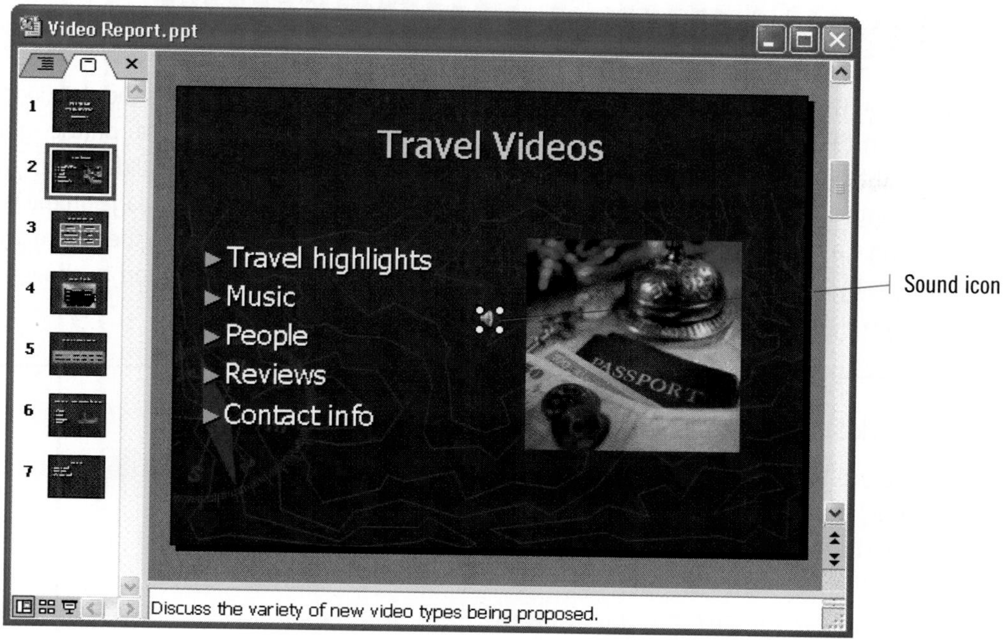

FIGURE G-13: Slide showing resized and repositioned sound icon

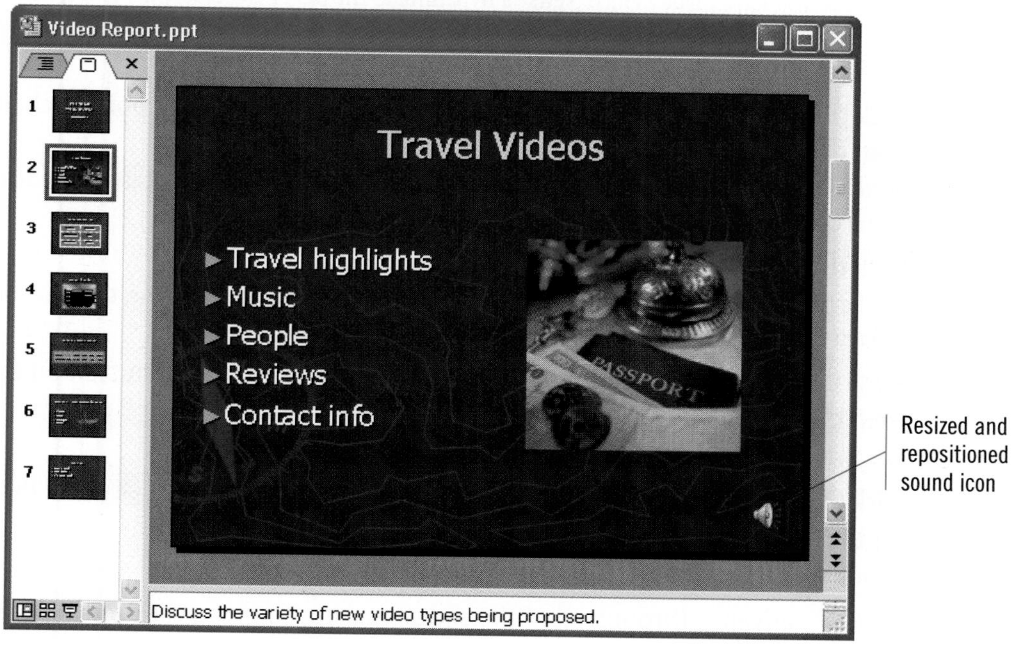

Clues to Use

Playing music from a CD

You can play a CD audio track during your slide show. Click Insert on the menu bar, point to Movies and Sounds, then click Play CD Audio Track. The Insert CD Audio dialog box opens. Select the beginning and ending track number and the timing options you want. See Figure G-14. When you are finished in the Insert CD Audio dialog box, click OK. A CD icon appears on the slide. You can indicate if you want the CD to play automatically when you move to the slide or only when you click the CD icon during a slide show. The CD must be in the CD-ROM drive before you can play an audio track.

FIGURE G-14: Insert CD Audio dialog box

Inserting a Hyperlink

Often you will want to view a document that either won't fit on the slide or is too detailed for your presentation. In these cases, you can insert a hyperlink, a specially formatted word, phrase, graphic, or drawn object that you click during your slide show to "jump to," or display, another slide in your current presentation; another PowerPoint presentation; a Word, Excel, or Access file; or a Web page on the World Wide Web. Inserting a hyperlink is similar to linking because you can change the object in the source program after you click the hyperlink. You decide to add a hyperlink to the presentation to show a recent product review, which is in a Word document.

STEPS

1. **Click Slide 7 in the Slides tab**
2. **Select Video News on the slide, click the Insert Hyperlink button on the Standard toolbar, then click Existing File or Web Page**
   The Insert Hyperlink dialog box opens. Compare your dialog box with Figure G-15. You want to hyperlink to another file.
3. **Select the file PPT G-6.doc from the drive and folder where your Data Files are stored, click OK, then click in a blank area of the slide**
   Now that you have made "Video News" a hyperlink to the file PPT G-6.doc, the text formatting changes to a light green color, the hyperlink color for this presentation's color scheme, and is underlined. It's important to test any hyperlink you create.
4. **Click the Slide Show button, point to Video News to see the pointer change to, then click the Video News hyperlink**
   Microsoft Word opens, and the Word document containing the review appears on the screen, as shown in Figure G-16. The Web toolbar appears below the Formatting toolbar.
5. **Click the Back button on the Web toolbar**
   The Reviews slide reappears in Slide Show view. The hyperlink is now light blue, the color for followed hyperlinks in this color scheme, indicating that the hyperlink has been used.
6. **Press [Esc] to end the slide show, right-click the Word program button on the taskbar, then click Close on the shortcut menu**
   The Word program closes.
7. **Click Slide 1 in the Slides tab, click the Slide Sorter View button, click in the Zoom box on the Standard toolbar, type 50, then press [Enter]**
   Compare your screen to Figure G-17.
8. **Click, advance through all of the slides, making sure you click the hyperlink on Slide 7, then click to return to the slide show**
9. **Add your name to the notes and handouts footer, click File on the menu bar, click Print, click the Print what list arrow, click Notes Pages, then click OK**
10. **Save your changes, then close the presentation**

FIGURE G-15: Insert hyperlink dialog box

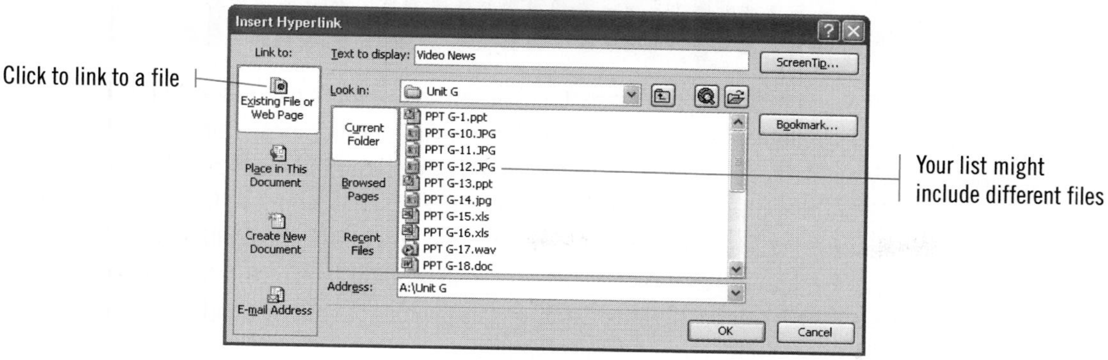

FIGURE G-16: Linked review in Word

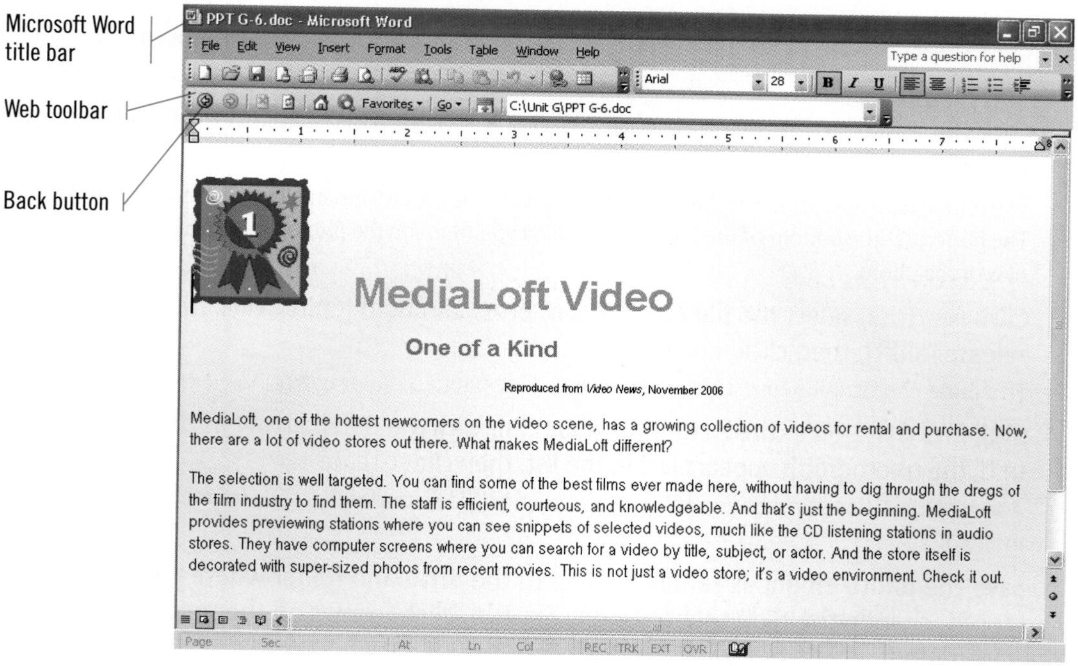

FIGURE G-17: Final presentation in Slide Sorter view

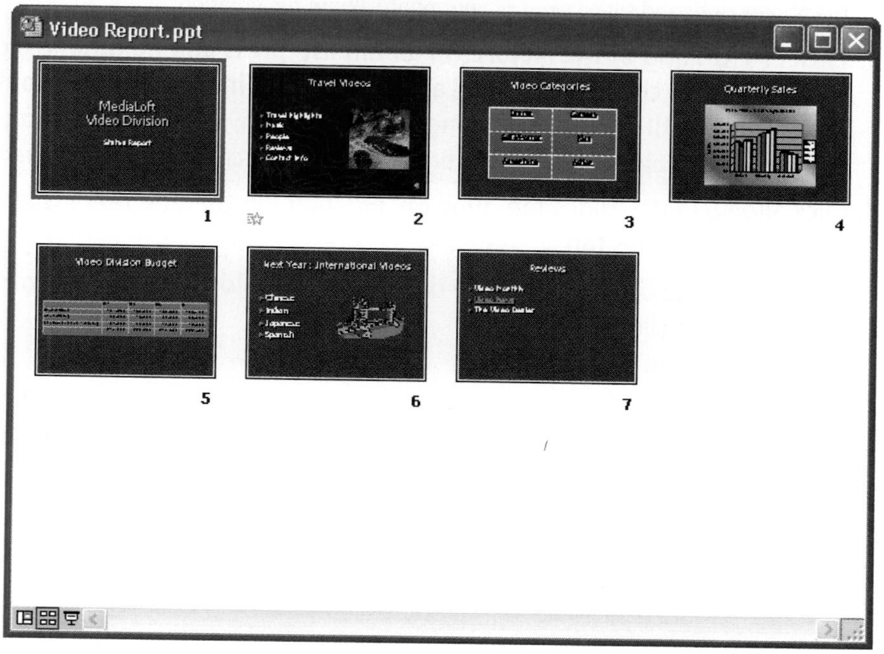

UNIT G

PowerPoint 2003

Creating a Photo Album

You can use PowerPoint to create a presentation using your favorite pictures. A **PowerPoint photo album** is a special presentation designed specifically to display photographs. You can add pictures to a photo album from your hard drive, digital camera, scanner, or Web camera. As with any presentation, you can customize the layout of a photo album by adding title text to slides, applying frames around the pictures, and applying a design template. You can also format the pictures of the photo album by adding a caption below the pictures, converting the pictures to black and white, rotating the pictures, and changing their brightness and contrast. You have a little extra time at the end of your day and you decide to use PowerPoint to create a photo album of a recent family ski trip.

STEPS

1. **Click Insert on the menu bar, point to Picture, then click New Photo Album**

   The Photo Album dialog box opens.

2. **Click File/Disk button, select the file PPT G-7.jpg from the drive and folder where your Data Files are stored, then click Insert**

   The photograph appears in the Preview box and is listed in the Pictures in album list as shown in Figure G-18. The buttons at the bottom of the Preview box allow you to rotate the photo, or change the contrast or brightness of the photo.

3. **Click File/Disk, select the file PPT G-8.jpg, press and hold [Shift], click the file PPT G-12.jpg, release [Shift], then click Insert**

   Five more photographs appear in the dialog box. One photo is out of order.

> **TROUBLE**
>
> If the files in the Insert New Picture dialog box are not sorted by File Name, select pictures PPT G-8, PPT G-9, PPT G-10, PPT G-11, and PPT G-12 in the list.

4. **Click PPT G-12.jpg in the Pictures in album list, click the down arrow button below the list until the photograph appears last in the list, then click Create**

   A new presentation appears. PowerPoint creates a title slide along with a slide for each photograph that you inserted.

5. **Save the photo album as Family Ski Trip to the drive and folder where your Data Files are stored, change the slide title to Family Ski Trip, click Format on the menu bar, then click Photo Album**

   The slide title changes and the Format Photo Album dialog box opens. You can use this dialog box to format the photographs and slide layout of your photo album presentation.

> **QUICK TIP**
>
> If you want others to have access to your photo album on the Web, you can save the photo album presentation as a Web page.

6. **Click PPT G-7.jpg in the Pictures in album list, press and hold [Shift], click PPT G-12.jpg, release [Shift], click the Picture Layout list arrow in the Album Layout section, click 1 picture with title, click the Frame shape list arrow, click Corner Tabs, then click Update**

   Notice that all of the slides now have a title text placeholder and all of the photographs have corner tabs.

7. **Click Slide 6 in the Slides tab, type My big jump! in the title text placeholder, then click Slide 7 in the Slides tab**

8. **Type My rescue off the hill in the title text placeholder, then enter your own title text on the other four slides**

   All of the slides now have a title.

9. **Click Slide 1 in the Slides tab, click the Slide Show button, advance through the slides, click the Slide Sorter View button, then add your name to the notes and handouts header**

   Compare your screen to Figure G-19.

10. **Save your changes, click File on the menu bar, click Print, click the Print what list arrow, click Handouts (1 per page), click OK, close the presentation, then exit PowerPoint**

FIGURE G-18: Photo Album dialog box

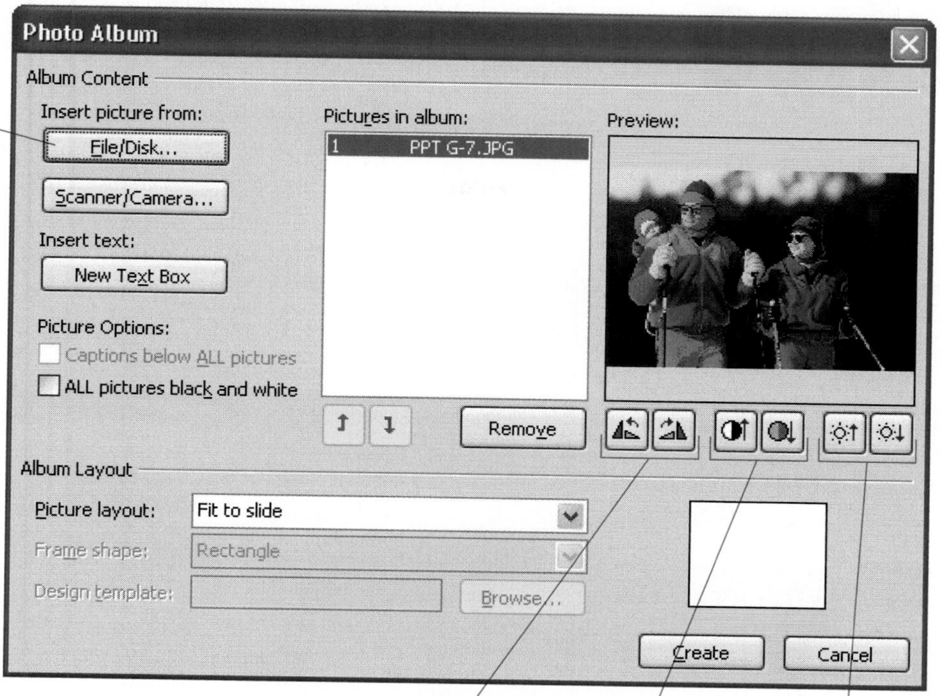

FIGURE G-19: Completed photo album presentation

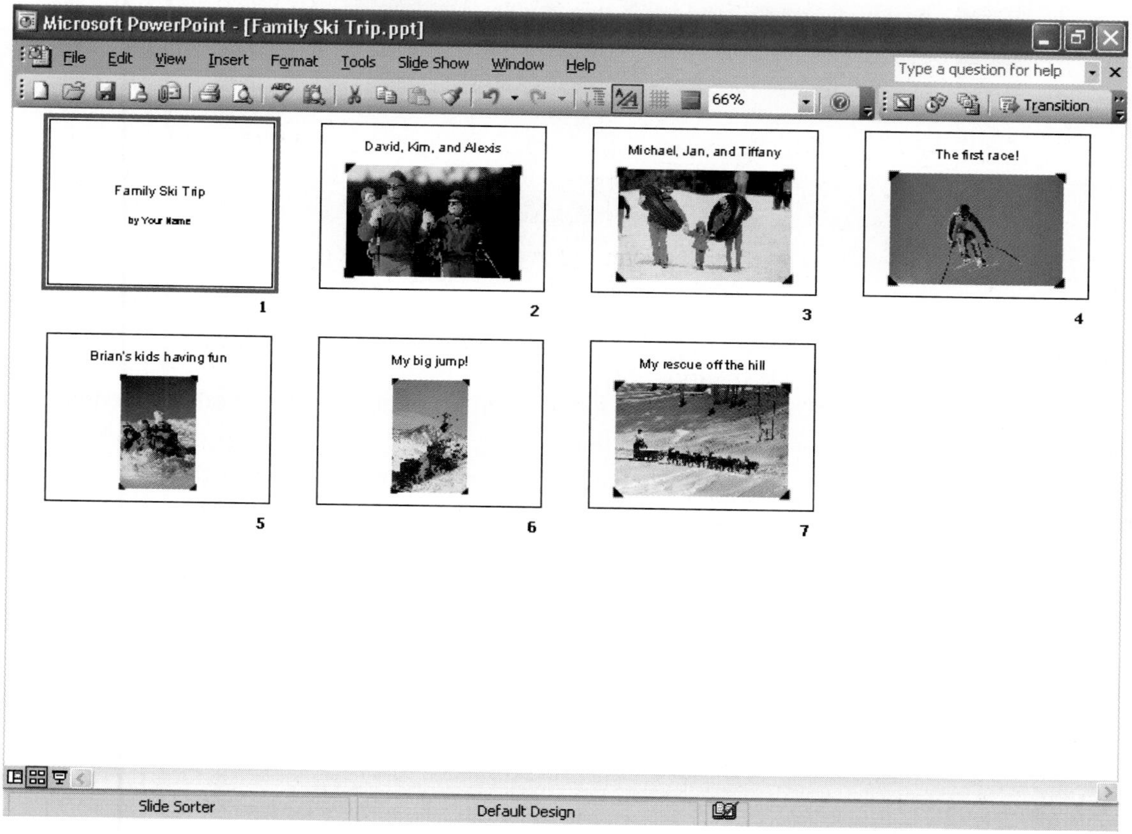

PowerPoint 2003

Practice

▼ CONCEPTS REVIEW

Label each element of the PowerPoint window shown in Figure G-20.

FIGURE G-20

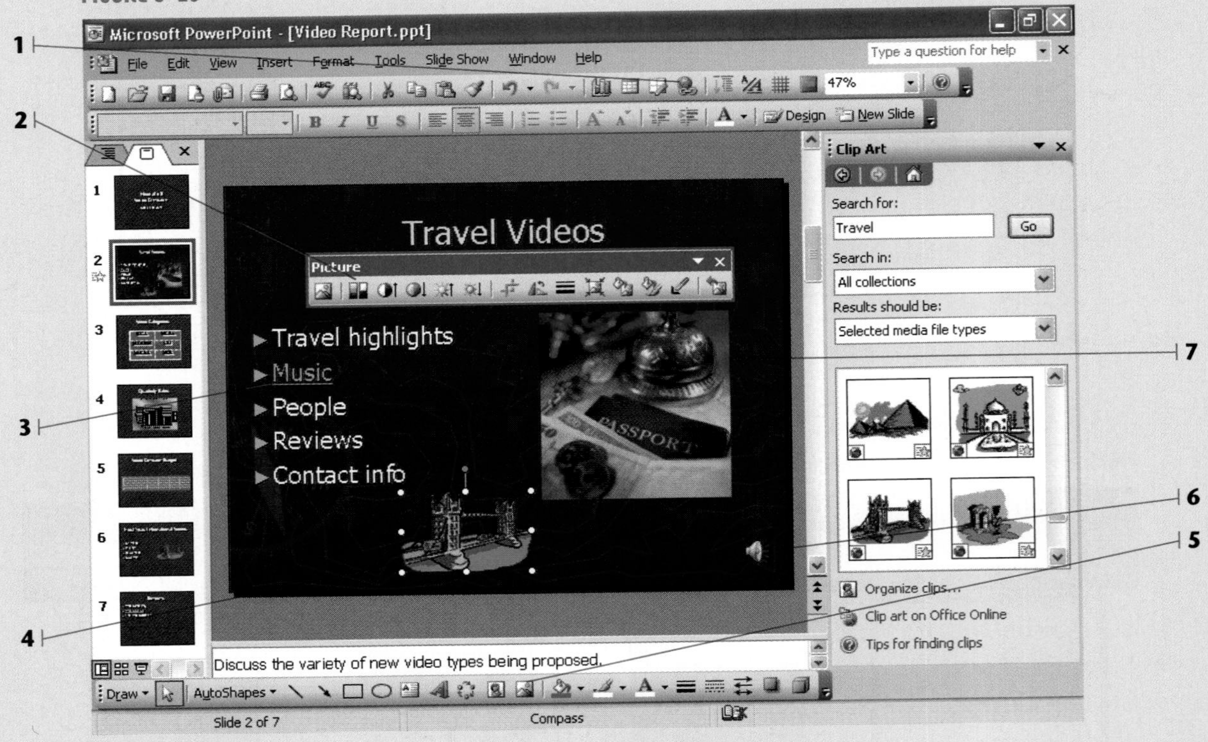

Match each of the terms with the statement that best describes its function.

8. **Movie**
9. **Hyperlink**
10. **Animation**
11. **Photo Album**
12. **Linked object**
13. **Source program**
14. **Destination program**

a. A specially formatted word or graphic that you can click to jump to another document
b. A representation of an object stored in its source file
c. A special presentation designed specifically to work with photographs
d. Multiple images that move when you run a slide show
e. Live action captured in digital format by a movie camera
f. The program that you use to create an embedded file
g. The program into which an embedded file is inserted

Select the best answer from the list of choices.

15. Which statement about embedded objects is not true?

a. Embedded objects can be edited in their source program.
b. Embedded objects always have the latest information.
c. Embedded objects are not a part of the presentation.
d. Embedded objects can be edited even if the original file is not available.

16. Which statement about linked objects is true?

a. To edit a linked object, you must open its source file.
b. A linked object substantially increases the size of your presentation file.
c. You can access a linked object even when the source file is not available.
d. A linked object is an independent object inserted directly on a slide.

17. Which statement best describes a hyperlink?

a. A hyperlink is a type of animation.
b. A hyperlink is a type of chart that you embed using Graph.
c. A hyperlink is a portal button that you click on a slide when you want to search the Web.
d. A hyperlink is a specially formatted word that you click to display a Web page.

18. The best way to display your photographs using PowerPoint is to create

a. An animation.
b. An embedded object.
c. A photo album.
d. A hyperlink.

▼ SKILLS REVIEW

1. Embed a picture.

a. Start PowerPoint, open the presentation PPT G-13.ppt from the drive and folder where your Data Files are stored, then save it as **Marketing 2006**.
b. Go to Slide 4 and insert the image PPT G-14.jpg.
c. Resize the picture so it fits in the blank area of the slide, then use the arrow keys on the keyboard to adjust its position.
d. Save your changes.

2. Embed an Excel chart.

a. Insert a new slide after Slide 5 using the Blank slide layout.
b. Embed the chart from the file PPT G-15.xls.
c. Using Excel tools, enlarge the chart title text to 24 points and the Value and Category axes to 14 points.
d. Change the Value axis title and Legend text to 18 points and reposition the legend so it is at the bottom of the chart (*Hint*: Click the Placement tab in the Format Legend dialog box.)
e. Resize and reposition the chart so it is centered horizontally and vertically on the slide.
f. Save your changes.

3. Link an Excel worksheet.

a. Create a new slide after Slide 6 with the Title Only layout.
b. Title the slide **Basic P & L**.
c. Link the spreadsheet file PPT G-16.xls from the drive and folder where your Data Files are stored.
d. Resize the object so that it fills the slide width.
e. Reposition the object so it is centered vertically. (*Hint:* To center it more precisely, hold down [Alt] while you drag, or hold down [Ctrl] while you press the arrow keys.)
f. Fill the spreadsheet object with light gray (the Follow Accent and Followed Hyperlink Scheme Color).
g. Save and close the Marketing 2006 presentation.

▼ SKILLS REVIEW (CONTINUED)

4. Update a linked Excel worksheet.

a. Start Excel, then open the worksheet PPT G-16.xls.

b. Replace the value in cell B4 with **95,000**.

c. In cell D7, enter **1,350,000**.

d. Close Excel after saving your changes.

e. Open the Marketing 2006.ppt presentation file in PowerPoint, updating the link as you do so.

f. Go to Slide 7 and view your changes. Save the presentation.

5. Insert an animated GIF file.

a. Go to Slide 8.

b. Insert an animated GIF file of your choosing on the slide. Use the word **email** to search for an appropriate animated GIF.

c. Resize and reposition the GIF file as necessary.

d. Preview it in Slide Show view. Save the presentation.

6. Insert a sound.

a. Go to Slide 2.

b. Insert the sound file PPT G-17.wav from the drive and folder where your Data Files are stored. Set the sound to play when you click the sound icon.

c. In the Format Picture dialog box, scale the sound icon to 125% of its original size.

d. Drag the sound icon to the lower-right corner of the slide.

e. Test the sound in Slide Show view. Save the presentation.

7. Insert a hyperlink.

a. Go to Slide 7 in the presentation, then add a new slide with the Title and Text layout.

b. Title the slide **Reviews**.

c. In the first line of the main text placeholder, enter **Jeff Sanders, Web Cheese Review** and on the second line enter **Jorge Fonseca, Online Cheese Today**.

d. Select the entire main text placeholder, and change its font size to 36 points.

e. Resize the text placeholder to fit the text, then center it on the slide.

f. Convert the Jeff Sanders bullet into a hyperlink to the file PPT G-18.doc.

g. Click in the notes pane, then type **The hyperlink links to Jeff's cheese review of the 2006 Camembert**.

h. Run the slide show and test the hyperlink.

i. Use the Back button to return to the presentation.

j. End the slide show.

k. Exit Word.

l. Run the spellchecker, view the presentation in Slide Show view, and evaluate your presentation. Make any necessary changes.

m. Add your name as a footer to notes and handouts, print the slides as Notes Pages, then save and close the presentation.

8. Create a photo album.

a. Create a new photo album, then insert the files PPT G-19.jpg, PPT G-20.jpg, PPT G-21.jpg, and PPT G-22.jpg from the drive and folder where your Data Files are stored.

b. Make sure the pictures appear in descending order.

c. Change the title on the title slide to **Jeff's Playoff Game**.

d. Format the album layout to one picture with a title on each slide.

e. Format the frame shape to Rounded Rectangle.

f. Enter a title of your choosing on each slide with a photograph.

g. Save the photo album as **Jeff's Playoff Game** to the drive and folder where your Data Files are stored.

h. View the photo album in Slide Show view, then add your name to the notes and handouts header.

i. Save your changes, print the photo album handouts, close the presentation, then exit PowerPoint.

▼ INDEPENDENT CHALLENGE 1

D & K Engineering is a mechanical and industrial design company that specializes in designing manufacturing plants in the United States and Canada. As the company financial analyst, you need to investigate and report on a possible contract to design and build a large manufacturing plant in Belize. The board of directors wants to make sure that they can make a minimum profit on the deal. It is your job to provide a recommendation to the board.

Create your own information using the basic presentation provided and assume the following about D & K Engineering:

- The new manufacturing plant in Belize will be 75,000 square feet in size. The projected cost for D & K Engineering to design and build the plant in Belize is about $280.00 per square foot based on a four-phase schedule: planning and design, site acquisition and preparation, underground construction, and above-ground construction.
- Factors that helped determine D & K Engineering's cost to build the plant include: D & K Engineering payroll for 45 people in Belize for 24 months; materials cost; hiring two Belizean construction companies to construct the plant; and travel expenses.
- Factor in a $1.5 million dollar profit margin for D & K Engineering above the cost of the building.

a. Open the file PPT G-23.ppt, then save it as **Belize Plant**.

b. Think about what results you want to see, what information you will need to create the slide presentation, and how your message should be communicated. In order for your presentation to be complete, it must include the following objects: (i) an embedded picture; (ii) an embedded Excel chart; and (iii) a sound from the Clip Organizer.

c. Use Microsoft Excel and PowerPoint to embed objects into your presentation. Use the assumptions previously listed to develop information that would be appropriate for a table.

d. Give each slide a title and add main text where appropriate.

e. Make the last slide in the presentation your recommendation to pursue the contract, based on the financial data you present.

f. Add your name as a footer to the notes and handouts, save your changes, then print the final slide presentation as handouts (two slides per page).

Advanced Challenge Exercise

ACE

- Click File on the menu bar, point to Send To, then click Microsoft Office Word.
- Click the Blank lines next to slides option button, then click **OK**.
- Save the Word document as **Belize Plant Proposal ACE**. then add your name to the document footer.

g. View the presentation in Slide Show view, then exit PowerPoint.

▼ INDEPENDENT CHALLENGE 2

You are the director of operations at The Templeton Group, a large investment banking company in Texas. Templeton is considering merging with Redding, Inc, a smaller investment company in Arizona, to form the 10th largest financial institution in the United States. As the director of operations, you need to present some financial projections regarding the merger to a special committee formed by Templeton to study the proposed merger.

Create your own information using the basic presentation provided on your Project Disk. Assume the following facts about the merger between Templeton and Redding:

- Templeton earned $7 million dollars in profit last year. Projected profit this year is $5 million dollars. Templeton's operating expenses run approximately $31 million dollars each year.
- Redding earned $3 million dollars in profit last year. Projected profit this year is $4 million dollars. Redding's operating expenses run approximately $22 million dollars each year.
- Templeton has a 19% share of the market without Redding. Redding has a 6% share of the market without Templeton. Combined, the companies would have a 25% share of the market.
- With the merger, the projected profit next year is $12 million dollars. Templeton would need to cut $7.6 million dollars from its annual operating costs and Redding would need to cut $2 million dollars from its annual operating costs.

▼ INDEPENDENT CHALLENGE 2 (CONTINUED)

a. Open the file PPT G-24.ppt from the drive and folder where your Data Files are stored, then save it as **T & R Merger**.

b. Think about what results you want to see, what information you will need to create the slide presentation, and how your message should be communicated. In order for your presentation to be complete, it must include the following objects: (i) a linked Excel worksheet; (ii) an embedded PowerPoint table, chart, or other object; and (iii) a hyperlink.

c. Use Microsoft Excel to link a worksheet to your presentation. Use the preceding assumptions to develop related information that would be appropriate for the worksheet. Use the profit and operating expense figures to create your own revenue figures. (Revenue minus operating expenses equals profit.)

d. Hyperlink to the file Redding, Inc.ppt. Choose the slide in the presentation where the hyperlink should be placed. You can use existing text or create a drawn or other object to use as the hyperlink.

e. Give each slide a title and add main text where appropriate. Create slides as necessary to make the presentation complete.

f. Add your name as a footer to the notes and the handouts, save your changes, then print the final slide presentation.

g. View the presentation in Slide Show view, then exit PowerPoint.

▼ INDEPENDENT CHALLENGE 3

You have just been promoted to the position of sales manager at Import Express, a U.S. company that exports goods and professional services to companies in Japan, South Korea, China, and the Philippines. One of your new responsibilities is to give a presentation at the biannual finance meeting showing how the sales department performed during the previous six-month period.

Plan and create a short slide presentation (six to eight slides) that illustrates the sales department's performance during the last six months. Identify the existing accounts (by country), then identify the new contracts acquired during the last six months. Create your own content, but assume the following:

- The majority of goods and services being exported are as follows: food products (such as rice, corn, and wheat); agriculture consulting; construction engineering; and industrial designing and engineering.
- The company gained five new accounts in China, South Korea, and the Philippines.
- The sales department showed a $4.2 million dollar profit for the first half of the year.
- Department expenses for the first half of the year were $3.5 million dollars.
- The presentation will be given in a boardroom using a projection machine.

a. Think about what results you want to see, what information you will need to create the slide presentation, and how your message should be communicated. In order for your presentation to be complete, it must include the following objects: (i) an embedded Excel chart; (ii) a sound from the Clip Organizer; (iii) an embedded picture; and (iv) an animated GIF file or embedded movie.

b. Use the movies provided for you in PowerPoint, or if you have access to another media source that does not infringe on copyright laws, choose an appropriate movie from that source to embed in your presentation.

c. Give each slide a title and add main text points where appropriate.

d. Add a template, background shading, or other enhancing objects to make your presentation look professional.

Advanced Challenge Exercise

- With your PowerPoint file open, open the Excel file PPT G-25.xls from the drive and folder where your Data Files are stored, then select and copy the data on Sheet 1.
- Display your open PowerPoint file, create a new slide, then use the Paste Special command to paste the object.
- Use the same operation to paste the data on Sheet 2 of the PPT G-25.xls file to a new slide in your presentation.

e. Save the presentation as **Imports** to the drive and folder where your Data Files are stored.

f. Add your name as a footer to the slides and notes and handouts, save your changes, then print the final slide presentation.

g. View the presentation in Slide Show view, then exit PowerPoint.

E-QUEST ▼ INDEPENDENT CHALLENGE 4

You are the business manager for Partners Inc., a large nonprofit educational organization in Los Angeles, California. One of your duties is to purchase new and used computer equipment for the organization every three years. Partners Inc. has allotted some money in the budget this year to upgrade some of the computer equipment. Your job is to prepare a brief presentation, outlining the cost of purchasing new and used equipment and selling the old equipment, for the board of directors' next monthly meeting.

Develop your own content, but assume the following:

- Ten computer systems need to be sold.
- The old computers are configured as follows: Pentium III, 866 MHz, 64 MB RAM, 10 GB HDD, IDE CD-ROM with Sound and 4 MB Video, 56 K Modem 10/100 3Com Network Card, Windows 2000.

The 15 replacement computer systems need to be configured as follows: Pentium 4, 2.0 GHz - 2.5 GHz, 128 MB RAM, 50+GB HD, DVD CD-RW with Sound and 24 MB Video, 56 K Modem 10/100 3Com Network Card, Windows XP.

- Add $50.00 to the price of each purchased computer for tax and shipping.
- You are allowed to spend up to $1000.00 per new computer.

You'll need to find the following information on the Web:

- The average price of the old computer systems that need to be sold.
- The prices of the new computer systems.
- Auction Web sites where the old computers can be sold.

a. Open a new presentation, and save it as **Partners** to the drive and folder where your Data Files are stored.
b. Add your name as the footer on all slides and handouts.
c. Connect to the Internet, then use a search engine to locate Web sites that have information on used computer systems.
d. Think about what results you want to see, what information you will need to create the slide presentation, and how your message should be communicated. Review at least two Web sites that contain information about used computers. Print the pages of the Web sites you use to gather data for your presentation. (Remember to gather information on the old computers as well as the new computers.)
e. In order for your presentation to be complete, it must include the following objects: (i) an embedded picture; (ii) an embedded Excel worksheet or chart; (iii) a GIF animation or movie; and (iv) a sound.
f. Create an Excel worksheet that describes the difference between the purchase of the new systems and the sale of the old systems.
g. Give each slide a title and add main text where appropriate. Create slides as necessary to make the presentation complete.
h. Apply an appropriate slide design. Change the slide design colors as necessary.
i. Spell check the presentation, view the final presentation in Slide Show view, save the final version, then print the slides as handouts.
j. Close the presentation, exit PowerPoint, and disconnect from the Internet.

▼ VISUAL WORKSHOP

Create two slides that look like the examples in Figures G-21 and G-22. Save the presentation as **Expenses**. Add your name as a footer on the slides, then save and print the slides. Submit the final presentation output.

FIGURE G-21

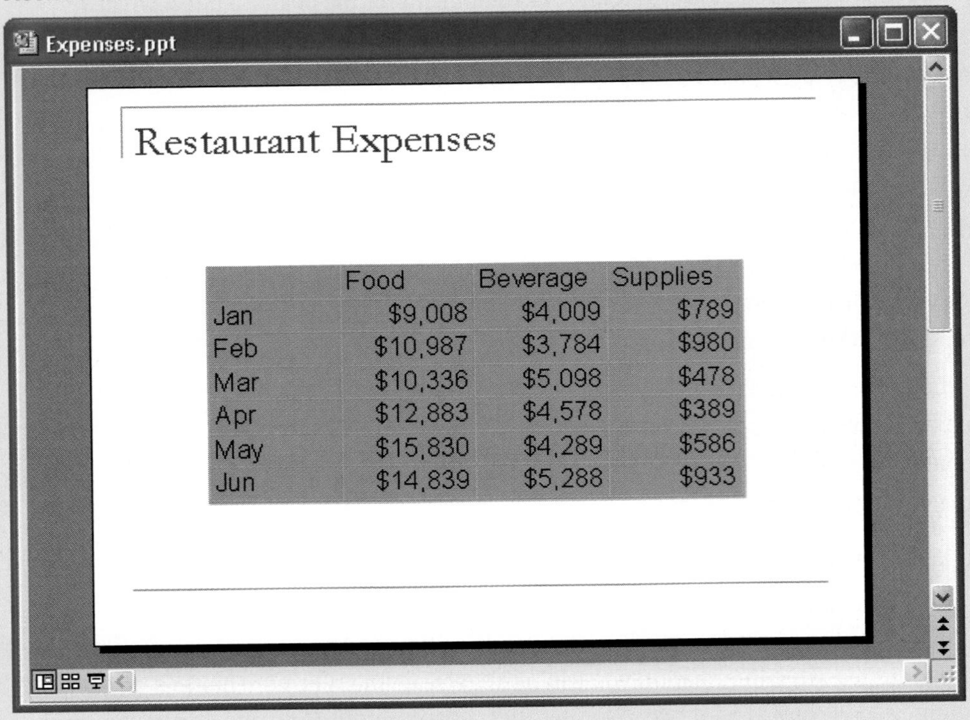

FIGURE G-22

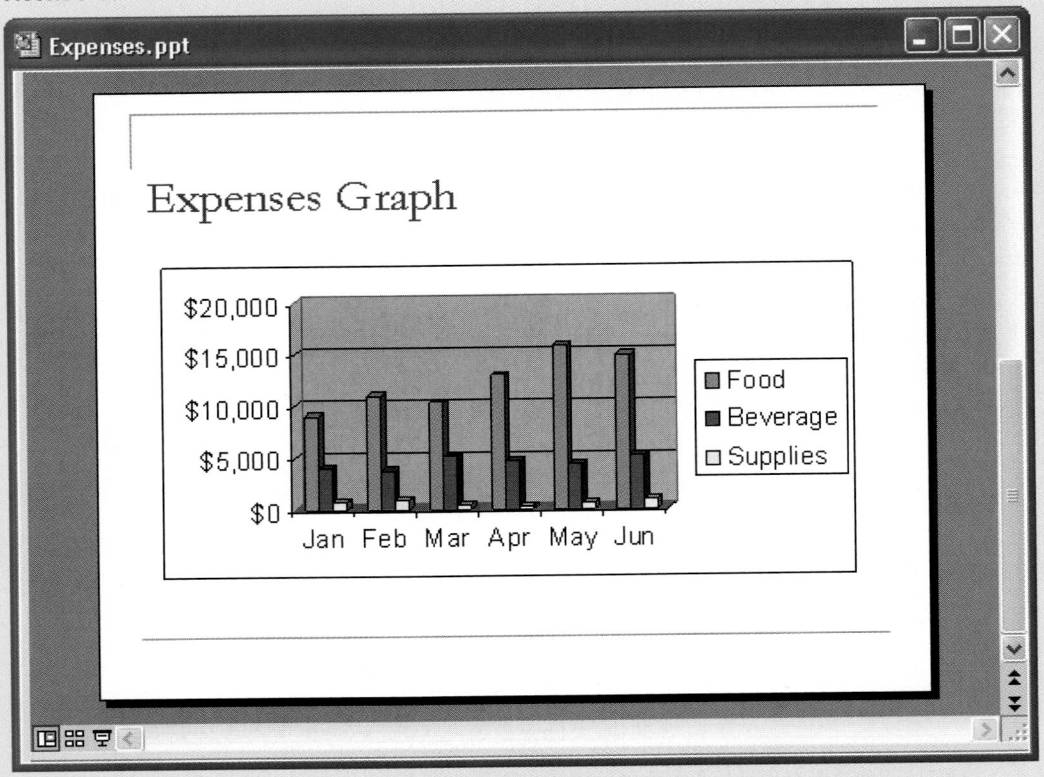

UNIT H

PowerPoint 2003

Using Advanced Features

OBJECTIVES

- Send a presentation for review
- Combine reviewed presentations
- Set up a slide show
- Create a custom show
- Rehearse slide timings
- Publish a presentation for the Web
- Package a presentation
- **Broadcast a presentation**

SAM

If you have a SAM user profile, you may have access to hands-on instruction, practice, and assessment of the skills covered in this unit. Log in to your SAM account and go to your assignments page to see what your instructor has assigned.

After your work on a presentation is complete, you have the option of sending the presentation over the Internet for others to review and send back to you. Reviewers can add comments as well as make changes to the presentation that you can review and accept or reject. Once you are finished changing the presentation, you need to produce the final output that you will use when you give your presentation. You can print the presentation, display it as a slide show using a computer or projector, publish it on the Web for others to view, or broadcast it live over the Web. You have finished creating the content for the MediaLoft Video Division presentation. Now you need to send it to your supervisor, Maria Abbott, and to the marketing manager, Alice Wegman, for review. After you incorporate the reviewer's comments and changes, you produce an on-screen slide show, and publish it for viewing on the World Wide Web.

UNIT H

PowerPoint 2003

Combining Reviewed Presentations

Once a reviewer has completed their review of your presentation and sends it back, you can combine the changes into your original presentation using the Compare and Merge Presentations command. You can apply individual changes, changes by slide, changes by reviewer, changes on the slide master, or changes to the entire presentation. You can continue to combine changes to your original presentation until you have applied all the changes, deleted all the changes markers, saved the presentation, or ended the review. You sent out the Final Status Report presentation to your supervisor and another manager in MediaLoft to review. Now you want to combine the two reviewed versions with your original presentation.

STEPS

1. **Click Tools on the menu bar, then click Compare and Merge Presentations**
   The Choose Files to Merge with Current Presentation dialog box opens.
2. **Click the Look in list arrow, navigate to the drive and folder where your Data Files are stored, click PPT H-2.ppt, press [Ctrl], click PPT H-3, then click Merge**
   The two reviewed presentations are merged with your original presentation. The Revisions task pane opens on the right side of the screen. It is divided into two tabs: the List tab and the Gallery tab. The List tab displays individual changes by reviewer for the current slide. The Gallery tab displays a thumbnail of the current slide and shows what the slide would look like if all the suggested changes were made. Each reviewer's changes are identified by a different color marker on the slide. If more than one reviewer made a change on the same object, the change is identified by a white color marker. There are no revisions on Slide 1.
3. **Click the Next button in the Revisions task pane, then click the MA1 comment icon in the Slide changes section of the Revisions task pane**
   Slide 2 appears. The open item on this slide is a comment made by Maria Abbott as shown in Figure H-3. Each comment or reviewer change has a change description box that appears on the slide next to its corresponding color comment icon or reviewer marker. Since this is a comment, no action is required by you.

> **QUICK TIP**
> To undo one change or all the changes made on a slide, click the Unapply button list arrow on the Reviewing toolbar, then select one of the options.

4. **Click the Next Item button on the Reviewing toolbar, then click the All changes to Text 2 check box in the change description box**
   A check mark appears on the reviewer color marker, in the check boxes in the change description box, and on the reviewer color marker in the Revisions task pane, which indicates that all of the changes by Maria Abbott have been made to the slide.
5. **Click the twice on the Reviewing toolbar**
   Slide 6 appears and a change description box opens. This is an animation setting change made by Alice Wegman, which you don't want to incorporate into the presentation, so you decide to move to the next change.
6. **Click the Delete Marker button on the Reviewing toolbar, click the white reviewer marker on the slide, click the check boxes in the change description box as shown in Figure H-4, then review the changes in the body text box**
   The reviewer color marker is white, indicating that the marked change contains more than one reviewer's changes. Compare your screen to Figure H-4.
7. **Click the End Review button End Review... on the Reviewing toolbar, read the information in the dialog box, then click Yes to end the review**
   The Reviewing toolbar and Revisions task pane close and the color markers on the slide are deleted.
8. **Save your changes, click View on the menu bar, click Task Pane, click Window on the menu bar, then click Arrange All**
   Now your screen will match the rest of the figures in this book.

FIGURE H-3: Figure showing Revisions task pane

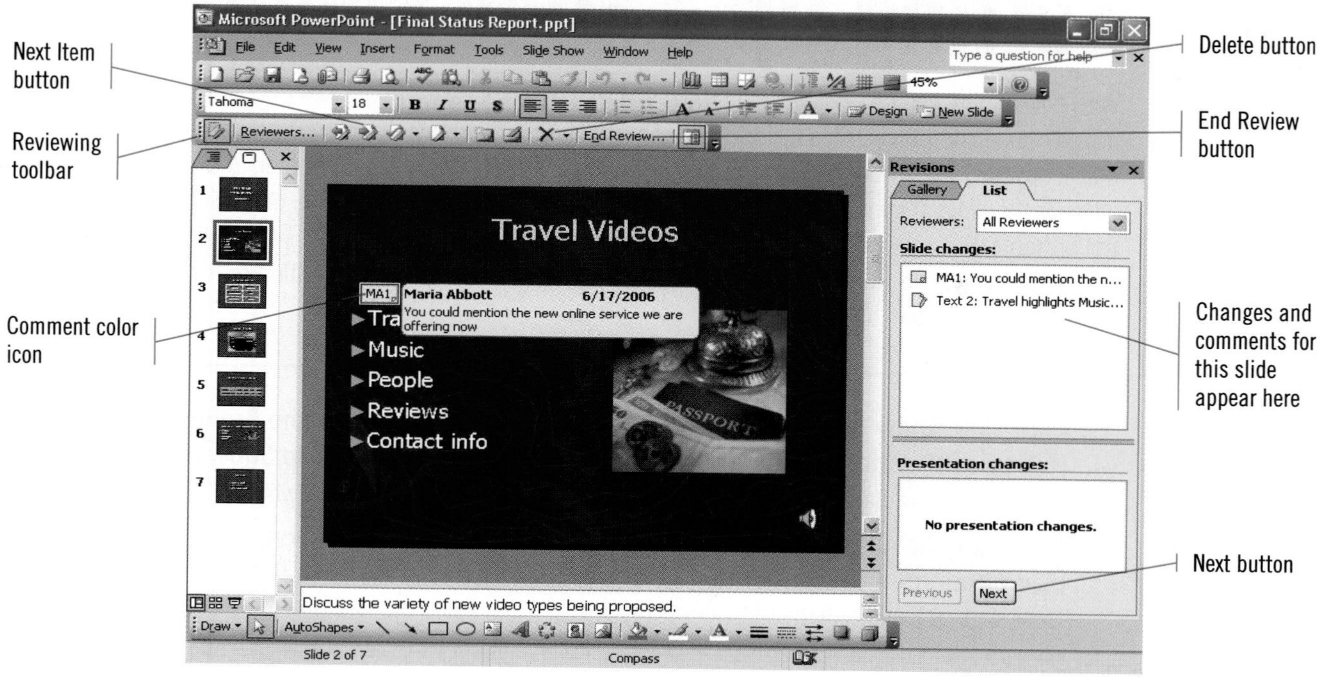

FIGURE H-4: Figure showing revised slide

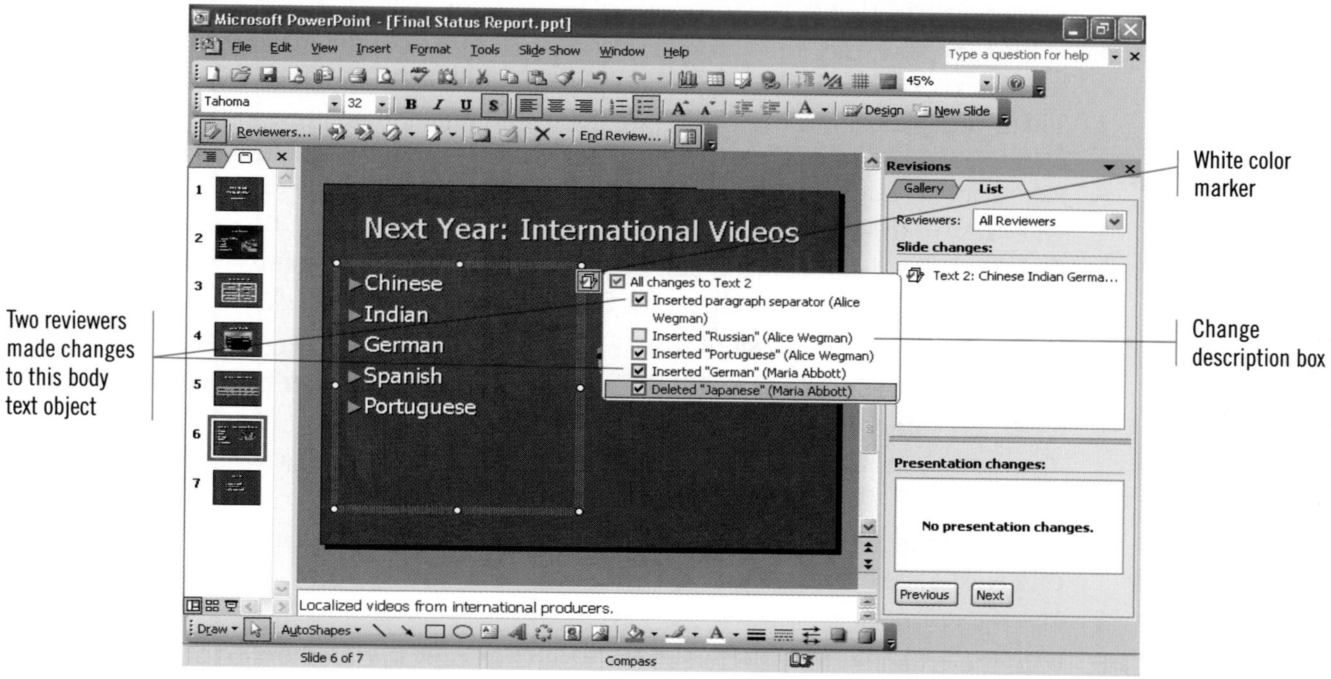

Clues to Use

Reviewing a presentation

To evaluate a presentation someone sends for your review, simply open the presentation in PowerPoint and make your changes. The Reviewing toolbar will automatically open when you open the presentation. When you are finished making changes, save the presentation. Next, click File on the menu bar, point to Send To, then click Original Sender to send the presentation back to its original owner using Outlook. If you want to edit the message in the e-mail before you send the presentation back, you can click the Reply with Changes button on the Reviewing toolbar.

Setting Up a Slide Show

With PowerPoint, you can create a slide show that runs automatically. Viewers can then watch the slide show on a stand-alone computer, called a kiosk, at a convention or trade show. You can create a self-running slide show that loops, or runs, through the entire show, without users touching the computer. You can also let viewers advance the slides at their own pace by pressing the Spacebar, clicking the mouse, or clicking an on-screen control button called an action button. A self-running slide show is also useful when you publish a presentation to the Web for others to view. You prepare the Final Status Report presentation so it can be viewed at an upcoming trade show.

STEPS

1. **Click Slide Show on the menu bar, click Set Up Show, then click the Browsed at a kiosk (full screen) option button in the Show type section of the Set Up Show dialog box**
   The Set Up Show dialog box has options you can set to specify how the show will run.
2. **Make sure the All option button is selected in the Show slides section, then make sure the Using timings, if present option button is selected in the Advance slides section**
   These settings include all the slides in the presentation and have PowerPoint advance the slides at time intervals you set.
3. **Click OK, click the Slide Sorter View button, then click the Slide Transition button on the Slide Sorter toolbar**
   The Slide Transition task pane opens.
4. **In the task pane, click the Automatically after check box in the Advance slide section to select it, click the Automatically after up arrow until 00:08 appears, click Apply to All Slides, click Slide Show, view the show, let it start again, then press [Esc]**
   PowerPoint advances the slides automatically at eight-second intervals, or faster if someone advances the slide manually. There may be times when you want users to advance slides by clicking a button that is actually a hyperlink to jump to the next slide.
5. **Click Slide Show on the menu bar, click Set Up Show, click the Manually option button in the Advance slides section, then click OK**
6. **Double-click Slide 1, click Slide Show on the menu bar, point to Action Buttons, click Action Button: Forward or Next button, then drag the pointer to draw a button in the lower-left corner of Slide 1**
   A new action button appears on the bottom of the slide and the Action Settings dialog box opens, as shown in Figure H-5.
7. **Make sure the Hyperlink to option button is selected, click the Hyperlink to list arrow, click Next Slide if necessary, then click OK**
   Compare your screen to Figure H-6.
8. **With the action button selected, press [Ctrl][C] to copy it, click the Next Slide button, press [Ctrl][V] to paste the button on Slide 2, repeat for slides 3-7, then click the Slide 1 thumbnail in the Slides tab**
9. **View the slide show, click the action buttons to move from slide to slide, press [Esc] to end the slide show, then save your changes**
   Make sure you wait for the animated objects to appear on the slides before you click the action buttons.

QUICK TIP

If your computer has a sound card and a microphone, you can record voice narrations to play during your slide show by clicking Record Narration on the Slide Show menu. Voice narrations can be helpful for self-running slide shows and presentations on the Internet. You can link or embed the narration.

QUICK TIP

You must be in Slide Show view to use action buttons.

FIGURE H-5: Action Settings dialog box

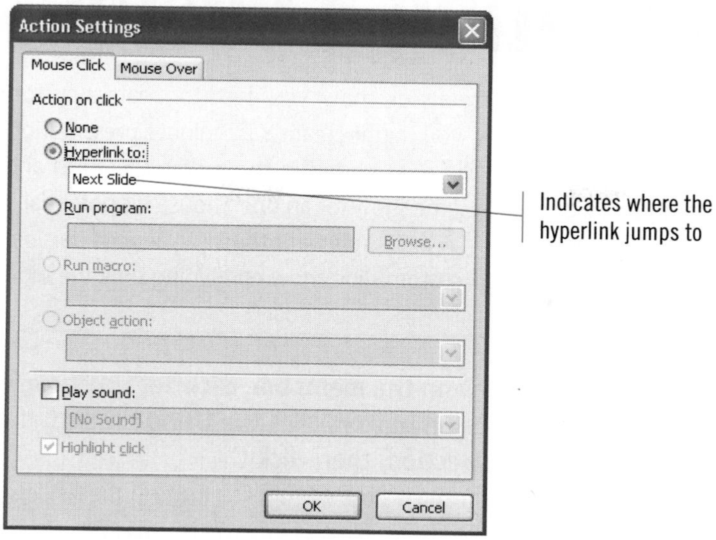

FIGURE H-6: Slide 1 showing new action button

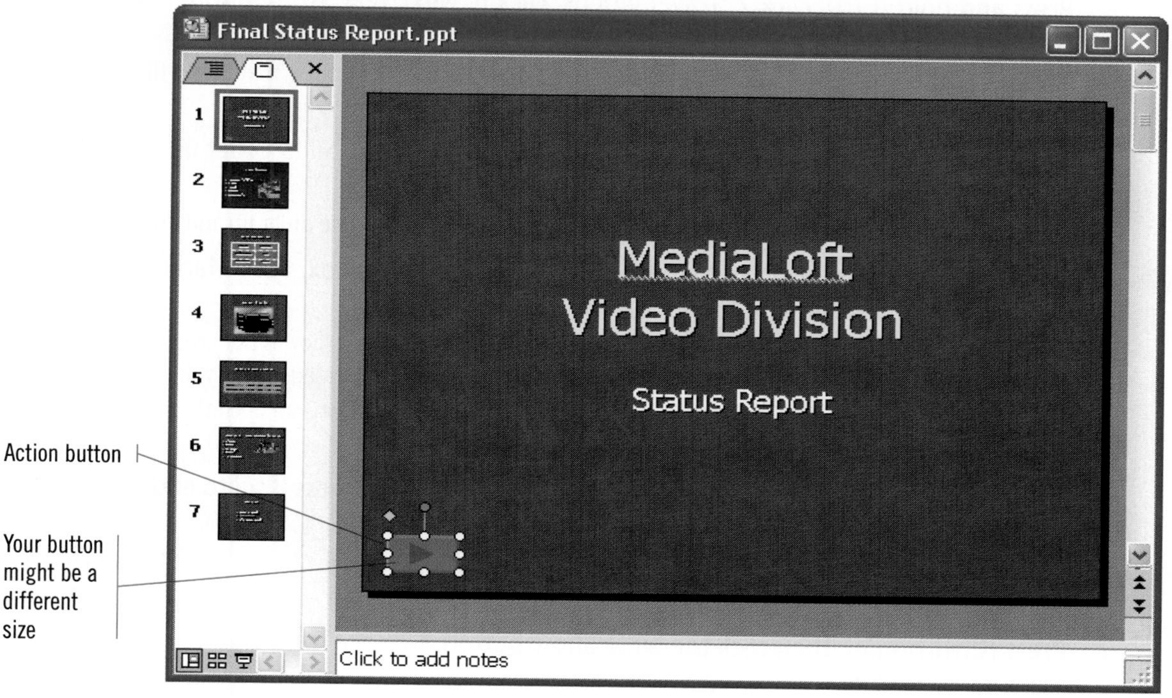

Clues to Use

Hiding a slide during a slide show

During a slide show, you can hide slides you don't want the audience to see. Hidden slides are not deleted from the presentation; they just don't appear during a slide show. The easiest way to hide a slide is to right-click the slide thumbnail in Normal view or Slide Sorter view, then click Hide Slide. When a slide is hidden, its slide number has a hide symbol—a gray box with a line through it—over it. To unhide the slide, right-click the slide thumbnail, then click Hide Slide. You can display a hidden slide during a slide show by right-clicking the slide prior to the hidden slide, pointing to By Title, then clicking the title of the hidden slide.

UNIT
H
PowerPoint 2003

Creating a Custom Show

Often when you create a slide show, you need to create a custom version of it for a different audience or purpose. For example, you might create a 20-minute presentation about a new product to show to potential customers who will be interested in the product features and benefits. Then you could create a five-minute version of that same show for an open house for potential investors, selecting only appropriate slides from the longer show. You want to use a reduced version of the slide show in a marketing presentation, so you create a custom slide show containing only the slides appropriate for that audience.

STEPS

1. **Click Slide Show on the menu bar, click Set Up Show, click the Presented by a speaker (full screen) option button, click the Using timings, if present option button in the Advance slides section, then click OK**

   This turns off the manual kiosk settings you made in the last lesson.

2. **Click Slide Show on the menu bar, click Custom Shows, then click New in the Custom Shows dialog box**

   The Define Custom Show dialog box opens. The slides that are in your current presentation are listed in the Slides in presentation list box.

3. **Press and hold [Ctrl], click 2. Travel Videos, click 6. Next Year: International Videos, click 7. Reviews, release [Ctrl], then click Add**

   The three selected slides move to the Slides in custom show list box, indicating that they will be included in the new presentation. See Figure H-7.

4. **Click 3. Reviews in the Slides in custom show list, then click the Slide Order up arrow button one time to move it up one position in the list**

   You can arrange the slides in any order in your custom show using the Slide order up and down arrows.

> **QUICK TIP**
> To print a custom show, click Print on the menu bar, click the Custom Show option button in the Print Range section, select the custom show you want in the Custom Show list box, set any other printing preferences, then click OK.

5. **Drag to select the existing text in the Slide show name text box, type Marketing Presentation, then click OK**

   The Custom Shows dialog box lists your custom presentation. The custom show is not saved as a separate slide show on your disk even though you assigned it a new name. To view a custom slide show, you must first open the presentation you used to create the custom show in Slide Show view. You then can open the custom show from the Custom Shows dialog box.

6. **Click Show, view the Marketing Presentation slide show, then press [Esc] to end the custom show after you view the Next Year: International Videos slide**

   The slides in the custom show appear in the order you set: Slide 2, 7, then 6. After pressing [Esc] you return to the presentation in Normal view.

7. **Press [Ctrl][Home], then click the Slide Show button**

   Slide 1 appears and the text animation on the slide begins.

8. **Right-click anywhere on the screen, point to Custom Show, then click Marketing Presentation, as shown in Figure H-8**

   The Marketing Presentation custom show appears in Slide Show view.

9. **Press [Esc] after viewing the Next Year: International Videos slide, then save your changes**

FIGURE H-7: Define Custom Show dialog box

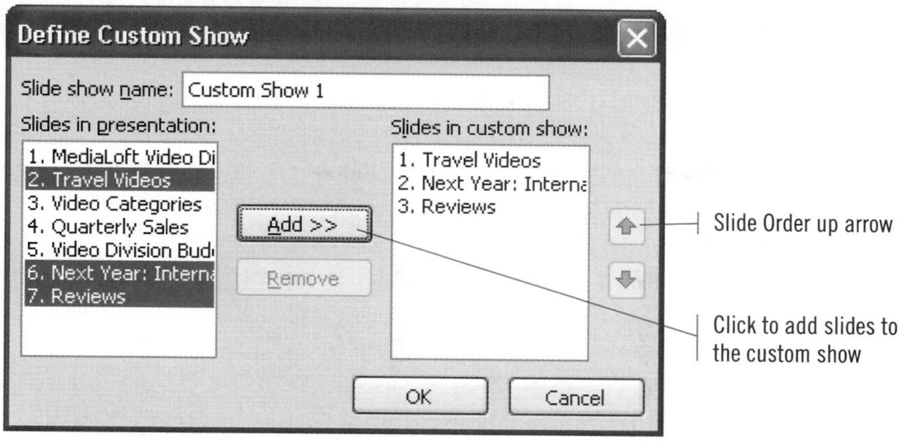

FIGURE H-8: Switching to the custom slide show

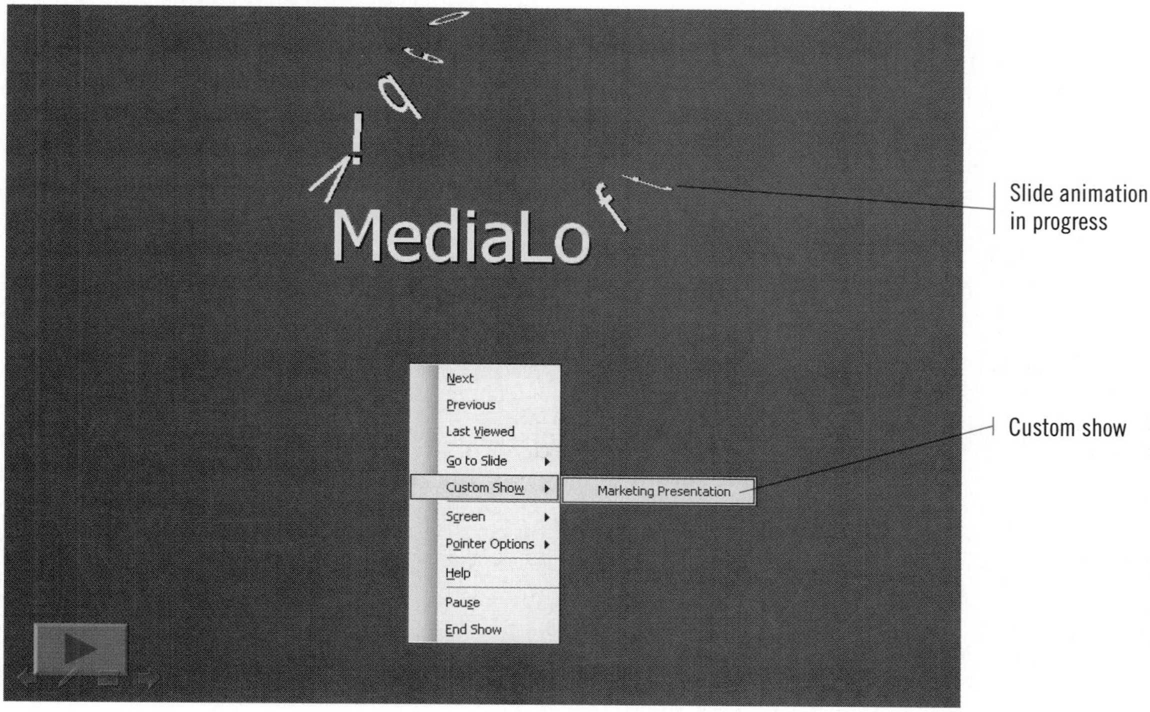

Clues to Use

Using action buttons to hyperlink to a custom slide show

You can use action buttons to switch from the "parent" show to the custom show. Click Slide Show on the menu bar, point to Action Buttons, then choose any action button. Drag the pointer to draw a button on the slide, then, in the Action Settings dialog box, select Custom Show in the Hyperlink to list box. Select the name of the custom show to which you want to hyperlink, then click OK. When you run the show, click the hyperlink button you created to run the custom show.

UNIT H

PowerPoint 2003

Rehearsing Slide Timings

Whether you are creating a self-running slide show or you're planning to talk about the slides as they appear, you should rehearse the slide timings, the amount of time each slide stays on the screen. If you assign slide timings to your slides without actually running through the presentation, you will probably discover that the timings do not allow enough time for each slide or point in your presentation. To set accurate slide timings, use the PowerPoint Rehearse Timings feature. As you run through your slide show, the Rehearsal toolbar shows you how long the slide stays on the screen. When enough time has passed, click the mouse to move to the next slide. You decide to rehearse the slide timings of the presentation, but first you decide to modify Slide 2 a little more.

STEPS

1. **Click Slide 2 in the Slides tab, right-click the comment icon, then click Delete Comment**
   The reviewer comment is deleted.
2. **Click Travel in the title text object, click Tools on the menu bar, then click Thesaurus**
   The Research task pane opens displaying a list of synonyms for the word travel.
3. **Point to the word tour, click the tour list arrow, then click Insert**
   The word Tour replaces the word Travel and now appears in the title text object.
4. **Click the Slide Sorter View button, then click Slide 1**
   Before you complete the steps of this lesson, first read the steps and comments so you are aware of what happens during a slide show rehearsal.
5. **Click the Rehearse Timings button on the Slide Sorter toolbar**
   Slide Show view opens, and Slide 1 appears. The Rehearsal toolbar appears in the upper-left corner of the screen, as shown in Figure H-9 and starts timing the slide. Be sure to leave enough time to present the contents of each slide thoroughly.
6. **When you feel an appropriate amount of time has passed for the presenter to speak and for the audience to view the slide, click the Next button on the Rehearsal toolbar or click your mouse anywhere on the screen**
   Slide 2 appears and the timing counter begins for this slide.
7. **Click at an appropriate interval after Slide 2 appears, click after viewing Slide 3, then continue setting timings for the rest of the slides in the presentation**
   At the end of the slide rehearsal, a Microsoft PowerPoint message box opens, it displays the total time for the slide show, and asks if you want to keep the slide timings. If you save the timings, the next time you run the slide show, the slides will appear automatically at the intervals you specified during the rehearsal.
8. **Click Yes to save the timings**
   Slide Sorter view appears showing the new slide timings, as shown in Figure H-10. Your timings will be different. When you run the slide show, it will run by itself, using the timings you rehearsed. The rehearsed timings override any previous timings you set.
9. **Click the Slide Show button, then view the presentation with your timings**
10. **Save your changes, add your name to the Notes and Handouts footer, click File on the menu bar, click Print, click the All option button, then print the Handouts (4 slides per page)**

TROUBLE

Make sure you wait until the animations are finished on each slide before clicking the Next button.

TROUBLE

If too much time has elapsed, click the Repeat button on the Rehearsal toolbar to restart the timer for that slide. You can also set the time for each slide by typing it in the Slide Time text box.

QUICK TIP

To move to the next slide before your rehearsed slide timing has elapsed, click the slide to advance to the next slide.

FIGURE H-9: Rehearsal toolbar in Slide Show view

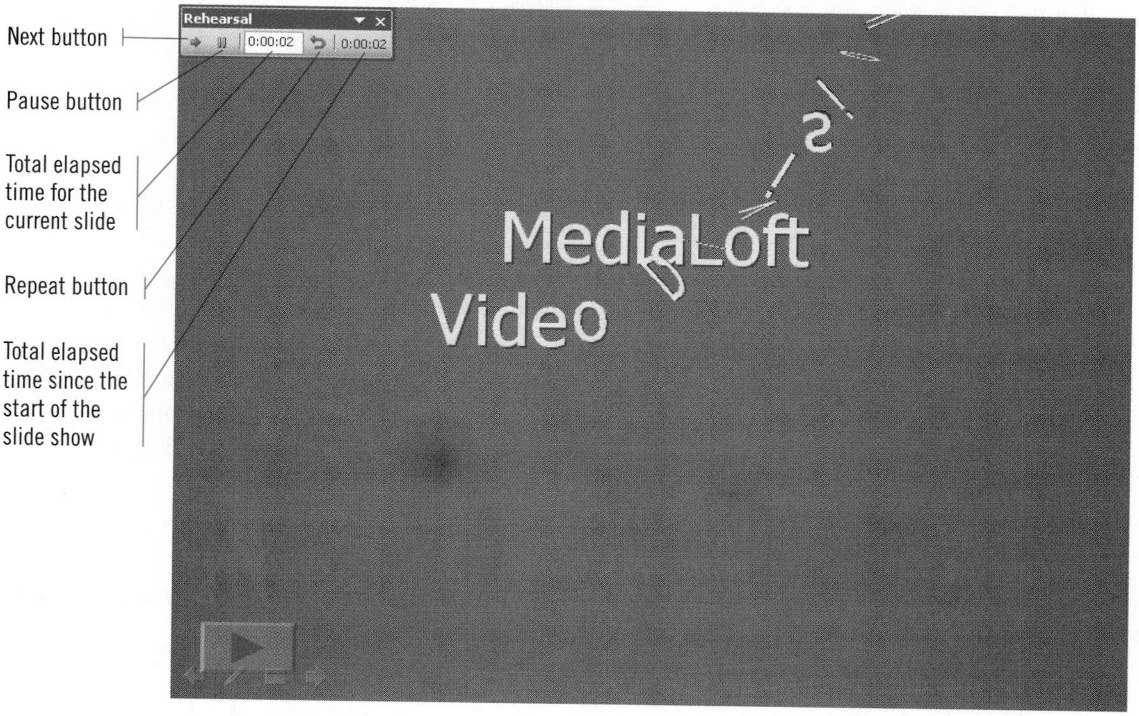

FIGURE H-10: Final presentation in Slide Sorter view showing new slide timings

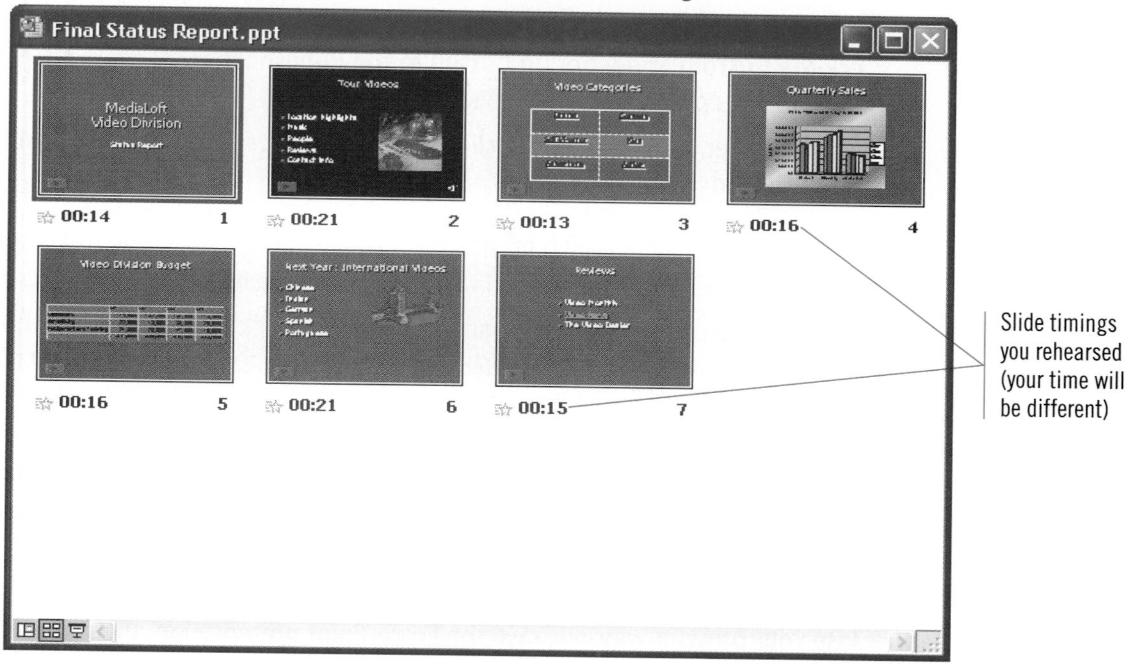

Clues to Use

Changing the page setup

When you need to customize the size and orientation of your presentation you can change its page setup. Click File on the menu bar, then click Page Setup to open the Page Setup dialog box. In the Page Setup dialog box, you can change the width and height of the slides to ten different settings, including On-screen Show, Letter Paper, and 35mm Slides. You can also set a custom slide size by determining the height and width of the slides. You can also change the orientation of the presentation. There is an orientation setting for the slides of the presentation and then another separate setting for the notes, handouts, and outline.

UNIT H

PowerPoint 2003

Publishing a Presentation for the Web

You can use PowerPoint to create presentations for viewing on the Web by saving the file in Hypertext Markup Language (HTML) format. To save the entire presentation, click File on the menu bar, click Save as Web Page, then click Save in the dialog box that opens. This creates a single file Web page. Once published to a Web server, others can view (but not change) the presentation over the Web. If you want to customize the version that you are saving as a Web page (for example, if you wanted to save only the custom show, or if you wanted to make adjustments to how the presentation will look as a Web page), click the Publish command in the Save As dialog box. You want to create a version of the Final Status Report presentation that can be viewed on the MediaLoft intranet page. You do not want to include the information on Slides 2, 3, 4, and 5, so you use the Publish feature to publish the Marketing custom show you created earlier.

STEPS

QUICK TIP
At this point, you can click Save in the dialog box to save a presentation in HTML format, but you can only save the whole presentation, and you don't get to choose which browser is supported.

1. **Click File on the menu bar, click Save as Web Page, click the Save in list arrow, then select the drive and folder where your Data Files are stored**
   The Save As dialog box opens.
2. **Make sure the filename in the File name text box is selected, then type webpres**
3. **Click Publish**
   The Publish as Web Page dialog box opens.
4. **Click the Custom Show option button in the Publish what? section, then click the Display speaker notes check box to deselect it**
5. **In the Browser support section, click the All browsers listed above (creates larger files) option button**
   You want to make sure most browsers can view the HTML file you publish. At the bottom of the dialog box, notice that the default filename for the HTML file you are creating is the same as the presentation filename, and that it will be saved to the same folder in which the presentation is stored. Compare your screen to Figure H-11.
6. **Click the Open published Web page in browser check box to select it, then click Publish**
   PowerPoint creates a copy of your presentation in HTML format and opens the published presentation in your default Internet browser similar to Figure H-12, which shows the presentation in Internet Explorer. Your original presentation remains open on the screen. The slide titles on the left are hyperlinks to each slide.
7. **Click the slide title hyperlinks on the left side of the screen, or the Slide Show button at the bottom of the browser screen, or the Next and Previous buttons at the bottom of the screen, to view each presentation slide in the browser**
   Because each slide in this presentation has an action button, you can also click them to advance the slides.
8. **Close your browser window, save the PowerPoint presentation, then close the presentation**

QUICK TIP
To change the format of elements on the Web page, click Web Options in the Publish as Web Page dialog box.

QUICK TIP
Once you publish a presentation and create the HTML files, you'll need to copy it to a Web server so others can open it from the Web.

FIGURE H-11: Publish as Web Page dialog box

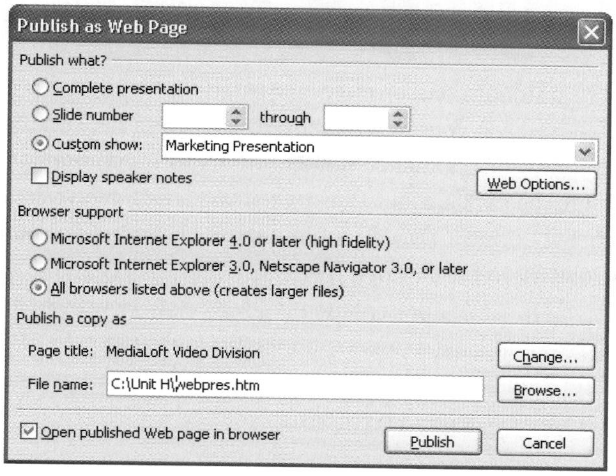

FIGURE H-12: Custom show from Video Division presentation in Internet Explorer

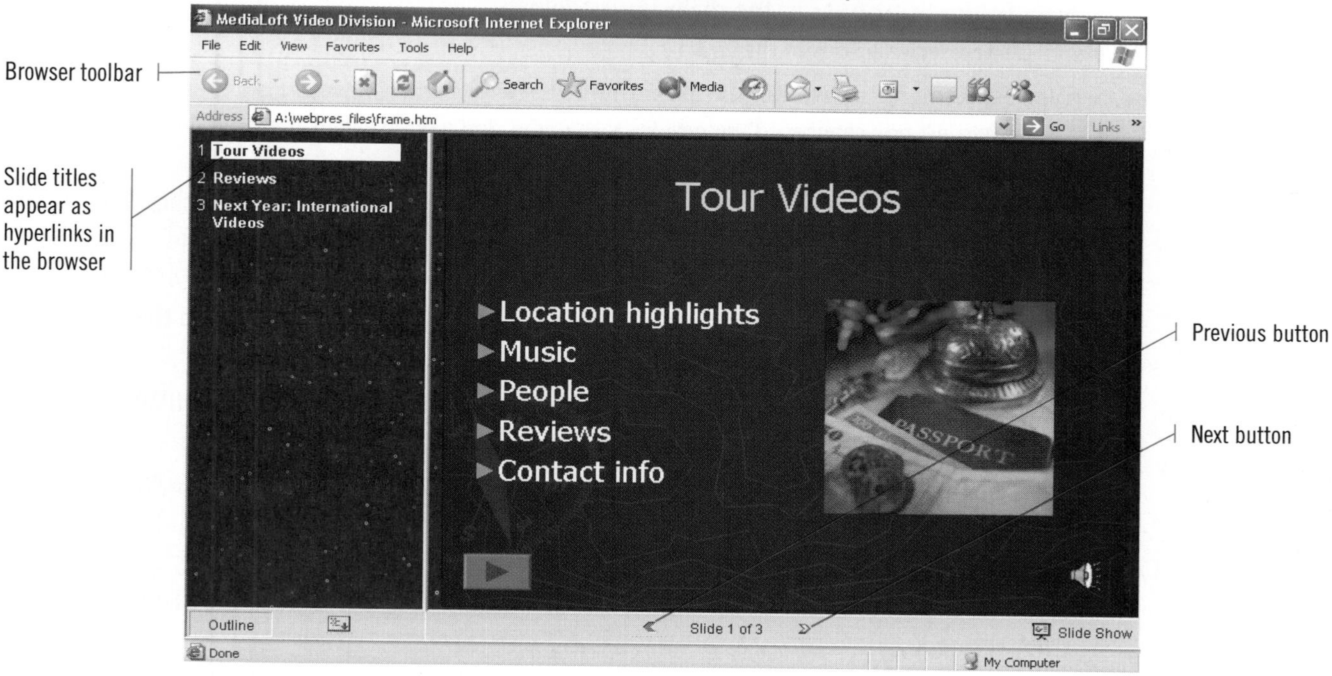

Clues to Use

Online meetings

If you are on a network, you can use Windows NetMeeting and PowerPoint to host or participate in meetings over an intranet or the Web. As the host of a meeting, you can share a presentation in real time with others who may be located in another office in your building or across the country. If you are the host of a meeting, you are required to have NetMeeting (a program automatically installed with Office), the shared document, and its application installed on your computer. As a participant in a meeting, all you are required to have installed on your computer is NetMeeting. As the host, you can schedule a meeting by clicking Tools on the menu bar, pointing to Online Collaboration, then clicking Schedule Meeting. Follow the steps in the dialog boxes to send an e-mail message to the person you are inviting to the meeting. To start an unscheduled online meeting from within the presentation you want to share, click Tools on the menu bar, point to Online Collaboration, then click Meet Now. Follow the steps in the dialog boxes to call participants to the meeting. If the participants accept your meeting invitation, the Online Meeting toolbar opens and the meeting begins.

UNIT
H
PowerPoint 2003

Packaging a Presentation

When you need to distribute one or more presentations or present a slide show using another Windows computer, you can package your presentation to a CD or a network folder. To package everything you'll need to run a slide show on another computer (including your presentation, embedded and linked objects, and fonts), you'll use the Package for CD feature. If you are running Microsoft Windows XP or later and have the ability to create your own CDs, you can use the Package to CD feature to make a CD of your presentation. The PowerPoint Viewer is included by default with the presentation. The PowerPoint Viewer is a program that allows you to view a presentation in Slide Show view even if PowerPoint is not installed on the computer. You package a presentation using the Package to CD feature so you can present it at an off-site meeting. You don't have the ability to create a CD, so you package the presentation to a new folder that you create on your computer's hard drive.

STEPS

TROUBLE

If you decide to place the Package folder in a different location, make sure the folders in the path name have a maximum of eight characters and contain no spaces.

1. **Open the presentation Video Division Report Offsite.ppt from the drive and folder where your Data Files are stored, click File on the menu bar, click Save As, then click the Create New Folder button in the dialog box toolbar**

   The New Folder dialog box opens.

2. **Type Package in the Name text box, then click OK**

   The Save in list box changes to the new Package folder. You will save your packaged presentation in this new folder.

3. **Type Video Division Report Packed Version in the File name list box, then click Save**

   If your original presentation is on your hard disk, you can place the packaged version directly on a floppy disk. If the presentation is too big for one disk, PowerPoint lets you save across multiple floppy disks.

4. **Click File on the menu bar, click Package for CD, then read the information in the dialog box**

   The Package for CD dialog box opens as shown in Figure H-13.

5. **Type Packed Report in the Name the CD text box, then click the Options button**

   The Options dialog box opens.

6. **Read the information in the dialog box, click the Embedded TrueType fonts check box, click OK, then click Copy to Folder**

   The Copy to Folder dialog box opens as shown in Figure H-14.

7. **Click the Browse button, locate and click the Package folder you created, click Select, then click OK**

   PowerPoint packages the presentation to the Package folder you created and then displays the Package for CD dialog box.

8. **Click the Close button, close the presentation, then exit PowerPoint**

9. **Open Windows Explorer, navigate to the Packed Report folder, then view the contents as shown in Figure H-15**

   All the files needed to run this presentation are in this folder.

FIGURE H-13: Package for CD dialog box

FIGURE H-14: Copy to Folder dialog box

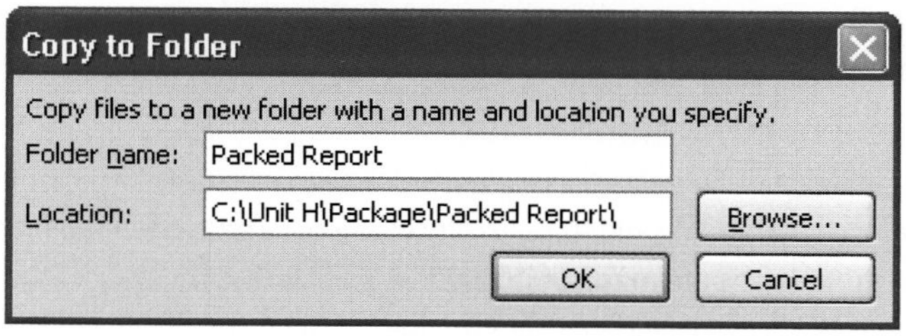

FIGURE H-15: Windows Explorer window showing Packed Report Folder

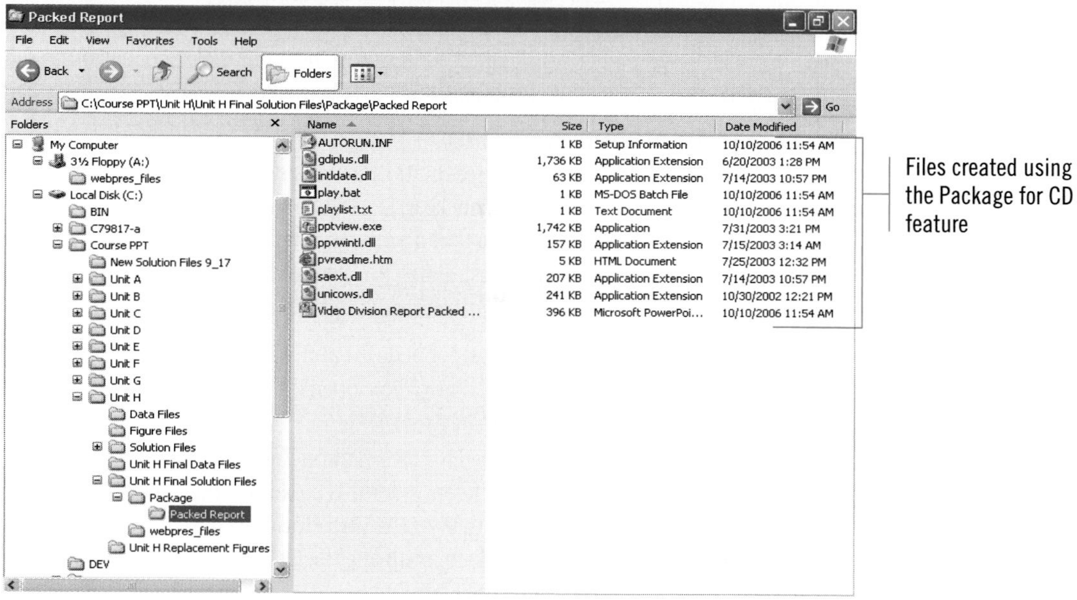

PowerPoint 2003

Clues to Use

Using the Microsoft PowerPoint Viewer

The Microsoft PowerPoint Viewer is a program used to show a presentation on a computer that doesn't have PowerPoint installed. The PowerPoint Viewer is a free program distributed by Microsoft from the Office Web site. You can include the PowerPoint Viewer with your presentation by choosing the Viewer for Microsoft Windows in the Pack and Go Wizard. To view a presentation slide show using the PowerPoint Viewer, open the PowerPoint Viewer dialog box by double-clicking the pptview.exe. From the Microsoft PowerPoint Viewer dialog box, you can run a slide show, set Viewer options, and print a presentation. To show a packaged presentation using the PowerPoint Viewer, you must first unpackage the presentation. Locate the folder that contains the packaged presentation, then double-click the pngsetup icon. Extract the presentation to a folder. A message dialog box appears asking if you want to run a slide show; click Yes.

Broadcasting a Presentation

You can use PowerPoint as a communication tool to broadcast the presentation over an intranet or the Web. You can start an unscheduled broadcast at any time, or use NetMeeting to schedule a broadcast to take place at a specific date and time. If you want your presentation broadcast available for on-demand viewing, you can record and save it to a network server where others can access the broadcast and replay it at their convenience. In preparation for hosting a presentation broadcast next month, you learn the basics of broadcasting.

DETAILS

QUICK TIP

To broadcast a presentation, you must first download an add-in from the Web. In PowerPoint, open the PowerPoint Help task pane, then click the Downloads link to view the Microsoft Office Online Web site. Search the Web site to locate the "PowerPoint 2003 Add-in: Presentation Broadcast," click the add-in link, then follow the directions to download and install the add-in.

- **Set up a presentation broadcast**
  Using the PowerPoint broadcasting feature, you can set up a presentation broadcast for a small group of up to 10 computers that are all on the same intranet or have access to the Web. As the presenter, you will need PowerPoint 2003, Microsoft Internet Explorer 5.1 or later, Microsoft Outlook, or another e-mail program, a shared computer or server, and a connected video camera and microphone if you want to broadcast live video and audio. To broadcast a presentation to more than 10 computers at one time, you'll need to have access to a Windows Media Server or a third-party Windows Media Server provider.

- **Schedule a presentation broadcast**
  To give the members of your audience plenty of time to prepare for a presentation broadcast, you can schedule the broadcast for a specific date and time. To schedule a broadcast, open the presentation that you want to broadcast, click Slide Show on the menu bar, point to Online Broadcast, then click Schedule a Live Broadcast. In the Schedule Presentation Broadcast dialog box, click Settings to open the Broadcast Settings dialog box. Indicate your audio, video, and display preferences. Use the File Location section to enter your server or shared computer information. See Figure H-16. If you will be using a Windows Media Server or including audience feedback, click the Advanced tab, then enter the necessary information. Click OK, then click Schedule. A dialog box similar to an e-mail message box opens. Add participants' e-mail addresses to the To text box, change other settings in the dialog box as necessary, then click the Send button on the toolbar.

- **Begin a presentation broadcast**
  When you are ready to begin your presentation broadcast, you start by clicking Slide Show on the menu bar, pointing to Online Broadcast, then clicking Start Live Broadcast Now. If Outlook is your e-mail program, a message dialog box opens telling you that a program is trying to access your e-mail addresses; click Yes to continue. The Live Presentation Broadcast dialog box opens and lists the available presentations ready for broadcast. Select the presentation you want to broadcast, then click Broadcast.
  - If the broadcast has been previously scheduled and you are using a microphone or camera in your broadcast, the Broadcast Presentation dialog box opens. Complete the testing of the equipment, then click Start. The presentation broadcast begins.
  - If the broadcast is unscheduled, the Live Presentation Broadcast dialog box opens similar to Figure H-17. Click Settings, select the appropriate preferences for this broadcast, then click OK. Click Invite Audience and let the people you want to attend know that you are broadcasting. When you are ready to start the broadcast, click Start. If you are using audio and video, complete the testing of the equipment, then click Start.

- **View a presentation broadcast**
  The easiest way to participate in an online broadcast is to open the e-mail message that contains the broadcast invitation and click the Uniform Resource Locator (URL) for the broadcast. The lobby page of the online broadcast appears in your browser. At the scheduled broadcast time, the presentation appears on your screen. During the meeting, you are able to send e-mail messages to the presenter. Figure H-18 shows how your screen might look if you were participating in an online broadcast.

FIGURE H-16: Broadcast Settings dialog box

Indicate your audio and video preferences in this section

Enter server or shared file location here

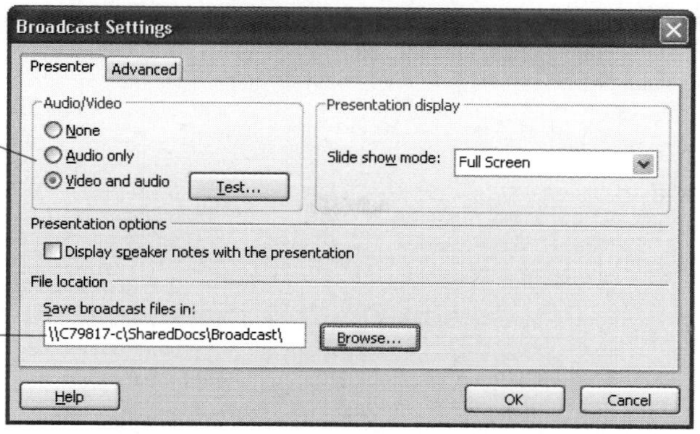

FIGURE H-17: Live Presentation Broadcast dialog box

Click to open the Broadcast Settings dialog box

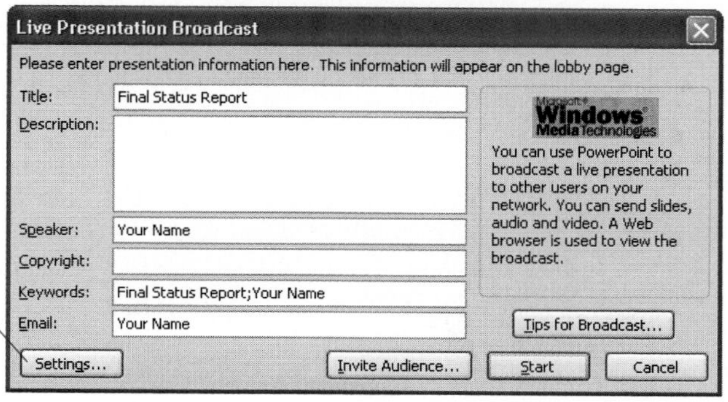

FIGURE H-18: Presentation broadcast in Internet Explorer

If the online broadcast includes live video, the video appears here

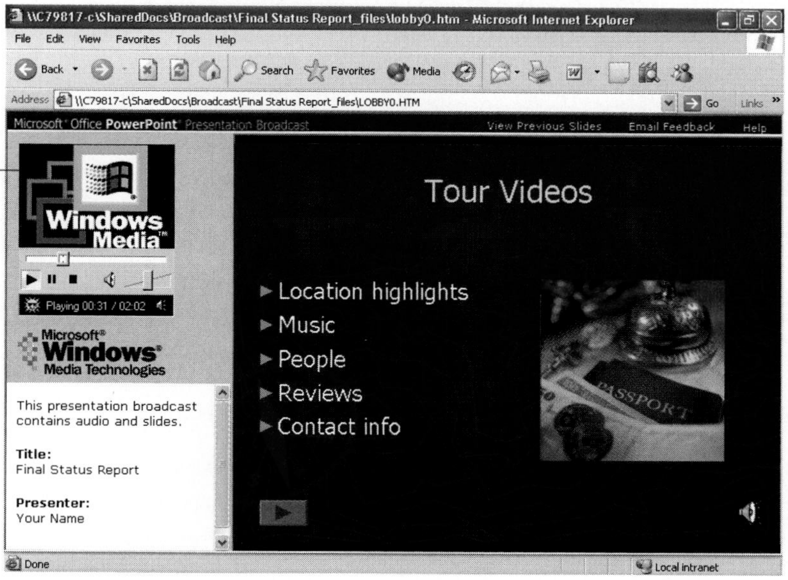

PowerPoint 2003

Clues to Use

Record and save a broadcast

If you don't want to broadcast your presentation live, you can record it and save it to a network server where others can access it at any time. Open the presentation you want to broadcast, click Slide Show on the menu bar, point to Online Broadcast, then click Record and Save a Broadcast. The Record Presentation Broadcast dialog box opens. Change the information as necessary. Click Settings, change any of the video, audio, and display preferences, then identify the server or shared computer where the broadcast files will be stored. Click Record, complete the equipment testing, then click Start. Record your broadcast. When you want others to view the recorded broadcast, you will need to send an e-mail and identify the link to the starting page of the broadcast. To view the broadcast, the audience member clicks Replay Broadcast on the start page of the presentation.

Practice

▼ CONCEPTS REVIEW

Label each of the elements of the PowerPoint window shown in Figure H-19.

FIGURE H-19

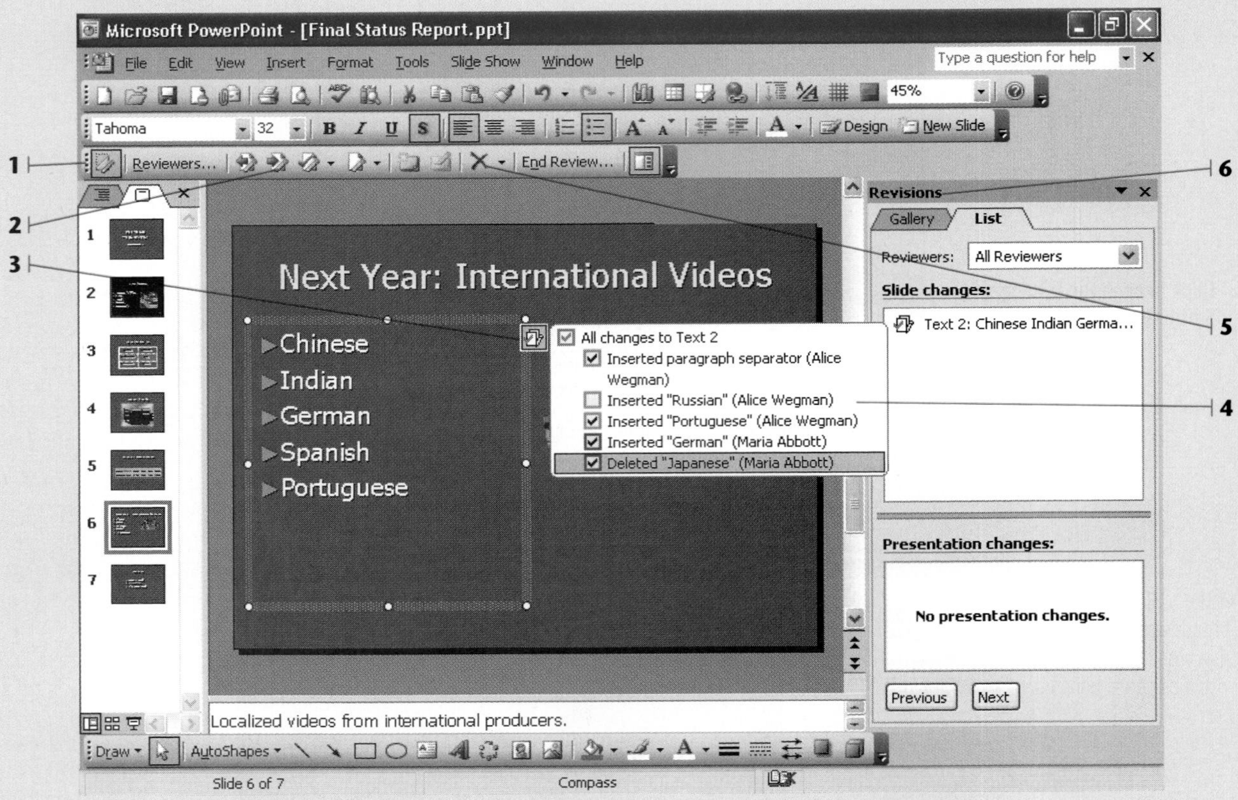

Match each of the terms with the statement that best describes its function.

7. **Online Collaboration**
8. **Custom show**
9. **Package to CD**
10. **Online Broadcast**
11. **Kiosk**

a. A stand-alone computer that runs a slide show
b. To host or participate in a Web meeting, you must use this feature
c. A special slide show created from selected slides in a presentation
d. To present a presentation over the Web for up to 10 computers, you need to use this feature
e. A feature that packages a presentation to take it to another computer

Select the best answer from the list of choices.

12. Which of the following statements about reviewing presentations is false?

- **a.** You can use any 32-bit e-mail program to send a presentation out for review.
- **b.** Reviewers must use PowerPoint 2003 to review presentations.
- **c.** Outlook automatically creates a review request e-mail message.
- **d.** Reviewers can make changes and add comments to a presentation.

13. How do you know that more than one reviewer made a change to the same item?

- **a.** The change is highlighted in yellow.
- **b.** Each reviewer's change is identified by a different color marker.
- **c.** A thumbnail of the changes automatically appears on the slide.
- **d.** A white color marker appears.

14. Which of the following statements about rehearsing your slide timings is true?

- **a.** Rehearsing the slides in your presentation gives each slide the same slide timing.
- **b.** During a rehearsal, you have no way of knowing how long the slide stays on the screen.
- **c.** If you give your slides random slide timings, you may not have enough time to adequately view each slide.
- **d.** If you rehearse your presentation, someone on another computer can set the slide timings.

15. How is a reviewer's change identified on the slide?

- **a.** A color marker
- **b.** A message box
- **c.** Reviewer's changes are italicized.
- **d.** The only place a reviewer's change is identified is in the Revisions task pane.

16. Which of the following statements about hiding slides is false?

- **a.** You know a slide is hidden if you see a hide symbol over the slide number in Slide Sorter view.
- **b.** Hidden slides don't appear during a slide show.
- **c.** Hidden slides are deleted if you save a presentation with a hidden slide.
- **d.** It's possible to view a hidden slide during a slide show.

17. How do you create a presentation so it can be viewed on the Web?

- **a.** Copy the presentation to a network server.
- **b.** Save the presentation as an HTML file.
- **c.** Import the presentation to a Web page.
- **d.** Open the presentation in a Web browser.

18. What does the Package for CD feature allow you to do?

- **a.** View a presentation on the Web.
- **b.** Create an online broadcast.
- **c.** Burn music CDs.
- **d.** Distribute a presentation for others to view.

19. What does the PowerPoint Viewer allow you to do?

- **a.** View a presentation on the Web.
- **b.** View and participate in an online meeting.
- **c.** View a presentation in Slide Show view on any compatible computer.
- **d.** View a presentation in all four views at the same time.

▼ SKILLS REVIEW

1. Send a presentation for review.

- **a.** Open the presentation PPT H-4.ppt and save it as **SF Series Proposal**.
- **b.** Click File on the menu bar, point to Sent To, then click Mail Recipient (for Review) to send the presentation via e-mail to yourself for review.
- **c.** Open Outlook, or your compatible e-mail program, make sure the e-mail message was received, then close your e-mail program.

▼ SKILLS REVIEW (CONTINUED)

2. Combine reviewed presentations.

a. Compare and merge the presentation PPT H-5.ppt to SF Series Proposal.

b. Click the Next Item button on the Reviewing toolbar to read all the comments, and accept all other suggested changes from the reviewer.

c. End the review, then save your changes.

3. Set up a slide show.

a. Set up a slide show that will be browsed at a kiosk, using slide timings.

b. Set the slides to appear every five seconds.

c. Run the slide show all the way through once, then stop it.

d. Set the slide show to run manually, presented by a speaker.

e. Put a Forward or Next action button, linked to the next slide, in the lower-right corner of Slide 1.

f. Copy the action button, then paste it onto all of the slides except the last one.

g. Select Slide 2 and place an Action Button: Back or Previous in the lower-left corner. Have it link to the previous slide. Resize the button so it is the same size as the button you created in Step e, and place it near the bottom of the slide, approximately one inch from the left side and bottom.

h. Copy the Back button, then paste it on all of the slides except the first one.

i. Run through the slide show from Slide 1 using the action buttons you inserted. Move forward and backward through the presentation, watching the animation effects as they appear.

j. When you have finished viewing the slide show, save your changes.

4. Create a custom show.

a. Create a custom show called **New Series** which includes Slides 3, 4, 5, 6, and 7.

b. Move the two slides that discuss performances above the lecture slides.

c. View the show from within the Custom Shows dialog box, using the action buttons to move among the slides and waiting for the graphics animations. Press [Esc] to end the slide show after viewing the Financing Lectures slide.

d. Move to Slide 1, begin the slide show, then, when Slide 1 appears, go to the Custom Show.

e. View the custom slide show, then return to slide view and save your changes.

5. Rehearse slide timings.

a. Open the Rehearsal toolbar, set new slide timings, then save your new timings and review them.

b. Add your name as a footer on notes and handouts, then save your changes.

c. Print your New Series custom show as handouts (6 slides per page.)

d. Print all the slides in the presentation as handouts (6 slides per page.)

6. Publish a presentation for the Web.

a. Publish the entire SF Series Proposal presentation for the World Wide Web as **sfpropsl**. Do not include speaker notes, and make it viewable using all browsers listed.

b. Open the mht file in your browser and navigate through the presentation.

c. Close your browser, then close the presentation and PowerPoint.

7. Package a presentation.

a. Create a new folder on your hard drive and name it **Pack2**.

b. Save the **SF Series Proposal** presentation in the Pack2 folder you created.

c. Open the Package for CD dialog box, then change the options so that Truetype fonts are embedded.

d. Click the Copy to Folder button, then change the name of the folder to **SF Series Proposal**.

e. Click the Browse button to locate the Pack2 folder, then click OK.

f. Close the SF Series Proposal Packed presentation.

g. View the contents of the **Pack2** folder using Windows Explorer.

▼ INDEPENDENT CHALLENGE 1

You work for Island Tours, an international tour company that provides specialty tours to destinations throughout Asia and the Pacific. You have to develop presentations that the sales force can use to highlight different tours at conferences and meetings. You will use some PowerPoint advanced slide show features such as slide builds and interactive settings to finish the presentation you started. Create at least two additional slides for the basic presentation provided on your Data Disk using your own information. Assume that Island Tours has a special (20% off regular price) on tours to Bora Bora and Tahiti during the spring of 2006. Also assume that Island Tours offers tour packages to the following countries: the Philippines, Japan, Australia, and New Zealand.

a. Open the presentation PPT H-6.ppt, then save it as **Pacific Islands** to the drive and folder where your Data Files are stored.
b. Merge the presentation PPT H-7.ppt to the Pacific Islands file. Accept all the suggested changes.
c. Use the assumptions provided to help you develop additional content for your presentation. Use pictures, movies, and sounds provided on the Office CD-ROM or from other media sources to complete your presentation.
d. Animate the entire chart object so that it dissolves in and has an appropriate sound effect play as it appears.
e. Create a custom version of the show that can be shown at a trade show kiosk.
f. Rehearse slide timings for the presentation.
g. View the presentation in Slide Show view.
h. Use the Package for CD feature to package your presentation.
i. Add your name as a footer on all notes and handouts. Print the final slide presentation and all related documents in the format of your choice.

▼ INDEPENDENT CHALLENGE 2

You work for BreakAway Travel Services, a travel service company. BreakAway Travel is a subsidiary of Globus Inc. Every October, BreakAway Travel needs to report to Globus Inc. on the past year's activity. Create your own information using the basic presentation provided in the Project File. Assume the following:

- BreakAway purchased major routes from Canada to Asia and the Far East from Canadian AirTours.
- BreakAway's average revenue runs about $12 million dollars per quarter.
- Twelve new tour packages to Eastern Europe were created this year. Two of the new tours are The Great Wall Tour and The Trans-Siberian Rail Tour.
- BreakAway increased its staff by 8% during the year.

a. Open the presentation PPT H-8.ppt, then save it as **Breakaway**.
b. Use the assumptions provided to help you develop additional content for your presentation on two separate slides. Use pictures, movies, or sounds provided on the Office CD-ROM or from other media sources to complete your presentation.
c. Rehearse slide timings.
d. Create a custom version of your show to run continuously at a conference kiosk, using the timings that you rehearsed.
e. Create a custom version of the show for a specific audience of your choice.
f. Publish the presentation in HTML format, save it as **Breakaway**, preview it in your browser, then close your browser.

Advanced Challenge Exercise

ACE

- Send your presentation to another student in your class for review using the Send To feature.
- Have the student review your presentation, add at least one comment and make at least one change, then send it back to you.
- Use the Compare and Merge Presentations feature to combine the presentations.

g. View the presentation in Slide Show view.
h. Add your name as a footer on all notes and handouts. Save the presentation, then print the final slide presentation and all related documents in the format of your choice.

▼ INDEPENDENT CHALLENGE 3

You are the assistant director of operations at Pacific Cargo Inc., an international marine shipping company based in San Francisco, California. Pacific Cargo handles 65% of all the trade between Asia, the Middle East, and the West Coast of the United States. You need to give a quarterly presentation to the company's operations committee which outlines the type and amount of trade Pacific Cargo handled during the previous quarter. Plan and create a 10- to 15-slide presentation that details the type of goods Pacific Cargo carried, how much was carried, which companies (foreign and domestic) purchased goods, which companies (foreign and domestic) sold goods, and how much revenue Pacific Cargo earned. You also need to identify the time it took to deliver the goods to their destinations and the delivery cost. Create your own content, but assume the following:

- Pacific Cargo hauled automobiles from Tokyo to San Francisco during the last quarter. A car-carrier ship can hold 184 cars or 166 pickup trucks.
- Pacific Cargo hauled large tractor equipment and parts made by Caterpillar Tractor and John Deere Tractor from the United States. One ship went to Brazil and one went to Kuwait.
- Typical household goods carried by Pacific Cargo include electronic equipment, appliances, toys, and furniture.
- The cost of hauling goods by ship is $3,380 per ton. Pacific Cargo owns five cargo ships that can operate simultaneously. All five ships were in operation during the last quarter.
- Pacific Cargo hauled a total of 980,000 tons during the last quarter.

a. Create a new presentation, then save it as **PC Report Q1**.
b. Use clip art or shapes to enhance your presentation.
c. Use the assumptions provided to help you develop the content for your presentation. Use movies and sounds provided on the Office CD-ROM or from other media sources to complete your presentation.
d. Use Excel to embed or link objects into your presentation. Use the preceding assumptions to develop related information that would be appropriate for a table or worksheet.
e. Set transitions and animations, and rehearse slide timings.
f. View the presentation in Slide Show view.

Advanced Challenge Exercise

- Open the Page Setup dialog box.
- Change the size of the slide to Letter Paper (8.5 × 11 in).
- Change the orientation to Portrait. See Figure H-20 for an example of a slide with Portrait orientation.
- Resize the objects on the slides as necessary.

g. Add your name as a footer on all notes and handouts. Print the final slide presentation and all related documents in the format of your choice.

FIGURE H-20

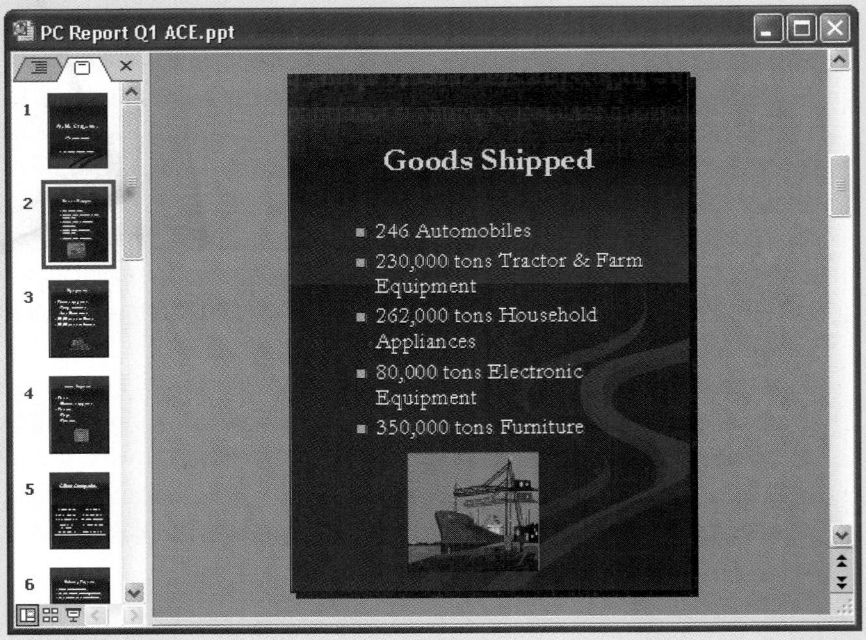

▼ INDEPENDENT CHALLENGE 4

You are the sales manager for Música Internacional, an international music distributor of South American music located in Brasilia, Brazil. This year the M.I. music festival, which showcases different musical groups and styles from all over Central and South America, is being held in Brasilia. Your boss wants you to create a presentation that highlights the variety of musical groups and styles distributed by Música Internacional for the festival. There is wide international appeal for South and Central American music, especially in Europe and Asia. The music festival attracts thousands of artists, presenters, recording company representatives, promoters, and fans every year.

- **a.** Open a new presentation, and save it as **Festival Pres**.
- **b.** Add your name as the footer on all slides and handouts.
- **c.** Connect to the Internet, then use a search engine to locate Web sites that have information on South American music. You'll need to find the names of at least five South American musical groups.
- **d.** Think about what results you want to see, what information you need to create the slide presentation, and how your message should be communicated. Print the pages of the Web sites you use to gather data for your presentation.
- **e.** In order for your presentation to be complete, it must include the following objects: (i) an embedded table; (ii) a GIF animation or movie; and (iii) sound.
- **f.** Title each slide and add main text where appropriate. Create more slides to make the presentation complete.
- **g.** Apply an appropriate slide design. Change the slide design colors as necessary. See Figure H-21 for an example of a slide.
- **h.** Create a custom show that focuses on the interest in South American music in Europe and Asia.
- **i.** Spell check the presentation, then view the final presentation in Slide Show view.
- **j.** Save the final version, then print the slides and handouts.
- **k.** Publish the presentation for the Web as **music**, then view the presentation using your Internet browser.
- **l.** Close the presentation, exit PowerPoint, then disconnect from the Internet.

FIGURE H-21

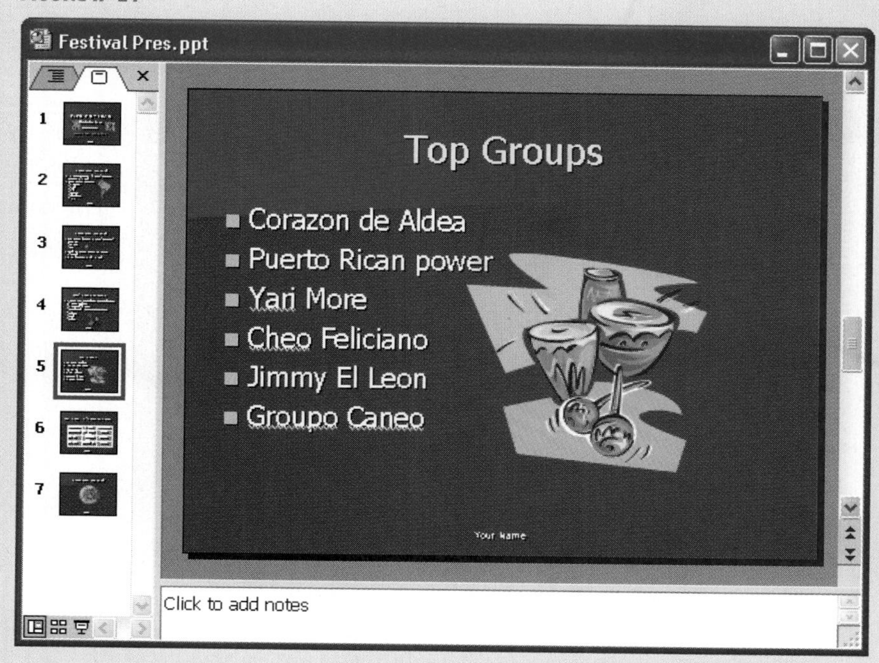

PowerPoint 2003

▼ VISUAL WORKSHOP

Create the slides shown in Figure H-22. Save the presentation as **Mountain Tours**. The clip art is in the Clip Organizer. Set transitions, animations, and slide timings. Insert forward and backward action buttons for the slides. View the presentation in Slide Show view. Print the presentation as handouts (3 slides per page).

FIGURE H-22

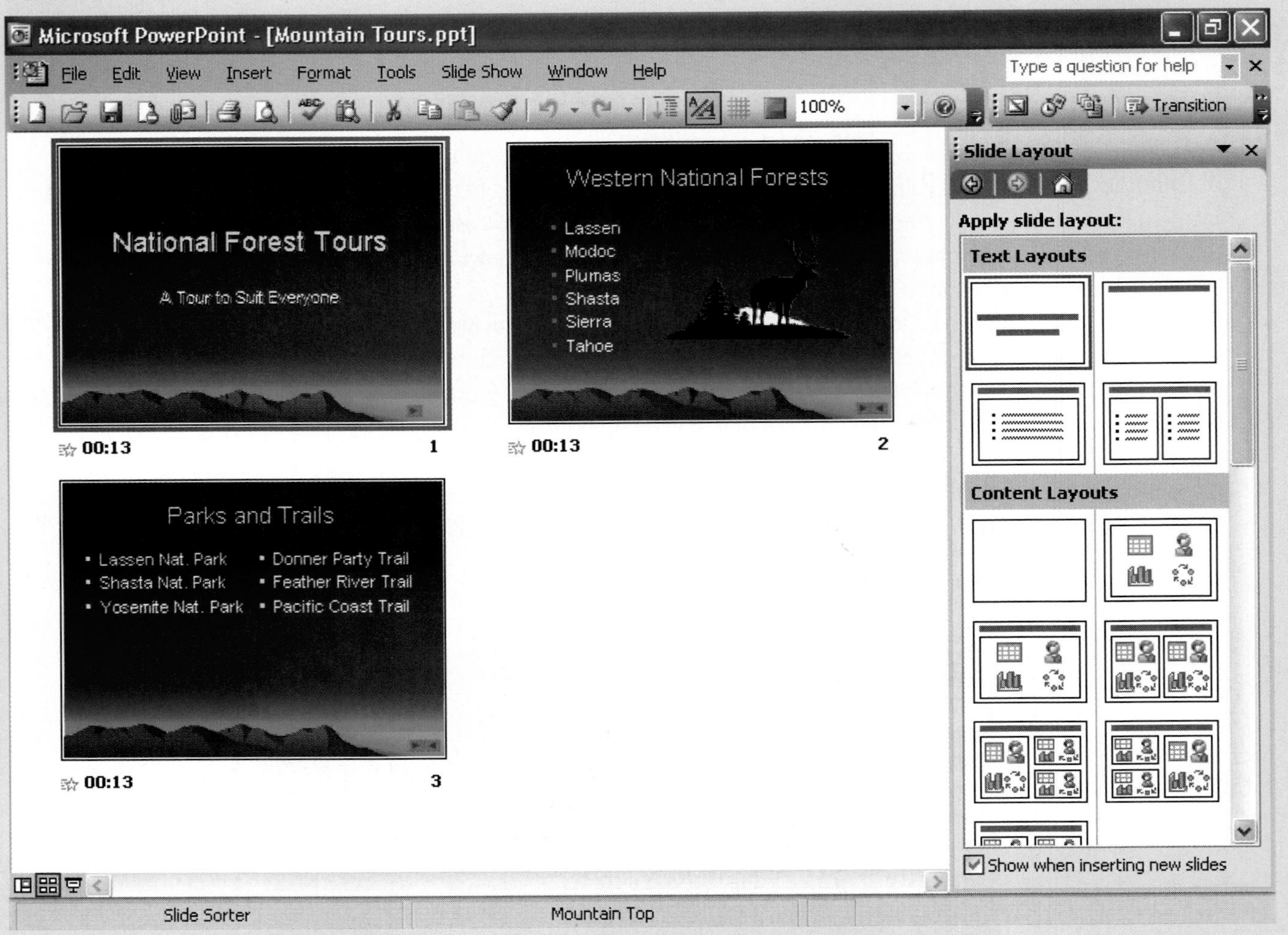

Glossary

A

Action button An on-screen control button that you click in Slide Show view to perform an activity, such as advancing to the next slide.

Active cell A selected cell in a Graph datasheet or an Excel worksheet.

Adjustment handle A small yellow diamond that changes the appearance of an object's most prominent feature.

Align To place objects' edges or centers on the same plane.

Animation The illusion of making a static object appear to move. Some graphics, such as an animated .gif (Graphics Interchange Format) file, have motion when you run the slide show.

Animation scheme A set of predefined visual effects for a slide transition, title text, and bullet text of the slides in a PowerPoint presentation.

Animation tag Identifies the order in which objects are animated on a slide during a slide show.

Annotate A freehand drawing on the screen made by using the Annotation tool. You can annotate only in Slide Show view.

AutoContent Wizard A wizard that helps you get a presentation started by supplying a sample outline and a design template.

B

Background The area behind the text and graphics on a slide.

.bmp The abbreviation for the bitmap graphics file format.

Body text Subpoints or bullet points on a slide under the slide title.

Body text placeholder A reserved box on a slide for the main text points.

Bullet A small graphic symbol, usually a round or square dot, often used to identify items in a list.

C

Category axis The horizontal axis in a chart.

Cell The intersection of a column and row in a worksheet, datasheet, or table.

Chart A graphical representation of information from a datasheet or worksheet. Types include 2-D and 3-D column, bar, pie, area, and line charts.

Chart boxes In Organization Chart, the placeholders for text. The placeholders can contain names and positions in an organization's structure.

Clip art Predesigned graphic images you can insert in any document or presentation to enhance its appearance.

Clip Organizer A library of art, pictures, sounds, video clips, and animations that all Office applications share.

Color scheme The series of eight coordinated colors that make up a PowerPoint presentation; a color scheme assigns colors for text, lines, objects, and background. You can change the color scheme on any presentation at any time.

Column heading Gray boxes along the top of a datasheet.

Crop To hide part of a picture or object using the Cropping tool.

D

Data label Information that identifies the data in a column or row in a datasheet.

Data series A column or row in a datasheet that is converted into a graphic and shown as a chart.

Data series marker A graphical representation of a data series, such as a bar or column.

Datasheet The component of a chart that contains the numerical data displayed in a chart.

Design template Predesigned slide design with formatting and color schemes that you can apply to an open presentation.

Destination program The program a file or object is embedded into.

Dialog box A window that opens when a program needs more information to carry out a command.

Drawing toolbar A toolbar that contains buttons that let you create lines, shapes, and special effects.

E

Embedded object An object that is created in one application and copied to another. Embedded objects remain connected to the original program file in which they were created for easy editing.

Exception A Formatting change that differs from the slide master.

File The presentation you create using PowerPoint.

File format A file type, such as .bmp, .jpg, or .gif.

Filename The name of a presentation file.

Folder A subdivision of a disk that works like a filing system to help you organize files.

Formatting toolbar A toolbar that contains buttons for the most frequently used formatting commands.

G.gif The abbreviation for the graphics interchange format.

Grid Evenly spaced horizontal and vertical lines that appear on a slide when it is being created to help place objects. Lines do not appear when slide is shown or printed.

Gridlines Horizontal and/or vertical lines within a chart that make the data series markers easier to read.

Group To combine multiple objects into one object.

Handout master The master view for printing handouts.

Hanging indent The first line of a paragraph begins to the left of all subsequent lines of text.

Hyperlink An object or link (a filename, word, phrase, or graphic) that, when clicked, "jumps to" another location in the current file or opens another PowerPoint presentation, a Word, Excel, or Access file, or an address on the World Wide Web.

Indent levels Text levels in the master text placeholder. Each level is indented a certain amount from the left margin, and you control their placement by dragging indent markers on the ruler.

Indent markers Small triangles on the horizontal ruler that indicate the indent settings for the selected text.

Insertion point A blinking vertical line that indicates where text appears in a text placeholder in PowerPoint.

J.jpg The abbreviation for the JPEG (Joint Photographic Experts Group) File Interchange Format.

Kiosk A freestanding computer used to display information, usually in a public area.

Leading The spacing between lines of text in a text object.

Link A "live" connection between a source file and its representation in a target file; when the source file is updated, the representation can be updated in the target file. Can also refer to a hyperlink (*see also* Hyperlink).

Master text placeholder The placeholder on the Slide Master that controls the formatting and placement of the Main text placeholder on each slide. If you modify the Master text placeholder, each Main text placeholder is affected in the entire presentation.

Master title placeholder The placeholder on the Slide Master that controls the formatting and placement of the Title placeholder on each slide. If you modify the Master title placeholder, each Title placeholder is affected in the entire presentation.

Master view A specific view in a presentation that stores information about font styles, text placeholders, and color scheme. There are three master views: Slide Master view, Handout Master view, and Notes Master view.

Menu bar The bar beneath the title bar that contains menus from which you choose program commands.

Microsoft Graph The program that creates a datasheet and chart to graphically depict numerical information.

Movie Live action captured in digital format.

Normal view A presentation view that divides the presentation window into three sections: Slides or Outline tab, Slide pane, and Notes pane.

Notes master The master view for Notes Page view.

Notes Page view A presentation view that displays a reduced image of the current slide above a large text box where you can type notes.

Notes pane The area in Normal view that shows speaker notes for the current slide; also in Notes Page view, the area below the slide image that contains speaker notes.

Object An item you place or draw on a slide that can be manipulated. Objects are drawn lines and shapes, text, clip art, imported pictures, and embedded objects.

Organization chart A diagram of connected boxes that shows reporting structure in a company or organization.

Outline tab The section in Normal view that displays your presentation text in the form of an outline, without graphics.

Pane A section of the PowerPoint window, such as the Slide or Notes pane.

Photo album A type of presentation that displays photographs.

Placeholder A dashed line box where you place text or objects.

PowerPoint Viewer A special application designed to run a PowerPoint slide show on any compatible computer that does not have PowerPoint installed.

PowerPoint window A window that contains the running PowerPoint application. The PowerPoint window includes the PowerPoint menus, toolbars, and Presentation window.

Presentation software A software program used to organize and present information.

Publish To save a version of a presentation in HTML format. You can save the HTML files to a disk or save them directly to an intranet or Web server.

Range A continuous group of cells.

Rotate handle A green circular handle at the top of a selected object that you can drag to rotate the selected object upside-down, sideways, or to any angle in between.

Row heading The gray box containing the row number to the left of the row in the datasheet.

Scale To change the size of a graphic to a specific percentage of its original size.

Scroll To use the scroll bars or arrow keys to display different parts of a PowerPoint window.

Selection box A slanted line border that appears around a text object or placeholder, indicating that it is ready to accept text.

Series in Columns The information in the columns of a datasheet that are on the Value axis; the row labels are on the Category axis.

Series in Rows The information in the datasheet rows that are on the Value axis; the column labels are the Category axis.

Sizing handles The small circles that appear around a selected object. Dragging a handle resizes the object.

Slide layout This determines how all of the elements on a slide are arranged, including text and content placeholders.

Slide Master A template for all slides in a presentation except the title slides. Text and design elements you place on the slide master appear on every slide of the presentation. See also Title Master, Notes Master, and Handout Master.

Slide pane The section of Normal view that contains the current slide.

Slide Show view A view that shows a presentation as an electronic slide show; each slide fills the screen.

Slide Sorter view A view that displays a thumbnail of all slides in the order in which they appear in a presentation; used to rearrange slides and add special effects.

Slide timing The amount of time a slide is visible on the screen during a slide show. You can assign specific slide timings to each slide, or use the PowerPoint Rehearse Timings feature to simulate the amount of time you will need to display each slide in a slide show.

Slide-title master pair The title master and the slide master slides in Slide Master view.

Slide transition The special effect that moves one slide off the screen and the next slide on the screen during a slide show. Each slide can have its own transition effect.

Slides tab The section in Normal View that displays the slides of a presentation as small thumbnails.

Source program The program in which a file was created.

Standard toolbar The toolbar containing the buttons that perform some of the most commonly used commands such as Cut, Copy, Paste, Save, Open, and Print.

Status bar The bar at the bottom of the PowerPoint window that contains messages about what you are doing and seeing in PowerPoint, such as the current slide number or a description of a command or button.

Subtitle text placeholder A box on the title slide reserved for subpoint text.

Task pane A separate pane available in all the PowerPoint views except Slide Show view that contains sets of menus, lists, options, and hyperlinks for commonly used commands.

Tab indicator Cycles through the tab alignment options.

Text anchor The location in a text object that determines the location of the text within the placeholder.

Text box Any text object you create using the Text Box button. A word processing box and a text label are both examples of a text box. Text box text does not appear in the Outline tab.

Text label A text box you create using the Text Box button, where the text does not automatically wrap inside the box. Text box text does not appear in the Outline tab.

Text placeholder A box with a dashed-line border and text that you replace with your own text.

Thumbnail A small image of a slide. Thumbnails are visible on the Slides tab and in Slide Sorter view.

Timing *See* slide timing.

Title The first line or heading on a slide.

Title bar The bar at the top of the program window that indicates the program name and the name of the current file.

Title Master A template for all title slides in a presentation. Text and design elements you place on the Title Master appear on all slides in the presentation that use the title slide layout.

Title placeholder A box on a slide reserved for the title of a presentation or slide.

Title slide The first slide in a presentation.

Value axis The vertical axis in a chart.

View A way of displaying a presentation, such as Normal view, Notes Page view, Slide Sorter view, and Slide Show view.

View buttons The buttons at the bottom of the Outline tab and the Slides tab that you click to switch among views.

Window A rectangular area of the screen where you view and work on the open file.

Wizard An interactive set of dialog boxes that guides you through a task.

.wmf The abbreviation for the Windows metafile file format, which is the format of some clip art.

Word processing box A text box you create using the Text Box button, where the text automatically wraps inside the box.

Index

▶A

action buttons, POWERPOINT H-6, POWERPOINT H-9
Action Settings dialog box, POWERPOINT H-7
Add command, POWERPOINT B-15
Add words to command, POWERPOINT B-15
adjustment handle, POWERPOINT C-6, POWERPOINT C-7
aligning objects, POWERPOINT C-8, POWERPOINT C-9
All Programs menu, POWERPOINT A-4, POWERPOINT A-5
animation effects, POWERPOINT D-18–19
  charts, POWERPOINT F-12, POWERPOINT F-13
  inserting animated GIF files, POWERPOINT G-10–11
animation schemes, POWERPOINT D-18
annotations
  saving, POWERPOINT D-14
  Slide Show view, POWERPOINT D-14
area charts, POWERPOINT D-7
arrow keys, moving objects, POWERPOINT D-2
audience impact, POWERPOINT B-17
AutoContent Wizard, POWERPOINT A-8–9
AutoCorrect command, POWERPOINT B-15
AutoShapes
  advanced drawing tools, POWERPOINT E-10–11
  applying shaded background, POWERPOINT C-16
  changing default attributes, POWERPOINT E-10
AutoShapes menu button, POWERPOINT E-14

▶B

Back button, Save As dialog box, POWERPOINT A-13
background
  colors, POWERPOINT D-4
  customizing, POWERPOINT C-16, POWERPOINT C-17
bar charts, POWERPOINT D-7
bitmapped objects, colors, POWERPOINT D-4
black and white, viewing presentations, POWERPOINT A-17
.bmp files, POWERPOINT G-2
body text placeholders, POWERPOINT B-6, POWERPOINT B-7
broadcasting presentations, POWERPOINT H-16–17
Broadcast Settings dialog box, POWERPOINT H-16, POWERPOINT H-17
bubble charts, POWERPOINT D-7
bullet(s)
  picture, POWERPOINT E-4
  size, POWERPOINT E-4
bulleted list placeholder, POWERPOINT B-7
buttons. *See also specific buttons*
  Slide Show menu, POWERPOINT D-14

▶C

Category Axis Gridlines button, POWERPOINT F-8
CDs, playing music from, POWERPOINT G-13
cells, tables. *See* table cells
Center tab stop, POWERPOINT E-6
Change/Change All command, POWERPOINT B-15
chart(s), POWERPOINT F-1–17
  adding sounds, POWERPOINT F-12, POWERPOINT F-13
  animating, POWERPOINT F-12, POWERPOINT F-13
  changing options, POWERPOINT F-8–9
  changing type, POWERPOINT F-6–7
  customized types, POWERPOINT F-7
  customizing data series, POWERPOINT D-11
  elements, POWERPOINT F-10–11
  embedding, POWERPOINT D-6–7
  Excel. *See* Excel charts
  formatting, POWERPOINT D-10–11, POWERPOINT F-5
  formatting datasheets, POWERPOINT F-4–5
  gridlines, POWERPOINT F-8
  inserting data from files into datasheets, POWERPOINT F-2–3
  organization. *See* organization charts
  types, POWERPOINT D-7
chart placeholder, POWERPOINT B-7
Chart Type dialog box, POWERPOINT F-6, POWERPOINT F-7
checklist for presentations, POWERPOINT D-19
clip art
  cropping, POWERPOINT D-4, POWERPOINT D-5
  inserting, POWERPOINT D-2–3
  online sources, POWERPOINT D-3
  scaling, POWERPOINT D-4, POWERPOINT D-5
clip art placeholder, POWERPOINT B-7
Clip Organizer, POWERPOINT G-10
closing files, POWERPOINT A-16, POWERPOINT A-17
color(s)
  background, POWERPOINT D-4
  bitmapped objects, POWERPOINT D-4
  printing files, POWERPOINT A-16
Color button, POWERPOINT F-10
color scheme(s)
  applying to another presentation, POWERPOINT E-13
  applying to selected slides, POWERPOINT C-16
  customizing, POWERPOINT C-16, POWERPOINT C-17
column charts, POWERPOINT D-7
column width, datasheets, POWERPOINT D-8, POWERPOINT F-4
comments, editing, POWERPOINT F-10
cone charts, POWERPOINT D-7
content placeholder, POWERPOINT B-7, POWERPOINT D-2
Copy to Folder dialog box, POWERPOINT H-14, POWERPOINT H-15
correcting errors, spelling, POWERPOINT B-14–15
Create New Folder button, Save As dialog box, POWERPOINT A-13
cropping clip art, POWERPOINT D-4, POWERPOINT D-5
customizing
  background, POWERPOINT C-16, POWERPOINT C-17
  color scheme, POWERPOINT C-16, POWERPOINT C-17
  data series in charts, POWERPOINT D-11
  presentations, POWERPOINT E-1
custom slide shows, POWERPOINT H-8–9
Cut button, POWERPOINT C-10
Cut command, POWERPOINT C-10
cycle diagrams, POWERPOINT F-16
cylinder charts, POWERPOINT D-7

▶D

data series, POWERPOINT F-3
  customizing, POWERPOINT D-11
data series markers, POWERPOINT F-3
datasheets, POWERPOINT D-6, POWERPOINT D-7
  column width, POWERPOINT D-8, POWERPOINT F-4
  editing data, POWERPOINT D-8, POWERPOINT D-9
  entering data, POWERPOINT D-8, POWERPOINT D-9
  formatting, POWERPOINT F-4–5
  inserting data from file into, POWERPOINT F-2–3
dates, entering, POWERPOINT B-10
Decimal tab stop, POWERPOINT E-6
Define Custom Slide Show dialog box, POWERPOINT H-8, POWERPOINT H-9
Delete button, Save As dialog box, POWERPOINT A-13
Delete Master button, POWERPOINT E-3
design templates, POWERPOINT B-1, POWERPOINT B-12–13
desktop, creating shortcuts, POWERPOINT A-4
destination program, POWERPOINT G-4
Diagram Gallery dialog box, POWERPOINT F-16
diagram placeholder, POWERPOINT B-7
displaying
  rulers, POWERPOINT C-6
  slide master, POWERPOINT E-2
  title master, POWERPOINT E-2
doughnut charts, POWERPOINT D-7
drawing objects, POWERPOINT C-4, POWERPOINT C-5
  editing drawn objects, POWERPOINT C-6–7
  freeform shapes, POWERPOINT E-11
Drawing toolbar, POWERPOINT A-6, POWERPOINT A-7

▶E

editing
  comments, POWERPOINT F-10
  data in datasheets, POWERPOINT D-8, POWERPOINT D-9
  drawn objects, POWERPOINT C-6–7
e-mail, sending presentations for review, POWERPOINT H-2–3

embedding
charts, POWERPOINT D-6–7
Excel charts, POWERPOINT G-4–5
linking versus, POWERPOINT G-6
organization charts, POWERPOINT F-14–15
pictures, POWERPOINT G-2–3
worksheets, POWERPOINT G-5
ending slide shows, POWERPOINT D-14
End Show button, POWERPOINT D-14
error correction
spell checking, POWERPOINT B-14–15
undoing changes on slides, POWERPOINT H-4
evaluating presentations, POWERPOINT B-16–17
Excel charts, embedding, POWERPOINT G-4–5
exiting PowerPoint, POWERPOINT A-16, POWERPOINT A-17
exporting presentations, POWERPOINT G-3

►F

file(s). *See also* presentation(s)
closing, POWERPOINT A-16, POWERPOINT A-17
graphics, formats, POWERPOINT D-5
lost, recovering, POWERPOINT A-15
printing, POWERPOINT A-16, POWERPOINT A-17
saving, POWERPOINT A-12–13
filenames, POWERPOINT A-12
Fill Effects dialog box, POWERPOINT C-16
First line indent market, POWERPOINT E-6, POWERPOINT E-7
font(s)
saving with presentations, POWERPOINT A-12
selecting size, POWERPOINT C-12
Font Color button, POWERPOINT C-12
footers, slides, POWERPOINT B-10–11
Format AutoShape dialog box, POWERPOINT E-8, POWERPOINT E-9
Format Number dialog box, POWERPOINT F-4, POWERPOINT F-5
Format Painter, POWERPOINT E-13
Format Table dialog box, POWERPOINT D-12
formatting
advanced tools, POWERPOINT E-12–13
charts, POWERPOINT D-10–11, POWERPOINT F-5
datasheets, POWERPOINT F-4–5
organization charts, POWERPOINT F-16–17
text, POWERPOINT C-12–13
Formatting toolbar, POWERPOINT A-6, POWERPOINT A-7
freeform shapes, POWERPOINT E-11

►G

GIF files, POWERPOINT G-2
animated, inserted, POWERPOINT G-10–11
Graph (program), POWERPOINT D-6, POWERPOINT D-7, POWERPOINT F-4
graphics formats, POWERPOINT D-5
grayscale, viewing presentations, POWERPOINT A-17
gridlines, charts, POWERPOINT F-8
grouped objects
animating parts, POWERPOINT D-18
grouping, POWERPOINT C-8, POWERPOINT C-9
guides, adding to slide, POWERPOINT C-8

►H

hanging indents, POWERPOINT E-6
header(s), slides, POWERPOINT B-10–11
Header and Footer dialog box, POWERPOINT B-10, POWERPOINT B-11
Help system, POWERPOINT A-14, POWERPOINT A-15
hiding slides, POWERPOINT H-7
HTML (Hypertext Markup Language) format, saving presentations in, POWERPOINT H-12
hyperlink(s), POWERPOINT G-14–15

►I

Ignore/Ignore All command, POWERPOINT B-15
importing text from Word, POWERPOINT C-14–15
indent(s), hanging, POWERPOINT E-6
indent levels, Master text placeholder, POWERPOINT E-6–7
indent markers, POWERPOINT E-6, POWERPOINT E-7
Insert CD Audio dialog box, POWERPOINT G-13
Insert Chart button, POWERPOINT D-6
Insert Hyperlink dialog box, POWERPOINT G-14, POWERPOINT G-15
Insert New Slide Master button, POWERPOINT E-3
Insert New Title Master button, POWERPOINT E-3
Insert Object dialog box, POWERPOINT G-6, POWERPOINT G-7
Insert Picture button, POWERPOINT D-4
installing PowerPoint, POWERPOINT A-9

►J

.jpg files, POWERPOINT G-2
jumping to slides, POWERPOINT D-14

►L

leading, POWERPOINT E-8
Left indent marker, POWERPOINT E-6, POWERPOINT E-7
Left tab stop, POWERPOINT E-6
lightbulb symbol, meaning, POWERPOINT B-9
line charts, POWERPOINT D-7
Line Spacing dialog box, POWERPOINT E-8, POWERPOINT E-9
Line Style button, POWERPOINT F-10
linked files, sending presentations for review, POWERPOINT H-2
linked worksheets, updating, POWERPOINT G-8–9
linking
embedding versus, POWERPOINT G-6
objects using Paste Special, POWERPOINT G-7
worksheets, POWERPOINT G-6–7
Links dialog box, POWERPOINT G-9
Live Presentation Broadcast dialog box, POWERPOINT H-16, POWERPOINT H-17
lost files, recovering, POWERPOINT A-15

►M

master layout, restoring, POWERPOINT E-7
Master Layout button, POWERPOINT E-3
Master layout dialog box, POWERPOINT E-7
master text, formatting, POWERPOINT E-4–5
Master text placeholder, POWERPOINT E-2, POWERPOINT E-3
indent levels, POWERPOINT E-6–7
Master title placeholder, POWERPOINT E-2, POWERPOINT E-3
Master view, POWERPOINT E-2–3
formatting text, POWERPOINT E-4–5
media clip placeholder, POWERPOINT B-7
meetings, online, POWERPOINT H-13
menu(s), POWERPOINT A-6, POWERPOINT A-7. *See also specific menus*
menu bar, POWERPOINT A-6, POWERPOINT A-7
Microsoft Office Web page, clip art, POWERPOINT D-3
Microsoft PowerPoint Viewer, POWERPOINT H-14, POWERPOINT H-15
movies, inserting, POWERPOINT G-10, POWERPOINT G-11
moving
chart elements, POWERPOINT F-11
objects, POWERPOINT D-2
text, POWERPOINT C-10
music, playing from CDs, POWERPOINT G-13

►N

narrations, POWERPOINT F-13
recording, POWERPOINT H-6
New Presentation task pane, accessing, POWERPOINT A-8
Normal view, POWERPOINT A-6, POWERPOINT A-7, POWERPOINT A-10, POWERPOINT A-11
Outline tab, POWERPOINT B-8–9
Slide Design task pane, POWERPOINT B-12, POWERPOINT B-13
notes, POWERPOINT B-11
Notes page view, POWERPOINT A-11
Notes pane, POWERPOINT A-6, POWERPOINT A-7, POWERPOINT B-11
Nudge button, POWERPOINT D-2

►O

objects, POWERPOINT B-4, POWERPOINT C-5
aligning, POWERPOINT C-8, POWERPOINT C-9
changing order of animation, POWERPOINT D-18
drawing. *See* drawing objects
embedding. *See* embedding
grouped. *See* grouped objects
linking. *See* linking
modifying, POWERPOINT C-4, POWERPOINT C-5
moving, POWERPOINT D-2
resizing, POWERPOINT C-4, POWERPOINT C-5
selected, POWERPOINT G-4
online meetings, POWERPOINT H-13
opening
existing presentations, POWERPOINT C-2–3
Save As dialog box, POWERPOINT C-2
Order menu, POWERPOINT C-7
organization chart(s)
embedding, POWERPOINT F-14–15
modifying, POWERPOINT F-16–17
organization chart placeholder, POWERPOINT B-7
Outline tab, POWERPOINT A-6, POWERPOINT A-7
entering text, POWERPOINT B-8–9
Outlining toolbar, POWERPOINT B-8
Outlook window, POWERPOINT H-2, POWERPOINT H-3
overhead transparencies, printing slides sized for, POWERPOINT A-16

►P

Package for CD dialog box, POWERPOINT H-14, POWERPOINT H-15
packaging presentations, POWERPOINT H-14–15
page setup, changing, POWERPOINT H-11
panes. *See also specific panes*
Normal view, POWERPOINT A-6, POWERPOINT A-7
Paste button, POWERPOINT C-10
Paste command, POWERPOINT C-10

Paste Special, linking objects, POWERPOINT G-6, POWERPOINT G-7
permissions, setting, POWERPOINT C-3
photo album(s), POWERPOINT G-16–17
Photo Album dialog box, POWERPOINT G-16, POWERPOINT G-17
picture(s)
embedding, POWERPOINT G-2–3
inserting, POWERPOINT D-4, POWERPOINT D-5
picture bullets, POWERPOINT E-4
pie charts, POWERPOINT D-7
planning presentations, POWERPOINT B-2–3
PowerPoint
exiting, POWERPOINT A-16, POWERPOINT A-17
features, POWERPOINT A-2, POWERPOINT A-3
installing, POWERPOINT A-9
starting, POWERPOINT A-4
PowerPoint photo albums, POWERPOINT G-16–17
PowerPoint window, POWERPOINT A-4, POWERPOINT A-5, POWERPOINT A-6–7
presentation(s). *See also* file(s)
broadcasting, POWERPOINT H-16–17
checklist for, POWERPOINT D-19
customizing, POWERPOINT E-1
evaluating, POWERPOINT B-16–17
existing, opening, POWERPOINT C-2–3
exporting, POWERPOINT G-3
packaging, POWERPOINT H-14–15
planning, POWERPOINT B-2–3
publishing for Web, POWERPOINT H-12–13
reviewed, combining, POWERPOINT H-4–5
reviewing, POWERPOINT C-11, POWERPOINT H-5
saving, POWERPOINT A-12–13
saving fonts with presentations, POWERPOINT A-12
sending for review, POWERPOINT H-2–3
viewing in grayscale or black and white, POWERPOINT A-17
presentation software, POWERPOINT A-2–3
Preserve Master button, POWERPOINT E-3
Preset option button, Fill Effects dialog box, POWERPOINT C-16
Print button, POWERPOINT A-16
Print dialog box, POWERPOINT A-16, POWERPOINT A-17
printing
color, POWERPOINT A-16
custom slide shows, POWERPOINT H-8
files, POWERPOINT A-16, POWERPOINT A-17
notes, POWERPOINT B-11
Print Preview window, POWERPOINT B-14, POWERPOINT B-15
Publish as Web Page dialog box, POWERPOINT H-12, POWERPOINT H-13
publishing, for Web, POWERPOINT H-12–13
pyramid charts, POWERPOINT D-7
pyramid diagrams, POWERPOINT F-16

R

radar charts, POWERPOINT D-7
radial diagrams, POWERPOINT F-16
recording broadcasts, POWERPOINT H-17
recovering lost files, POWERPOINT A-15
Rehearsal toolbar, POWERPOINT H-11
rehearsing slide timings, POWERPOINT D-17, POWERPOINT H-10–11
Rename Master button, POWERPOINT E-3
replacing text and text attributes, POWERPOINT C-13
Research task pane, POWERPOINT A-14, POWERPOINT A-15
resizing objects, POWERPOINT C-4, POWERPOINT C-5
restoring, master layout, POWERPOINT E-7
review, sending presentations for, POWERPOINT H-2–3
reviewing presentations, POWERPOINT C-11
Right tab stop, POWERPOINT E-6
rotate handle, POWERPOINT C-6, POWERPOINT C-7
rulers, displaying, POWERPOINT C-6

S

Save As dialog box, POWERPOINT A-12, POWERPOINT A-13, POWERPOINT E-16, POWERPOINT E-17
opening, POWERPOINT C-2
saving
annotations, POWERPOINT D-14
broadcasts, POWERPOINT H-17
fonts with presentations, POWERPOINT A-12
presentations, POWERPOINT A-12–13
scaling clip art, POWERPOINT D-4, POWERPOINT D-5
scatter charts, POWERPOINT D-7
Search Results task pane, POWERPOINT A-14, POWERPOINT A-15
Search the Web button, Save As dialog box, POWERPOINT A-13
selected objects, POWERPOINT G-4
Series in Columns command, POWERPOINT D-9
Series in Rows command, POWERPOINT D-9
Shadow Style menu, POWERPOINT C-7
shapes
advanced drawing tools, POWERPOINT E-10–11
freeform, POWERPOINT E-11
margins around text in, POWERPOINT E-8
shortcuts, creating on desktop, POWERPOINT A-4
size, bullets, POWERPOINT E-4
sizing, chart elements, POWERPOINT F-11
slide(s)
hiding during slide shows, POWERPOINT H-7
jumping to, POWERPOINT D-14
new, POWERPOINT B-6–7
notes, POWERPOINT B-11
from other presentations, inserting, POWERPOINT C-15
Slide Design task pane, POWERPOINT B-12, POWERPOINT B-13
opening, POWERPOINT B-12
slide footers, POWERPOINT B-10–11
slide headers, POWERPOINT B-10–11
slide layouts, POWERPOINT B-6, POWERPOINT B-7
inserting clip art, POWERPOINT D-2
slide master(s), POWERPOINT E-2, POWERPOINT E-3
displaying, POWERPOINT E-2
exceptions, POWERPOINT E-5
preserved, POWERPOINT E-2
Slide Master View toolbar, POWERPOINT E-3
Slide pane, POWERPOINT A-6, POWERPOINT A-7
slide show(s)
custom, POWERPOINT H-8–9
ending, POWERPOINT D-14
printing, POWERPOINT H-8
setting timings and transitions, POWERPOINT D-16–17
setting up, POWERPOINT H-6–7
Slide Show menu, buttons, POWERPOINT D-14
Slide Show view, POWERPOINT A-11
annotations, POWERPOINT D-14
commands, POWERPOINT D-14–15
Slide Sorter view, POWERPOINT A-10, POWERPOINT A-11
Slides sized for list arrow, Page Setup dialog box, POWERPOINT A-16
Slides tab, POWERPOINT A-6, POWERPOINT A-7
slide timings. *See* timings
slide-title master pair(s), POWERPOINT E-2
slide transition(s), setting, POWERPOINT D-16–17
Slide Transition task pane, POWERPOINT D-16, POWERPOINT D-17
sound(s), inserting, POWERPOINT G-12–13
sound effects, charts, POWERPOINT F-12, POWERPOINT F-13
source program, POWERPOINT G-4
speech recognition, POWERPOINT B-5
spell checking, POWERPOINT B-14–15
Spelling dialog box, POWERPOINT B-14, POWERPOINT B-15
Standard toolbar, POWERPOINT A-6, POWERPOINT A-7
starting PowerPoint, POWERPOINT A-4
status bar, POWERPOINT A-6, POWERPOINT A-7
stock charts, POWERPOINT D-7
Style Checker, POWERPOINT E-15
Style menu, POWERPOINT C-7
subtitle text placeholders, POWERPOINT B-4, POWERPOINT B-5
Suggest command, POWERPOINT B-15
surface charts, POWERPOINT D-7
Symbol dialog box, POWERPOINT E-4, POWERPOINT E-5

T

tab indicator, POWERPOINT E-6, POWERPOINT E-7
table(s)
cells. *See* table cells
changing cell height or width, POWERPOINT D-12
creating, POWERPOINT D-12–13
table cells
changing height or width, POWERPOINT D-12
diagonal line through, POWERPOINT D-12
table placeholder, POWERPOINT B-7
target diagrams, POWERPOINT F-16
task panes, POWERPOINT A-6, POWERPOINT A-7. *See also specific task panes*
templates
applying from another presentation, POWERPOINT E-17
creating, POWERPOINT E-16–17
multiple, POWERPOINT B-12
supplied with PowerPoint, POWERPOINT B-1, POWERPOINT B-12–13
from Web, POWERPOINT B-3
text
changing margins around, in shapes, POWERPOINT E-8
entering, POWERPOINT B-8–9
formatting, POWERPOINT C-12–13
importing from Word, POWERPOINT C-14–15
master, formatting, POWERPOINT E-4–5
Master view, formatting, POWERPOINT E-4–5
moving, POWERPOINT C-10, POWERPOINT C-11
replacing, POWERPOINT C-13
replacing attributes, POWERPOINT C-13

text anchor feature, POWERPOINT E-8
Text Anchor Point command, POWERPOINT E-8
text labels, without text wrap, POWERPOINT C-10
text objects
adding, POWERPOINT C-10, POWERPOINT C-11
arranging, POWERPOINT C-10, POWERPOINT C-11
resizing, POWERPOINT C-4, POWERPOINT C-5
text placeholders, POWERPOINT B-4, POWERPOINT B-5
3-D styles, POWERPOINT E-12
thumbnails, POWERPOINT A-6
timings
rehearsing, POWERPOINT D-16–17, POWERPOINT H-10–11
setting, POWERPOINT D-16–17
title bar, POWERPOINT A-6, POWERPOINT A-7
title master, displaying, POWERPOINT E-2
title placeholders, POWERPOINT B-4, POWERPOINT B-5
toolbars, POWERPOINT A-6, 17. *See also specific toolbars*
Tools button, Save As dialog box, POWERPOINT A-13
transitions
slide shows, setting, POWERPOINT D-16–17
viewing, POWERPOINT D-14

►U

Unapply button list arrow, POWERPOINT H-4
Undo button list arrow, POWERPOINT B-8
updating, linked worksheets, POWERPOINT G-8–9
Up One Level button, Save As dialog box, POWERPOINT A-13

►V

Venn diagrams, POWERPOINT F-16
view(s), POWERPOINT A-6, POWERPOINT A-7. *See also specific views*
view buttons, POWERPOINT A-6, POWERPOINT A-7
viewing presentations, POWERPOINT A-10–11
in grayscale or black and white, POWERPOINT A-17
viewing transitions, POWERPOINT D-14
Views button, Save As dialog box, POWERPOINT A-13
voice narrations, POWERPOINT F-13
recording, POWERPOINT H-6

►W

Web page(s), changing format of elements, POWERPOINT H-12
wizards, POWERPOINT A-8, POWERPOINT A-9. *See also specific wizards*
Word, importing text from, POWERPOINT C-14–15
WordArt, POWERPOINT E-14–15
WordArt Gallery dialog box, POWERPOINT E-15, POWERPOINT E-16
WordArt Shape button, POWERPOINT E-15, POWERPOINT E-16
worksheets
embedding, POWERPOINT G-5
linking, POWERPOINT G-6–7

►X

XY charts, POWERPOINT D-7

Some of the exercises in this book require that you begin by opening a Data File. Follow one of the procedures below to obtain a copy of the Data Files you need.

Instructors

- A copy of the Data Files is on the Instructor Resources CD under the category Data Files for Students, which you can copy to your school's network for student use.
- Download the Data Files via the World Wide Web by following the instructions below.
- Contact us via e-mail at reply@course.com.
- Call Course Technology's Customer Service Department for fast and efficient delivery of the Data Files if you do not have access to a CD-ROM drive.

Students

- Check with your instructor to determine the best way to obtain a copy of the Data Files.
- Download the Data Files via the World Wide Web by following the instructions below.

Instructions for Downloading the Data Files from the World Wide Web

1. Start your browser and enter the URL www.course.com.
2. When the course.com Web site opens, click Student Downloads, and then search for your text by title or ISBN.
3. If necessary, from the Search results page, select the title of the text you are using.
4. When the textbook page opens, click the Download Student Files link, and then click the link of the compressed files you want to download.
5. If the File Download dialog box opens, make sure the Save this program to disk option button is selected, and then click the OK button. (NOTE: If the Save As dialog box opens, select a folder on your hard disk to download the file to. Write down the folder name listed in the Save in box and the filename listed in the File name box.)
6. The filename of the compressed file appears in the Save As dialog box (e.g., 3500-8.exe, 0361-1d.exe).
7. Click either the OK button or the Save button, whichever choice your browser gives you.
8. When a dialog box opens indicating the download is complete, click the OK button (or the Close button, depending on which operating system you are using). Close your browser.
9. Open Windows Explorer and display the contents of the folder to which you downloaded the file. Double-click the downloaded filename on the right side of the Windows Explorer window.
10. In the WinZip Self-Extractor window, specify the appropriate drive and a folder name to unzip the files to. Click Unzip.
11. When the WinZip Self-Extractor displays the number of files unzipped, click the OK button. Click the Close button in the WinZip Self-Extractor dialog box. Close Windows Explorer.
12. Refer to the Read This Before You Begin page(s) in this book for more details on the Data Files for your text. You are now ready to open the required files.

Macintosh users should use a program to expand WinZip or PKZip archives. Students, ask your instructors or lab coordinators for assistance.